BLUE COLLAR,
THEORETICALLY

Blue Collar, Theoretically
A Post-Marxist Approach to Working Class Literature

John F. Lavelle

McFarland & Company, Inc., Publishers
Jefferson, North Carolina, and London

LIBRARY OF CONGRESS CATALOGUING-IN-PUBLICATION DATA

Lavelle, John F., 1950–
  Blue collar, theoretically : a post-marxist approach to working class literature / John F. Lavelle.
    p.   cm.
  Includes bibliographical references and index.

  ISBN 978-0-7864-4885-2
  softcover : acid free paper ∞

  1. Working class writings — History and criticism.
  2. Working class in literature.   3. Social classes in literature.   4. Marxist criticism.   I. Title.
  PN56.L22L38 2012
  809'.93355 — dc23   2011040802

BRITISH LIBRARY CATALOGUING DATA ARE AVAILABLE

© 2012 John F. Lavelle. All rights reserved

No part of this book may be reproduced or transmitted in any form or by any means, electronic or mechanical, including photocopying or recording, or by any information storage and retrieval system, without permission in writing from the publisher.

Cover image © 2012 Shutterstock; front cover design by TG Design

Manufactured in the United States of America

McFarland & Company, Inc., Publishers
  Box 611, Jefferson, North Carolina 28640
    www.mcfarlandpub.com

To my parents Gerald Francis Lavelle and Christine Marie (Crogan) Lavelle, to my brothers and sister — Jim, Rick, Ron, and Sandy, all proud working-class people — and to all those diverse and individual people I've worked with on the factory floors all these years. I also dedicate this book to my grandparents, my aunts and uncles, great aunts and great uncles, and those lost ancestors strong enough and individually minded enough to board a ship to come to the New World and work in the mines of Pennsylvania. Without any of you this book could not have been written.

Table of Contents

Acknowledgments viii
Preface 1

1. The Praxis of Class 9
2. A Study in New Working-Class Studies 45
3. A Review of the Discourse of Working-Class Literature 97
4. Postmarxist Theories of Class 150
5. Postmodern/Poststructuralist Theories of Class and a Theory of the Working Class 179
6. A Working-Class Reading of *Maggie: A Girl of the Streets* and *The Great Gatsby* 215

Conclusion 247
Chapter Notes 257
Bibliography 260
Index 271

Acknowledgments

I'd like to acknowledge the help of many friends and colleagues, including Clai Rice, Joseph Andriano, and Yung Hsing Wu, for their help with the original manuscript. I'd also like to thank Jason Harris, Wynn Yarbrough, Michael Howarth and Liberty Kohn for their input and for keeping me sane during the initial drafting and revisions.

Preface

This book is an effort to solve problems now plaguing the study of the working class, specifically in literature studies. It does not propose any revolutionary theory of class in its deconstruction of the study as it now stands, but instead gathers theories from those already existing in disciplines such as sociology, cognitive science, anthropology, and psychology, theories that overlap and, in many cases, come to the same conclusions, opening up a more fecund area of research in what is being called new working-class studies and working-class literature studies.

This book is an attempt to construct a new theory of class that might be applied to both the general study of class and the study of class in literature, specifically the study of the class designated as the "working class."[1] It advances an alternative to macro theories, specifically Marxism, that define class in terms that limit both our understanding of its real-world implications and our analysis of its operation in literature.

Being philosophical in its creation, Marxism employs metaphor, symbolism, analogy, abstract constructions, and ideas not meant to be applied directly in day-to-day living. As a political doctrine it is utopian on the one hand and, paradoxically, radically militant on the other, grounded within ideology and dependent on the same ideology it attempts to repudiate.

The hegemony of Marxism is due not only to the existence of a political power structure within academia, but also to its discourse, which creates a field of power that survives underground within the ebb of a cycle to emerge again as a quick and simple (if not simplified) solution when other metanarratives have been shown to be false. That is to say, it appears when society experiences a crisis in mainstream metanarratives. Marxism is then put forward as an alternate discourse with alternate "truths." This generates a circular movement, a cycle, from Enlightenment republican ideals to utopian Marxist ideals, a movement always mediated by individual agency and subjective well-being. The "worker," whoever this may be, achieves a "goal" of changing certain "truths" of the existing hegemony's discourses precipitating a dissolution of the revolutionary impulse. This causes a movement back toward republican ideals, which in time are co-opted by conservative capitalistic forces moving the hegemony toward the right, thus marginalizing more and more people until "truths" fail and the cycle begins again. This failure, if it can be called a failure, is caused by ideology in two senses. The first is ideology preventing any movement in Western culture from extending to revolution by creating tension between competing ideologies effectively canceling each other out. The second, and for revolutionary Marxists the most frustrating, is that people act as individuals within a group with their own conception of happiness (subjective well-being) constructed through ideology. Once personal subjective well-being is reached, the group starts to disintegrate.

The argument of this text comes out of the many real-world inconsistencies of Marxism and the way it has been applied to working-class studies and working-class literature studies in America. Being from the working class, coming from the working class myself, I found working-class studies and working-class literature studies to not represent — or to *misrepresent*— me, my family, the many people I worked with and still call my personal friends, and the acquaintances I worked alongside during thirty-plus years in Northeast factories. Because Marxism has effectively closed off the discourse to new rules in the language game, working-class studies, as it now exists, is prone to, at best, stereotyping working-class people or, at worst, caricaturizing them by stripping them of their individuality and applying a preconceived representation that, no matter how noble, renders them less than human, as demonstrated by Rebecca Harding Davis in *Life in the Iron Mills*.

However, many other discourses concerned with class and the working class do exist, and many Marxists have moved away from Marx, reinterpreting his corpus and adding and subtracting theoretical points in an attempt to address the inconsistencies and contradictory aspects of Marxism, while paradoxically still calling themselves Marxists. The theories put forth by the postmarxists, poststructuralists, and postmodernists correct these inconsistencies and contradictions without having to recover Marxism.

Three theorists — Thorstein Veblen, Max Weber, and Emile Durkheim — are as relevant to voices within working-class studies as Marx, if not more so, having better credentials than Marx and having produced work based on empirical research rather than philosophical thought. Their major disagreement with Marx is his construction of class through economics and the position of the means of production, all generalized statements only viable at the macro level. They argue that class is created within status groups at the micro level and economics is an epiphenomenon of status groups allowing or denying access to life chances. Although not stated, all three touch on some mechanism working within small groups, separating people into classes. For Durkheim it is evolution. For Veblen and Weber it is not that simple.

The postmarxists, starting with Antonio Gramsci, noticed the proletariat seemed all too culpable for their own enslavement. Returning to Weber, Veblen, and Durkheim, these postmarxists realized the mechanism of separation was ideology, and it was more complex than Marx's false consciousness. Ideology produces narrations of the self pretending to be natural, a fable masquerading as a history. Disciplines such as sociology, anthropology, cognitive science, and psychology have integrated the concept of ideology into their work while working-class studies and working-class literature studies have held the door shut.

Because Marxism is hegemonic within working-class literature studies, this book begins by addressing the way the argument has been constructed, as well as the semantics used. While there is some slippage of the signifiers in the significant terms used in the study ("work," "labor," "worker," "laborer," and "class"), an attempt is made to define the terms rigorously and to elucidate how these terms cause slippage within many of the arguments concerning the working class.

The text, then, presents the fields of working-class studies and working-class literature studies and shows how they are now constructed, pointing out the inconsistent usage of these terms, as well as the paradoxes, contradictions, and inconsistencies plaguing the studies precipitated by the use of what can be labeled vulgar Marxism. In truth, these studies only exist at all (despite being marginalized by mainstream literature studies) because of the refusal to actually acknowledge the inconsistencies, paradoxes, and contradictions within the arguments presented in the studies.

In these studies class is often theorized at a macro level, allowing for what might be called a surface level of theorizing — an acceptance of Marxism without questioning the theories — forcing researchers to attempt to find data (ignoring contradicting data) or to adjust data to fit the theory. As the population level of the study is reduced, however, more inconsistencies and contradictions surface using macro theories of class. A second level of theorizing allows the data to question the theory, adjusting tenets of the theory to fit the data when generalized statements no longer hold true, but at the same time researchers still cling to the theory. As the level of population reaches the individual level, even this adjustment is not enough. The data must either be ignored or, following the example of some theorists, the theory must be scrapped and a new theory constructed that fits the data.

Chapter two discusses the way the working class is now theorized within the studies, addressing the popular arguments through a critique of three texts that propose totalizing arguments and five books with twenty-three essays that propose various arguments moving from surface-level theorizing to theorizing at the micro or individual level. Some essays contradict themselves and others, sometimes implicitly and sometimes explicitly. Some essays contradict their own arguments. Many contradict other essays' arguments, while still other essays construct their arguments at deeper levels of theorizing, giving hints of a possible direction the study might follow in order to reconcile this problem of undercutting itself.

The third chapter discusses how the working class is represented through literature — specifically, how it is configured and defined through the literature academics propose is "working-class literature" through their construction of working-class canons. These canons are constructed, most times, within a vulgar Marxist paradigm in a circular argument independent of the discourse and dependent on performativity. Academics frequently gain authority through performativity, including citing each other as authorities, thus enhancing their personal status and, therefore, the ability to be "right." They lay out theories using Marxist tenets of victimization, exploitation, and manual labor, then proceed to gather literature bolstering their position while ignoring any literature that contradicts their argument.

The major weakness, as the study is now configured, is its narrowness of scope. A Marxist configuration of the working class consists only of the industrial proletariat, a minority of the population until 1920. Those who study the working class have attempted to expand on this idea while still attempting to maintain Marxist parameters in both scope and time. They have extended the scope of the working class by including other occupations, such as non-factory agricultural workers, service workers, domestic workers, and all unskilled labor. These new working-class occupations seem to fall neatly into a working class based on economics and lack of autonomy in the workplace. However, this parameter now excludes those traditionally of the working class, the skilled workers, because these occupations generally earn wages above the idealized occupants of the working class and many occupations considered middle class, such as teachers, some clerical occupations, nurses, and so forth. This economic criterion for a configuration of the working class has introduced the concept of poverty into the discourse. However, poverty is a condition, not a class designation, and needs to have its own area of study. Gender, sex, and race have frequently better explicated the reasons for poverty and marginalization than class has done. Finally, once the exceptions are removed, the study becomes one concerned with the white, male, industrial proletariat, a very small group that has existed in literature for a very short time.

Many academics studying the working class in literature have also attempted to expand the range of working-class literature not only in the occupations and economic conditions this literature includes, but also in the time span it takes place in. Realist texts of the late nineteenth and early twentieth centuries fall neatly into the Marxist parameters now used for working-class literature and buttress its positions. However, as academics move the study beyond this epoch, finding texts fitting their parameters becomes more difficult, thus bringing to light another inherent weakness within the study's tenets.

Having expanded the parameters to include nonindustrial workers as part of this class, their argument must claim the working class has existed before industrialization in both occupations and time. This means that if a working class is to indicate all those economically below others, those who must sell their labor to others, those exploited and victimized, then the working class must have existed throughout history, and literature of and about the working class that fits into a Marxist paradigm should exist throughout history. As the examples of working-class literature move away from the golden period of proletariat writing, texts reflecting Marxists tenets become more difficult to find. This usually causes those studying working-class literature to try to shoehorn texts not really fitting within their tenets into the parameters, often making assertions with little or no textual evidence.

The other contradictory impulse in working-class literature studies is to attempt to create a canon of literature based on authors supposedly from the working class or having written about the working class. No definitive answer seems to exist as to who or what a working-class author might be. Are all authors who write about the working class thereby working-class authors, such as William Carlos Williams, who, by occupation, was a doctor? Are only authors from the working class allowed to be working-class authors? What of authors from the working class who do not write about the working class? Is an author such as Langston Hughes a working-class author when he writes of class but not when he writes of race?

The major point that might be garnered here is that both configurations are poor ways to construct parameters of the study. A better way is to discard the ideas of a canon of works or authors and to subject all works to a working-class reading. Although some academics might insist canons of Native American, feminist, African American, and postcolonial literature exist, the important aspect of these studies is a set of assumptions allowing for all texts to be scrutinized for representations of Native Americans, women, African Americans, and others.

Chapter three considers how the study of the working class in literature is configured using the concepts from chapter two concerning the depth of theorizing at decreasing levels of population. Since most of what is called working-class literature is Marxist in content, only two texts will be critiqued: one anthology purporting to be a textbook for college students (*American Working-Class Literature: An Anthology*, by Nicholas Coles and Janet Zandy) and one study supposedly of American working-class literature from 1620 to the present (*Labor Texts: The Worker in American Fiction*, by Laura Hapke). Both texts theorize the working class at a surface level with parameters constructed from generalized statements. Although workable at a macro level, they fall apart at the micro level, and because literature is written at the micro level of the population, at the level of the individual, both texts have obvious problems, inconsistencies, contradictions, and readings of texts without textual support.

A text at a deeper level of theorizing concerned with the signs of class in literature shown through language (specifically, poetry) is *The Stamp of Class*, by Gary Lenhart. This book has been included as a literary counterpoint to the way most academics theorize class in literature and as an example (if only a hint) of alternatives. Finally, two ethnographic works (*Working: People Talk About What They Do All Day and How They Feel About What They Do*, by Studs Terkel, and *Gig: Americans Talk About Their Jobs*, by John Bowe, Marisa Bowe, and Sabin Streeter) have been included as a way to counter Marxist theories making up many of the tenets of the current parameters of working-class studies and working-class literature studies and to counter the stereotypical construction of the working class itself by showing many of the assumptions of, about, and who the working class are to be false and detrimental both to the study, and, more importantly, to the people designated as the working class.

Chapter four brings into the discussion alternate theories of class based on ideas derived from Weber, Veblen, Durkheim, and Nietzsche. Moving away from Marxism, these theorists are usually referred to as postmarxists, a term sometimes disputed by Marxists who either dispute the theories outright or dispute that the theories are postmarxist at all. However, postmarxist theories find in Marxism the same irreconcilable contradictions Gramsci does. Although many academics would argue against labeling Gramsci a postmarxist, he brings in to the discussion a more complex reading of ideology and social structure, prompting movement away from the simplicity of Marx's construction of society as directly dependent on the mode of production and false consciousness.

Theorists such as Louis Althusser take up the idea of ideology being the mediating factor in the construction of class, specifically through the construction of identity and the subject. Pierre Bourdieu and Michel Foucault, the two theorists discussed at length in this chapter, both base much of their theories on ideology. They have developed theories based on Weber's "stande" (status groups) as class. Bourdieu develops a theory of social fields that includes habitus (Veblen's propensities); cultural, symbolic, and social capital; and signs manifested through what he names "practice"—all mediated by ideology. These signs become differences for inclusion and exclusion, the true delineator of class. Foucault, using concepts of "discourses," shows how ideology is inscribed within the discourses in society perpetuating "truths." These discourses—narratives—create Subject/subject positions.

Both theorists are concerned with the idea of power and how power is created and transmitted in society. For Bourdieu, social fields exist within the larger social field of power, and people and groups attempt to take up positions near power centers within a social field. Foucault's ideas of power come from Nietzsche, although he attempts to avoid the Enlightenment thinking that trapped Nietzsche.

Nietzsche, although somewhat culpable for the situation the world is in today through his theories of the will-to-power, did recognize that two separate ideologies seem to exist in society. He called them moralities, naming these two ideologies "noble" and "slave," forever damning the altruistic ideology. Caught up in the Enlightenment idea of evolution and history as teleological and working toward some ultimate goal for mankind, Nietzsche sees altruism as detrimental to the evolution of mankind. Paradoxically (although he denies it), his theories need some supreme being to guide this evolution/history, if not give it purpose, contradicting his "death of God" proposition.

Chapter 5 expands on the ideas raised in chapter 4, using theories from postmodernists and poststructuralists to propose a new theory of class, suggesting that a class named "working class" might only exist at the locus of interpellation. Thus the theory becomes a theory of "class." The chapter starts by explaining postmodernity, how it fits into a theory of class, and the leading theories and theorists; although some theorists argue against postmodernity existing, most accept its existence but argue about what it might be. The debate over how to configure postmodernity centers on whether postmodernity, as Hutcheon seems to believe, is a liberating turn or, as Jameson believes, is only another manifestation of capitalism. The position of this chapter contends the population of the Western world allows for multiple narratives, and thus they are both correct.

Postmodernism illuminates the metanarratives, once considered "truths," as only narratives marginalizing a multitude of voices within a polyphonic world. Thus postmodernism takes up questions of identity and considers how ideologies inform and create identities while still allowing, or unable to stifle, individual agency. Identity in most of the social sciences—sociology, anthropology, cognitive science, and psychology—is seen as fluid and mutable, becoming salient at the locus of interpellation through an exchange of signs filtered through prototypes and schemas garnered through habitus, power systems, social structures, and mass media providing the major signs for in-group/out-group separation.

This chapter constructs an alternate way to view class, seeing it at the micro level as access to power and in-group/out-group selection. It sets up tenets to be used in a working-class reading of any text, with class decided through difference and power, mediating agency through social structure. This chapter shows how two core ideologies produce differing signs used for the separation of people within social fields. These two ideologies are called "privileged" and "equalitarian" according to the way they view reality. The chapter does not, however, argue that only two poles exist, but ideology, thus identity, exists on a continuum from one core ideology to the other and a character's ideology might change throughout a story. This change frequently becomes the crux of the story.

Chapter six applies this tenets of the theory to two texts, *Maggie: A Girl of the Streets* and *The Great Gatsby*, the former chosen because it reflects realist literature and might be considered a type of social realism, thus lending itself to a Marxist reading, although few have been produced. Two readings are presented of *Maggie: A Girl of the Streets*, one internal to the text and one external, showing two different approaches this new theory might take.

A reading of *The Great Gatsby* is presented to show just how a reading might be done. *The Great Gatsby* has been chosen because it does not fit well into a Marxist paradigm and much of the book must be ignored or bent to fit a Marxist reading. However, the new theory has little trouble unpacking the novel's depictions of multiple classes and the subtle divisions between a multitude of classes. The reading uncovers two core ideologies — privileged (seen in Tom, Daisy, Jordan, and Nick) and equalitarian (seen in Wilson, Gatsby, Myrtle, and those people Nick meets at the apartment and many of the new rich at Gatsby's parties). This reading of *The Great Gatsby* elucidates the way class is constructed within the story through difference, such as in the names of the East Eggers and West Eggers, the clothes, automobiles, neighborhoods, and houses, but especially through lineage.

This book, constituting a different way to conceive class, is an attempt to begin a new conversation in working-class literature studies, hoping the study might move in a new and more fecund direction. It grounds class within status and sees class operating through signs of difference at the small-group level. It hopes, through presenting a new theory of class, that working-class studies and working-class literary studies will be invited to the "diversity banquet" within mainstream academia (Russo and Linkon 4).

Chapter 1

The Praxis of Class

A situation exists within the study of the working class and working-class literature allowing for the prevalent stereotyping of people designated, for various reasons, as the working class. When considering that "there is no unambiguous body of thought called Marxism, and most of those who have called themselves Marxist have fashioned a selective vision that has matched their own circumstances and objectives," the underlying cause for this stereotyping within the study becomes apparent: the hegemonic use of these Marxisms within the study (Hyman 27). Marxist theorists still dispute the theories of Marxism within the field and have modified the theories immeasurably. "In any event there is a vast literature giving many different interpretations of 'what Marx really meant'" (Hyman 28). In recent decades postmodernist and poststructuralist theories have challenged the old hegemonic discourses and fresh voices have added new rules to the language game of the discourse of class. There have been "developments that present clear challenges to contemporary theories of work [...] a fall in the relevance of work-based concepts of class [and] the growing interest in consumption rather than production, together with an interest in personal identities" (Korczynski, Hodson, and Edwards 2).

These new theories of Marxism, whether correct or incorrect, are mostly ignored in the field of working-class and working-class literature studies. This use of vulgar Marxism in its original nineteenth-century form has caused the development of a more profound symptom of the study, an underlying cause of the dispersion and lack of rigor in the study of both the working class and class in literature. This symptom is the slippage of the signifier and signified within the signs "work," "class" and "worker." This slippage in turn has created within the fields of study contradictions and inconsistencies, not a "mosaic of class," as Janet Zandy has postulated (19).

"All too often Marxism becomes ossified as dogma" (Hyman 27). In the study of class and class in literature, Marxism has become dogmatic along with hegemonic because Marxism provides a ready-made niche with established theories, and "'traditional' theory is always in danger of being incorporated into the programming of the social whole as a simple tool for the optimization of its performance" (Lyotard 12). Specifically, "all formal systems have internal limitations" (Lyotard 43). Regarding the hegemony of Marxism in academia, Lyotard states that "the struggles in question [against Marxism] have simply been deprived the right to exist" because "the weight of certain institutions imposes limits on the [language] games [...] requir[ing] supplementary constraints for statements to be declared as admissible within its bounds" (Lyotard 13, 16). Under these limitations the "production of proof" is "designed to win agreement for the addressees" and since "performativity increases the ability to produce proof, it also increases the ability to be right" (Lyotard 46). Those academics conducting working-class studies within a Marxist parameter do not question the signs of their study ("work," "labor," and "class"), but assume the meanings are clear, though these meanings and the usage of these terms are different for different academics discussing class, and sometimes change within an argument itself. This slippage allows many uncontested assumptions.[1]

The major problem, then, starts with the closure of the discourse of working-class studies to alternative language games other than those proposed by Marxists. Yet this Marxist language game lacks continuity across the depth and breadth of the field of study and creates contradictory arguments when compared, not complementary arguments. This is due to, and creates, a lack of rigor in the discipline caused by the lack of rigor in defining the rules of the language game, allowing for "looseness" in the definitions of the three basic terms used in the study, thus permitting looseness and slippage in the arguments themselves. To start to reconstitute a theory of the working class, the basic terms of the argument—"work," "worker," and "class"—must be defined accurately.

"Work"

Marx

The term "work" seems straightforward: "W = Fd," or work equals force times direction, the expending of energy (Finney, Weir, and Giordano 454). However, according to footnote one by Engels in volume one of *Capital* (part one, "Commodities and Money," chapter 1, "Commodities"), the German word "work" does not translate directly into English. The English words "work" and "labor" are two separate aspects of the German word "labor": "the labour [sic] which creates Use-Value and counts qualitatively is *Work*, as distinguished from Labour; that which creates value and counts quantitatively" (qtd. in Marx, *Capital* 1: 47). For the argument presented in this text, the terminology of Marx will be used and because this argument need not separate the two ideas, the word "labor" will be synonymous with the word "work," an expenditure of energy in an effort to produce something.

To Marx work is the defining, or primary, unit of measure in society, allowing him to make the assertion that labor (work) becomes congealed within the product of the labor, a very important assumption of Marx's theories. Jean Baudrillard questions several inconsistencies and paradoxes in Marx's assumptions, arguing Marx is attempting to control the nature of the discourse by defining what is "true" within the discourse of class, disallowing other concepts of truths. Baudrillard claims that Marx creates a new system of interpretation — a new metanarrative of humanity and society rather than a simple economic or social theory. Baudrillard states of Marx's theories, "But isn't this dominant scheme which metaphorizes all azimuths, itself merely a metaphor? Is the reality principle it imposes anything but a code?" believing "all the fundamental concepts of Marxist analysis must be questioned" (18, 21). Andrew Brown, when defending Marx's theory of value from other Marxists who sometimes "dispense entirely with abstract labour as substance of value," states, "According to Marx's preface to *Capital*, the commodity is the 'cell-form' of the capitalist economy, thereby making the capitalist economy analogous to an organism" (126 and 127). Brown, then, restates one of the numerous metaphors often taken as reality, and thus his and many Marxist arguments must depend on an analogy between a thing of nature and an abstract philosophical construct. The analogy and metaphor must cease to be analogy, metaphor, or philosophical construct and become "real." Once these ideas and theories move beyond the metaphorical and philosophical into the real, inconsistencies abound.

Marx argues man's labor gives rise to meaning and through his base and superstructure to reality itself. Baudrillard questions this construction. "Isn't this a similar fiction [...] another wholly arbitrary convention [...] all human material and every contingency of desire and exchange in terms of value, finality and production?" (19). Although other animals use tools and produce things with "use-value" through labor, such as honeybees (Marx's example); Marx considered what could be termed cognitive or conscious labor — the deliberate and reasoned production of something of value — as separating humans from other animals. The difference between humans and bees, according to Marx, is that the human "raises his structures in imagination before he raises it in reality" (*Capital* 1: 178). However, Marx's formal definition of labor does not fit with his operational definition of the term. While Marx argues all labor is in an effort to produce something, if only an idea, he does not separate distinct types of labor, such as intellectual labor or skilled labor, from unskilled labor, asserting all labor in the abstract "remains the same," so "a general or a banker plays a greater part, but a *mere* man, on the other hand, a very shabby part" (*Capital* 1: 44). Labor for Marx is man's natural state of being. Baudrillard, along with Weber, questions this assumption, believing "these prodigious metaphors of the system that dominates us are a fable of political economy retold to generations of revolutionaries infected even in their political radicalism by the conceptual viruses of the same political economy" (Baudrillard 22). Weber sees these Marxist concepts of labor as ideological, coming out of the theologies of later Protestantism and the philosophies of Enlightenment thought.

Labor for Marx could only be defined in the abstract. First, he contests the idea that the "value" of a commodity is determined by the amount of labor expended to produce it. "The more idle and unskillful the labourer, the more valuable would the commodity be. The labour that forms the substance of value is homogeneous human labor" (Marx, *Capital* 1: 38). Thus, "the value of a commodity would therefore remain constant if the labour-time required for its production has remained constant" (*Capital* 1: 40). Marx understands labor-time by itself cannot be the decider of a commodity's value. Second, because of this, basing the idea of human labor on the expenditure of energy to produce a product of use-value, Marx must create an abstraction he calls "value" (*Capital* 1: 44). Baudrillard contends use-value is a fiction predicated on the idea that man is a singular human not tied to a group society and had originally created tools for his own use. Since the natural primitive state of humans has always been in some way communal, a human existing on his or her own and satisfying all his or her needs is a fiction. In Marx's theories "the same fiction reigns in the three orders of production, consumption, and signification" (Baudrillard 30). "In fact use-value of labor power does not exist anymore than the use-value of a product" (30). If use-value does not exist, then the idea of an abstraction called "value" must be doubted.

This "value" abstraction allows Marx to construct labor as universal and a "value" constant allows a labor constant to exist. This postulation becomes a slippage within the idea of labor. "With reference to value [of a commodity], it counts only quantitatively and must first be reduced to human labour pure and simple. [...] [I]t is a question of [...] How much?" (*Capital* 1: 45). This configuration also allows him to suggest "the coat is worth twice as much as the ten yards of linen. [...] It is owing to the fact that the linen contains only half as much labor as the coat" (*Capital* 1: 45). For Marx "labour-power must have been expended during twice the time necessary for the production of the former," although this is not necessarily true — obviously the production of a coat's worth of linen would not, or does not, take half as long to produce as all coats costing twice as much, and all coats costing twice as much as the linen would not necessarily take twice as long to make (*Capital* 1: 45). Thus, this value constant has already been proven incorrect.

In this way Marx configures the value of the labor as the value of the commodity divided by the time the labor took to produce the commodity because, for Marx, a product or a commodity is actually congealed labor. However, he postulates that for each commodity an average amount of labor exists — the amount taken to produce the commodity — and thus the value of the labor is contingent on the exchange value of the commodity. Only when the product is produced for exchange — exchange value — does labor have a definitive value, the exchange value of the commodity divided by the hours of labor, meaning the value of the commodity sets the value of labor instead of labor setting the value of the commodity.

Several problems are created when configuring a commodity as nothing but congealed labor and exchange value as directly determining labor value. The two major problems are the cost of raw material and the added cost of skills because of supply and demand. Marx regulates raw material in all its forms to a nonentity. Marx states, "If we take away the useful labor [...] a material substratum is all that is left, which is furnished by Nature without the help of man" (*Capital* 1: 43). In this way he can marginalize the risk/reward of investments (such as the investment in raw material) and simplify the idea of alienation of labor without having to confront the possibility that a laborer sells his labor as a commodity voluntarily rather than have to participate in another field of labor involving risk/reward. Naturally, the time of the writing of this book and the time of Marx are different and thus Marx, working in a social field entrenched in Enlightenment thought, a world just shifting to mass production, would construct his reality differently from someone 150 years later. Possibly when he thought of raw material he thought of the diamond mines in Brazil or other areas of imperialism allowing for the taking of raw material without paying for the right to take it or paying for the material itself. However, now, and in most instances in Marx's time, according to Weber, costs beyond labor existed in producing a commodity. Once commodity futures, the speculation on the price of raw material, are considered, Marx's configuration can easily be seen as faulty.

Though raw material, for Marx, inevitably comes from the land, sometimes from a convoluted series of treks (one might say wool is only congealed wheat and grass), costs inherent with the land must be borne by the commodity, including taxes and payment to the owner of the land for the taking of the material. Obviously the argument as to whether the land is the congealed labor of the owner, and the taxes the commodity of the congealed labor of the tax man and other city officials, can be argued ad nauseam. This same idea might be turned on its head, though, and rather than seeing labor in the commodity, one might see all the material in the "commodities," such as wheat in bread or the iron ore in the plow used to plow the wheat field, as producing the laborer. The energy for labor was once raw material and paid for as a commodity with cost added for labor. Either way a commodity can never exist as only congealed labor. Marx correlates the cost of material with the cost of the labor to procure the material, using the example of diamonds as a model, being rare and thus difficult (meaning taking more labor) to acquire. However, DeBeers' effort to control the diamond market is well known and undermines Marx's simplistic configuration of the cost of congealed labor in the market as the determining factor of the price of the commodity, or even excess labor power. Also, an argument might be constructed postulating that the costs of raw material can be subtracted from the commodity and what is left is labor-value — raw material being a commodity of exchange. As seen in the stock market, materials' price might have nothing to do with their cost or procurement (labor), but everything to do with their supply and demand.

Marx makes much of the money equivalent. It is the universal commodity, not necessarily having any use-value in itself, but rather in its ability to be a medium of exchange between commodities. Although he also considers labor a commodity to be exchanged for the promise of payment later,[2] in many ways he does not configure the idea of capitalism and the use of money in the same way. A person's concept of money, whether correct or incorrect, determines its use. Is money a commodity, as Marx sees it, or raw material? A laborer once exchanged his labor for a commodity with use-value — a shirt, tool, a bushel of corn — and, according to Weber, always a money equivalent in some form having only exchange-value. The laborer may very well see money as a commodity whose use-value is its ability to be exchanged for other commodities, as his labor is exchanged for money. However, a capitalist sees money as both commodity and raw material. It is raw material when it is invested to create more money through the production and exchange of a commodity, no less or no more than Marx's consideration of iron in its different forms, although Marx refuses to see money as raw material. In this way Marx and Marxists have closed the discourse to differing concepts of money and labor, as well as a myriad other differing concepts. This closure of the discourse finally alludes to the missing component in Marx's works: "ideology" and the effect of ideology on people. Although he does address ideology, he marginalizes the ideas of ideology within the idea of false consciousness. Ideology is much more than false consciousness. It is the driving force behind motivation and narration of reality and thus behind all concepts.[3]

Marx hopes to solve the first problem by contending that raw material, coming from nature, is free and thus its cost cannot be considered in the cost of the product. He attempts to solve the second problem by generalizing all labor as a constant. Marx's position and training as a philosopher must not be forgotten. His concepts of labor and commodities and other aspects of manufacturing are philosophical in nature and allow for the abstraction of a commodity as congealed labor, as well as the abstraction of labor itself, of use-value, exchange-value, and value itself. To abstract use-value, labor-value, and even exchange-value is possible because they existed for Marx only at the level of abstraction. When they are placed within a complex real world where contradictions are produced, they suffer. For Marx "skilled labor counts only as [...] multiplied simple labor" (*Capital* 1: 44). Thus, in abstraction, the tailor worked "more intensely," or twice as long, as the weaver (*Capital* 1: 44). In reality this is not possible. The weaver may work twice as long as the tailor to earn the same money; however, Marx's assumption that the tailor works twice as long as the weaver in the same amount of hours is not true even in abstraction. Thus the abstraction of labor or labor-power, for the purpose of placing labor within the commodity or in positioning the laborer as the natural owner of the commodity, is fraught with problems. This tailor sold his theoretical coat for twice as much as the weaver sold his bolt of cloth and theoretically did not work any longer. Thus labor is not homogeneous and the tailor's labor is worth more than the weaver's.

In the labor market, supply and demand determines the price of labor. While Marx does consider supply and demand of labor in the marketplace, he also, as stated before, considers the exchange-value of the commodity as determining the value of labor and not of seeing supply and demand as the determinant of the worth of labor. As an abstraction, these configurations work fine, but in reality they are contradictory. If the price of labor is determined by the supply, then it is free of the exchange-value of the commodity even in abstraction while the price of the commodity is determined by the supply and demand of the market. This can be seen in the "The Statute of Artificers" (1563), which aimed to not only control the apprenticeships and flow of workers into certain occupations, but also ensure an adequate supply of labor for agriculture by allowing officials to "assess wages every Easter" (K. Brown 15, 19). These assessments of wages were not concerned with the minimum wage. Rather, they were concerned with the maximum wage caused by a continual labor shortage and the demand it put on the market, having nothing to do with the price of the commodity in a Marxist configuration, and in this case the price of the commodity, would depend on the cost of labor (although unless the market could support this price, the commodity would be sold at a loss).

Marxist theories depend on piecework, a piece per hour, or hour-per-piece configuration. The price of the labor-power for an hour is equal to the price of the commodity (or commodoties) produced in that hour. While he believes one can then correlate the difference in the price of skilled labor with this configuration, one cannot. According to one configuration, this would mean a universal price for a labor hour, but this configuration works only when all things are abstracted. His other configuration, suggesting skilled labor might be considered labor-power times the amount of the minimum wage of labor per hour (that is, a skilled laborer's hour is only a nonskilled laborer's hour times by some number, or skilled labor theoretically works more hours than nonskilled), cannot be applied to the real world of work either.

For all of Marx's radical thought, he was an orthodox economist. The orthodox economic approach to the labor market looks for equilibrium within the market between supply and demand, stating "a higher wage would result in too many workers competing for jobs (supply exceeds demand) and a lower wage would result in there being too few workers to fill the job slots available (demand exceeds supply)," the one condition driving the price down and the other forcing it up (Machin 184). This equilibrium of workers is part of the "Invisible Hand" theory of Adam Smith. However, it too assumes a direct relationship between profits and labor, believing that higher wages decreasing the number of laborers employed. The relationship, if any, can only be tangential, even if it looks as though, in many cases, it is direct, as Marx assumes. It is, in fact, a fallacy existing because of a disparity between theory and the real world.

This model of "the higher the wage the fewer workers are employed" is the assumption against raising the minimum wage. Of course this contends that several suppositions are related when no relationship actually exists. The first supposition suggests labor markets should work on competition of laborers for work and thus the market for labor floats through supply and demand — normally true. The second suggests supply and demand is tied to profit. It is not, although it seems to be. In actuality it is tied, or "roped," to the profit margin. Profit is the selling price of the commodity in the market minus the cost to make the commodity.[4] The selling price of the commodity in the market is only tangentially associated with its cost, but is directly associated with its demand. The profit margin is an arbitrary goal set by managers, and is frequently set by bonus goals of the managers and not according to what could or should rightfully be the selling price of a commodity figured through cost and reasonable profit. This philosophy has been a direct cause of America's industrial infrastructure becoming antiquated through the refusal of managers to reinvest profits into updating the infrastructure and is also the reason for the shoddy quality of American goods due to the never-ceasing quest to make the product cheaper, or to take "cost" out of the product, not put "value" in. This antiquation is usually blamed on workers' wages, but, as can be seen in countries like Germany, most of the blame, according to Dr. Deming and others, can be put squarely on management (Walton 33–39). The orthodox approach shows labor is a commodity within the market, as Marx contends. It also assumes "workers are free to switch between jobs costlessly in response to any wage changes" (Machin 184). Marx also agrees with the assumption that "all workers are the same (their labor is homogeneous)" (Machin 184). However, "the limitations of the orthodox approach have long been recognized by economists" and later models of the labor competition model have had to incorporate the effect of heterogeneous labor (labor is not all the same) and imperfect competition (Machin 185).

Baudrillard, along with other theorists, considers Marx to have been a prisoner of Western rationalist or Enlightenment thought, "an entire civilization that comprehends itself as producing its own development and takes its dialectic force toward completing humanity in terms of totality and happiness" (33). This allows a "Marxist dialectic [to] lead to the purest Christian ethic. [...] [T]his aberrant sanctification of work has been the secret vice of Marxist political and economic strategy from the beginning" (Baudrillard 36). As Tester states, considering Weber, "there is no rational justification for the principle that it is virtuous to work hard in order to make money other than that justification which is offered by the principle itself" (46). Baudrillard suggests "at the same time it produces the abstract universality of labor our epoch produces the universal abstraction of the concept of labor and the retrospective illusion of the validity of this concept for all societies" (85). Marx, and Marxists, are caught up in the very ideology he and they hope to discredit— bourgeoisie Christian/Enlightenment thought constructing humanity as charged with a divine purpose of laboring to a utopian end. Thus "Marx's concept of labor (like that of production, productive forces, etc.) must be submitted to a radical critique as an *ideological* concept" and not as a social or economical theory (Baudrillard 43).

Veblen

Thorstein Veblen was a late-nineteenth/early-twentieth-century thinker who, like Marx, attempted to explain, scientifically, the working of society and to understand the paradoxes embedded in it. The difficulty in reading Veblen is that he is always a study in understanding subtle satire. Sometimes defending Veblen's positions becomes a chore because the defender must pluck the serious core of Veblen's theories from his satirical writing.

Veblen differs from Marx in several ways. Veblen's discourse in *The Theory of the Leisure Class*, in all seriousness, concerns itself with the actions of the individual — class at the micro level, not contingent on class antagonisms and exploitation, but rather on status, emulation, conspicuous consumption, conspicuous waste, and institutions of thought, theories that seemingly anticipate postmarxism.

Marx postulates five epochs of civilization, while Veblen believes only two conditions need be worried about — the age of the peaceable savage and this prolonged barbarian age of civilization. Marx invests in a utopian future. Veblen makes no such claim. Although Veblen does not contest Marx's idea of primitive communism, he contests ownership as an "innate idea deeply implanted in mans' nature. On the contrary, it is an acquired cultural trait that must be learned" (Diggins 119).

Veblen's theory of workmanship leads to the contestation of Marx's theory of value. Whereas Marx places labor-value within the product itself, Veblen does not. Marx, by placing labor into the product as solidified labor, can contend that profit is actually surplus labor. By controlling the means of production and by ownership of the product produced, capitalists thus alienate the laborer from his labor. Veblen believes, though, that once a product is made for others (to exchange), whether through labor or ownership of the means of production, it loses its own intrinsic value and the joy of workmanship; thus alienation is not dependent on capitalism. Diggins explains, "When a product is made to satisfy others, it loses its own intrinsic value and the joy of workmanship cannot be an end in itself. [...] The laborer now assumes he can realize himself not in production but in consumption" (131).

Thorstein Veblen constructs a definition of labor, unlike Marx, based on anthropology, sociology, and evaluation. Both men are limited in the scope of their thinking by bourgeois ideology (as many other thinkers were up until almost the postmodernist era), giving to men a higher purpose and claiming that work is the natural state of man (this is more applicable to Marx than Veblen).

The idea of labor begins, for Veblen, as it does for Marx, by going beyond the scientific definition of the expenditure of energy to specifically shaping nature to human will. Here Veblen and Marx part. Marx's definition of labor must congeal in use-value first and commodity exchange-value second, so the commodity's value will somehow equal the labor-value put into it. The laborer must inherently desire to own the product of his labor and thus the means of production. Marx's definition of the laborer allows for a moral position asserting the laborer's inherent right to own both the means of production and the commodity itself. This position vilifies the group paying for work as a commodity and retaining ownership over the means of production and the commodity. This configuration does not allow the construction of the labor to be the end of the commodity chain for the laborer and does not allow the laborer to be divorced from the product. It, in fact, disallows labor as commodity in itself.

Veblen, however, never sees, as Marx does, a time before a product was a commodity and created for its use-value alone. Use-value presupposes humans were solitary creatures and did not share labor or tools, but rather made tools strictly for their own use and only later exchanged them, but in reality tools were made as much for exchange, if only as communal objects, as for use. In the primitive production of tools Veblen believes "this does not mean the shaping of things by the individual to his own individual use simply; for archaic man was necessarily a member of a group" (Veblen, "Instinct" 194). Science has proven humans were never solitary animals and always cooperated, which is crucial to the idea of the primacy of labor and thus the moral right or need to own the means of production.

Veblen argues that through skill in labor comes praise of dispraise, self-esteem, and finally emulation. He sees a movement from alienation to workmanship once tools and weapons are made. Paradoxically a movement toward a disdain for work evolves in an "elite" class, a contention opposite Marx's proposals. Although Veblen saw a propensity for workmanship as a "comparison of the abilities," this propensity becomes the comparison of "the force [one] is able to put forth" through a "canon of meritorious conduct" ("Instinct" 187–88). Although the use of energy and force in hunting and war would seem to be considered work, Veblen believes early humans, specifically males, did not see hunting or battle as work. As Marx moves away from the scientific definition of work as energy spent, to energy spent consciously making something, Veblen moves away from the same definition in the same way, contending labor must be a conscious effort to produce something. Although hunting and war produce something, the production of the effort is subordinate to the effort itself, of gaining praise. Therefore "the able-bodied barbarian [...] severely leaves all uneventful drudgery to the women and minors of the group" ("Instinct" 200). Thus "industrial employments are women's work," bringing about the belief that "labor is ignoble" and the "prerequisite of the poor" ("Instinct" 200, 201). Veblen's chauvinistic presumptions aside, this idea of "work" being ideological is an important aspect of competing ideologies, which will be taken up in later chapters.

Max Weber

Max Weber has little to say on the primary definition of work or whether it separates humans from beasts. Where Marx and Veblen were seemingly driven to find some redeeming feature, if not goal, in the impulse of humanity's drive to produce, other than just greed (in Veblen's case, evolution), Weber made no such claims and saw no cosmic end in which history and humanity drove itself, or no evolutionary march (as claimed by Marx and Durkheim). Swedberg argues that the gist of Weber's theory stated in "Marginal Utility Theory and The Fundamental Law of Psychophysics"

> rests [...] on three perfectly common experiences of people in their everyday lives: (1) that human beings are motivated by needs that can be satisfied through scarce material means; (2) that the more of something that is consumed, the more a need is usually filled; and (3) that people allocate scarce goods in accordance with the importance they attach to different needs [21].

As Weber explains, this theory is not universal through time, and although it seems to support Marx's idea of use-value and exchange-value, marginal utility theory is feasible only if and when it is applied to a capitalistic society — it is not a universal concept. Work for Weber is not an evolutionary impulse or drive, but a necessary evil; thus the motivation to work comes from a necessity of filling a need, whether physical or psychical. These needs, however, have been satisfied outside capitalism. "An individual economy may be conducted along capitalistic lines to the most widely varying extent; parts of the economic provision may be organized capitalistically and other parts on the handcraft or manorial pattern" (Weber, *General* 207). The "capitalistic beginnings [...] found in earlier centuries were merely anticipatory" and "may be removed in thought from the economic life of the time without introducing an overwhelming change" (Weber, *General* 208). No march of progress exists through stages of social or economic history. Weber believed anti-capitalist economists and philosophers such as Marx misunderstood modern capitalism. Their ideas were "a conflation of its modern rational form with pre-modern robber capitalism. Unlike robber capitalism, the pursuit of gain through rationally disciplined labour [sic] is grounded in an ethic of responsible professionalism" (Scott 38).

Weber viewed society as a system, as did Durkheim, although their configurations differed. Durkheim saw capitalism — the division of labor along with the morality and ethics producing capitalism — as a natural evolution of society. Weber made no such claim. One of Weber's more noteworthy contributions to the science of sociology and society states that late Protestantism is the driving force behind modern capitalism. In *The Protestant Ethic and the*

Spirit of Capitalism Weber "endorses the Protestant work ethic not merely on the grounds of its inescapably and aptness to modern circumstances — i.e. because it is our fate — but also because it is an ethic in more than just a sociological sense" (Scott 38).

"From the economic standpoint, industry — in the sense of transformation of raw materials — developed universally in the form of work to provide for the requirements for a house community. In this connection it is an auxiliary occupation" (Weber, *General* 97). In pre-capitalistic society work was done within one's own property until needs were filled. Sometimes this was not possible, especially for small independent farmers, necessitating that they become workers for hire "attached to the village [...] receiving a share in the products or money payments. This we call dermerlogical labor" (Weber, *General* 97). Notably, for Weber, a commodity is not congealed labor. No theoretical labor-value exists. This position frees labor from the tyranny of the commodity and allows labor to be valued separately from the product it creates. This, then, allows labor to be relocated to the realm of legitimate commodity in itself, also freeing labor from the tyranny of universal labor-value and allowing for the creation of skilled labor, or "crafts work," as a separate commodity from unskilled labor, "carried on [...] through differentiation of occupations or technical specialization [...] whether it be free or unfree workers, and whether for a lord, or for community, or on the worker's own account," and thus subject to a different market and the market's fluctuations (Weber, *General* 97). The division of labor was created through the central market of the village where excess products were brought to be traded. This later developed into professional traders who could exploit their location and their mobility, not tied to a communal house or village (Weber, *General* 98–99).

Weber does not see the exchange of services or commodities within a principality or village as commodity exchange in the Marxist sense. This is duty, similar to the duty of a prince or lord to reign, to order things, and to "protect." Thus, a mixture of duties exists within the village or principality, including the duty of violence, if only implied. This construction of pre-capitalist society finally brings into the conversation the idea of power as commodity and posits violence as the dominant skilled trade, an important point when considering dominant ideologies constructing the realities of a social space.

Weber takes the discussion of labor out of the realm of philosophy and economics and places it within sociology, allowing it to expand beyond speculative thought and orthodox economy, using observation and data to study the workings of humans individually and in groups. Unlike orthodox economics, sociology allows for agency among the individual actors. Sociology, along with social anthropology, meets humans on their own ground, hopefully separating their actions from theology and philosophy, from predestination and higher purpose.

Work as Occupation

According to the *Random House Webster's Unabridged Dictionary*, second edition, no less than fifty-three meanings for the word "work" exist. Of the term "work," only the first meaning has been discussed — the exertion of effort directed to produce or accomplish something; labor, toil. However, the fourth definition of work in this dictionary is one often mixed and conflated with the first definition in working-class studies and working-class literature studies. The fourth definition states that work is "employment in some form of industry, especially as a means of earning one's livelihood." This conflation allows for confusion or, often, the slippery use of the term, especially with another much-misused term: "class."

Marx, Veblen, Weber, and especially Durkheim believe a division of labor must exist to produce commodities at any level. Marx, Veblen, and Weber concede that this division of labor creates a certain type of society. Durkheim sees it as an essential part of the evolution of society. He evokes the metaphor of a living thing, comparing society to an organism not only in its function, but also in its evolution to higher forms — again an Enlightenment conceptualization of life on Earth marching toward a higher order of which humanity is the supreme end, and, as of this time, is still working itself toward some goal of potentiality.

Durkheim cites Herbert Spenser, believing he has "not without justice qualified as a physiological contract the exchange of materials which is made at every instant between the different organs of the living body" (Durkheim, *Division*, 125). Durkheim bases his metaphor of society on the "natural" division of labor:

> [People] are sometimes so marked off that the individuals among whom work is divided form a great many distinct and even opposed species. [...] What resemblance is there between the brain thinking and the stomach digesting? Likewise, what is there in common between the poet entirely wrapped up in his dream, the scholar entirely in his researches [sic] the workman spending his life making pin-heads, the plowman wielding his plow, the shopkeeper behind his counter? [Division 264].

Obviously there is a distinct "classism" within Durkheim's metaphor, even if only what might be called "soft classism," since "species" implies a person born into a family functioning as laborers cannot hope to function as a poet or a scientist. These suppositions are based on a certain type of ideology, elitist and privileged, remaining today as a cornerstone of a certain view of class in America.

Durkheim then ties this natural division of labor into the idea of evolution. Borrowing from social Darwinism, Durkheim states that "if work becomes divided more," the cause is "because struggle for existence is more acute" (*Division* 266). Durkheim also switches between the metaphor of the body and that of the biosphere, at once seeing natural competition and cooperation, although both contradictory to the other. Durkheim's metaphor of society as a body, an organism or a system of cells or molecules evolved to work together, assumes any action seeming disruptive to the function of the organism or its evolving to a higher form is aberrant — actions such as strikes, walkouts, revolutions, and so forth. These are seen as malfunctioning cells within the organism, as are overproduction, exploitation, and dominance of classes by others, to the point of creating a whole class of "cells" with little or no function, malnourished and detrimental to the organism, and another group of cells, according to Veblen, employed at nothing except garnering praise.

Yet Durkheim's "biosphere evolution" analogy allows for the conditions he felt aberrant in his "organism" analogy. Although Durkheim believes types of individuals "can be produced only in the midst of a society, and under the pressure of social sentiments and social needs," these "needs" are not necessarily for the betterment of all of society or help to create a healthy society (*Division* 277). Although society has "evolved" in the last twenty-five thousand years in certain aspects, an argument can be made that in other aspects it has not, since this evolution has not come about through necessity or strict adherence to the changing natural environment. It evolved through competition of humans against humans and, although seemingly natural, the result is unnatural, creating a class of humans (not species) whose ideology leans toward a penchant for violence, greed, and subjugating other humans beyond what is needed to survive, and who for thousands of years have nurtured violence as a profession. By dominating, they have had the opportunity to place within society, as the dominant ideology, metanarratives giving honor to them and justifying their actions by making them seem not only logical but also honorable.

Weber is in agreement with Veblen, stating that "the oldest form of specialization is a strict division of labor between the sexes" (Weber, *General* 97). However, Weber states, "The earliest specializations by no means implies skilled trades" (*General* 98). These skilled trades "developed within the large households of a chieftain or landed proprietor" or "may have evolved with the opportunity for exchange" (*General* 98–99). This is as close as Weber,

Durkheim, or Marx comes to admitting that skill in violence, as it is somewhat today, was the predominant skill.

According to Veblen, in ancient times the dominant occupational group would have been the group whose occupation was to garner honorific praise through deeds and trophies gained through violence — the violent group. "A honorific act is in the last analysis little if anything else than a recognized successful act of aggression" (Veblen, *Theory* 11). The violent group, being violent, allotted to themselves the largest share of goods in complete ownership. Other than honorific portions of goods, the shares included territory and slaves. Although the violent group lorded over the other groups in the small communities or communal households, it cannot be seen as parasitic relationship altogether, for it also had semiotic aspects. By protecting their own interests, they also protected those other people involved within their interests.

Laborer

The stratification of occupations requires the definition of a second term, one often misused and confused in working-class studies — the "worker" or "laborer." The words "worker" and "laborer" carry with them the weight of their binary opposites, the "non-worker" or "non-laborer." For most arguments of class, "worker" obtains a privileged position in the argument, allowing for an assumption that other classes do not work and their labor is not labor. *Working: People Talk About What They Do All Day and How They Feel About What They Do,* by Studs Terkel, or its later incarnation *Gig,* by Bowe, Bowe, and Streeter, contend all people work, and most unprivileged definitions of labor, or work, seem to claim that all people involved in an occupation work. Thus no division exists between intellectual work and physical work.

Marx

For Marx a free laborer has nothing to exchange but his labor. The laborer, "instead of being in the position to sell commodities in which his labor is incorporated, must be obliged to offer for sale as a commodity the very labour-power, which exists only in his living self" (*Capital* 1: 168–69). Marx's configuration of use-value in a product, and labor-value congealed within a commodity, suggests, if given the choice, or chance, all humans would own the means of production. This is not borne out by historical fact. By arguing that a laborer is forced to sell his or her labor, he closes the discourse to the idea that a laborer would sell his labor rather than invest money in a risk/reward venture of ownership of the means of production and commodity.

Marx predicted, correctly, the future domination of employment in industrial production over other jobs in the Western world. He did not see, however, its end in a postindustrial-postmodern world. Rather, he predicted the rise of the proletariat and the creation of a communistic world where all humans shared the wealth and owned the means of production, assuming industrialization and human production of commodities would go on forever, not predicting the extent or possibilities of automation. His revolution has not happened and with the Industrial Age ending, at least in the West, it is unlikely to happen, as many postmarxists have predicted. This result cannot simply be blamed on direct interference of the bourgeois.

Marx had three conditions a person must meet to be a laborer, despite his idea that all humans labor. The first condition concerns the labor of the laborer, "its possessor, the individual whose labour-power it is, offers it for sale, or sells it, as a commodity" and "the labourer and the owner of money meet in the market, and deal with each other as on the basis of equal rights" (Marx, *Capital* 1: 168). The second condition concerns the ability of the laborer to choose, if only in theory.

Marxists have made much of Weber's statement concerning the forced selling of labor by the laborer "under the compulsion of the whip of hunger." The statement is often misinterpreted to mean the laborer prefers to own the means of production, but, as discussed later in this chapter and as Baudrillard suggests, for Weber, it is labor itself the whip of hunger must initiate, whether a person with a "traditional" psyche owns the means of production or not.

The second condition allows Marx, first, to configure the laborer as somehow a victim, presuming that anyone possessing the ability to own the means of production would do so. This assumption does not hold up to scrutiny now or then. As Weber states, "The capitalistic economy of the present day is an immense cosmos in which the individual is born, which presents itself to him, at least as an individual, as an unalterable order of things in which he must live" (*Essays* 57). Two ideological propositions meet the newborn person in the Western world. The first is that labor, in all its forms, is the personal and thus real commodity to be sold and the commodity, the product, is to be bought and consumed. The second ideological proposition greeting many people entering into society is that work, a thing in itself, not necessarily capitalism, is the norm. Marx seems to suggest just this when proposing his teleological history, from primitive communism to modern communism. He is a child of the same ideology and proposes work as the norm through the lens of Protestantism/Enlightenment, basing almost all his assumptions on the premise of a natural human drive for success. This drive being, in fact, only ideological.

Of the paradigm shift that allowed capitalism to become the dominant metanarrative of the mid–19th, 20th, and 21st centuries, Weber states, "The origin and history of such ideas is much more complex than the theorists of the superstructure suppose" ("Spirit" 58). The major impediment to the metanarratives of capitalism permeating society was that older narratives still held sway, produced by an older "religion [which] still had a firm grip on people's minds. [...] [T]he making of money was looked upon with considerable suspicion" (Swedberg 23). Until Protestantism came along with its "work ethic," working hard, spending wisely and accumulating money to invest was looked upon as bordering on sin. Weber's consummate example of this change is Ben Franklin.

Weber noticed when workers were confronted with raises in the earnings per piece, those workers still ensconced in "traditionalism" did not increase their labor output, but rather decreased it because, for these traditional laborers (pre-capitalistic spirit), the opportunity of earning more was less attractive than working less because "a man does not 'by nature' wish to earn more and more money, but simply to live as he is accustomed to live and to earn as much as is necessary for that purpose" ("Spirit" 62). When Weber is confronted with the opposite scenario, decreased wages, he discovers, from a purely quantitative point of view, the "efficiency of labour decreases with a wage which is physiologically insufficient" ("Spirit" 63). Finally, for capitalism to work, "labour must, on the contrary, be performed as if it were an absolute end in itself. [...] But such an attitude is by no means a product of nature" (Weber, "Spirit" 63). If, then, ideas or metanarratives permeating Marx's thinking and that of other Protestant/Enlightenment thinkers are no more natural than the traditional metanarratives of old Catholicism, this traditional ideology probably still exists today, and, as Baudrillard believes, Marxist thought is only another metanarrative, another ideology, and since empirical research proves much of the assumptions Marx based his assertions on were only ideological, much of what is considered gospel about the working class is probably incorrect. Thomas Wright, a machinist writing in the 19th century, contests most vulgar Marxists' configurations of the working class, specifically their penchant to add "another layer of tinsel to any of the philanthropically or oratorically highly-gilt and embellished pictures of the 'working man' which represent him as having virtues and advantages which he really does not possess" (5).

The truth is that laborers do see their labor as a commodity in itself (again Marxists confine this idea to false consciousness). Intellectual labor is an obvious example of this condition. If all who work are laborers, then intellectual laborers can only have their labor congealed in books, articles, or some other physical form or else, importantly, feel alienated from their labor if it cannot be congealed in a commodity. This leaves occupations such as teachers, consultants, psychologists, and many others in a liminal space since their labor produces, at best, an ephemeral "commodity." Certainly the possibility exists of considering a teacher's work congealed in the student's product, as if the work were grass and the product mutton. However, this is quite convoluted (something Marxists have become very adept at) and does not make much real sense. Importantly, these occupations sell only expertise, Marx's labor-power multiplied.

The third condition requires the free laborer to be free, "that as a free man he can dispose of his labour-power as his own commodity" (Marx, *Capital* 1: 179). Importantly, Marx sees the true value of the labor-power being "determined, as in the case of every other commodity, by the labour-time necessary for the production and consequently also reproduction, of this special article"— the laborer (*Capital* 1: 170). Marx finally proposes that "the value of labor power is the value of the means of sustenance necessary for the maintenance of the labourer" (171). The excess labor-power produced within the commodity (labor) is taken as profit by the owner of the means of production, or the seller of the congealed labor-power — a capitalist, merchant, or a trader. If this assertion seems correct, it then brings into contention, again, the assumption that a laborer only sells his or her labor-power sans skills, and this selling of labor-power is not an end in itself, not the commodity in which the laborer prefers to deal, and if he or she might choose between owning the means of production or letting someone else worry about maintaining the means of production and selling the product or commodity on the open market, the laborer would choose to own the means of production. Capitalists, then, might be looked at as agents or investors for the laborer and at times this was exactly what they were. This can be seen in Weber's explanation of development of skilled trades "evolv[ing] in connection with the opportunity for exchange" (*General* 99). This exchange depends on access to finished goods markets and raw material markets and on having money or other commodities in abundance to invest (meaning the ability to put aside material in any form, including the money form, to be used later rather than for immediate survival). Although a "skilled craftsman may produce freely for stock and for market," this was an "extreme case" rather than the norm (Weber, *General* 99). For skilled craftsmen to be totally independent of a lord or a guild, he or she would have to own not only the means of production but also the land it sat upon, and be capable of acquiring the necessary stock of raw material and access to the market. Only lords, merchants, and guilds had the wherewithal to purchase and stock raw material. For the skilled tradesperson, selling his or her labor becomes more efficient than, in a Marxist sense, purchasing the raw material (or the congealed labor-power of another person) that will congeal his labor-power within the commodity and then attempting to sell it on the open market. A laborer, then, sees selling his or her labor as the most efficient form of labor.

Finally, and most importantly, if the value of labor-power is only the cost of maintaining and reproducing the laborer and everything beyond this is excess labor-value, the laborer's profit is anything he or she can negotiate with the buyer of the labor-power beyond the cost to maintain and reproduce him- or herself. In this negotiation between the laborer and the capitalist, skill sets bring more to the market than just labor-power. If labor-power is the cost of maintaining and reproducing the laborer, then all labor-power supposedly costs the same. For Marx this is based on hours worked by formulating an hourly rate based on the hours it took to make a commodity and the price of the commodity on the market. Thus labor-power's worth fluctuates while the cost of maintaining the laborer does not, unless prices for such staples as shelter, food, and clothing fluctuate. "The value of labour-power resolves itself into the value of a definite quantity of the means of subsistence. It therefore varies with the value of these means or with the quantity of labour requisite for its production" (Marx, *Capital* 1: 172). Yet skilled labor earns more than unskilled labor while the cost of the reproduction of the skilled laborer is not much more, over a lifetime, than the unskilled laborer. Obviously the only real difference between the skilled and unskilled is the cost of their labor on the open market. Thus skilled or unskilled labor is regulated as a commodity, as an end in itself, and depends on the market. This may be reflected in the cost of the commodity produced by the skill set, but it is not always true. Marx proposes that this difference in the cost of the commodity comes from the cost of the difficulty of procuring the raw material in labor-power and not the labor-power itself. Marx suggests education/apprenticeships are only congealed labor-power to be congealed in the commodity sometime in the future. However, the time/capital spent on education subtracted from the time and wages of the skilled worker, compared to the wage differential of the unskilled worker is by no means equal. This can easily be seen in the differences in material goods owned by the skilled worker compared to the unskilled. The skilled laborer does not necessarily get a larger percent of the excess labor-value (profit), since the laborer has little control of the selling price of the commodity on the market. This, then, contradicts Marx's assertion of all labor-power, labor, and labor-value, no matter the occupation, being the same.

The question, then, is how does Marx get from the idea that all humans labor to the idea of the "laborer" as the "worker"? This falls into the realm of semantics. In *Capital*, the laborer is anyone who labors, excluding the capitalist. When writing the "Manifesto," Marx ignores this configuration and opts for the connotation/metaphor of the "worker," a signifier now charged with political and moral undertones. These workers become the proletariat. They are a certain group made up of people who are skilled, but do not own the means of production, and who are unskilled attempting to organize into a large enough political grouping to bargain for better wages and working conditions. In note one of the "Manifestos's" 1888 English edition Engels writes, "By the proletariat, [it is meant] the class of modern wage laborers who have no means of production of their own, are reduced to selling their labor power in order to live" (7). Again this definition becomes rather slippery, since many people earn wages or salaries by selling their labor in occupations not considered working-class or laborer occupations. The proletariat becomes "the modern working class" (Marx and Engels, "Manifesto" 14). Marx, however, means strictly those unskilled workers forced to work long hours who are "an appendage of the machine" ("Manifesto" 14). Marx's final configuration of the working class, the proletariat, was a small portion of the population. Most historians "have exaggerated the number of wage earners" (K. Brown 2). Most people at the time were employed in rural areas, in domestic service jobs (as skilled tradesmen), or in general nonproduction jobs. "Capitalist manufacturing was still an emergent system when Marx wrote" (Hyman 29). Also, to be a proletariat, a person of the working class had to be more than just a worker tied to a machine. He or she had to be collectively conscious of being a proletariat. Specifically, these workers were not considered true proletariats (of a class) until they became conscious of being of the class and of their shared class interests.

> The proletariat goes through various stages of development. With its birth begins its struggle with the bourgeoisie [...] becoming concentrated in greater masses its strength grows, and it feels the strength more until finally it centralizes into all the same character, into a national struggle between classes [Marx and Engels, "Manifesto" 15, 16].

This configuration has commonly been used for almost all arguments concerning wage disputes, exploitation, and victimization of one group by another. The term "working class" becomes as ephemeral as the term "capitalist," the edges smoky and ill defined. This configuration not only allows the working class to be reconfigured in any way that buttresses the argument at hand, but, when looked at across the discipline, these multitudes of constructions of the parameters of the working class also become troublesome and contradictory. To deal with another contradiction in his arguments, the petite bourgeoisie, who could not be defined as either capitalist or proletariat, a contradiction he had no real answer for, Marx argued, "The lower strata of the middle class — the small trades-people, shopkeepers, and retired tradesmen, generally the handicraftsmen and the peasants — all these sink gradually into the proletariat" (Marx and Engels, "Manifesto" 15).

Veblen

Veblen and Weber seem to find common ground in the discussion of a history of society, asserting the first laborers to be women. Since both Veblen and Weber believe the first division of labor was probably sexual, with women doing some work and men doing other work (Veblen believed that any labor done for honorific reasons was not labor at all), the first laborers had to be women and the men who did not participate in the violent acts. Neither Weber nor Veblen explicates a definite theory concerning how males became nonviolent, or if nonviolent males had always existed. The study of other great apes has shown the existence of subordinate males in all groups, but all participated in some form of violence when the condition called for it. For Veblen men had always worked at crafts to some extent and probably moved out of the violent group, the hunter/warrior group, after agriculture was developed, although they would have defended the community. These skilled laborers also became valuable as slaves. Although some slaves probably did defend the community or hunt, many probably could not be trusted not to flee and thus needed to be put to work at crafts to be useful. At some point, Veblen believes, through the proclivity to value workmanship, men started to value the ownership of this work. As time passed, property became "more and more a trophy of success scored in the game of ownership" (Veblen, *Theory* 18). For Veblen, then, "esteem is gained and dispraise is avoided by putting one's efficiency in evidence" (*Theory* 10).

This separation of people into these rudimentary classes questions the idea of exploitation, one of the criteria for defining the working class — one class being unfairly exploited by another, specifically the lower economic classes by the upper economic classes, or laborers by capitalists. According to the *Random House Webster's Unabridged Dictionary*, the verb "exploit" means "to utilize for profit." Thus everyone exploits his or her position or his or her skills, or other people's skills, and this type of exploitation exists within any society with a division of labor, including a communistic one. An example would be exploiting the skill of a mechanic to fix an automobile. However, the connotation Marxists provide as the meaning of exploitation naturally means unfair exploitation. Again, this definition suffers when tested. If exploitation is, as Marx states, the taking of excess labor-value, then almost all those who work are exploited. Obviously some people are exploited more than others, or are paid better for this exploitation (again contradicting Marx's theory of labor value). This suggests a threshold between fair exploitation and unfair exploitation. If, then, a threshold of unfair exploitation might exist — dependent upon many factors, such as wage and benefits compared to subjective well-being,[5] investment in education, money and time, and occupational responsibility — many people in occupations generally considered to be working class cannot be offhandedly categorized as exploited unfairly. Instead, each person in each occupation must be considered. Unfair exploitation, then, becomes an ideological argument assuming those designated as the working class feel exploited beyond a metanarrative telling them they are exploited. If the capitalist (or owner of the means of production) can be seen as an agent, a go-between for the laborer and the raw material and commodity markets, then it is the capitalists' money/investment, time and know-how that are exploited, but often more than fairly.[6]

How can the laborer be defined against the other classes? The capitalist owns the means of production and the laborer does not, but neither do the other classes. Once a communal group developed and humans evolved to a stage in which they could communicate with each other at the level of discussion, the violent faction of the group, probably existing well before humans were humans, used the threat of violence to establish their metanarratives contending violence is an honorific pastime as "truths."

The "petite bourgeoisie" as a designation likewise has rough edges, as rough as the designation "laborer." Still, these designations ignore the managerial class, those paid well for their labor and expertise, although some theorists lump them in with the petite bourgeoisie, though they are not in a Marxist sense. The Marxist configuration also ignores the skilled trades, historically able, through the market, to demand better wages and benefits. The problem with defining the "laborer," then, turns attention to the third term needing to be discussed before a conversation of the working class might be initiated with any rigor. The term is "class."

Class

If "work," "laborer," and "worker" are slippery terms within the discourse of working-class studies, created through the inability to rigorously define a term that works in all instances, and does not create contradictory arguments, then "class," seemingly the least difficult term to define, becomes the slipperiest term of all.

> Generally, all statements that have as their subject a collective — People, Class, University, School, State, etc. — presuppose that the question of the existence

> of this group have been solved and conceal [a] sort of "metaphysical fallacy" [...] The spokesperson is the person, who, speaking about the group, speaking on behalf of the group, serendipitously posits the existence of the group in question, institutes the group, through that magical operation which is inherent in that act of naming [Bourdieu, *Language* 250].

Academics suppose a "class" exists in the configuration in which they have conceived it for the argument at hand, contradicting many other theorists who have already conceived "class" in their own way. For those academics scrutinizing the plethora of meanings of the term in working-class studies, "class" becomes the most difficult term to pin down to a direct and precise meaning within the field of working-class studies.

Robert Nesbit states, "The term *class* is now useful in historical sociology, in comparative and folk sociology, but it is nearly valueless for the clarification of the data of wealth, power, and society status in the contemporary United States and much of Western society in general" (qtd. in Pakulski and Waters 667). Class in America is now a shifting, almost unclassifiable, entity.

> We argue that in advanced societies there has been a radical dissolution of class in two senses: a decentering of economic relationships, especially property and production-based relationships as determinants of membership, identity, and conflict, and a shift in patterns of group formation and lines of social political cleavage. We are arguing not merely for the demise of the *old* industrial classes [...] but for the *radical dissolution* of what might be called the "class mechanism" [Pakulski and Waters 668].

Pakulski and Waters question whether the mechanisms creating class (in the Marxist sense) still exist. However, once agency and empirical evidence are obtained from theorists, such as Weber, the question becomes: "Did this type of class ever exist outside of theorizing?"

An argument might be made concerning the notion of Weber's "ideal types" in Marxist theories. However, when Weber discusses "ideal types" in economic theory, he claims that "this is not meant in the sense of empirical validity [...] but in the sense that when equally "exact" theories have been constructed for all the other relevant factors [such as agency, ideology, and culture], all these abstract theories together must contain the true reality of the object" (Weber, *Essays* 246). Marxism's hegemony in the discussion of class has closed off the discourse to other "exact" theories. Thus what is being discussed in Marxist theories is not an ideal group. Also, while an "ideal" group may work in a theoretical discussion, it is not always reflective of a real groups because, through the closure of the discourse, certain real-world factors are excluded. Many of the "ideal" groups now in working-class studies have no counterpart in reality and the assertions and theories do not reflect the complex truth of reality at this time. If, in fact, these ideal groups are the types used to make the rules, then the other types, the real groups the ideal groups are supposed to represent, a plethora of in reality, are divergent, and thus exceptions to these rules. This conundrum, though, can easily be overcome by looking at class positions in the real world and matching theories or constructing theories that fit the real-world evidence.

Marx

Marx proposed three class positions: the bourgeois/capitalists, the petite bourgeois, and the working class or proletariat. Other theorists, such as Goldthorpe, have proposed as many as seven classes, while Geoffrey Evans and Colin Mills have proposed four. All configurations of class still retain the vestiges of Marxist thought, constructing groups by occupation into finer delineations. However,

> Marx's theory makes a mistake quite similar to the one Kant denounced in the ontological argument or to the one for which Marx criticized Hegel: it makes a "death defying leap" from existence in theory to existence in practice, or as Marx put it, "from the things of logic to the logic of things" [Bourdieu, *Practical* 11].

The history of the lower class contests the Enlightenment position arguing humans naturally want to produce, disproven by the sociological research of Weber. This does not mean these classes were, or are, lazy (an Enlightenment conclusion), but rather that they had a different philosophy, and, although "radical in its *logical* analysis of capital, Marxist theory nevertheless contains an anthropological consensus with the options of Western rationalism with its definitive form acquired in eighteenth century bourgeois thought" (Baudrillard 32).

Marx's foundational analysis of class, the one usually evoked by most working-class scholars, comes from the "Manifesto". "History," Marx states, "is the history of class struggle" (7). However, when other theorists concerned with the history of the civilization are considered, class becomes a complex idea if only in their disagreement and separate constructions of class designations. Marx states that once a gradation of "society into various orders" existed ("Manifesto" 7). Now, however, in this epoch (a point of argument as to whether the present is still part of Marx's epoch), the "bourgeois have established new classes, new conditions of oppression, new forms of struggle in place of old ones" ("Manifesto" 8). The result has been that this "epoch of the bourgeoisie, possesses, however, this distinctive feature: it has simplified class antagonisms. Society is more and more splitting into two great hostile camps, into the two great classes directly facing each other: bourgeoisie and proletariat" ("Manifesto" 8).

Finally, Marx insists what is needed for a group to constitute a class is a class consciousness, one of aligned self-interest. He is adamant that until the time the proletariat — the working class — understands itself as a class, it does not constitute a class. Thus, although plenty of room exists for several manifestations of class using criteria within the works of Marx, class, for Marx, is ultimately political.

Veblen

Marx and Veblen also move in different directions in their concepts of the interfacing of classes. While Marxists see the mode of production, ownership of the product and exploitation leading to unequal distribution of wealth and power as defining class and class antagonisms, Veblen discounts class consciousness and class antagonisms, asserting that classes exist through status.

For Veblen class stems from what he saw as a proclivity of workmanship. "As a matter of selective necessity man is an agent [...] possessed for a taste for effective work, and a distaste for futile effort. [...] This aptitude or propensity may be called the instinct of workmanship" (Veblen, *Theory* 9). This belief has caused some critics to see Veblen as a social Darwinist for assuming certain attributes could be instincts and thus inherited genetically, as opposed to inherited through the habitus.[7] Many contemporary evolutionists in anthropology, sociology, and psychology have started to revive this same controversial belief. Many evolutionary physiologists believe different genetic propensities across races or sexes are not, strictly speaking, social Darwinism. Pinker states:

> The existence of inborn talents, however, do not call for Social Darwinism. The anxiety [...] is based on two fallacies [...] the likelihood that inborn differences are *one* contributor to social status does not mean it is the *only* contributor. [...] [Second] that the success is deserved in a moral sense [150].

This statement, though, still smacks of social Darwinism if inborn talents are considered to be inherent in a race, ethnicity, or sex, and especially if inborn talents are subscribed to a class.

Veblen's construction of class is a result of looking at individual people and their habits, including habits of thought, and noticing common patterns. Veblen states, "Habits of thought with the respect to the expression of life in any given direction unavoidably affect the habitual view of what is good and right in life in other directions also" (Veblen, *Theory* 71–72). According to Veblen, habits of thought based in institutions (of thought), ideology or habitus will steer thinking, opinion, and beliefs in certain directions as well.

Veblen's institutions of thought in postmarxist terminology are dominant discourses that produce habits of thought or habitus, viewpoints, and paradigms that produce certain discourses. Thus these institutions of thought construct metanarratives closing off other possible discourses used in the narration of the self. Whereas Marxism relegates ideology to false consciousness, Veblen, as the postmarxist would have to discover later, bases his theories, if only implicitly, on the ideological aspect of civilized humans as actors and agents within social structure.

Almost all theorists agree stratification was a violent act in one form or another. The exception was Durkheim, who sees it as a natural evolution of society, believing "that any adequate explanation of society must include an account of the evolution, the nature and function of the moral norms and beliefs of members of that society" (Hall 13). Veblen, Weber, and Durkheim all had access to greater scientific knowledge than Marx, and used this knowledge to ground their theories (even if some were erroneous). This had the effect of minimizing the philosophical underpinnings in their theories, although less so for Durkheim. In the end, while Marx saw "class" as its position to the means of production, Veblen sees class as having worked its way from production early on to consumption.

Veblen hypothesizes a time of primitive communism during the early development of human society. This position is supported by empirical research, such as Weber's, on early civilization in and around Germany; however, this primitive communism never was, nor did it reach, the theoretical prescriptions of Marx of equality for all. As Weber shows, this Veblenian communism has less to do with sharing equally and more to do with the need for support within the community by the exchange of goods by those skilled at certain labors and the lack of the concept of money. This primitive division of labor includes the someday-to-be-elite class, of Veblen's leisure class the violent class.

"There is no point in cultural evolution prior to which fighting does not occur. But the point in question is not as to the occurrence of combat, [but] to an habitual bellicose frame of mind — a prevalent habit of judging facts and events from the point of view of the fight" (*Theory* 12). Thus humanity moved from this peaceable phase through the progression of ideology to a "predatory phase" (Veblen, *Theory* 12). For Veblen, only when the ability to make tools and grow food evolved beyond the needs of the group, enough to allow for "a margin worth fighting for, above the subsistence of those engaged in getting a living," did civilization begin to change in its ideological viewpoint (*Theory* 12). The idea that excess spurred aggression might have been true to an extent, but with the advent of tools for killing, the taking of food from others as a way of subsisting might have also been a motivation, especially after agriculture was developed, making control and protection of a producing area more important than running. In either scenario, for Veblen, this is the birthing place of class distinctions and separation, with a leisure class (violent class) whose general occupations are government and war "at least in part, carried on for the pecuniary gain of those who engage in them; but it is gain obtained by the honourable method of seizure and conversion" (*Theory* 26).

Violence within a violent world would seem an indigenous part of the world and because communal differentiation exists in many of the other higher apes, the existence of a peaceable communistic savage stage, even before the time of *Homo sapiens*, is doubtful. This inconsistency, though, is not really a point of contention and Veblen's supposition that we now live in a savage barbaric stage can hardly be contested. This stage exists "when the predatory attitude has become the habitual and accredited spiritual attitude for the members of the group; when the fight has become the dominant note in the current theory of life" (Veblen, *Theory* 12).

The struggles over territory, the result of agriculture, and the penchant for violence in war and hunting are two distinct ideological positions. Veblen does not see war or hunting as work. Those men participating in these professions are not workers or laborers because hunting and war have become honorific and their products are considered trophies of their prowess and courage. Trophies create ownership — personal items of honorific value even if they are useful, such as material garnered from animals, and ownership of slaves. Although Veblen considers a penchant for workmanship innate to humans, through events changing the ideology of communities, only those activities bestowing honor on the person became worthy of pursuit. Acquiring meat or successfully acquiring slaves or defending territory was an epiphenomenon of the penchant for violence of a certain group of men.

Women soon became trophies and thus ushered in the beginning of the ideology of ownership. They became trophies, supposedly, not for their reproductive abilities, but for their ability to create what Marx calls excess labor-power. Since both the mortality rate of women during childbirth and the mortality of children were high, not prizing women for their reproductive abilities seems unlikely. The ownership of women is followed by general slavery and the ownership of the product of labor and finally the idea of personal wealth. However, in any discussion of the working class, to see the slaves as akin to the proletariat and those of the violent class as the bourgeois is inaccurate.

Veblen's leisure class compares to Marx's bourgeoisie only in its position in a hierarchy. Marx is concerned with the exploitation of the lower classes by this class. Veblen brings this exploitation into question by questioning the compliancy of the other classes in this game of exploitation, stating,

> The motive that lies at the root of ownership is emulation; and the same motive of emulation continues active in the further development of the institutions [and] of the social structure which these institutions of ownership touches. The possession of wealth confers honour [Veblen, *Theory* 17].

Among the violent class, Veblen's proto-leisure class, "labor comes to be associated in man's habits of thought with weakness and subjection to a master [...] a mark of inferiority [...] labor is felt to be debasing" (*Theory* 24). In the lower classes "whose ordinary means of acquiring goods is productive labor [...] they take some emulative pride in a reputation for efficiency of their work" (*Theory* 23). Yet, according to Veblen, this "frugality and industriousness" weighs little in the placement of the person within the class situation [*Theory* 23].

Notably, both Marx and Veblen see accumulation as developing within the higher or elite class; for Marx, this meant the feudal lords and later the bourgeoisie. Yet, although Marx sees accumulation as intrinsic to capitalists, he cannot explain why other classes emulate this behavior other than through commodity fetishism and false consciousness. Veblen's theory illuminates this seemingly paradoxical philosophy of accumulation.

> The opportunities for gaining distinction by means of [...] direct manifestation of superior force grow less and less. [...] And it is even more to the point that property now becomes the most easily recognized evidence of a reputable degree of success. [...] It therefore becomes the conventional basis for esteem. [...] Thus wealth is now intrinsically honourable and confers honour on its possessor [*Theory* 19].

This property, evidence of success for Veblen, is Bourdieu's cultural, social, and symbolic capital.

For Veblen, emulation in modern society revolves around conspicuous consumption and conspicuous waste. Conspicuous consumption involves the purchase of a usable item not so much for its utilitarian aspects, but rather for its honorific endowments, while conspicuous waste can only have honorific qualities not adding to the survival of the human or family. This propensity for ownership for praise should not be confused with Marx's theory of commodity fetishism, whereas, like labor-value and use-value, the value of the fetish, as Freud sees it, is within the commodity. For Veblen the value remains outside the commodity.

Veblen believed "the tendency in any case is constantly to make the present pecuniary standard the point of departure. [...] This in turn gives rise to a new standard of sufficiency and a new pecuniary classification of one's self as compared with one's neighbors" (Veblen, *Theory* 20). An ideology of emulation blinds people to the possibility that others might not consider the same goals important. As will be seen in Berger's text and Terkel's text in the following chapters, the goals of the working class are not always the goals of the middle class because goals are ideologically constructed.

The placement in class is due, in part, to a person's conspicuous consumption — the ability to put one's wealth or abilities on display. Veblen states, "A certain standard of wealth in one case and prowess in the other is a necessary condition of reputability, and anything in excess of this normal amount is meritorious" (*Theory* 20). If the person fails to live up to the standard of the class, they "suffer in esteem of their fellowmen; and consequently they suffer in their own esteem, since the usual basis of self-respect is respect accorded by one's neighbors" (*Theory* 20).

Class, then, for Veblen, is based on conspicuous consumption and honorific pursuits. This turns the ideas of class and of life chances (the chance of moving up in, if not class, then economic situation) tied to economics on their heads. Although the idea of conspicuous consumption would seem to be tied directly to the economic class position, it is not in the sense most Marxists would argue. An example is the ability for a person from one economic position to purchase the signs of another economic position or to develop personal signs and exist within a class outside their economic station. This can only mean that class, defined through consumption, although existing across societies, must actually come to be through and within small groups with honorific pursuits being judged at this small-group and individual level in the social field through the signs reflecting the values of the small group, signs now distributed through the media and state ideological apparatus — for the former, television is the most powerful, while the education systems are most powerful for the latter.

In America class positioning, being more mutable than in some other countries, takes on the form of the reading of signs. These signs may give clues to economic class positions or may also hide economic class positions. Thus, in America, class exists in the Veblen sense, and considering Marx and Veblen are opposed to each other when speaking of the definition of class and what constitutes a class, a person can only be constituted into Marx's theoretical classes through the actions of Veblen's real classes.

Weber

Weber attempts to deal with these opposing ideas by dividing them into "class," a group whose political actions are based on their economic status, and "status group," a group of people displaying similar signs, including types of conspicuous consumption, and who are in a similar position to power systems allowing or disallowing access to life chances. Weber's theories are based on the observation and accumulation of empirical data, such as artifacts unearthed in Germany and elsewhere, of communities founded on small village systems and communal households or farmsteads. In different regions different systems appeared.[8] Many of these constructions were not communistic, as Veblen and Marx proposed, but feudalistic in division. Neither Marx nor Veblen situates their communistic "epochs" within an actual time period, therefore not allowing for any real discussion of accuracy of their theories. Weber found that, although the land surrounding a village or communal house was doled out in shares, these shares were not given to everyone in the household or village, but rather "to the members in full standing or to the freemen of the village. These included only those who held title to some share in each of the three fields of arable [land]" (Weber, *General* 24). Thus, even in this early time period certain people and groups were entitled to land while others were not and "the peasants very early fell into a position of dependence on a political superior or feudal overlord" (Weber, *General* 28).

Weber concurs with Veblen, seeing hunting and fighting creating a male-centric society, although Weber does not believe people were threatened with violence, if only implied threats, as a way to dominate them, as would be necessary in the principalities he claims existed. However, this communal arrangement is not considered by Weber, as it is by Veblen, to be based on ownership. For Weber ownership comes with the idea of exchange. "From the evolutionary standpoint, money is the father of private property [...] there is no object with the character of money that does not have that of individual ownership" (Weber, *General* 179). Ownership does not immediately imply commodity even if the goods were exchanged, since exchange does not necessarily mean the goods were produced for exchange and for Weber commodity exchange itself does not imply that the modern idea of capitalism existed within the purpose of the exchange or the production of the goods.

In *The Protestant Work Ethic and the Spirit of Capitalism* Weber argues, "Until the late 1500s and the 1600s capitalism was of a traditional character [...] the goal for the individual merchants, as well as the individual laborer, was primarily to satisfy one's needs" (Swedberg, *Essays* 22). Before the Protestant work ethic, the desire to make money went against the principles of Christianity. Weber proposes capitalism to be a distinct outcome of Protestantism — specifically Calvinism. The accumulation of money and power by the Catholic Church was not capitalism. Rather, capitalism begins with rational thinking and accounting. With the advent of Protestantism, the making of money becomes an obligation. "The earning of more and more money along with the strict avoidance of all enjoyment in life, is above all completely devoid of eudemonistic, not to say hedonistic, admixture" (Weber, *Essays* 56). This making of money not only becomes a virtue and obligation, but its results also become attributes of "good" and "bad" people. With Calvinism this accumulation, or lack thereof, becomes a sign from the major transcendental signifier (God) of reward or punishment. This allows a division of people along (mostly unspoken) moral lines in what are considered social classes and allows the moral closure of life chances to an "undeserving" group by a "deserving" group. These groups are, to Weber, not classes, but status groups — *Stände*.

> In contrast to classes, status groups ... are normally groups. They are, however, often of an amorphous kind. In contrast to the purely economically determined "class situation" we wish to designate as status situation every typical component of the life of men that is determined by a specific, positive or negative, social estimation of honor. [...] But status honor need not necessarily be linked with class situation. On the contrary, it normally stands in sharp opposition to the pretentions of sheer property [Weber, *Essays* 88].

Weber's delineation and configuration of "status groups" brings to light one of the major problems with most Marxist theories of class when applied to what is actually happening in the real world. At the individual level and small-group level, class is not decided economically, but economics may be decided through status groups or what is commonly called "class," Weber's definition aside. The power derived from class position, the economic conditions, "is not, of course, identical with 'power' as such. On the contrary, the emergence of economic power may be the consequences of power existing on other grounds" (Weber, *Essays* 83). For Weber class comes to exist through status groups. As class is configured today in the Western world, "class" is actually status groups, and what might be considered an economic class is a facet of a status group.

In any case, "a class does not constitute a group (Gemeinschaft). To treat 'class' conceptually as being equivalent to 'group' leads to distortion" (Weber, *Essays* 86). The fact that "men in the same class situation regularly react in mass actions [...] must not lead to the kind of pseudo-scientific operation with the concept of class and class interest which is so frequent these days and which has found its most class expression in the statement of a talented author" (Weber, *Essays* 86). Configuring class in strictly economic ways has dire effects on most social programs hoping to "help" an underprivileged "class."

Again, what Weber speaks of as "status groups" is what, in social situations, is called "class." This social class is the maker of the social condition of an individual and places him or her within a social class through in-group/out-group separation. This construction of class dynamics is the polar opposite of that of most theorists who use Marxism as a basis of their assumptions, whether conscious of this usage or not. Finally, ideology and the signs of this ideology are the separators of people into like groups within a social field and these social fields deny others, or are themselves denied access to, power systems allowing for life chances, and such signs as modes of dress, living in certain neighborhoods, speech (and what is spoken of and how it is spoken of), and even deportment are important signs for in-group/out-group separations.

Durkheim

Emile Durkheim's views of class are vague. His system of separation is configured into "occupational groups." Occupational groups are not the same as Marx's configuration of classes. They are not a designation of people across humanity based on economic position, but rather groups within a society based on occupations; thus the individual of one occupation supposedly in one class could very well be in a higher status group or a lower one depending on other factors than occupation. Durkheim's division of labor is a natural state. Yet, because of a lack of a "moderating order or regulator" of, not just worker to employer, but also employer to worker, these states exist in an "anomic state that is the cause [...] of the incessantly recurrent conflicts, and multifarious disorders of which the economic world exhibits so sad a spectacle" (*Division* 2). Although class struggle exists in this Durkheim configuration of the world and humanity, this struggle is an aberrant situation and "the division of labor cannot be held responsible, as is sometimes unjustly charged; that it does not necessarily produce dispersion and incoherence, but the functions [...] tend to regulate themselves" (*Division* 4).

However, "when a certain number of individuals in the midst of a political society are found to have ideas, interests, sentiments, and occupations not shared by the rest of the population, it is inevitable that they will be attracted toward each other" (*Division* 14). Occupations, which once had more influence on the formation of these social groups, if only because those of certain occupational groups congregated within the same neighborhoods, are now much less influential. Rather ideas, interests and sentiments — again, ideology — have much more influence. "Once the group is formed, a moral life [ideology] appears naturally" (*Division* 14). Occupational groups are only tangential to the social world; social groups exist within the social world and are closely related to Weber's status groups in that Durkheim also sees power held by those in society having similar interests — that is to say, the way they narrate their reality is the same. Durkheim considers these similar interests and narrations as morality.

Postmodern Ideas of Class

Many academics disagree as to which theorist can be considered the first postmodernist or postmarxist, although the two designations are not exclusive. Although postmarxist theorists have turned their attention on work and the worker, they have also given much of their attention to the scrutiny of class since class is directly concerned with identity, and thus class becomes an excellent field to dissect the workings of identity.

Antonio Gramsci, with *The Prison Notebooks*, was one of the first to move away from the vulgar Marxist viewpoint of worldwide revolution and the ending of the capitalistic epoch. Gramsci developed the idea of hegemony, complicating Marx's theory of false consciousness and contending that workers had culpability in their own enslavement. Gramsci believes political historical blocs compete through the dissemination of their ideologies throughout the populace. His thinking on ideology, like that of later postmarxists goes far beyond Marx.

Marx believed ideology to be "an imaginary construction whose status is exactly like the theoretical status of the dream among writers before Freud. For those writers, the dream was the purely imaginary, i.e. null result of the 'day's residues'" (Althusser 8). Marx felt that, although we live inside ideology, one might get outside of it. Althusser contends "ideology represents the imaginary relationship of individuals to their real conditions of existence" (109). He proposes one can never be outside ideology.[9] Since ideology permeates a person's "being," each historical bloc attempts to control the ideological makeup of the population, and in the case of a capitalistic society, the dominant ideology of capitalism is spread not only by the capitalists, but also by the proletariat themselves even if this ideology is detrimental to their best interests.

Althusser also contends that the ideological state apparatus allows the dominant group or class to disseminate their ideology through the other classes.[10] Until the middle of the 19th century the major state apparatus was the church, which was replaced by the state educational system in the 20th century, and now in the 21stß the educational system and church have been joined and augmented by mass media. The dissemination and acceptance of the dominant ideology is accomplished at the level of the symbolic order, according to Althusser, who employs a Lacanian reading of Freud through Saussure, postulating that, rather than the unconscious being a state-of-being of repressed desire and urges, it is governed by the order of the signifier. Importantly, interpellation begins before birth by willing subjects "hailing" the new subject within an ideology disseminated by ideological state apparatus. Althusser states, "All ideology hails or interpellates concrete individuals as concrete subjects [...] constituting concrete individuals as subjects" (115–16). Each person enters into ideology at the time of birth believing his or her ideological makeup is natural, and considering the way he or she perceives the world as reality. "The individual is interpellated as a (free) subject in order that he shall submit freely to the commandments of the Subject [...] in order that he shall (freely) accept his subjection [...] in order that he shall make the gestures and actions of his subjection 'all by himself'" (Althusser 123).

The Redefinition of the Term "Working Class"

Among authors and scholars concerned with class, including those disagreeing adamantly and those whose theories are fraught with inconsistencies, almost all believe a class system exists in America (everywhere in some form). The problem, then, is to understand "class" as it is conceived in America (for this book only deals with American literature). An approach to understanding the term "working class" is to first realize that it began as a political designation of a small and very specific portion of the population — the proletariat — or nonskilled labor employed in the factories. Next is understanding that Marx's vision was through a utopian lens, believing in a teleological history with an ultimate goal for civilization — an end of history. The term "working class" is used to describe those persons not owning the means of production, yet relegated to a narrow concept, considering only the people employed in industrial jobs. However, because the Marxist lens has been turned to view all people in a certain economic designation and working for wages, the term "working class" has become a politically correct term used by most in place of the term "lower class," a term no longer politically correct enough to be used in the discourse of class. This adds to the confusion now going on in the study, for the sign "work" now takes on the connotative meaning of "lower" while still holding on to the meaning of producing, while contradictorily including those with no jobs or occupations, the ill and those persons unable to work for one reason or another. Thus "working class" stands for these theoretical people conceived in arguments as somewhat disadvantaged in the world, and this text does not deny that a portion of the population in advantaged countries are not given the same life chances as others. This text does, however, contest a theory proposing a simplistic and inherent victimization, direct and purposeful, by an elitist group dominating through hegemony with political and economic clout. This text also contests the belief that class is constructed merely on economic terms and considers economic situations to be the direct result of ideological situations based on both social and ideological positions of persons within power structures and systems. The use of "class" by the rank and file to mean "status groups" might be accused by some of being of conflation of terms, "class" meaning class and "status groups" meaning status groups, but this book's use of class to connote status groups is actually less of a conflation of terms than is seen in most texts, supposedly studies of the working class, using the term "class" or the terms "labor," "work," "laborer," and "worker." This use of "class," in fact, is a more rigorous use of the term and reflects more accurately the way most people view class.

Chapter 2

A Study in New Working-Class Studies

Chapter 1 presented the problem of the inability or refusal to rigorously define the terms used in the study of class. This problem of ill-defined terms might be associated with a level of theorizing of class within the argument. Chapter 2 focuses on the closure of the discourse to other rules of the language game of class caused by these levels of theorizing and perpetuated by the desire for "a unitary and totalizing truth" (Lyotard 12). This desire "lends itself to the unitary and totalizing practice of the system's managers" in which "the state of power relations depends on the overall degree of autonomy possessed by the field," allowing for the creation of an authority defining what constitutes knowledge within the field (Lyotard 12; Bourdieu, *Field* 40). Many times this knowledge is assumed without question, to be the truth.

Because the effect of this closure of the discourse is to stereotype the working-class individual, this closure has ramifications beyond academics. Because academics are given authority over the subject of the working class, they affect the concept of the class itself through the conceptualization of prototypes of people singled out as "working class," thus affecting these people and the attitude toward them. The "social power of the actors involved is important: expectations are more likely to lead to a self-fulfilling prophecy if the expectation is held by a higher status person [such as an author]. [...] Lower status individuals have less power with which to combat false expectations held by others" (Hollander and Howard 345). A real danger exists of perpetuating a false stereotype, especially if it is one of victimization and powerlessness. It does damage to all aspects of those people who are singled out as working class by influencing how they perceive themselves and how others perceive them because "social construction is an interactional process; self-presentations are shaped by conceptions held by others [and] create a powerfully reproductive system whereby preconceptions and stereotypes [...] are enacted and maintained" (Hollander and Howard 345). Nothing may be more victimizing to people of the "working class" than to propose theories of class, to write or promote literature representing them within a narrow stereotypical classification.

In attempting to deal with the contradictory configurations of class now existing within the study caused by this closure of the discourse, Ira Katznelson contends in the preface and introduction of *Working-Class Formation: Nineteenth-Century Patterns in Western Europe and the United States* (a text reviewed later in this chapter) that the constructions of class have "made it possible to use the term as a convenient label for an unsorted kitbag of findings" (10). He believes certain academics have "also substituted for a direct confrontation with important issues of class conceptualizations and comparative analysis" (10). Katznelson states, "'Class' as a term is too frequently used in a congested way, encompassing meanings and questions that need to be separated from each other" (vii). Paradoxically, to speak as Katznelson does, and as this text does, attempting to find and develop a noncontradictory way to study and speak of class, is to add yet another voice to the cacophony. Sadly, and detrimental to the study, constructing theoretical working classes has become an argument in itself. Aage Sørensen states:

> there is an enormous [sic] literature on the concept of class that consists mostly of debates about which properties should be included in the concept. The result is a variety of class schemes and arguments that center around which class scheme is most appropriate for capturing the class structure of modern society [1523].

Katznelson considers the inherent problem of writing about class, stating, "Because it is employed without a clearly specified definition, debates about class often become conversations in which people talk past each other" (14). This chapter, as Katznelson does, questions the way class is being theorized in academia. It also reviews and critiques different texts taking various positions in their approach to the study of class as it concerns theorizing class.

The approaches to the theorizing of class can be divided into two rough categories, both contingent to each other. The first concerns the authority given to the theory used, whether its ethos is challenged or accepted. The second category is concerned with creating generalized positions at levels of populations. The first is the level of the investigation of the theories used in developing an argument, which proceed from no investigation of the theory used to a dismantling of the theory. The second category deals with theorizing human wants, needs, and movements and the efforts to gain these wants and needs in ever-decreasing segments of the population.

Those who do not investigate the theory they apply to class assume that the tenets of the theory are correct because, many times, they seem to support the argument at hand. Vulgar Marxism is usually the theory of choice. Marxism provides a ready-made niche with established theories and works well as a totalizing theory because "the struggles in question [against Marxism] have simply been deprived the right to exist" (Lyotard 13). Those who close the discourse to other language games position themselves as authorities to legitimize and thus control and maintain the narrative. In doing so they not only legitimize their positions but also legitimize the knowledge itself. This legitimation of knowledge is "the process by which a 'legislator,' dealing with scientific [in this case, academic] discourse, is authorized to prescribe the stated conditions [...] determining whether a statement is to be included in the discourse for consideration" (Lyotard 8). Whether purposeful or accidental, this legitimating and the placing of themselves as authorities allows for the creation of knowledge as cultural capital, often exchanged for publication and promotion. As Lyotard states, "Knowledge is and will be produced in order to be sold; it is and will be consumed in order to be valorized in a new production: in both cases the goal is exchange" (4). He also argues, "Knowledge and power are simply two sides of the same question: who decides what knowledge is, and who knows what needs to be decided" (8–9).

This impulse is sometimes derived from the need to anchor identity in a postmodern world where all anchoring metanarratives are questioned. Marxism has had spikes in popularity in America, at least among academics, during the 1930s, 1960s, and, for working-class studies, the present time. The first was the Great Depression. The second was near the beginning of the postmodern era and during the counterculture of the 1960s. The third, the present time, is post-industrial and postmodern with a proclivity toward "incredulity toward metanarratives" (Lyotard xxiv). All three epochs had or have a crisis of metanarratives, a disruption of the grand narratives used to construct ideology and thus identity. Many working-class academics have identified a type of anxiety they claim derives from movement out of the working class and into the middle class, specifically through occupations in academia. This angst, many times, is not caused by a movement from one class to another as much as it is by the dissolution of the metanarratives, including those of class position, causing a wholesale unanchoring of identity in society. Working-class academics mistakenly attribute the postmodern disruption of their identity through the loss of a metanarrative to their movement out of the working class and into middle-class academia, seeking to reestablish their identity through the reestablishment of a metanarrative of class. Many academics from the middle class (i.e., outsiders) attempt to quantify this unanchoring of this identity into a class problem, again purposefully ignoring the ideological depths of the people they study and their own ideological biases, "grossly simplifying reality" (Metzgar 200).

At this surface level of theorizing working-class studies is the impulse to reconstruct a metanarrative of society — a clean and easily understandable division of peoples — a way to construct an identity anchored in class and not free floating. Lyotard, speaking of Marxists, states, "We cannot conceal the fact that the critical model in the end lost its theoretical standing and was reduced to the status of a 'utopia' of 'hope'" (13). Marxism has become a convenient port in which to anchor, having established a metanarrative through a metaphoric and somewhat reconstructed view of history and a projected utopian vision of the future. It also gives the study, through established theoretical criteria, legitimacy, thus allowing for a base onto which a new metanarrative might be anchored, but, as Hitchcock contends, "those who project a unified or undifferentiated working-class subjectivity have been thwarted by representation's profusions" (22).

Those who argue at a surface level of theorizing do not investigate the theory they are using. They simply find data fitting the theory, ignoring all that does not, and adjusting much of what is used. Those academics who apply this type of theorizing to an argument already know the answer to the inquiry (if they have an inquiry) and only seek the proof. The arguments developed at this level usually marginalize agency to foreground victimization and exploitation, constructing working-class people as hapless victims who, because of their lack of agency, cannot be culpable for their situation. At the same time those who use vulgar Marxism to structure their argument, assign to this class some "native intelligence" and sometimes a separate culture without investigating why a native intelligence or separate culture might exist. Christopher and Whitson, in "Toward a Theory of Working Class Literature," perceive the working class as a "non-individualist class" (76). They do not question the appearance of paradoxes and inconsistencies when the statement is subjected to real-world studies. Two texts reviewed in this chapter developing arguments at this surface level of theorizing are *What's Class Got to Do with It? American Society in the Twenty-First Century*, edited by Michael Zweig, and *New Working-Class Studies*, edited by John Russo and Sherry Lee Linkon, although several of the contributing authors in each book do manage to break from a strict vulgar Marxist approach.

The second level of theorizing questions the established theory and often modifies the theory in some form. Some empirical research produces data seemingly showing a theory, or at least part of the theory the author based his or her hypothesis on, to be erroneous. The researcher then seeks to modify the theory while attempting to maintain aspects of the original. *The Trouble with Diversity: How We Learned to Love Identity and Ignore Inequality*, by Walter Benn Michaels, is such a text. Michaels questions the idea of a working-class culture and sees it as just a reconfiguration of categories allowing for exclusion of people from certain life chances. Bennett M. Berger's *Working-*

Class Suburb: A Study of Auto Workers in Suburbia not only questions the configuration of the working class using a Marxist paradigm but also suggests class may be more than an economic or occupational position, and individual histories might be involved, and by contending the foundational hypothesis of the study was in error and thus a second hypothesis must be formulated from the evaluation of date rather than changing the data to fit the original hypothesis, the text points to the problem of many studies of the working class — the lack of rigor in the formulation and solution of the argument. *Working-Class Formation: Nineteenth-Century Patterns in Western Europe and the United States*, edited by Ira Katznelson and Aristide R. Zolberg, while maintaining aspects of Marxism, questions how class is conceived in working-class studies. It also questions the simplified constructions of the argument through its construction of the history of the working class as complex. Although the book deals with the development of the industrial working class in America and Europe, only those essays dealing with the development and history of the American working class will be considered. Significantly, both Amy Bridges and Martin Shefter show, through the recounting of history, that American exceptionalism did exist.

The third level of theorizing, through research and data, questions the established theory altogether. At this level data are the foundation on which a theory must be built, the theory being subordinate to the facts. If at this level the theory cannot be modified, it must be scrapped and a new one developed that better fits the data. *Cultural Studies and the Working Class: Subject to Change*, edited by Sally R. Munt, although contending that it retains vestiges of Marxism (being British and thus influenced if only politically by the New Left), questions both explicitly and implicitly much of what is assumed in vulgar Marxism by suggesting class exists within a social field at the micro level, and is dealt with through individual narratives and ideology within the social field. Like *Cultural Studies and the Working Class*, the text *Culture Matters: How Values Shape Human Progress*, edited by Lawrence E. Harrison and Samuel P. Huntington, looks at class and the problems of poverty and inequality as a cultural phenomenon, although the use of the word "culture" in both texts is problematic.

Noticeably, as researchers segment the population into smaller and smaller groups, such as when considering the intersections of occupations, economics, power, education, subjective well-being, gender, race, and class, theories are stressed to maintain accuracy. At the macro levels of population, such as a theoretical historical worldwide working class, general statements can be made without fear of much contradiction. But at some point of decreasing population groups, macro theories start to become contradictory and the theorist or researcher must either ignore these contradictions in the theory or data, modify them, or develop a new theory altogether. As researchers divide humans into smaller interacting and interconnecting groups (if contradictory groups are not ignored), the more complexity the theory gains.

Katie Quan, whose essay is reviewed in this chapter, was involved at the rank-and-file level of unionism. Her essay is concerned with the exodus of good jobs in America and the treatment of foreign workers. In her essay Quan sees a need for transnational unions. A vulgar Marxist approach to theorizing the working class insists on the need for revolution and the ownership of the means of production by the proletariat. However, Quan does not promote either of these positions, questioning, among many things, the Marxist idea of a class consciousness, and the socialistic or non-individualistic view of unions and the working class. She also questions what "inequality" means to the working class.

Paradoxically, other arguments at this surface level ignore certain Marxist edicts by foregrounding certain republican and capitalistic narratives inherent in working-class ideology, whether in America or Western Europe. These narratives offer a capitalistic solution to inequality. This configuration of this surface-level study of theorizing, which provides insight to the contradictory nature of theorizing at this level and also at deeper levels of theorizing, proposes both explicitly and implicitly that the best solution for the working-class person is to leave the working class. This philosophy is one of the major underlying precepts in *Cultural Studies and the Working Class: Subject to Change* and in several other essays concerning class.

This anti–Marxist solution to the inequality of a class system reveals another paradox of theorizing at this level. While the working class is generally configured as having a culture of sorts, along with a certain amount of pride in being working class, for some authors and academics working within the hegemonic Marxist discourse of antagonistic struggle, the concept of the American Dream still exists, the dream of upward mobility reflected most blatantly through Horatio Alger's *Ragged Dick* stories of rags to riches. While authors like Aronowitz and Zweig portray this concept as a fool's errand, others either (explicitly or implicitly) promote this concept through the positions of their arguments. Importantly, Bennett M. Berger's workers in *Working-Class Suburb: A Study of Auto Workers in Suburbia* and Terkel's interviewees and the narrators of the stories in *Gig: Americans Talk About Their Jobs* give weight to the proposition demanding that subjective well-being and what might constitute happiness for each individual be considered. "*Subjective well-being* is a person's evaluation of his or her life. [...] Subjective well-being results from people having a feeling of mastery and making progress toward their goals" (Diener, Sapyta and Suh 34).

Once subjective well-being is considered, no hard-and-fast concept of what might be called inequality can exist. This brings into the discussion the use of argumentative fallacies of straw man (either/or) arguments and sacred cow arguments, many times used at the first and second level of theorizing. The straw man argument depends on the use of extremes cases — either/or — closing the discourse to the discussion of positions between polarizing the population into rich and poor, victimized and victimizer, and so forth. The sacred cow argument positions any discussion of the working class being culpable for their situation as untenable by configuring the working-class person as an innocent victim. Thus the argument degenerates to a comparison of extremes, a homeless person compared to a billionaire, but lifestyles are many times dependent on subjective well-being. The concept of subjective well-being is ignored by almost all the authors of these studies in favor of a concept of a hyper–American Dream. This hyper–American Dream sometimes drives the approaches of many authors, such as Russo and Linkon in *Steel-Town U.S.A.* and *New Working Class Studies*, and is the sticky, unanswerable question in *Culture Matters: How Values Shape Human Progress* and *The Trouble with Diversity: How We Learned to Love Identity and Ignore Inequality*.

This chapter identifies the different ways in which the study of the working class is theorized. The texts chosen for review have been selected as a cross section of both the breadth and width of the studies at differing levels of theorizing and approaches to the working class and differing levels of population studies. Although this critique cannot possibly be comprehensive, it does try to cover the leading academics in what is being called new working-class studies, and the most common threads of thought. The difficulty in reviewing these texts is that no text is completely right or wrong. Enough acceptable information exists in each to create an air of legitimacy and enough incorrect information to put this legitimacy in doubt. Some texts make major points, especially concerning poverty, but, again, the poor and the working class are different.

The books to be reviewed can also be divided into texts written in an attempt to sustain a totalizing argument or collections of essays attempting to expound an overall argument binding the articles under some overarching thesis. The former are usually divided into chapters and subheadings of some sort, while the latter are divided into sections of similarity. Eight books will be elucidated sufficiently to constitute a critique. Five of the books are collections of essays. Of these essays, twenty-three will be given attention. The other essays are either not germane to the argument of this book, such as ones concerned with multinational corporations and the supposed subjugation of the workers of the world, or else have their positions covered through reviews of other texts. These texts and essays range from somewhat rigorous studies of the working class, such as Bennett M. Berger's study *Working-Class Suburb: A Study of Auto Workers in Suburbia*, to creative nonfiction narratives passed off as ethnographic studies with little rigor.

The texts reviewed will be scrutinized for the level of theorizing, their positive and negative contributions to the study of class, how they impact the study, and how, as the study seems to now stand, they elucidate or contradict other texts (and sometimes themselves) in the study. The texts are ordered from those theorizing at a surface level concerned with large segments of the populations using generalizing prototypes to those theorizing at the deepest level and concerned with the individual.

First-Level Theorizing

What's Class Got to Do with It? American Society in the Twenty-First Century, Edited by Michael Zweig

Zweig divides the eleven essays contained in his book into four sections, addressing several of the standard problems in working-class studies while also addressing the directions in which the study is moving and the possible directions it should or may move toward in the future. After an extended introduction by Zweig, the book divides into sections discussing the intersection of race and gender with class, the working class's role in the new global economy (taking up two sections), and finally how class intersects with youth.

Zweig and other authors in the book theorize class at a surface level using an uncontested Marxist viewpoint as a cornerstone of their argument. In his introduction, Zweig evokes the "social abstractions" of race and gender to construct this same social abstraction for class. He asks, "Suppose [...] you didn't recognize the existence of class. You would be blind to the most important characteristic of the individual workers and employers you were observing" (2). He contends that class cannot be divided through simple economics, but must be conceived through power relations; however, these power relations are strictly Marxist in nature, immediately closing the discourse of class by creating a dichotomy of workers versus employers. Zweig does question the three-tiered system as it now exists, although he actually reconstructs the classes into the classic three-tiered system through the power relationships of both the middle class and working class to the capitalist class (3). He states, "Working class is made up of people, who [...] have comparatively little power or authority" (4). Middle class for Zweig are those professions "in the middle of the power grid" (5). He defines them as having autonomy through their profession or occupation, such as "doctors, lawyers, accountants, and university professors" (6). Zweig does not delve into the underlying reasons why some children grow up to be doctors, lawyers, accountants, and university professors and others factory workers, welders, and plumbers. His autonomy in the workplace is not a factor in the schools where many of the life choices determining occupations are made.

By prioritizing autonomy as the deciding attribute for class definitions, Zweig somewhat addresses the problem of using a straight economic/occupational approach to defining class, which is problematic when considering certain occupations historically defined as middle class, such as managers, who might earn much less and have less autonomy than certain occupations historically defined as working class, such as welders. Zweig's concept of class allows for the reconstruction of the parameters of classes, creating a working-class plurality. He believes 36% of the population is middle class and 2% are of the capitalist class and thus 48% are working class. He admits to "fuzzy borders with the working class and the capitalists" (7).

Zweig's argument begins to unravel at this point. Because this is an edited collection, he must bring under one overarching argument of class several different essays, many of which contradict each other. His text does, however, move the study a bit forward toward legitimacy — when it is not also moving it away from legitimacy. David Moberg in the *Progressive* states, "Zweig [...] pins his hopes — overwhelmingly and unrealistically — on the new Labor Party and offers, at best, a general strategy for reducing capitalist domination" (43). David Camfield warns that in Zweig's book, "a number of authors conceptualize the working class in an overly narrow manner" (199). Although Zweig states that "classes are not monolithic collections of socially identical people," he attempts to constitute his argument as if they were, not bothering with obvious contradictions (8). "Outside the classroom, where class struggle takes place, his definition [of the working class] disintegrates" (Tyler 27). The text has no binding overall theory; even Zweig's theory proposing class is determined by power or the lack of power, and not economics, is contradicted by several of the essays in the book. David Camfield states:

> In addition to the uneven quality and different understandings of important issues[...] that one expects to find in collections such as this one, there are a number of respects in which [the text] is less than satisfactory. Zweig's definition of class in terms of power is vulnerable to criticisms of class theory [199].

Zweig must finally simplify his power relations and ignore the petit bourgeois, as many other Marxists must. Zweig first creates three classes, and then marginalizes the middle class for a construction of two antagonistic classes.

The first is "the working class [...] made up of people who [...] have comparatively little power or authority. [...] On the other side of the basic power relation [...] is the capitalist class" (4). While Zweig claims that too much stereotyping exists through economics of class, he must do exactly this with his use of power as concerning occupation as a signifier of class, falling back on stereotypes, such as the floor manager and the worker as examples of power relations. He believes that with "no union to protect them, workers are employed 'at the pleasure of the boss'" (9). He ignores labor laws protecting wage earners from just this scenario.

Zweig attempts to corral the disparate theories in this collection of essays under one overarching theory of class. The book not only fails at this but also makes clear the difficulties inherent in most of the underlying constructs of Marxist theories presented in the essays, as one essay often deconstructs or contradicts another. This derails any chance of class being studied in a rigorous and analytical manner in the text; instead it becomes a fractured discipline ricocheting in different directions under the umbrella of Marxism.

Zweig argues that when economics is used as a basis to divide class, "we open the door to some of the most common and pernicious misunderstandings about American society; that most poor people are black or Hispanic and that poverty is a women's issue. In fact [...] two thirds of all poor people were white, and more than three quarters of all black people were not poor" (19, 20). According to the statistics of the United States Census Bureau, only 4.2 percent of whites are in poverty while more than 10.4 percent of blacks are in poverty (1). By Zweig's estimate, nearly 25 percent of African Americans are in poverty. Importantly, these statistics are based on a $25,000 baseline and do not elucidate the amount or ethnicity of people living in true abject poverty.

Zweig manipulates the data, if not outright changing it. These figures, rather than arguing poverty is a class problem, position it as a race problem since a much greater number of minorities exist in poverty by percentage of their race than whites. The reason for the 4.2% of whites in poverty is not indicated and must take into account those unable or willing to work for medical reasons and emotional reasons, as well as other criteria having nothing to do with class, including those of other classes who have fallen into temporary poverty. The figure of 10.4 percent (or Zweig's 25 percent) for one race in poverty points toward a large contingent of people who, for one reason or another, are in poverty because of discrimination.

The first section of the text, "The Mosaic of Class, Race and Gender," contains three essays. The first, by Dorothy Sue Cobble, deals with gender and class while the next two essays deal with race and class, and since both are much the same, only Bill Fletcher's essay will be discussed. Dorothy Sue Cobble's essay "When Feminism Had Class" is a short history of the "other labor movement," the women's labor movements and the "heroes" of the movement (26, 27). It is a historical essay of women's role in labor[1] and unions, and should not be misconstrued as an essay on class. She questions why women's labor history has been ignored, believing "in part the absence results from long-standing gender biases that are still operative among labor historians" (25). Cobble writes a lucid account of the history of women as instigators and supporters of the labor movement in the United States, such as Myra Wolfgang ("the battling belle of Detroit"), Esther Paterson, Dorothy Lowther Robinson, Gladys Dickason, and Anne Draper (19, 27). However, her essay is not about the working class. Cobble, along with many other authors who attempt to write about class, does not investigate her theoretical assumptions, and assumes that to speak of the working class is to speak of labor from a Marxist paradigm, labor being the "all" of the working class. Her essay is about labor and does not cover the complexity of class other than to bring to light the discriminatory practices of males as concerns gender and work within the working class.

The question readers might ask after reading Cobble's essay is "What's class got to do with it?" Although the essay foregrounds a power struggle, the struggle here is not working class against capitalists, but rather industrial wage-earning women against industrial wage-earning men. If the essay had not been in a book, one on the working class, as this text supposedly is, but in one of labor, or a text concerned with the struggle of women's rights, it might be a shining example of the women's labor struggle. It deconstructs the idea of a victimized and powerless class by illuminating how much power males exercised over women of their own class.

Cobble also deconstructs the relationship between race and class. She narrates an anecdote, not of gender or class, but of race. She speaks of Addie Wyatt and how she put in a grievance because she was replaced on the line by a white woman, reflecting a position Fletcher takes up on race relations in the next essay (27). Both accounts of race and gender deconstruct the position contending race or gender might be synonymous with and within class, lending credence to race and gender being the extenuating factors of these people's situation at the moment of interpellation. As Cobble's women had been "hailed" as women in the labor movement, Addie Watts was hailed as an African American at this moment of contention.

The essay is an example of how at this level of theorizing, race and gender studies can frequently address inequalities better. It also brings to light a great weakness of working-class studies as it is theorized at this level, a weakness many academics argue is the major underlying reason working-class studies has been marginalized within academia. When approached through Marxist's macro theories, race and gender, once extracted from class, leave class as the study of white males, leaving the proposition of any study of the working class in a very precarious state.

Cobble contends the women's movement was started by women who are "white middle-class and elite to solve their *own* problem," demonstrating that the problem in this text, supposedly a class problem, exists throughout all classes (25). As Nan Lin has noted, "males associate in networks with other males and females associate with other females in the occupational networks," indicating that class is only a very weak contributor to gender inequality (788).

Bill Fletcher's essay, "How Race Enters Class in the United States," questions this easy conflation of race and class, although he constructs his argument using a Marxist paradigm and his essay ultimately conflates race with class. He quotes Ben Fletcher: "Organized labor [...] be it radical or conservative, thinks and acts in terms of the white race" (35). Bill Fletcher believes "class speaks [...] to issues of power" (36).

Fletcher believes many working-class academics just ignore this problem, unable to come to terms with the deconstruction of class once race and gender have entered the discourse. Through his discussion Fletcher finally deconstructs class as a homogeneous group and unintentionally questions a Marxist construction of class, stating, "To talk about 'working-class interests' in the absence of a racial context has been, for the most part, an abstraction" (38). To do so, he believes, is an "'empire' or 'imperial consciousness'" (41). For the most part Fletcher's theories are lucid, but he does construct his "imperial consciousness" to avoid directly stating that class is not the issue in racial discrimination. To retain a juncture between class and race, his discussion finally degenerates into a conspiracy theory of capitalists pitting white against black, a Marxist supposition of the capitalists' tendency to divide and conquer. Capitalists have had no need to divide and conquer. Bigotry has existed since long before the capitalistic epoch came about, as slavery attests.

Fletcher recounts the history of America, arguing subject positions came to exist as a dichotomy within the narrative of Americans constituted as settler versus race (37). Through false thought material, the settlers construct their imperial consciousness. For Fletcher this imperial consciousness, in the seventeenth century, allowed for the concept of slavery, including within its parameters, for Fletcher and also for Coles and Zandy (authors of *American Working-Class Literature: An Anthology*, reviewed in the next chapter), the concept of indentured servants (37–38).[2] Fletcher ignores the fact that racial enslavement of people has existed much longer than America's history and the concept of race, especially the concept of superior/inferior races, allowed for perpetual enslavement rather than just indenturing.

Fletcher's divide-and-conquer scenario argues, "The competition [of capitalism] for limited resources places one section of the working class at odds with the other sections. This internal contradiction in the working class is a source of delight for the capitalists" (36). Time and again, though, throughout the written history of America examples turn up contradicting the assumption that racism gives an advantage to capitalism. In works such as Frederick Douglass', racism in the working class is shown to be detrimental to capitalism by not allowing the capitalists access to the cheapest forms of labor — black slaves. Racism has always disallowed capitalists access to the cheapest labor, as also indicated in *Steel-Town U.S.A.*

Fletcher suggests right-wing populism instituted the belief in the working class that "under the working class there should be a cushion. This cushion should be workers of color" (42). If, as Cobble suggests when recounting the incident of racial prejudice of Addie Watts within the rank and file of a union shop, which would seem to be more leftist than right-wing, this belief by white workers that a cushion of black workers should exist below them has little to do with right-wing populism and more to do with racism directly. Finally, the popular Marxist line of reasoning arguing capitalism invented competition, pitting one person or a group against another, has little historical value. Obviously war is an extreme form of this type of competition. Racism and sexism are old ideological constructs going back to the mists of history.

Section two of Zweig's book is titled "Class and the Global Economy." The three essays ("Neoliberalism and Anticorporate Globalization as Class Struggle," "September 11 and Its Aftermath Through the Lens of Class," and "Global Strategy for Workers: How Class Analysis Clarifies Us and Them and What We Need to Do") concern themselves with globalization of capital and the proletariat, and are beyond the scope of this text since this chapter is not concerned with labor movements, especially those outside of the United States, other than to point out that they are examples of the impracticality of attempting to apply a theory whose formulation depends on a homogeneous class. However, Panitch's essay, "September 11 and Its Aftermath Through the Lens of Class," implicitly questions the reductionism of class studies in its refutation of the importance of being middle class to the actions of the 9/11 terrorists. Panitch states, "This argument operates on the truly reductionist premise that a person's immediate class membership and immediate thoughts and actions are directly related to one another without any impact on them from the society and the world in which the person lives" (81). He questions all theories that assume a class acts as a class or people act as classed people. This deconstructs Zweig's stated position as well as that of others who depend on class separation through class action. To suppose working-class people act as only working-class people means their identity is mediated only by work and class position is reductionist. The 9/11 terrorists were motivated by many other factors than their class, all helping to formulate their ideology and identity. This essay suggests, then, that economics is a poor way to speak about the differences in people's worldviews, in their actions and beliefs.

Quan's essay, "Global Strategy for Workers: How Class Analysis Clarifies Us and Them and What We Need to Do," is interesting in its elucidation of some missteps in the use of Marxist theories at a surface level of theorizing. She was a "garment worker in New York City sewing zippers and waistbands into hundreds of pants each day on piece rate" (95). She lost her job because of what she calls "squeeze" (97). The contractors get "squeezed" to produce for the manufacturers the same goods for less money. The manufacturers are squeezed by distributors, who are squeezed by the retailers. She believes this squeeze is the reason (or excuse) for moving factories off shore (102). Quan suggests one answer to this squeeze is stronger unions crossing international borders (107–8). Through creating global unions the problems of workers all over the world might be addressed at once.

The troubles for workers in Asia are far different from those in America. In the 1970s Quan was making $18.00 an hour when minimum wage went from $2 to $2.50 an hour. The minimum yearly wage was around $4,000–$5,200 a year. Quan's wage would have equaled this in a little over a month and a half. Even if seasonal, the $720 gross a week left plenty of surplus to be put away for the lean times, subsidized with unemployment insurance. This is hardly the scenario in third-world countries, and the idea that a garment worker in Thailand making a few dollars a day might agree to go on strike so her "sister" in America might have her wages raised to $20 an hour is doubtful.

Quan is very pro-union, but she does not advocate worldwide revolution, nor does she advocate government involvement in the negotiations between workers and companies. Her ideological beliefs are not Marxist or socialist in the sense of wanting to own the means of production. Her ideas of a union's main purpose would regulate unions to what Aronowitz (reviewed later) would call an interest group.

As most authors do, she purposely leaves out the final link in her chain of "squeeze": retailers squeezed by consumers. The U.S. consumer, driven by marketing (this does not eliminate culpability), squeezes the retailer for the lowest prices. This, then, asks whether the capitalists are only the scapegoat for our refusal to take responsibility for our actions as consumers, buying foreign and non-union-made goods, if we are so concerned about the working class in America.

In the third section of Zweig's book, titled "Class and Working People," Frances Fox Piven's essay "Neoliberal Social Policy and Labor Market Discipline" argues that the welfare policy instituted by the Bush administration and other disparate policies of government during that time, such as getting tougher on crime, privatizing pensions, and raising the age of retirement, are of one political philosophy. "Only when we consider these different policies together does the underlying logic of contemporary American social policy emerge" (Piven 113).

Piven concludes that this change in the welfare program is indicative of larger "social policy" developments whose logic is "of enforcing low-wage work in a changing and deteriorating labor market" (115, 113). Understandably, she wonders why so much fuss was made over a "national program to provide cash assistance to families headed by impoverished mothers" since it only accounts "for a mere 1 percent of the federal budget and an additional small percentage of state budgets" (113). Piven tabulates what she considers attacks on programs to help the poor with the "dumbing-down of schools" and the "three decades long assault on unions" to finally postulate, overall, that it is "to intensify work discipline" by the government (117, 116, 120). She believes the government, in cahoots with capitalists, is forcing more laborers into a declining labor market, forcing down the price of labor.

Although Piven makes cogent points, her essay, like Fletcher's, smacks of conspiracy theories, not allowing for complexities in her theorizing and depending on a simplified Marxist explanation. A connection might exist between such programs as welfare reform and anti-unionist policies in that both take profits from the business sector, the former through taxes and the latter through wages and benefits, but not even a weak connection exists tying these to the rise in the age of retirement and the dumbing down of schools. The decision to raise the retirement age came well before her presumed starting point of the "conspiracy," the early 1970s. She suggests some conscious effort has been made to dumb-down schools. The crisis in education is much too complicated even to attempt to elucidate here, but Piven uses this crisis and other dissimilar data in a way prevalent in much of the theorizing of the working class at this surface level. Her essay not only makes a claim to unproven assertions but it also assumes certain tenets of Marxism to be true without scrutinizing them.

DeFreitas and Duffy's essay, "Young Workers, Economic Inequality and Collective Action," is divided into three sections. The first is concerned with inequality of wages for young people pertaining to working-class occupations, specifically (but not stated) unskilled labor. The second section deals with class identity of young people in America. The third is involved with youth and unions. DeFreitas and Duffy's argument unintentionally brings to light another paradox of the theorizing within working-class studies at this level. While one pole of the study insists on a legitimation of the working class as a cultural destination, the other pole insists that rather than the legitimation of the working class as a destination, it needs to be an origin — a place from which to leave. The unstated assumption in the text — the working class, rather than being a cultural destination, is a place to leave — is problematic because, again, the statement assumes poverty and working class are one and the same, but it is notable for contradicting those who romanticize this class and its "culture." DeFreitas and Duffy attempt to straddle the fence. They state, "College education is the most widely accepted solution to unstable jobs and low wages" (148). They contend, though, that the cost of college makes it unattainable for many poor young people, although they do not back up this assertion other than to note the rising cost of tuition and do not mention grants and loans available to children of low-income families.

By stating that many young people have no way out, DeFreitas and Duffy can argue that working-class young people are pro-union. DeFreitas and Duffy seem to predict an upsurge in unionism in years to come based on their observation of working university students or young minority workers' organized protests. However, their level of theorizing depends on allowing definitions to slide and overlap within their discourse — specifically, their definition of their subjects, who are sometimes defined as "teenagers," "young people," and "high school graduates," whatever construction fits the point being made at the moment. Although these terms are possibly the same, they are not used as such. The decline in jobs for teenagers is suggested to indicate both high school graduates who are on their own and teenagers who are still living with their parents and work part-time. "Young people" also sometimes include teenagers. They state, "Three out of four Americans over twenty-five still do not have a college degree," a very misleading quote since their statistics take in three generations of people, many of whom did not need to go to college to secure a good job (148). They also contend that a third of the minimum-wage earners are teenagers and only 5.2 percent of workers 16–24 years olds are in unions (152). For the most part teenagers work part-time, and, as DeFreitas and Duffy admit, the work done by young people still in school "may have little relation to their intended career path" (150). These young people are also extremely unskilled and are employed in areas where unionizing would do little good. Unions have little value for them, and many work fewer hours and earn less money than the cost of union dues.

While attempting to build an argument of youth as working class dependent on their supposed position within a class system based on earning, power, and occupations, DeFreitas and Duffy illuminate the contradictions in their theorizing while undercutting the supposition that class in America is constructed through economics, power, or occupation. They conducted a survey of students in a private liberal arts college where more than two out of three college students they surveyed were employed. Yet "70%" of the students surveyed considered themselves middle class, debunking the assumption that class, in this case, might be constructed in a Marxist sense (151). Because the answers to their first survey do not produce the wanted data, DeFreitas and Duffy offer another survey, a "second more indirect approach," rather than admitting, as Berger does (reviewed later in the chapter), that their hypothesis may be incorrect (151). This survey asked students to "judge their 'solidaristic sentiments' toward employers and workers" (151). The results were "two thirds of the students said their 'employers don't do enough' in sharing profits with employees. And two fifths [less than half] don't do enough in three other important areas: providing affordable health care [...] treating pro-union employees fairly and providing family friendly workplaces" (151). Without a discussion of the science of survey methods, an obvious fault in their methodology was surveying individuals from a private college of liberal arts who were mostly middle-class students who, at this point in their lives, subscribed to the discourses of a liberal arts college. Thus they would see themselves as middle class, but with very liberal leanings disappearing as they transition into the workplace and return to immersion in middle-class discourses, as the teenagers of the 1960s have gone from left leaning to right leaning.

DeFreitas and Duffy's essay, if anything, reflects common faults indigenous to this aspect of working-class theorizing. In attempting to become part of the conversation of the working class in academia, they and many others contribute to the closure of the discourse of the language game through performativity. Lyotard sees "the weight of certain institutions [of thought] imposes limits on the [language] games [...] requir[ing] supplementary constraints for statements to be declared as admissible within its bounds" (16). For academics to become members in the working-class language game, they must anchor their conversation in a Marxist prototype because "all formal systems have internal limitations" (Lyotard 43). Under these limitations the "production of proof" is "designed to win agreement for the addressees" and since "performativity increases the ability to produce proof, it also increases the ability to be right" (Lyotard 46). Lyotard believes "such behavior is terrorist. [...] By terror I mean the efficiency gained by eliminating, or threatening to eliminate, a player from the game one shares with him" (63). Rather than attempting to move the study along in any meaningful way, creating new modes of discourse, the language game demands performativity. DeFreitas and Duffy's problem, and the problem for many others, proceeds from an "established theory" within an established discourse, and rather than attempting to bring new and alternate rules into the language game, they try to re-prove the old utterances of the discourse, to enhance its performativity. Their performative act is not questioned even when it consists of contradictory statements or statements taken out of context and biased research.

Although DeFreitas and Duffy do not state directly that movement into the middle class becomes the only option for the working class, Tokarczyk does see "a college education offer[ing] the possibility [...] that poor youth may escape from poverty and that working-class youth may enter the middle class" (161). The thrust of her essay engages the problem of barricades blocking working-class students from attaining an advantageous degree in higher education. Her essay, "Promises to Keep: Working Class Students and Higher Education," divides universities into elite and working-class colleges, seeing the elite colleges as the prototypical model of how people view higher education (162). The working-class student is alienated because "some faculty at state and less elite private institutions behave as though they were indeed teaching in an elite institution" (162).

Tokarczyk believes that while the difficulty for working-class students, as it concerns elite institutions, is acceptance into the university, the difficulty for students at "working-class" institutions, along with the "elitism of faculty," is "the scarcity of resources" (162). Although Tokarczyk does not directly say working-class students are not prepared for college, she assumes that because working-class students are relegated to "mediocre high schools," they are ill prepared to enter college. This supposedly keeps the working-class student out of "elite" universities (163, 162). In the "state schools" of higher education, "the lack of resources force overloaded professors to teach overenrolled classes, giving 'little time for mentoring'" (162). Because these state schools have little time or resources, they "often do nothing to help working-class students adapt to college expectations" (163).

Tokarczyk grounds her argument on unstated stereotypical assumptions prevalent within first-level theorizing. She believes faculty do not care that most students must work (163). This statement depends on the assumption that those students who work are all working class, refuted in DeFreitas and Duffy's essay and in Tokarczyk's own essay citing a national survey where four fifths of students in both elite and non-elite schools were employed outside of the university (163). More importantly, she sets up a contradiction in her argument, at one time arguing college standards need to be changed for the working youth, and then refuting this statement when complaining working-class colleges "sometimes dumb down their courses" for the working-class student (163). She also assumes all public school systems are segregated along class lines. This can only be true in major cities and not in the small cities or towns.

Tokarczyk does, however, bring to the surface several unstated contentions of working-class studies at this level of theorizing. In many arguments "working class" is synonymous with "poor." She doesn't subscribe to this idea and separates the two designations. While DeFreitas and Duffy straddle the fence as to whether the working class has a culture, Tokarczyk takes as her starting point the assumption that no working-class cultural locus exists.

Although Jensen's essay, "Across the Great Divide: Crossing Classes and Clashing Cultures," reads more like an article in a popular magazine, using anecdotal evidence to generalize about a large population, of all the authors in Zweig's book, she suggests, implicitly, that the real difference between classes is ideology rather than power or economics, although she attempts to construct a homogeneous class by lumping different people's experiences with different circumstances under the umbrella of "working class 'crossover' experience" (170). While *Culture Matters*, a text reviewed later, does give evidence that this experience exists, Jensen's anecdotal evidence does little to prove it.

In one example Jensen conflates age and gender with class. The anecdote involves an older woman who returns to college to "get her piece of paper" to save her job as a legal secretary (168–70). College has, supposedly, precipitated a crisis in her marriage by causing a change in her. This experience supposedly stems from not knowing "what [one] was getting into [...] [to] fall in love with a new world [...] *to become someone else*" (170). Most of this woman's trouble stems from her husband's disrupted emotional state. Two older women in the class tell her about how they "had to leave their husbands because they needed to 'find themselves' and 'get a new start'" (168–69). None of this is necessarily caused by class differences and might be attributed to the woman's age and changing gender assumptions. The only reason Jensen even proposes it is a class issue is because the woman's husband was supposedly angry when she did not go "bowling" or "watch TV," stereotyped activities of the working class (168).

Another anecdote Jensen uses as an example of the problem of class passing cannot be isolated from race or gender. Jensen endeavors to explain Geraldine Piorkowski's "attempt to describe the psychological barrier for the upward mobile student," a barrier she calls "survivor guilt"—a charged term suggesting that somehow those of the working class are not, or need to be, surviving something (172). The anecdote Piorkowski relates is of a "minority student" who is also female (175). The student feels guilty for leaving her family behind and "becomes an object of ridicule by family members who feel threatened by such differences from family norms" (qtd. in Jensen 175). Suggesting the emotion the student is experiencing is "survivor guilt" is pejorative. The threatening of "family norms" is an overly simplistic explanation of a conflict of core metanarratives.[3]

In Zweig's book of essays on class, a continuum exists from very leftist positions, such as his introduction, to decidedly centrist text with positions contradicting Marxist leftist assumptions, such as Katie Quan's essay — although concerned with the plight of workers around the world, it is unconcerned with Marxist doctrine or revolution or a wholesale change in society. Several essays, like Jensen's, Tokarczyk's, and DeFreitas and Duffy's, in their focus on the problems with working-class persons becoming upwardly mobile, take, if only accidentally, an opposing position to Marx and socialism. This continuum, then, cannot help but deconstruct itself as one assumption must contradict or counteract another. However, Zweig's text does give the careful reader a view of the state of working-class studies as conceived within a narrow discourse.

How Class Works: Power and Social Movement, by Stanley Aronowitz

Aronowitz also moves away from a strict Marxist doctrine of class into a Gramscian configuration of political blocs vying for power. He "understands power in three principal dimensions: who constructs the rules of inclusion and exclusion [...] who tells the story of present and past [...] and who has the power to define the future" (Aronowitz 53). Although this statement is true as far as it goes, these power dimensions are much more complex than Aronowitz asserts. In Aronowitz's configuration of power, power exists within the workplace or within large political blocs. For Aronowitz class only comes into being within the struggle for political power and ceases to exist once the struggle is over. According to Weber and other theorists, this is true. However, this working of class takes place at a micro level. Aronowitz's theorizing is at a macro level and thus contradictions arise.

Power relations are central to Aronowitz's argument, as they are for many theorists, but again, for Aronowitz, the workings of these relations are at a macro level, because power relations conceived through Marxist theories incorrectly assume power is contested at the macro level, although sometimes, as Weber understands, power contested at the micro level through the gathering of people with similar grievances erupts at the macro level in what Marx would call antagonisms. The contestation of power at the micro level is alluded to by some of the authors in Zweig's text and most of the authors in *Cultural Studies and the Working Class: Subject to Change* (reviewed later).

Heidi J. Swarts believes "Aronowitz puts forward a sort of unified theory of class and social movements" (187). Carlson assumes that because Aronowitz puts forward this critical theory of class social movements, he is attempting to "breathe new life into the exhausted Left" (64). Aronowitz "broadens the notion of class to include those not directly involved or even completely excluded from production. For example the women's movement is a class movement when it fights for power" (Serravallo 515). Clawson states, however, that the "principle [how class works] is asserted rather than demonstrated" in Aronowitz's text (236).

The real thrust of Aronowitz's argument is the failure of labor to join with the other social movements, depriving "both movements [workers and social] of the possibilities of forging an alliance that could redefine freedom and effectively contest power" (159–60). He does not consider, for example, the opposing arguments within the feminist movement and labor movements, even leaving aside the fact that labor unions have been by nature male-centric. Nor does he consider that the makeup of many feminist organizations has been made up of mostly middle-class women whose husbands probably, in one form or another, are on the opposing side of labor.

Aronowitz believes "when movements become organizations with by-laws and elected officers, they cease to be movements and take their place in a pluralist polity as just another interest group" (157). For Aronowitz unions are nothing more than "interest groups," as are civil rights organizations and feminist organizations. "Now the worker becomes only one of the plurality of identities [...] with no particular privileged position with respect to historical transformation" (Aronowitz 162). Although he seems to construct social movements within a Gamscian paradigm, he appears a bit disappointed these social movements have succeeded in changing the discourses of the hegemony.

Aronowitz overlooks the ideological aspect of these groups. Although he has stated that social movements seek to modify existing power arrangements, he believes these movements sought to make wholesale changes in the power relations, when the majority, in their most militant stages, would have fallen under his definition of interest groups. This is evident in both Berger's and Quan's texts. Succeeding in altering the power structure is somewhat an epiphenomenon of these groups' attempts to alter the language of the discourse. Rather than trying to make changes within a power structure by revolution, they are a postmarxist/Gramscian hegemony contesting a dominant hegemonic power bloc, attempting to change the discourses at the level of subjectivity, causing changes in the power structure through changing the ideology of others.

For Gramsci, who brings ideology into the discussion of Marxism and thus initiates postmarxism, the struggle for the control of the discourse would result in the dominant power adopting aspects of the ideology and discourses of competing, subordinate powers to maintain its dominance and thus revolution becomes one of position rather than of dominance. For the civil rights movement, the struggle was against the ideologies, discourses, and metanarratives allowing discrimination to exist, as the feminist movement was against the opposing ideologies across all classes.

Because Aronowitz constructs his arguments based within a Marxist paradigm, he separates people into three opposing and antagonistic classes, stereotyping not only the working class but also the middle class and upper class by suggesting

> professional and managers do not mingle much with service or industrial workers, immaterial workers of all sorts are rarely in the company of blue-collar workers, and none of the above socialize with the poor, working or not. In sum, black or white, there is little blending of people from sharply disparate economic backgrounds [31].

Middle-class people, for Aronowitz, do not go to country-western concerts, while the working class does. One class plays golf and the others do not. Yet working-class people *do* pay for season tickets to sports venues and theaters, go on vacations to Disney World and the beach, stay in nice hotels, shop at the same stores as middle-class people and even make trips to Europe. As Bourdieu has shown, taste is ideological, formed and passed on through habitus and, importantly, in this postmodern world, it is formed through mass media and maintained through in-group/out-group dynamics.[4] Thus, for all Aronowitz's reconstruction of power relations, his divisions finally depend on the standard economic argument, showing himself to be a classist in the worst way by caricaturizing all classes, not just the working class. Aronowitz's argument, like that of other Marxist thinkers, depends on a discourse polarizing people into factions of them and us.

Aronowitz accuses the Right of disseminating propaganda insisting everything is fine in America, although for Aronowitz the Right is everyone right of Left, including the liberals, moderates, and centrists. According to him, they state "72% of the poor own their own homes and a much larger percentage own automobiles and television sets" (Aronowitz 35). He rebuts this contention by suggesting it shows the opposite:

> People [Americans] measure their well-being not on the living standards of an [East] Indian peasant, but according to whether their own situation is equal to

the historical level of material culture — the living standard to enjoy a decent life within a specific economical and cultural context [...] in America millions of dwellings are trailers, small mobile homes and flimsy prefabricated houses [35].

He creates a false dichotomy contending that only two sides exist — the Right's, disseminating absurd propaganda that claims "the poor" are doing well because they own their own home, and his, arguing the working class is mostly downtrodden and victimized. He evokes the image of tin boxes listing to one side or another, suggesting people living in them have been forced by circumstances (in this case, capitalism) to do so. He, like others, marginalizes agency. By polarizing the discourse to either/or, the argument becomes unrebuttable, a sacred cow, implicitly questioning the audacity of anyone suggesting these "poor people" would voluntarily live in this condition, when in truth "trailers," especially "double-wides," provide a nice second home for many retirees and those "flimsy prefabricated houses" are affordable starter homes for young couples hoping to move up to better homes in a few years by earning equity through mortgage payments and the normal rise in real estate values. Aronowitz, along with other academics who write about the working class, is an elitist, having problems understanding why someone would prefer to live in a prefabricated house rather than in some upscale neighborhood in Chicago or New York, and might only attribute it to false consciousness. He must discount agency and subjective well-being.[5] Aronowitz has bought into and dispenses the same rhetoric he accuses the Right of disseminating, refusing to believe his ideological standard of living is not a definitive standard. By discounting subjective well-being, Aronowitz conceptualizes the value of an object through its value as cultural capital. Once the fetishized worth of an object through its value as cultural capital is removed, a larger house or a more expensive car might be less desirable than a smaller house and less expensive car.

Aronowitz reconceptualizes class for each argument he makes, at one time suggesting the working class are the poor, while at another they are any worker. He slides from a construction of the middle class through work to one constructed through morals, what Metzgar (reviewed later in this chapter) will call the "middle-class two-step" (200). A problem with Aronowitz's text, according to Clawson, is the "haphazard and inadequate use of citations [...] for what has the appearance of hard fact" (237). Clawson, concerned with Aronowitz's figures for home ownership, states, "The rate for the entire population [...] is significantly lower than that [72%]" (237).[6]

Aronowitz foregrounds a problem also prevalent in working-class studies, the adjusting of data to build straw man arguments or to back weak arguments.

Clawson states of Aronowitz and other leftist thinkers, "If this as an example of what leading leftists produce," other academics "will develop contempt for the left," and if "this is a model of left scholarship, it will reinforce all the worst tendencies. To be critical [...] means that anything goes, when in fact [...] it must be more rigorous and more analytic than the mainstream" (237). As Clawson suggests in his review of *How Class Works*, this lack of rigor is common in working-class studies.

New Working-Class Studies, Edited by John Russo and Sherry Lee Linkon

John Russo and Sherry Lee Linkon should be applauded for attempting to come to terms with the phenomena of the Rust Belt. Russo and Linkon have published several texts concerned with the working class in this area, notably *Steel-Town U.S.A.* and the collection of essays reviewed here, *New Working-Class Studies*. These studies are theorized at a surface level assuming labor and the working class are one and the same (configured within a Marxist paradigm) and only the industrial working class exists. This text, by virtue of its title, assumes the role of defining what is now being called "new working-class studies," a coverall title for arguments concerned with the differing conceptualizations of the working class within a Marxist paradigm of class. Once again, the way the working class is constructed by one author of one essay in the text has the effect of deconstructing another author's argument. Russo and Linkon feel these interdisciplinary studies provide insight into the study of the working class defined as "experience and the social politics of power" (5). This is a Marxist configuration of power and powerlessness that does not investigate how ideologies and state ideological apparatus create, give access to, or deny relations to power because they assume, through their configurations of the victimized working class lacking power, that the working class is not culpable for their position or condition.

Insightfully, Russo and Linkon see the need for diverse disciplines to be involved with studies of the working class. They do, however, limit the disciplines to those having a leftist viewpoint, claiming that only those studies of "class conflict and intersections between class and race" are worthy of the study (8). Although they believe new working-class studies "embraces diverse and contradictory ideas," they attempt to close the discourse of the study to those theories promoting other views than Marxism (8).

Their position is decidedly leftist and labor oriented, believing "the most important foundation of new working-class studies is labor studies" (2). They go on to give their history of the development of working-class studies in

America, by which they mean labor studies. They then complain that few diversity studies programs in academia study "working-class life and culture," contending class has yet to be invited to the "diversity banquet" (4). Russo and Linkon make a leap in logic, asserting that this marginalization of the study stems from the shame certain academics feel in being from the working class and that those not from the working class feel in their privilege, as well as the fear of "whiteness studies" and lingering vestiges of the "red scare" (5). They do not back up this assertion with empirical data. Even though they then state that "defining who is or is not working class is a slippery, complex task," other than Jack Metzgar's struggle to define class against theirs, their construction of class, and those constructions of class by the authors in the text, lacks just this complexity (11). This deficiency in their theorizing of class may be the true reason class has not been invited to the "diversity banquet." Their theorizing disallows alternate theories of class while the "diversity banquet" insists on an open discourse.

Russo and Linkon's position is not only work-centric but also it is Rust Belt–centric. They study people indigenous to a certain place, ideology, and ethnic culture and extrapolate it to apply to all people who earn wages in the United States. In *Steel-Town U.S.A.* the people suffer from the collapse of a way of life. Although Russo and Linkon state, "Youngstowners were proud not only of what they produced, but also of the benefits brought by their efforts," they do not prove this pride has any more to do with occupation than with the objects their money provided. They make another leap in logic by assuming work, and not this lifestyle available to them through well-paid unionized heavy industry, determined their ideology and thus their identities (*Steel-Town U.S.A.* 2). What will be seen in the reviews of poetry by Lauter and Daniels in section two and three of *New Working-Class Studies*, respectively, is that most of what is deemed working-class literature concerns itself with a negative outlook toward work. In chapter 3, two out of three steelworkers interviewed in Terkel's text and Bowe, Bowe and Steeter's text have negative views of their occupations, putting into contention the assertions in both of Russo and Linkon's texts.

Although Russo and Linkon state in *New Working-Class Studies* that cultural and American studies offer "important models [...] about how individuals and groups negotiate complex identities, and for connecting power with identity, politics, and cultural practices," the essays in their book accomplish this at a superficial level using stereotyping criteria (4). As a counterargument to Russo and Linkon's and Zweig's text, reviewed later in this chapter, several texts using cultural studies as their approach to the study of class and inequality, show how, at a deeper level of theorizing, this approach elucidates the workings of identity.

Russo and Linkon's premise, in *Steel-Town U.S.A.*, is that those in poverty need to resurrect this working-class culture. Walter Benn Michaels, in *The Trouble with Diversity: How We Learned to Love Identity and Ignore Inequality*, claims the idea of a culture of the poor is absurd (167–68). Although Russo and Linkon's and Michaels' ideas concerning culture are slightly different, Michaels' point might be understood in light of Russo and Linkon's position. To resurrect a metanarrative as a way to construct a positive identity constrains identity making and is counterproductive.

Finally, it is this "framing efforts of academics" such Russo and Linkon, many authors in this text, and others like them that feeds the problem of the stereotyping of the working class (Russo and Linkon 11–12). Although Damian Williams, in his review of *New Working-Class Studies*, believes they are "emphasizing fluidity as opposed to static imagery implied in more traditional approaches," their "fluidity" is in fact static (102–3). As Conley contends in his review, Russo and Linkon "emphasize structure at the expense of human agency" (74). Their framing effort creates misconceptions of and by the working class. As Lyotard contends, many of these texts are efforts to close the discourse of working-class studies through performativity, allowing for a misconception of the working class.

In *New Working-Class Studies* Paul Lauter opens his essay, "Under Construction: Working-Class Writing," by asking the following question: "How does culture inflect a designation whose meanings generally are derived from economic and power relationships?" (63). Lauter sets his discourse within a vulgar Marxist philosophy of power and economics. He labels the writers within this framework "worker-writers." Although he has named them as such, they are not the same as working-class people who write. His name, which suggests worker-writers are the representation of the whole class, might be compared to lawyer-writers representing the whole of the middle class. Again, by proposing that the literature, as he defines it, produced by worker-writers is the sole representation of the working class, Lauter has closed the discourse both to alternate representations of the working class in literature, and to the working class itself.

While conceding the point that writers who are from the working class do not limit their writing to working-class subjects, Lauter is unable to concede that writers from outside the working class are also able to write working-class literature. To elucidate his point he compares the poems "The Orange Bears," by Kenneth Patchen, to "The Filling Station," by Elizabeth Bishop.

He states, "The primary contrast here is [...] working-class life observed from the inside and from the outside" (66). This, though, is not as obvious as it first seems. Bishop's poem does not include a first-person narrator, so "outside" has some legitimacy when discussing the poem, but Patchen's narrator, being a young boy, must remain outside the power struggle. The narrator's position allows Patchen to construct the older members of the family as heroic. The difference in viewpoint, then, is actually a political one for Lauter regarding the "limitations of a single angle of vision" (66).

Lauter feels that the defining differences between these poems, and thus between working-class literature and literature written of the working class, are "the details one chooses [...] the language one registers the details and thus responds to them" (66). These details, though, seem to need to be "details of industrial violence with its disorder injury and death" (67). Dirt and soot are central to Bishop's poem, but it is unimportant to Lauter because they are not "expressions of class violence as well as working-class consciousness about it" (67).

Work is also central to Bishop's poem, but what is lacking for Lauter in her poem is the violence, exploitation, alienation and oppression, or, importantly, the romanticizing of the struggle of the proletariat. Notably, Patchen's poem was published in 1948 while Bishop's was published in 1979. Patchen's poem comes directly out of the labor protest literature and proletariat literature with its romanticizing and propagandizing of the worker.

Lauter does not comment on the aesthetics of the poetry he brings into his discussion, foregoing this aspect for a reading of representation, reflecting one of the primary premises of academics who promote literature they deem working class — the refusal to allow the discussion of aesthetics into the discourse of working-class literature. Lauter finds fault with Bishop's poem because it does not restrict itself to a "limited set of working-class expressions" and does not romanticize the people who work in the garage as victimized proletariats (63). Bishop leaves the reader with a positive image of the inherent beauty of the common, creating a vivid still life. Through this still life the reader comes to realize that the unseen people of the garage have no less love for beauty and fine things than anyone else. She counterpoints the drabness of the garage, with its dirt and grease, with the delicateness of the doily and the beauty of the plant life, while the daisy in Patchen's poem becomes a heavy-handed symbol of innocence and beauty crushed.

Lauter, like others promoting a leftist political viewpoint, has no trouble using material out of context, misquoting Studs Terkel's book *Working: People Talk About What They Do All Day and How They Feel About What They Do.*[7] When Terkel wrote about work being violent, he was writing about all work through all the classes and the violence he was talking about was of the soul (Terkel xi). The quote itself deconstructs Lauter's parameters of what might be working-class writing by contending that violence and exploitation are prevalent in many occupations in many classes.

The other essay directed toward working-class literature is Jim Daniels' essay "Work Poetry and Working-Class Poetry: The Zip Code of the Heart." It considers poetry concerned with work in the connotation of wage-earning, blue-collar occupations, and poetry concerned with people at the low end of the income scale, not necessarily the poor, as working class. Daniels deconstructs Lauter's position by allowing poetry not directly involved with forms of exploitation or victimization to be considered working-class poetry, stating that "working-class poetry does not have to be about the job" (114). Because he also theorizes the working class at a surface level, he does seem to require certain stereotypical aspects of the working class, if only implicitly. He believes working-class poetry is written to lift "the curtain behind which our culture has often placed work and the lives of the workers" (114). Working-class literature for Daniels might be about anything or might be written by anyone, but it must be "about something" (114). It must not contain, though, "an emphasis on language at the expense of content and clarity," seeing this emphasis on language as the defining characteristic of mainstream poetry (114). But his argument does not explain why working-class poetry should not be put under the same scrutiny as all other poetry.

Daniels sees a danger in putting poets into a class, feeling it is a way to dismiss them (115). By this he means dismissing working-class poetry and poets altogether, although he has, in fact, closed the discourse of working-class literature in the same way he claims other discussions of poetry might marginalize poetry he designates as working class, while at the same time dismissing mainstream poetry as being about nothing. Daniels then concludes that a "bias against poetry about [...] working-class subjects in particular, exists in this country" (113). This is doubtful but strikes the victimized chord sounded so many times by these authors. It attempts to control what might be designated working-class poetry (or to use his new designation, "work poetry") and how it might be spoken about, controlling the discourse.

In his essay Daniels attempts to legitimize a canon, or "working-class" literature, by reviewing the different types of publications and giving examples of what he sees as consummate poetry of the working class. In fact it is, again, labor poetry, victimization and exploitation poetry. It is the poetry stereotyping these people as single-faceted human beings.

Jack Metzgar's essay, "Politics and the American Class Vernacular," in *New Working-Class Studies* is one of the more enlightened contributions in the book. When he discusses his theory of the middle class, he brings to light (sometimes intentionally, sometimes accidentally) the problem in academia of attempting to quantify classes through theories that insist class be framed. The problem for Metzgar is other academics' unreliable definition of the middle class and thus working class, shifting from a "'middle class' that includes almost 'everybody'" to a "'middle class' that enjoys a 'comfortable standard of living'" (195).

Still a problem in Metzgar's theorizing, also prevalent in all the other essays reviewed here, is the conception of class as solid. In actuality, one must "recognize that the structure is fluid and dynamic" (Crompton 578). Although Metzgar writes against a static conception of class, through his positioning of "middleness" he makes a hard-and-fast definition of class, insisting the working class is what the middles are not (198). Although he would deny reconfiguring class for each situation, as he accuses other of doing, he does just this, with each configuration having its own internal problems and contradictions; he states that the middle class should not be divided by a seat-of-the-pants ideal of "middleness," but rather by several different criteria such as college education, sometimes income, and sometimes autonomy, all for a "rough and ready" (seat-of-the-pants) definition of the working class (200). Metzgar then divides middle class and working class through culture, believing class is also "about the distribution of status" (199). Though he insinuates that economics create status, a gross and incorrect simplification, he indirectly suggests ideology is a determinant of class by contending the "moral and status connotations [of working class have] nothing to do with income or life circumstances" (204). Metzgar finally constructs the working class as all those without a four-year college degree. Included in the working class are those with two-year degrees, and other types of diplomas and certificates of educational accomplishment.

Paradoxically, Metzgar still attempts to construct his class schema in the three-tiered system. Yet his conception of the working class through education and ideology questions just this refusal of academics in working-class studies to divide classes into finer strata, constructing a small working class (not unlike his small middle class) of highly paid workers, including some unionized nonskilled workers and most skilled trades, other classes of lower paid workers above the poverty line and finally, as he suggests, the poor as a class by themselves. Evans and Mills, although using only four classes for their study, argue the standard for many sociological studies is seven, constructed by Goldthorpe (99). If, then, sociologists of class use multiple class designations, little reason exists for new working-class studies to cling to an outdated conception of class as comprising three tiers. This would not eliminate what Metzgar contends is "the middle-class two-step"—the re-theorizing of the framework of class during an argument to allow for contradictions within the argument—because certain occupations, for Metzgar, are middle class, such as college professors, but these individuals still earn less than some skilled trades, again setting up inconsistencies and contradictions within his argument (200).

Metzgar believes the professional middle class is generally more "status conscious" and "achievement oriented" than the working class (198). His argument, though, depends on a misconceived notion of what status conscious and achievement oriented might denote. As seen in *Cultural Studies and the Working Class: Subject to Change*, working-class people are no less status conscious than middle-class people, although this may be manifested in several ways. The first is through emulation of the middle class. The second, its opposite impulse, although still insisting on a status consciousness, is through the rejection of middle-class signs.

Metzgar's meaning of achievement oriented becomes problematic. Berger finds in his study *Working-Class Suburb: A Study of Auto Workers in Suburbia* that a more pragmatic philosophy of achievement exists among his working-class people. Berger believes if the goal of one's life is to achieve "most of what [one feels one has] a right to expect out of life," his workers have achieved the status and goals they set out to achieve (89). If status is based on achieving a goal, then, both classes seem equal, whatever their earnings, but if status involves the creation and decimation of cultural, social, and symbolic capital (the conscious developing and maintaining of privilege through what could be called "conspicuous achievement"), then a difference may exist, although Metzgar does not expand upon this position.

Metzgar does admit, though, that differing points of view exist concerning, if not being rich, then being well-off, believing people who earn a yearly wage near the poverty line ($25,000), "think $50,000 would be 'comfortable'" (195). Yet he overlays his personal philosophies upon the people he studies. Metzgar lists the "struggling working class" in table four as making from "$25,000 to $75,000" (203). $25,000 in 2005 represented the low end of a working class, but $75,000 (the upper scale for his working class) in most places could be considered better than comfortable and most people would see this as middle class (203). Metzgar, like Aronowitz, and later Michaels, takes the position of tying happiness not only directly to what money can buy but also to a mass media concept of what money should buy ("the kind of vacations you can take"), arguing that no one could possibly prefer a cabin in the woods or a week at the lake over several weeks in Paris (Metzgar 201).

Metzgar's table "Class Defined by Cultural Difference" gives a better definition of the differences between working class and middle class (207). Although he conceives culture as close to the level of ideology and identity, many of his attributes are stereotypical and problematic. Most importantly, though, Metzgar believes working-class people do not conceive reality in "the same way as the professional middle class does" (205). Metzgar finally questions the way new working-class studies theorizes class, considering as arbitrary the constructs in the discourse of academia only concerned with the performativity of this study. He suggests, through his questioning, that other ways of theorizing class may exist.

Second-Level Theorizing

The second level of theorizing questions the language game of the discourse of class, adding other rules or modifying older rules, and is precipitated by a crisis in applying the theory to the observations of class at smaller and smaller population levels. Data are gathered and scrutinized that create a disjuncture with the rules of the language game. Because contradictory date becomes available, the language game — the theory — is modified. A negotiation ensues between the needs of performativity and the data. Although the theory is questioned, it retains some of its credibility. This is not to say the part of a theory retained is right or wrong. Through power negotiations parts of an entrenched theory are retained, many times forcing the data to be adapted to fit it.

Working-Class Formation: Nineteenth-Century Patterns in Western Europe and the United States, Edited by Ira Katznelson and Aristide R. Zolberg

This book centers around the development of the idea of class, a class system, and class itself, attempting to understand how class came about — meaning how the modern working class came about, since class has probably existed since before language became available to articulate differences. The text deals with the formation, within the industrialized world of the 19th century, of what the authors consider to be the working class, as well as those wage earners in America involved, for the most part, in industrial manufacturing, although the authors do mention the rural agricultural worker but only in relationship to the industrial worker. The book seeks to cover the development of the working classes in different countries, such as Germany, France, England, and, as reviewed in this chapter, America.

This text, like many others, takes as its starting place Marx's theories, assuming the working class developed through exploitation, alienation, and victimization by the capitalist classes. This book, though, works out a more complex construction of the historical development of the working class, more so than many other texts attempting to discuss working-class history. Specifically, the book foregrounds the effect geography, population, and types of government have on the ideological makeup of the workers and thus the relationship of the working class to government, capital, and self. For this chapter, only the preface, introduction, and essays of *Working-Class Formation* concerned with the development of class in America will be considered, since the working class in America, its theoretical construction, and the problems of this construction are within the range and scope of the argument presented here and in other chapters of this book.

Working-Class Formation: Nineteenth-Century Patterns in Western Europe and the United States is less speculative in its theorizing of the working class and more grounded in empirical historic fact, if sometimes more pedantically than many other texts. Although vestiges of rigid Marxism still linger within the approach to the study because of the configuration of class using occupation and the relationship to the means of production, the authors avoid many of the clichéd and unquestioned assumptions concerning class.

According to the authors, several unique circumstances caused the development of class and the attitudes toward class to be different in America than in European countries. The conceptualization of America itself as a revolutionary ideal based on the rights of man, and what this ideal meant to people born into or immigrating to a world where personal freedom, individuality, universal rights, and equality are predominant metanarratives, produced the narrative of universal suffrage for men before industrialization took place. Dulles and Dubofsky agree: "No matter how much America changed […] workers retained their belief that they should be free and equal citizens in a democratic republic. Such beliefs endowed American workers and their institutions with a distinctive character" (2). Many people believed they had a right to individual regress. Thus republicanism and not socialism became the major discourse.

Both Amy Bridges and Martin Shefter argue that the concept of a continental nation with free or cheap open land gave people options not available in Europe. Finally, until the time of mass migration, the closing of the frontier, and the influx of immigrants whose ideological makeup had already been shaped by an entrenched class system and socialistic philosophy, a constant labor shortage existed. "The Puritan settlers in the Massachusetts Bay Colony in 1630 also had artisans and tillers of the soil. Despite this advantage the founders of New England soon felt, as those of Virginia, the scarcity of persons content in performing the humble task of society" (Dulles and Dubofsky 3).

Katznelson begins the book with a re-theorizing of class, attempting to negotiate between the data presented and the old Marxist configuration. Insightfully, he sees as a major problem the slippage in the definition of the terms used within the arguments. In the introduction, he divides class into "four connected layers of theory and history: structure, ways of life, dispositions and collective action" (Katznelson 14). These divisions or levels should not be confused or conflated with the divisions of theorizing proposed by this chapter. The first level, according to Katznelson, is the level of capitalism including "profit making," "proletarianization," and a "mechanism of exploitation" (14). At this level "it is impossible to infer ways of life" or lived experiences (Katznelson 15). The second level deals with how capitalism produces class relationships and societies, and how people of a class interact with those of their own class and those outside their class. However, this level is not concerned with class at the individual level (16–17). The third level shows "classes [as] formed groups, sharing dispositions" (Katznelson 17). This is not just the level of understanding the experience of the group, but also of "what is probable or improbable"—the notion, not of class consciousness, but of beliefs held by persons of a certain class within a certain geographical location (Katznelson 17). The fourth and final level deals with "collective action" or "people sharing motivational constructs" (19). Katznelson's third level of class ultimately contradicts his fourth level. The third level deals with ideology, while the fourth level deals with collective action. While the third level can be discussed at the level of the individual, the fourth cannot and must assume (often incorrectly) that a collective consciousness is present, not just a loose similarity of purpose, but rather a shared ideological position.

Bridges' and Shefter's essays dispute many theories used in the texts reviewed above and in new working-class studies, understanding that "there has never been a working class with a revolutionary consciousness in the fullest and the most demanding sense of the word" (Katznelson 7). The book, while contesting simplistic theories of historical classes, only investigates the working class at a large group level, dividing the working class into those skilled trades at the beginning of the 19th century, skilled trades before the Civil War, and those toward the end of the 19th century, dividing them again into the American-born and those who immigrated to the urban centers from other countries. Importantly, the book believes the American worker saw him or herself as an individual, but does not question why or how these individuals were motivated to participate in collective action. While Katznelson finally constructs class formation as political in the way the governing bodies and political rhetoric within the geographical location affected the formation and finally the ideological point of view of the working class toward their world, the two authors who deal with the working class in America in the 19th century seem to have a less strict view, if not in their positions, then in their examples of what constitutes class.

The authors cut the century roughly in two in their two essays, early and late, using the Civil War as a rough divider, with a bit of overlap. Amy Bridges recounts the history of the industrial working class in America from the beginning of powered industry to just past the Civil War, noting the similarities and differences between industrialization in America and Europe. Martin Shefter deals with post–Civil War industrialization and class reactions to industrialization. Both theorize class within the parameters of Weber's definition of class, as a political group, or *gesellschaft*, a loose organization of people brought together by individual self-interest. They explore the lives of these workers beyond that of class action, hinting that this class resembled a status group, not only in their exercising of power in their reaction to changes in their culture, but also in adhering to power groups outside class. Both authors contend religion, ethnicity, and ideology mediated people's concept of self and country and their position within it.

Bridges' theorizing concerns trade unions and skilled trades rather than unskilled workers and unskilled labor unions, few of which existed at the beginning of the 19th century. This does affect the perspective in which class is discussed since skilled workers and trade unions had much greater control over their work environment. In fact, it is just this control Bridges sees as instrumental to the owners' constant search for ways to deskill the jobs. Rather than accept the Marxist premise that capitalism naturally victimizes and exploits workers unfairly, only paying wages in the amount that will reproduce the laborer, Bridges investigates the interplay of power systems vying for control of the means of production and the lion's share of the profit. Unlike Marxists, Bridges finds laborers culpable for some antagonisms leveled against them by the capitalists and society at large.

Bridges argues, "The setting in which American workers encountered industrial transformation was a radically distinctive one" (160). Bridges suggests this setting affected the ideological and political disposition of the working class in America with the continual westward expansion of the nation and the population into rural areas and into agriculture, as well as the rhetoric of the Revolutionary War, the idea of equal rights, a classless society as it concerns rights, and, by the beginning of true industrialization, the right to vote for all white males. However, she observes that later in the century, as mass immigration moved people into large urban centers, ideology would change, influenced by European socialistic concepts and ethnic and religious loyalties.

According to Bridges, the effect of American suffrage for all white males created the idea of men as citizens rather than men as proletariats, for they already had a resource for recourse to grievances at the local, state, and national levels through the vote. Bridges notes much of the grievances taken up by wage organizations were couched in republican rhetoric rather than socialist ideals (164). The more militant unions, though, by mid-century, had European socialists as members and communistic leanings caused by the influx of immigration into urban areas where most large manufacturing was located (most of the industrial workforce in the latter half of the 19th century were immigrants or children of immigrants). They took on the rhetoric of socialism used today in class disputes and many studies.

If, according to Bridges, workers saw themselves as ethnic, raced, gendered, and Republicans and Democrats, several points may be garnered from Bridges' essay not explicitly stated in the text but taken up in the idea that class in America is unique. The first point is that the worker was and still is individualistic, a member of Weber's *gesellschaft*, not *gemeinschaft*, pursuing his or her personal agenda for his or her own purposes. Second, the theory of class struggle is only a theory, or theoretical, and the actual struggle is a personal struggle of individuals appearing as a class only when the perspective of the viewer is far enough removed. Workers did organize in different ways and in this sense were a class politically, as Weber assumes, but Bridges' argument suggests that not only did workers hold differing ideologies, narrating their identity and world differently, but their identities as workers were also salient only part of the time. The "working class" almost never saw itself as a class, but rather as citizens of America, and it still does, much to the chagrin of liberals and radicals who, for the life of them, can't understand why a "class" might vote against its own welfare.

Finally, as Bridges notes, most people who worked in the Unites States were rural, and, in fact, until 1920 rural workers, including farm workers and farmers, were greater in population than industrial workers. Studies of the industrial working class, then, are studies of a minority of people within an economic group. It questions any overgeneralized assumption about the historical condition of the working class as depicted in many studies that lets a minority of the class stand in for the majority. To really study the working class as a class at this level of theorizing, to make generalized statements with any hope of containing truths about class and class conditions, the study must include all the people of rural America, not just the industrial side, and not just rural migrant workers, but all rural workers, service workers, and other nonindustrial workers. Including all the working class, though, makes constructing an argument based on generalized statements using vulgar Marxism all but impossible.

The second essay in the book concerned with the American working class is "Trade Unions and Political Machines: The Organization and Disorganization of the American Working Class in the Late Nineteenth Century," by Martin Shefter. Shefter's essay picks up where Bridges' leaves off. He concentrates on working-class history of the late 19th century, constructing his discourse in the same mode as Bridges, more concerned with getting history correct in all its complexity than supporting certain uninvestigated assumptions that promote a stereotypical view of the working class in history. Like Bridges, he is thorough and attempts to remain somewhat neutral concerning any philosophical or political point of view. He stresses that, although by the end of the 19th century unions had become extremely confrontational, "American trade unions [...] were not revolutionary" (198).

Shefter contests the vulgar Marxist position that all workers were under the wills of the capitalists. He notes the market demand and organization of skilled workers "gave them leverage to extract high wages from employers, enforce work rules and to establish output quotas that restricted managerial discretion and further increased unit labor costs" (201). His historical evidence suggests many capitalists had little choice other than to enter into an antagonist relationship with workers. This is not to say that certain capitalists did not exert pressure on the laborers where they could to extract maximum profits. Shefter and Bridges contend the relationship between labor and capital has never been, or will ever be, as simple as most Marxists would have people believe. This historical relationship was in constant flux acted upon by outside forces. In the late 19th century, according to Shefter, "class divisions became more pronounced [...] not simply because manufacturers [...] sought to squeeze more output from their men, but also because workers themselves [...] took steps that sharpened the line between employers and employees" (235).

A condition somewhat overlooked by both Shefter and Bridges is the effect of the managerial class on the conditions of production, relationship to labor, and finally the ideology of all concerned. Shefter notices the massive movement of the new middle class away from the city center, the suburbanization of the middle class caused partially by innovations in transportation and roads. He does not discuss who these middle class were or how they were created, but some of these middle-class people must have been the managerial class, the industrial bureaucrats needed to oversee aspects of production, procure material, disperse product, and keep track of aspects of production. Little work has been done on the effect of ownership being divorced from direct involvement with manufacturing and the effect of Weber's accountants and the other employees whose only true function was, and still is, to secure profits for their bosses, pitting this class directly against the working class.

Shefter notes that by the late 19th century, trade unions had become powerful and had organized labor reform associations. They began to form local labor parties, but soon took on national significance, mostly noted in "the great strike wave of 1886" (227). Shefter argues that this wave of strikes provoked outrage among the upper and middle classes and caused them to stage counterattacks, leading to some of the most bitter and violent confrontations of the 19th century (237). Shefter elucidates how this backlash became more than just a capitalistic enterprise. The voting population of America seemed to have turned their backs on labor. The political inroads made by labor in both major parties were lost partially due to the influence, if only implied, of radical groups within the unions proposing the dismantling of the current wage system, if not the government.

In most works dealing with the working class, the situation is always that of a powerless working class victimized by an all-powerful capitalist class. In Bridges' and Shefter's essays the working class is given more complexity, although they still stereotype people of the working class. Their essays are a movement toward understanding the individual as it concerns class, though sometimes both authors fall into the trap of configuring the working class as non-individualistic. This stereotyping, however, can somewhat be attributed to the complexity of their argument dealing with a half-century of change in a time when change was rapid in manufacturing, communication, transport, philosophy, and ideologies. However, much of it is inherent in theorizing class at this level.

The question still remains as to how to theorize the working class in total and how to study them. To exclude all but the industrial working class from the discourse marginalizes a large section of the population. To include within the working class all persons in an economic stratum allows for many decidedly nonworking-class occupations to be included. The question of petite bourgeoisie remains unanswered. Where does an independent cooper or smith fit, or today an independent garage owner, baker, or computer repairman?

The Trouble with Diversity: How We Learned to Love Identity and Ignore Inequality, by Walter Benn Michaels

Michaels' text is of a different nature than previously discussed examples. It does not seek to establish a class framework, although it must in certain instances, which is a weakness in the argument. This weakness, though, brings to the surface the underlying question his book seeks to answer: why do the poor remain poor? This question is taken up on a global scale by *Culture Matters: How Values Shape Human Progress* (critiqued later). Michaels takes a different approach to the argument of divisions in America because his argument is different. He does not see it as a strict class division by economics into framed classes, although for him economics is the division. He divides class not into the Marxist three-tiered system, but rather the classical "haves" and "have nots." He argues that this inequality is ideological by asserting that through ideology, formed by metanarratives and discourses, we have come to love diversity and ignore inequality. Michaels questions the simplistic theorizing of many who study class and those who portray class as a culture (as if it were an ethnicity) and by doing so have allowed a "backdoor" racism to develop in this country.

He makes his point by establishing, scientifically, that race does not exist. Society has allowed for the establishment of race as "culture." This has permitted for the establishment of ethnicity as "culture" and thus finally class as culture. He maintains that this classism, in the guise of diversity, has allowed the liberals and conservatives to avoid the problem of inequality in America. Michaels seeks to deconstruct the idea of a class culture,[8] seeing the concept as "one of our strategies for managing inequality rather than minimizing or eliminating it" (10).

His argument is cogent and fairly factually based, but some problems persist. He openly discusses the connection between "poor" and "black," but adjusts the data. Again, as Aronowitz contends, Michaels notes that many more whites than black people in the United States live in poverty. Michaels believes getting rid of racism will not alleviate poverty. When considering the percentages, though, even Michaels admits only 8.65 percent of the population of whites live in poverty while blacks have 24.7 percent in poverty (171).[9] Michaels states that these numbers are "disturbing because they remind us of the degree to which both the legacy of racism and racism itself are a problem" (171–72). Although race is only an ideological construct, even Michaels admits it has effects in the real world. Truthfully, as he suggests, if one could end racism, poverty would not end, but only because many other circumstances go into creating poverty. It would, however, go down. Extrapolation of his numbers shows that if classism ended, poverty would still not end since racism and sexism would still continue to cause inequity.

Michaels, although he makes a cogent argument against the celebration of the culture of poverty, stumbles in the same way as do the majority of those promoting a Marxist viewpoint. To make his argument work, he must postulate that all working-class persons want exactly what he wants. In Michaels' case, $175,000 a year is not enough. Michaels believes his greediness has little to do with his argument being correct or incorrect (191). Logically this must be true, but his argument is incorrect because of the point of view produced by his lifestyle, his neighbors' lifestyle, and his inculcation into academia. Although Michaels falls into the top "3 percent of American [wealthy] population [...] [he] does not feel rich. [...] For one thing he is confronted on a daily basis by the spectacle of people who are much richer than he is" (192). Others are confronted with the same spectacle, but, as Metzgar states, they see $50,000 as comfortable. Within his book Michaels discusses a reality TV show, *Wife Swap*—specifically, an episode where a very well-to-do wife switches places with a working-class wife. The "rich" wife learns she needs to spend more time with her children and the working-class wife finds "money can't buy what I have" (102). Maybe because Michaels has moved into — and bought into — the paradigm that "more makes (you) better," he cannot fathom people finding a level of satisfaction below $175,000 per annum. What he misses is the differing levels and aspects of subjective well-being — the setting of goals and types of happiness of the individual.

Michaels is caught up in Veblen's emulation where "each class envies and emulates the class above it in the social scale, while it rarely compares itself with those below" (Veblen *Theory* 64). He does not feel rich despite making $175,000 a year. Michaels is

> a daily reader of the *New York Times*, and one of the primary functions the *Times* performs for its upper-middle-class readers is to make them feel poorer. It does this by publishing articles like "Is $200,000 the new $100,000?" or articles about the differences in status between people who have the nanny pick the children up after school and people who bring the nanny along [...] if you bring the nanny with you [...] you win [Michaels 192–93].

Michaels is caught up in a merry-go-round — not of money, but of status. His yearly $175,000 wage is secondary to his ideological conception of self-esteem.

Michaels, like others, ignores the changing epoch refusing to consider the effect of advancements in technology demanding that the rank and file acquire a degree beyond high school or skilled trade. The narrative of the heroically uneducated/unskilled working-class person is a type of nostalgia born of vulgar Marxism creeping into many arguments on class, a pseudo-legitimization of class as culture, exactly what Michaels works to deny. At some point in future discussions this heroic configuration of the working class must be modified if the situation of those in and near poverty is to be addressed.

When Michaels does speak of the need for education his slippery definition of education marginalizes the credibility of technical schools and two-year colleges as legitimate resources for alternative strategies to having to deal with the shrinking market for semi-skilled and unskilled labor. Metzgar,

Aronowitz, and Michaels theorize education along the lines of wealth and influence, using the Ivy League universities for their single example of inequality in education. When Michaels speaks of Harvard's affirmative action policy, he correctly deduces that "the problem with affirmative action is not [...] that it violates the principles of meritocracy; the problem is that it produces the illusion that we have a meritocracy" (85). Aronowitz believes "a baccalaureate from state colleges and universities [...] is not the equivalent of a degree from an Ivy League institute or a leading private university like Stanford or Chicago" (16). It may not be as good, but a degree from a state university may well be good enough for many. Because of his point of view, Michaels does not consider that a college degree provides many people with the opportunities for a profession and a way of life to their satisfaction without being expected to perform at the "supposed" Harvard level. William DeGenaro, an assistant professor at Miami University at Hamilton, sheds light on just this attitude in his opening paragraph of a review of three working-class books, including *Steel-Town U.S.A.*: "As I sit down to write this review, two students have just dropped my first-year composition class, one who plans to attend trade school and one who just got accepted into an apprentice program by the local bricklayers' union" (229). These students do not value college education as most academics do (the first commandment of the academic Ten Commandments) and prefer to earn their living through skilled trades. These occupations may or may not allow a person to earn as much or more money as a college degree would permit, but, in the end these former students may be happier working in skilled trades. To suggest this may not be so is reverse classism.

The underlying question Michaels wrestles with throughout his text may not be, for him, why he doesn't feel rich making three and a half times as much as his average worker, nor why someone might accept a degree from a state school rather than clawing and scratching to get into Harvard, nor even, finally, why anyone would put up with inequality at all even if diversity of culture has been foregrounded in identity making, but rather what the mechanism might be allowing for this inequality to exist or why the poor stay poor.[10]

Third-Level Theorizing

Finally, those who study how class works at the individual level must confront the irregularities and contradictions macro theories present. They do not propose to show how victimization, alienation, exploitation, and proletarianization are echoed by the individual. This would need to start with a theory, vulgar Marxism, and find data to fit. Rather, they observe, either under scientific conditions (as Berger does) or through close contact and personal experience, the lived experiences of people designated as working class. They are forced by the data to reconsider certain positions within their hypotheses or within learned theories, and then to modify these theories. In the first text reviewed, Bennett Berger starts with a hypothesis and must conclude that the hypothesis is incorrect. He then constructs another hypothesis better fitting the data. The second book, *Culture Matters: How Values Shape Human Progress*, although not about the working class directly, attempts to answer, from a global viewpoint, the question Michaels' text fails to answer: why the poor stay poor? The answer is not as simplistic as vulgar Marxists believe. The text finally confronts individual and group ideologies, although with questionable results. The advent of cultural studies supplies the final book of this chapter (*Cultural Studies and the Working Class: Subject to Change*) with a lens to finally look at the individual. Although it also sometimes conflates the working class with the poor and has echoes of Marxism still present (having been written about and published in Britain, where the New Left still holds a strong presence in academia), it opens the language game to discourses that explore ideologies and identities of the working class at the individual level. It changes the theorizing of class from non-individualistic collective consciousness to people narrating their existence in and around power systems.

Working-Class Suburb, by Bennett M. Berger

The preface of Bennett M. Berger's text opens with:

> The Ford division of the Ford Motor Company closed its assembly plant in Richmond California, and moved, taking virtually all its employees with it, to a brand new plant some fifty miles away. [...] It was my job to conduct a survey of the Ford workers with a view to discovering what changes in their lives and those of their families might be attributed to the move [v].

These workers moved to new tract homes in suburbia, a change from the urban lifestyle in Richmond.

> An interview schedule was designed based on the general assumption that these erstwhile working-class families, most of whom had lived in the drab industrial city of Richmond, would be learning middle-class behaviors, beliefs and aspirations as a result of the suburbanization process. [...] This assumption was mistaken [v].

Berger's text, although rather old, still retains its importance, if not for its study of working-class people, then for being ignored by many authors who came later and who study the working class. The study was done in the heyday of labor power in the 20th century as a scientific study concerned with how class is conceived in society. It is based on an ethnographic study conducted under scientific conditions. He gives a breakdown of the group studied by age, race, and family history. He also states his methodology and produces substantial evidence for his conclusion. He starts with a hypothesis based on other studies and theories, and when this hypothesis proves incorrect, he admits to this fact and formulates a different hypothesis according to the evidence presented in his study and modifies the theory used to correct the errors.

Another observation that might be taken from Berger's study is that not only did the working class not react as Berger first assumed, but they also did not react as many working-class academics have assumed. Berger found that workers did not move into the middle class, not because of class consciousness in a Marxist sense, but because they had diverse backgrounds and ages and saw themselves as different from one another, using diverse narratives to narrate their identity. Rather than class solidarity, the mediating factors in their stasis were family history, age, education, and ethnicity.

Berger argues that those academics who believed in the "myth of suburbia" controlled the discourse of the study, allowing the myth to persist and to be "very serviceable in public discourse as a highly evocative symbol" (xvi). Berger states, "Our society is wealthy enough to support a substantial class of intellectuals devoted to staying on top of contemporary events. [...] We get myths, which themselves become part of the ideology [Lyotard's performativity]" (xx).

Berger uncovered two aspects of these people's lives that have significance for the argument of this chapter — the lack of a socialistic attitude and its opposite impulse, the belief in the American Dream (although not the same dream constructed by mass media). Although the questions used in the interviews did not directly pertain to the worker's ideology, plenty of time and space was allotted for ideological opinions. Berger found these workers to have more allegiance to a kin network than to their fellow workers. Little solidarity existed other than being members of the union. Because many of those studied had little to do with neighbors and "friends," Berger questioned the standard assumption "that they were socially isolated and cut off from channels of power, information and growth" (67). He calls on Dotson's assumption, contending that "the role of informal participation, particularly within the family and kin group, has, we believe, consistently been underestimated" (qtd. in Berger 67). Finally, though, when the workers saw themselves as working class, it was not in a Marxist sense, but through status.

The workers and their families, rather than contesting the American Dream based in a capitalist philosophy, embraced it. Importantly, though, this American Dream was ideologically constructed. Berger claims the workers he studied had reached what they felt was the upper level of their achievement, and rather than considering this in negative terms (still having less wealth and property than many middle-class people), they believed they had reached their goal, and thus felt fulfilled and happy. "Owning a new home in a community of new home owners makes them more respectable and self-respecting people" (82). This feeling of subjective well-being through "goal achievement," for many theorists, is problematic since it contends that people of the working class do not always perceive themselves within an inequality framework. Although conspicuous consumption has now permeated the working class, courtesy of mass media, image management "presentation of self" is still less important to them than the middle class (Hollander and Howard 344).

Other differences Berger uncovered concerning the middle class and his working-class people were the concept of symbolic capital, or cultural capital, and the end goals of work. Cultural and symbolic capital are conspicuously missing when Berger writes about his working-class people. "Pride of ownership certainly might be thought of as evidence of heightened status consciousness; yet even here there is an ambiguity. Most respondents did not think of their homes primarily as status objects" (Berger 84). They saw their houses as "investments" or cheaper than renting, and, most importantly, these homes gave them a certain amount of freedom to "do as one pleased" (82).

Another notable discovery of Berger's is the hope of independence among the workers. "The service station owner is the local 'prince'; he has realized a dream" (89). While within the factory "the upper limit of the asperational framework is apparently foreman," one worker who took a foreman's job hated it (Berger 88). This suggests that neither the status of the promotion to a "management" position nor the extra money offset the negative aspects of being placed between workers and upper management. This also suggests one of the ideological aspects of a working-class person — the avoidance of power networks and power confrontations (taken up later in this book). The "garage owner" ideal presents itself as a refuge from power altogether, whether this is actually the case or not. Notably, this worker, rather than wanting more power (as Zweig suggests), was happier with less. The "garage owner" does not present a likely future of power or riches, but of autonomy. This cannot be the same autonomy Aronowitz or Zweig propose as a collective power position. For Berger's workers it is freedom from a power position. This ideological position cannot be simply attributed to the result of a lack of power by the working class. As shown by Evans and Mills when elucidating Goldthorpe's reasoning on his class divisions, the choosing of occupations is a dynamic action between the ideology of the potential employee and the demands and responsibilities of a job versus the benefits of the occupation (89, 90).

Culture Matters: How Values Shape Human Progress, Edited by Lawrence E. Harrison and Samuel P. Huntington

Culture Matters is not a book about the working class. It does, however, bring to light certain theories or aspects of theorizing germane to this chapter, although the authors' use of the word "culture" is problematic — they use culture where they mean ideology. The book hopes to elicit change in countries lacking personal freedom for citizens who are, for the most part, steeped in poverty. To change these cultural signs, such as dress and language, would only change the outward signs and do little to change the ideology of the people, as can be seen many times in poor neighborhoods with urban renewal. The text proposes different ideologies exist in different parts of the world among different people. To extrapolate from this text, if differing peoples have differing ideologies, differing classes also may have differing ideologies.

Culture Matters is motivated by what seems to be a large and paradoxical inequality existing in the world today as it concerns third-world countries, specifically the failure of certain countries to improve their conditions while others have made much improvement. The term the authors prefer to use is "progress." The sticking point, though, is the way progress is theorized within the text. In the introduction by Huntington, progress is defined as "a movement toward economic development and material well-being, social-economic equality and political democracy" (xv). However, many types of democracies, from laissez-faire democracy to social democracy, exist, as anyone who has listened to the debates within a democratic country can attest to, from maximizing freedom to adjusting or mediating it in some moral sense. Of course, economic progress does not necessarily usher in progress, as Marxists contend. If greater personal freedom is a measurement, economic development (in this essay the ability to produce and export commodities) can and does curtail freedom and can produce a society of have and have-nots.

Two other key terms are used within the arguments of the text. The first is prosperity, although "prosperity, after all, is hard to define" (Fairbanks 269). Fairbanks cites Debraj Ray's definition of prosperity, stating, "Prosperity is the ability of an individual, group, or nation to provide shelter, nutrition, and other material goods enabling people to live a good life according to their own definition" (qtd. in Fairbanks 270). Although prosperity would be easy to qualify and quantify for Westerners, prosperity, again, is an ideological concept. Some people measure their prosperity by cattle, some by children and grandchildren, others by money, and still others by power.

Fairbanks and other authors in the book take a decidedly Western philosophical viewpoint toward the concept of prosperity. If measured on the macro scale, conditioning and conditioned by micro conditions, it would be the ability for a nation to compete for resources in the global market and for individuals to compete for resources in the local market. Few countries can grow enough food to feed themselves; they must exchange products produced in their country outside their country. This means the people inside the state must export goods they have produced in exchange for money to purchase food from outside and other goods from within. The thesis of the text is concerned with the inability of certain nation states to compete in the global market, despite having opportunities to become competitive. The authors argue the problem must be ideological. Other than Shweder, most of the authors feel this inability to compete is caused by the inability to change to Western thought, to change their culture. The stumbling block to prosperity, as iterated by most of the authors of this book, is culture and the culture of these countries must be changed.

The second key term, which for this book is a very charged term, is culture.

> The term "culture," of course, has had multiple meanings in different disciplines and different contexts. [...] In this book, however, we are interested in how culture affects societal development; if culture includes everything, it explains nothing. Hence we define culture in purely subjective terms as values, attitudes, beliefs, orientations, and underlying assumptions prevalent among people in society [Huntington xv].

Although culture can be symbols and institutions — governmental, social, and religious — it is also the manifestation of values, attitudes and beliefs. When the authors of this text talk about culture, they are speaking of ideology driving the institutions and perceptions of people.

The thrust of this book is to understand and find solutions for third-world poverty and the failure of groups in the first world to extricate themselves from poverty. Most discussions in the text are beyond the scope of the argument presented in this chapter, the discussion and elucidation of the misconception of class and the working class through levels of theorizing by those who choose to study the working class. Yet *Culture Matters* is important to this argument in several ways. First, it theorizes differences in states and peoples as a complex phenomenon and not simply as economical. Second, the authors of the book take a Gamscian view, contending that the people of these third-world countries, and those in poverty in first-world countries, have some culpability for the problems along with the governments and religious authorities. This is not to relieve any first-world nation, or person in the nation, from blame. The real insight of *Culture Matters* is in its understanding that to change conditions within a country, ethnic group or class, the ideology needs to be changed; however, to what ideology is debatable.

Shweder, an anthropologist and self-proclaimed skeptic of the premise of the book, questions the "cultural developmentalism" of the text (162). He complicates the idea of studying culture by suggesting that many approaches exist to the study of both, such as "rational choice theorists" (163), "personality theorists" (163), "psychological anthropologists," "cultural psychologists" (164) and himself, a "cultural pluralist" (164). He "strongly believes in 'universalism,' but the type of universalism I believe in is 'universalism without uniformity.' [...] there are universally binding values but [...] there are just too many of them" (164). Certain values are always in conflict with others and must be subordinated to others at certain times. This subordination is situational as well as ideological. The placement of values finally depends on overarching metanarratives organizing these values in a complex matrix. The determining factor of what is good, what is prosperity, and what is progress finally depends on the ideological point of view, as Weber argues.

Shweder uses, as an example, mortality rates of children. Out of the womb a higher mortality rate for children in third-world countries exists than in first-world countries, while inside the womb a much higher mortality rate for children in first-world countries is realized. Shweder is not taking a side on the right-to-life/freedom-of-choice debate. He is questioning the proposition that certain cultures are considered barbaric while others are not. Obviously the point of view of those with the power to close the discourse to other views is ultimately considered the legitimate knowledge. Again, the argument can deteriorate into another straw man argument, such as comparing universal health care (putting the United States on the barbaric list) to genocide. Shweder's argument asks only to consider the point of view in which the argument is derived. The assumption is that our culture is better because we are more progressive. Yet the majority of wealth in the United States sits in the hands of a few while the world starves.

Another essay touching on the scope of the argument of this book is Glazer's "Disaggregating Culture," complicating the idea of culture as it deals with success or prosperity, suggesting other factors may be included besides culture, such as race. Significantly, many who study the working class subordinate race to class, relegating blacks and Hispanics to the working class as if their challenges are the same as whites at the same economic levels. *Culture Matters* seems to subordinate race and ethnicity to culture, or at least considers them to be the same thing; however, they are not. What must be determined in each instance is whether the condition of the person, family, community, and nation is caused by their ideology alone or their subjugation by another ideology.

Cultural Studies and the Working Class: Subject to Change, Edited by Sally R. Munt

Although this book is decidedly British in theory and scope, and heavily influenced by the New Left, thus, taking at its core the assumption that the discourse of class must be at some point Marxist, its attempt to reestablish cultural studies as a viable and legitimate way in which to study class brings to light an aspect of theorizing the working class missing from other areas of the discipline. This aspect is the study of identity — specifically, how people designated as working class see themselves in the world, how they see their world, and how they deal with competing discourses seeking to influence their narration of themselves and their world.

Cultural Studies and the Working Class: Subject to Change has much to add to elucidating the complexity of class. However, many of the essays take as their focus books or movies that admittedly have ideological axes to grind and thus are ideological constants, if not outright propaganda; as such, they are problematic as legitimate sources to elucidate points of arguments as used in essays by Bromley, Haylett, and others.

The book starts out questioning the criteria and categorization, if not the methodology, of defining class. Still, some authors fail to move beyond Marxism because, as Munt asserts, in Britain a belief still exists that Marxism has a "necessary place in university systems," but in America cultural studies is "firmly located within ethnic groups other than the white working class" (6). This configuration of a "white" (and male) working class has forced a reconceptualizing of "culture" in America. Most studies done in the United States are based on identity politics, sometimes accused, and rightfully so, of essentialism. When cultural studies is evoked in the study of class in America, the "academics still seem to look to Britain for working-class intelligentsia, whereas in Britain, within Cultural Studies, we have been busy incorporating the American model into our syllabi" (Munt 6). Cultural studies has meant different things in America and Britain. In America, sometimes it has meant a free-for-all with rigor thrown to the wind, where anything and everything becomes fair game and any argument, no matter how fleeting or shallow, is correct. Much may be learned from the study of disparate phenomena, but what is "learned" sometimes contains little value. In Britain cultural studies has always been connected to class, as have gender, sexuality, and race. Each study has had Marxist influences because of the New Left, and specifically the Birmingham Centre for Contemporary Cultural Studies, historically Marxist in thought; according to Munt, during the tenure of Stuart Hall, the center moved to Gramscian Marxism (4). This shift raises the question of why the study in Britain has not moved into the post–Althusserian stage as the rigorous strain of cultural studies in America has done, specifically GBLT and feminist studies.

Although the authors in this book move away from the standard stereotyping of class, most conflate the working class with poverty without inspecting their position. Munt believes that "it is the bread and butter work of Cultural Studies to refuse the victim position," but creating a non-revolutionary, non-victimized working-class person becomes difficult when everything available as a signifier within the language game, she believes, is either the "deserving poor" or "the underclass, which deserves nothing" (8). Time and again the essays become concerned with poverty and what it means to those affected by it and those who found a way out of it. People in poverty should not be included even within a subgroup of the working class. This suggests that all persons falling into poverty become working class, even those who are middle class. Their middle-class culture does not suddenly turn into a working-class culture because they've lost their means of income.

Munt, in the introduction, questions the assumptions of standard Marxist working-class theorizing, believing "no distinct working class [exists] to be operationalized in academic research [...] only many working classes" (10). This statement does not argue that classes exist in a hierarchy, but suggests many positions exist within a sphere of ideologies, agency, and social structures mediated by other influences, and "if you take 'class' from an exploration of gender [...] you ignore a crucial determining factor of the experience of being a woman, man or transgendered person," or if you remove race as a mediator of class, you ignore what it is to be subjugated for skin color (10).

The possibility exists in this form of theorizing of having a class position for each person in existence since most people are, in some way, unique. The problem, then, becomes a question of how class might be spoken about. Munt and the other authors in the book construct their positions within a cultural matrix of economics, education, ethnicity, gender, and sometimes geography. This construction of class asks how and why these multiple class positions exist, the real and important question in the theorizing of class. The book argues that culture creates class (meaning ideology), but does not truly investigate how this "culture" comes about, although at times it hints that narratives and belief systems are involved. Still, *Cultural Studies* opens the discourse in which class can be theorized by adding other dimensions and alternate rules to the language game even if vestiges of vulgar Marxism within the discourse still persist.

In the opening of his essay, "If Anywhere: Class Identifications and Cultural Studies Academics," Andy Medhurst questions the idea class is at all related to economics. His parents "did clerical jobs, which in other circumstances might have enabled them [...] to clutch at the especially anxious label, lower-middle class," though he starts by stating, "I come from a working class family" (19). He believes this because "we only had to mix with indisputably middle-class people to know that we belonged elsewhere" (19). Geography plays a role in Medhurst's working-class circumstances, not by forcing upon Medhurst a set of circumstances, but by allowing him access to what he calls working-class culture and by sheltering him from middle-class culture (again, he means ideologies). His parents felt more comfortable among working-class people because "class is never simply a category of the present tense. It is a matter of history, a relationship with tradition, a discourse of roots" (20). It is "a question of identifications, perceptions, feelings" (20).

Several essays in the book deal with the problem of "crossing over," including Medhurst's. Jensen's essay seems to argue that a sense of guilt or disloyalty exists; however, these examples might be attributed to changes in ideology (especially in the first example) caused by new rules of gender being added to the language game and, in the other example, racial guilt. The essays in this text seem to show that the idea of a sense of shame existing in being working class is perpetuated by academia.

Although economically, occupationally, and often geographically, the American working class emulates, if not strives to become, the middle class, in America, at least, middle class people, in part of their ideology, narrate themselves at certain times as working class, if only in the idea (usually false) of the independent individual perpetuated by mass media stereotypes. Many times, though, these people are "tourists" masquerading as working class. This is not unlike what several of the authors in this book feel, believing that they are masquerading as middle class, but for them this is not tourism — rather, it is deadly serious. Some, such as Andy Medhurst, do not feel middle class, but "cannot pretend to be working class any more" (20).

Joanne Lacey suggests narratives of one's life can be used as material to theorize class. Citing this method used by British feminists, she states, "Using the complexities and contradictions embedded in their own working-class histories to frame working-class identity within a poststructuralist paradigm, they present these class identities as now fragmented, contradictory, performed, lived as narratives and fantasies" (42). These narratives proposed by Lacey might argue that other narratives must be subordinated as a person's self is subordinated to the character claimed by the mask. The narrative of masquerading also proposes, at some level, that other narratives within the metanarrative of working class might oppose the metanarrative of the middle class, and produce signs allowing for small group separation.

John Cook's essay, "Culture, Class and Taste," touches on the assumption of a narrative or the narration of class. He begins his essay by taking the position that "distinctions of taste manifest[ing] distinctions of class" is backward and "taste" is "a hegemonic project, the making of a social world fit for the bourgeoisie class" (97, 99). What could have been investigated a bit more in Cook's essay is how taste takes on a moral position beyond allowing for authority and in-group/out-group separation. Obviously the argument of taste can be argued in extreme cases as the difference between someone playing Mozart and a child banging on a drum; it is a straw man or red herring fallacy. In a less extreme comparison, complexity is usually the determinant of taste, with less complexity usually valued less. However, the idea of knowing what is "better" moves from an understanding of aesthetics to some judgment of morality.

Cook seems to believe taste is an exclusionary project, or, at best, a segregating project. It is also a recognition of similar ideologies, if not a restriction by a certain authoritative position to power and of a power system. Beverly Skeggs asserts,

> Appearance has always mattered. It is the means by which others are recognized and it is a part of the way we want ourselves to be recognized. But this is not just a matter of interpersonal, or even dialogical construction of subjectivity; it is a matter of how symbolic violence may or may not occur [129].

As Cook states, a hegemonic project "must have the means for inviting people to join in" and "ways of making them obey the rules" (100). To have differing ideologies means nothing in a social field with contestations of power unless the signs of these differing ideologies are used for separation; separation can only be achieved through having the power to do so, and the power is given by an authority who becomes an authority through gaining power by asserting some form of taste expertise.

Cook believes myriad class positions exist. He suggests that class, then, is determined at the individual level or small-group level in what Althusser calls "interpellation." Importantly, "taste" and other signs of class, taking on moral aspects, allow for class separation through interpellation, allowing or denying opportunities in life, one of the reasons many of those authors in the text who claim to have "crossed over" live in fear of being exposed. The other fear of being exposed comes from the shame of being somehow less moral. This means that occupational positions, and thus economic positions, are the result of a complex interface of ideologies exclusionary to life chances or ideologies resisting the exclusion altogether by, paradoxically, excluding.

Cook turns the Marxist idea of class on its head, suggesting it is Weber's status groups that allow for life chances affecting the economic position of the person. However, Cook, referring to Bourdieu, believes there exists a "co-relation between economic class and taste" (102). This statement is an overgeneralization assuming that class exists in discrete categories in a hierarchy, where, in fact, if looked more closely, it does not. Many times class position is in flux. An example would be a comparison of a "well-dressed" Texan and a "well-dressed" New Yorker, remembering that class positions work on exclusion as well as inclusion of signs, down to the minutiae of apparel, speech, what is spoken of and how, and even walk and facial expressions. While the Texan produces signs of authority, power and wealth in Texas, his signs would be interpreted differently in New York City, where a $350 cowboy hat and $3,000 cowboy boots would be suspect.

When Cook states that "the taste of the social elites is not organized according to the same assumptions about value as the taste of the working class," he is suggesting that signs indigenous to some core metanarrative may exist (102). The assumption of different tastes in art is usually due to education or some natural inclination, but Cook believes the working class care about "what works of art are about over how they are formed" (102). He, however, does not go on to postulate "natural" (and thus moral) class differences, although his discussion of "punk" culture and other youth cultures moves in the direction of investigating what seem to be differing metanarratives. Cook does not critique this assumption that differing value systems produce signs that separate the classes. If his theory has credence, neither value system, as concerns taste, has the right to claim a position over the other. More importantly, this difference points to the existence of differing ideologies and core metanarratives producing different signs that allow for in-group/out-group separation. Nietzsche noticed the same phenomenon. Being disposed to prefer one core metanarrative over another, he named them "noble" and "slave" moralities.

Steph Lawler also deals with the concept of cultural and symbolic capital and the desire of the working class to emulate the middle class, although he contends that this is escapism from the drudgery of working-class lives, assuming working-class lives are drudgery. He believes middle-class "tastes and dispositions are coded as *inherently* 'right' and *inherently* 'tasteful'" because they become "knowledge and aesthetics themselves" (116). To not understand this is to "'fail' in the games of aesthetic judgment, of knowledge and of cultural competence" (116). If certain tastes are inherently right, emulation of the middle class is not escapism — from, for Cook and others, poverty — but, rather, as taste takes on a moral inference determining self-esteem, the "correct" thing to do. People will determine their self-worth against their perception of how morally middle class they are.

Although *Cultural Studies and the Working Class: Subject to Change* challenges the simplistic idea of class, moving beyond vulgar Marxism to what might be considered postmarxism in an Althusserian sense, it only touches on the mechanisms that create identity and maintain identity despite a person's movement in geography, economy, and education, as Berger maintains in his study of the working class. If, as Medhurst and others in this text assume, the real differences between the working classes and the middle classes are ideological, certain propensities natural to both ideologies should be manifest. For the working class of this book, a common narrative within their ideology is of "getting out"—specifically, through education.

Why worry about the way class is theorized? The question is not who benefits from the closure of this discourse of working-class studies to new rules of the language game, but rather who might suffer from the closure. The answer is the individual consigned by the study to a group said to be the working class. By closing off the discourse from other theories, those who write of the working class construct or reconstruct stereotypes and interpellate the working-class subject within a preconceived paradigm.

This situation is not alleviated within working-class literature studies. As the next chapter will show, the academics who are now studying working-class literature, like Daniels and Lauter, use this Marxist discourse to establish a knowledge/power base that stereotypes working-class literature by the use of simplified criteria. They also close off the discourse to alternate theories of the working class and alternate discourses of working-class literature; through performativity, they have erected a hegemonic discourse of working-class literature. Other books exist, though, that question the surface theorizing of many texts produced in the area of working-class literature and begin to theorize class at a much deeper level.

Chapter 3

A Review of the Discourse of Working-Class Literature

Working-class literature, as it is being defined today, takes its genre position from a reworking and capturing of characteristics derived from contemporary working-class studies (Marxism) and realist literature from the end of the first half of the last century, which often took its tenets from Marxism. Realism began with the attempt to record life as it "really was" over one hundred years ago as an effort mounted against Romantic literature in America. George Becker, quoted by Donald Pizer in "Late Nineteenth-Century American Realism: An Essay in Definition," lists three criteria for realism.

> The first is verisimilitude derived from observation and documentation. The second is an effort to approach the norm of experience — that is, a reliance on the representative rather than exceptional in plot, setting and character. The last is an objective, so far as an artist can achieve objectivity, rather than subjective or idealistic view of human nature and experience [263].

Yet much of early realism was very idealistic. Pizer, citing three canonical authors in 19th century literature (Howells, Twain, and James), states, "American Realism [...] is essentially subjective and idealistic in its view of human nature and experience" (264).

In the latter 19th century a strain of realism darkened into what Vernon Louis Parrington labeled "critical realism" (Carter 151). Howells' "literary horizons [post–Haymarket riot anarchists' hangings] were also extended to [...] force readers 'to examine the grounds of their social and moral opinions'" (Carter 160). Several later critics, though, saw Howells' influence as detrimental to the development of realism.

> Dreiser thought Howells well-meaning but ineffective; Sinclair Lewis said he was a piece of deadwood which Dreiser had to clear from the path of American literature before it could progress; and historians of literary theory have either ignored Howells. [...] or have repeatedly charged that he was a Victorian moralist or an uncritical optimist [Carter 151].

As realism shifted toward naturalism, Howells became less influential in the writings of his time.

Combined with the influence of Marxist socialism propagated by the socialist union movements and American communist parties, this realism became close in cause and content to what later would be called socialist realism, a genre of literature that generally was embarrassingly propagandist, if not, as Waldo Frank states, consisting mainly of "dull novels about stereotyped workers" (qtd. in Madden xviii). Other offshoots of this genre were proletariat and labor literature, written to disseminate a Marxist viewpoint of resistance, revolution, exploitation, alienation, and victimization. Proletariat writing of the early part of the 20th century, and somewhat in its regeneration in the 1960s, took the tenets of Marxism as the backbone of its writing.

Many working-class literary critics build the statutes of their canon or theory from concepts garnered through these subgenres of realism, labor literature, and socialist realism, allowing them to attempt to recover working-class literature as far back as the first settlers in America and co-opt literature from other genres, such as the African American genre. Coles and Zandy explain that they are "gathering three hundred texts [for their anthology] that span the centuries from colonial times to the early 2000s[;] this anthology presents a range of working-class literature that includes not only the industrial proletariat, but also enslaved and peonage labor, unpaid domestic work, immigrant and migrant labor, and low-paid service work" (xv).

Some academics studying working-class literature, such as Christopher and Whitson, give little credence to theory, although they propose "not a grand or totalizing theory, not a theory expressed in inaccessible jargon, but a theory aligned closely to the literature by writers with origins in the working class, a theory aligned with both our own intellectual orientations and our gut feelings" (73). Yet when the majority of working-class literary critics refer to established theory, they almost always evoke a Marxist critic or theory. Zandy explains, "I turn frequently to Raymond Williams, Mikhail Bakhtin, and Antonio Gramsci because they illuminate the relationality of class and culture" (3).

Marxist literary theory, when applied thoughtfully to a text, can generate insight into the text, although not necessarily insight into the ideology, identity, or even the real-life conditions of working-class persons. This application of Marxism usually takes two broad forms, either (as proletariat literature is mandated to do) reflecting class struggle through plot, narrative, and characterization, or contesting art as independent of the economic conditions of the time. As Marx suggests of the painter Raphael, he did not "produce his painting independently of the division of labor that existed in Rome at the time"; these paintings were "determined by the technical advances in art made before him [...] by the organization of society" (Marx and Engels, *German* 108).

Postmarxist theories complicate any scenario by adding ideology, power, and discourse to the list of determinants in proposing the ideology of the dominant class, or the contestations of this ideology by classes vying for dominance, determines the art of a moment in history. Although some collections of working-class literature seem to be attempting to question the text as historical product, few have investigated the forces producing and moderating the text, nor how the text reflects or resists the dominant ideology of the time other than to argue that this literature shows the victimization of the working people.

If the number of publications on working-class literature is any indication, the argument for a canon of "working-class" texts would seem somewhat settled. Yet even an author such as Jim Daniels, who seemingly represents the ideal author of the canon as it now stands, admits the concept is not as settled as many academics would have people believe. He maintains that "some poets embrace the designation 'working-class' poet while others reject that label" (115). If the authors, who have been designated as working class, and whose texts have also been designated as working class, reject this designation, the foregrounded question must be this: why do the academics of working-class literature studies insist on a classification of texts and authors?

Once arguments endorsing a canon of working-class authors and literature are scrutinized, they appear much like a defense against the lack of aesthetic value and literary seriousness of some works. Christopher and Whitson's article, "Toward a Theory of Working Class Literature," attempts to block the questioning of the aesthetic value of any work deemed to be working class by stating,

> Literary studies has not been willing — or able — to take on this class nature simply because embracing a classed approach would mean rethinking many of the most fundamental questions of literary theory, genre, and criticism. Working-class literature, at base, cannot simply fit into the status quo of literary criticism [72].

Again, by attempting to position working-class literature as a legitimate genre, the argument for and of a working-class canon of texts and authors closes the discourse in which working-class literature might be discussed. Coles and Zandy authoritatively declare that most disagreements with their text, and by association their construction of the tenets of working-class literature, might all be summed up as "class prejudice" (xxiii). Ironically, Laura Hapke quotes Carolyn Porter, who states, "It is [...] crucial in that regard to locate the plurivocal textual voices — that is, the ways in which the voice of power in the text also records other voices" (qtd. in Hapke 7). Yet, in attempting to join the ongoing conversation, Hapke and others become the power whose texts record or marginalize these other voices. Secondly, the control of knowledge, or the right to decide what knowledge is considered legitimate, becomes capital to be leveraged and sold, as Lyotard suggests. Knowledge is, as Bourdieu believes, a form of "social capital"—or "academic capital"—as will be seen when critiquing Gary Lenhart's book, *The Stamp of Class* (Bourdieu, *Practical Reason* 16, 17). Lenhart recounts being a participant in a working-class roundtable at a conference where the discussion centered mostly on who was and who was not a "real" working-class author, with those on the panel and in the audience endorsing themselves while disputing the claims of those not in attendance. To control the discourse of knowledge is to control the value of the capital. This control of the discourse controls the rules of the language game, of what may be spoken of and of how it may be spoken. As will also be alluded to in chapter 5, this text attempts to avoid just these pitfalls by positing that any theory of the working class in literature cannot expect or attempt to become hegemonic in its tenets, but must be open and on guard against any attempt to close it.

One of the focuses of this chapter is to locate the ways the voice of academic power records and controls the voices of the working class through control of the discourse, having constructed the genre through two paradoxical sets of criteria. The first set builds a single-faceted prototype of the working class that employs a simplistic categorization of labor struggle, work, poverty, exploitation, victimization, and manual labor by incorporating only texts including these criteria. The second set of criteria, which is contradictory to the first, constructs the genre by including any author supposedly coming from the working class regardless of whether his or her work includes any criteria from the first set. In the former construction, the study stereotypes the very people it proposes to study by essentializing what count as working-class experiences. In the latter construction, the authors are stereotyped by relegating their work to a certain genre. However, no corpora are constructed through Marxist critical realism, "the belief that a writer and work are the dialectical products of a particular historical moment, conditioned by economic-class realities" (Hull 148).

Yet through Marxism these academics create a language game within the study. These "various categories of utterance can be defined in terms of the rules [...] determining their properties" (Lyotard 10). Because this language game defines the working class within a narrow political bias, the discourse within these anthologies must suffer from forms of essentialization: overgeneralizations, faulty assumptions, misinterpretations, and slippery definitions protecting the discourse from outright challenges. This discourse cannot question itself or its premises, such as how race and gender complicate the essentialism within the study. This language game allows for those not questioning the premises to expand upon them in inflationary ways through performativity.

Finally, the discourse is incidentally incestuous because the "rules do not carry within themselves their own legitimation, but are the object of a contract, explicit or not, between players" (Lyotard 10). Within the rules of this language game, factions legitimize each other. Daniels not only cites the very anthologies in which he appears, but, by alluding to the authority of the editors and the authors in the anthologies as legitimate, he also legitimizes himself as an author of the working class. Six pages in *American Working-Class Literature: An Anthology* are dedicated to Daniels' poetry, which is more than are dedicated to the canonized writers included in the text.

Few anthologies exist that purport to be collections of working-class literature, and these are all the same. They use identical criteria to build their text (Marxism), emphasizing, whether consciously or unconsciously, "the dehumanizing aspects of the job and the cruelty of the bosses" (Daniels 118). Other texts, though not anthologies, have been published, that make an argument for such a designation as working-class literature, again using attributes that are Marxist in origin, such as Laura Hapke's *Labor's Text: The Worker in American Fiction* and David Madden's *Proletarian Writers of the Thirties*.

The anthologies and the studies may be cataloged into two rough groups — those unashamedly admitting to a Marxist bent, such as David Madden's *Proletarian Writers of the Thirties*, and those not admitting to a Marxist bent, but that unconsciously or unintentionally adhere to it by forming their ideas of the working class, the writers, and the literature from readings of realist, and social realist, literature. These texts argue for the representation of exploitation and oppression of the proletariat, creating a corpus of negative depictions of life for the working class. Very few, if any, anthologies or studies of working-class literature include very positive depictions of the working class. For example, included in *American Working-Class Literature: An Anthology* is a story by Hamlin Garland, "Under the Lion's Paw." It concerns a farm worker who rents a dilapidated farm and improves the property only to have the selling price of the farm raised beyond his ability to purchase it. Although this is an important story, in both its realist/naturalist writing and its depiction of life for some farmers (or farm workers) — the story shows only one aspect of the agrarian life. For an anthology to claim to be a true and honest text of the working class, positive depictions of the working class must be included, such as "Neighbor Rosicky," by Willa Cather. Academics' Marxist discourse implicitly argues either that positive depictions of the working class do not exist or, if they do, they must disqualify the text as working class. Yet positive depictions of working-class people abound in American literature. For other depictions of the rural working class counterpointing Garland's text, stories from authors like Sarah Orne Jewett and Alice Cary might be included.

The similarity of the anthologies and studies permits a review of a cross-section of the anthologies and the studies. Since this book concerns itself with American literature from 1620 to the present, one anthology and one study concerned with this wide epoch have been selected for analysis: *American Working-Class Literature: An Anthology*, edited by Nicholas Coles and Janet Zandy, and *Labor's Text: The Worker in American Fiction*, by Laura Hapke.

As a counterpoint to the Marxist hegemonic discourse perpetuated throughout much of the works available now in print, *Working: People Talk About What They Do All Day and How They Feel About What They Do*, by Studs Terkel, will also be reviewed as will, *Gig: Americans Talk About Their Jobs*, partially because the former book has been excerpted in Coles and Zandy's text and quoted in many works concerned with the working class and working-class literature, and the latter (when looked at with Terkel's book) is a comparison of attitudes toward work across thirty years. Literarily they place themselves between a contemporary anthology of nonfiction and an ethnographic study of the working class. As an effort to represent people who work, these texts are a more realistic and less biased accounting of working persons than many anthologies and studies in print.

Gary Lenhart's *The Stamp of Class* questions the idea of not only who might be a working-class author and what is a working-class text (in his case, poetry) but also how an author or a text might be defined. Although he, like many others, conflates working class with poor, he does delve into the real differences between poets today and throughout history. In his book he uses as his defining attribute of class, ideologies manifesting themselves in differing cultural attributes such as language and attitudes toward poetry itself. He does struggle, though, to elucidate a real stamp of class, until the last part of the book, where he is more at home with contemporary poets. Here he makes a rather good and solid argument for the stamp of class.

Although *American Working-Class Literature: An Anthology* by its title argues that its contents are of and from the working class, the criteria for many authors included in Coles and Zandy's text seem contradictory. Since the editors announce the text as a college textbook spanning American literary history from 1620 to the present, texts from America's earlier periods are included. Many of these texts, though, do not fall under even their wide-open criteria of working-class literature. Both Equiano's and Wheatley's texts have little to do with the working class and actually, undermine the Marxist argument presented within the preface and introduction.

Not so with Laura Hapke's *Labor's Text*. She outrightly expresses her leftist views. Although Hapke often unpacks a text using Marxist literary theory very well, like Coles and Zandy, she ties herself to a discourse demanding an interpretation of the text through exploitation, victimization, and struggle against capitalism, marginalizing other aesthetic attributes and deeper readings of more universal struggles. She sometimes does a cursory reading of a text, unable or refusing to see the more complex renderings of working-class characters, finding, for example, in Melville only negative renderings, such as how the sailors are depicted in *Redburn* or the slaves in "Benito Cereno" (34–35). Hapke does not allow for the proletariat (whom she is actually discussing) to be considered outside the folk-hero configuration. Like Coles and Zandy, she sometimes gets a bit overzealous in trying to constitute a canon of working-class literature, misinterpreting certain texts as representations of working-class people when, other than being placed in a factory or having characters who are constructed as poor, these stories are not of or about the working class.

The Marxist discourse in academia, concerned with working-class literature, causes both Hapke's text and Coles and Zandy's text to suffer greatly when attempting to shoehorn literature from 1620 until after the Civil War into the parameters of this discourse. With the advent of realism and social realism, with tracts and novels written with an overt political and social objective in mind of bringing to light the stark inequality and abject poverty existing at the time, finding texts that buttress their viewpoint becomes increasingly easier. Graham Thompson states of Hapke's book, "The problem with Hapke's working-class studies approach here is that it relies upon discourses of class distinction and economic organization much better suited to the pre–World War Two environment. [...] Nine chapters cover the ninety years between 1840 and 1930; just three are allotted to the next seventy years" (329). No chapters are dedicated to texts before 1840.

Whether these texts actually represent some people of the time or not is not what is in question here. Whether these texts accurately represent the majority of the working class is in question. Madden's warning against interpreting the texts written in the 1930s might be extended to all texts of all times. "We must avoid the preconception that it was primarily an era of radical action, thinking, and literature" (Madden xv). Madden is warning against constructing a history of a time and people based on one type of literature or point of view.

American Working-Class Literature: An Anthology

The opening sentences of the introduction of this text state:

> *American Working-Class Literature* invites readers to explore a work of writing that until recently has largely been left out of the mainstream literary canon. Workers have been singing, reciting, performing, telling stories, writing, and publishing since the beginning of the settlements that became the United States — and they are still doing so [Coles and Zandy xix].

Coles and Zandy also state in the preface:

> Gathering three hundred texts that span the centuries from colonial times to the early 2000s, this anthology presents a range of working-class literature that includes not only the industrial proletariat, but also enslaved and peonage labor, unpaid domestic work, immigrant labor and migrant labor, and low-paid service work. The writers are as diverse in race, gender, culture, and region as America's working class itself [xv].

They then attempt to establish a discourse demanding that working-class literature be about people who are part of industrial proletariat, enslaved, peonage or unpaid domestic labor.

> Like the term "*literature*," "*working class*" is also defined inclusively here. This is more than a "blue collar" collection. Collars — blue, white, pink, brown, or missing entirely — can be misleading signifiers. To categorize this writing as "labor literature," that is, work associated with organized labor movements, is too narrow as well [xx].

Although their anthology does represent many other types of workers besides "industrial" workers, such as farm workers, waitresses, and even housewives, it almost exclusively includes only work or work-related text (xx). The text also contains thirty-five authors considered canonical by even the strictest of criteria, such as Melville, Whittier, and Whitman. These texts are discussed within the discourse of work or struggle. Many non-canonical authors within Coles and Zandy's text are decidedly pro-leftist, pro-labor, and Marxist, such as Tillie Olsen and James Wright. Although Coles and Zandy deny their anthology centers on labor struggle, the bulk of the remaining texts represent the labor struggles of women and minority groups through the depictions of organized labor movements and exploitive working conditions. Thus "lived experiences" can only mean, for them, struggle, poverty, and so forth.

Coles and Zandy state that their text is "designed for the general reader, as well as the student" (xv). They quote Raymond Williams' belief that literature is not "an isolated aesthetic object but [...] 'writing in society'" (xv). They then argue "this collection of working-class literature not only expands the canonical understanding of students who are English majors, but offers all students a living connection to the legacy of American culture that may have been hidden from them" (xv). What they finally provide is an essentialist conception of the working class, one that causes more misunderstanding than understanding.

A major pillar of Coles and Zandy's argument is the fallacy of equivocation when attempting to align the working class with slavery. They first argue that "class is inseparable from other markers of identity: gender, sexuality, race, region, and ethnicity" (2). They do not, however, consider the aforementioned markers to be identity markers within the argument of this text, but ignore them altogether in their attempt to establish the dominance of class oppression. They create essentialist constructions of race, class, gender, and ethnicity as separate "class" categories, while in actuality these categories are not separate and complicate the idea of class within identity. Coles and Zandy's purpose is to establish, or rather disestablish, the differences between class and race to create a discourse grounded in the history of the working class as "white slaves" (3).

Coles and Zandy first seek to align white indentured servants with African slaves. They claim that most immigrants to America, "60 to 70%," arrived in America as indentured servants (3). This statement, along with Frederick Douglass' assertion that the working man was only a "white slave," and taking his assertion at face value without questioning the rhetorical or political conditions influencing his writing of the texts, they attempt to paint a picture of early America as a miserable place where the majority of people were enslaved or semi-enslaved (2). They quote Jacqueline Jones, contending that all workers were bound to "hard usage" (2).

Coles and Zandy focus on mostly unskilled labor, but do mention, in passing, sail makers and shipbuilders. While sail makers were considered tradesmen, the category "shipbuilder" encompasses occupations from unskilled to highly skilled trades.[1] "By the close of the eighteenth century, these journeymen were beginning to form local trade societies" (Dulles and Dubofsky 2). Unlike the later socialist unions, these societies contained masters, journeymen, and apprentices. They "acted together to maintain the standards of their craft, uphold price lists and generally protect themselves from unfair competition" (Dulles and Dubofsky 21). As Shefter and Bridges have noted, workers, through trade unions and the vote, asserted their will upon the government and capital. Pointedly, Coles and Zandy marginalize any discussion of the craftsmen and the guilds of this period. They only mention skilled trades in later chapters as industrial manufacturing was making them obsolete.

Importantly, regarding "hard usage," much of the evidence Coles, Zandy and others use to make their points depends upon using a contemporary point of view rather than attempting to "analyz[e] an event according to the multiple processes that constitute it" (Foucault, *Essential* 249). For Foucault, Coles and Zandy's argument depends on applying the standards of our time to a society of another time. If life was harsh in America, life was harder in Europe. Many people willingly indentured themselves for the chance of a new life. Dulles and Dubofsky state:

> Although [...] scholars emphasized the involuntary aspects of colonial immigration and the role played in the migration stream by paupers and criminals, the most recent research discloses a different reality. First, in the New World indentured servants largely replicated English patterns of rural employment. [...] Second, the immigration of indentured servants proved a rational response to the realities of seventeenth and eighteenth century markets. [...] It effectively redistributed labor from a sated English market to a hungry colonial one. Third, the indentured servants were a cross-section of the English laboring classes [6].

By seeking to establish indentured peoples as "white slaves," Coles and Zandy attempt to establish a relationship between them and real slaves, the Africans taken unwillingly from their homes and lands and placed into slavery. They posit that the only real distinction separating "white slaves [...] from enslaved blacks was the possibility of freedom for whites" (3). Yet Dulles and Dubofsky argue that, while cases of poor treatment of indentured servants existed, "the indentured servants were recognized as fellow Christians and were entitled to their day in court — in these respects, at least, their status was quite different from African slaves" (9). Also, many colonies had laws not only limiting the time for indenturing, but also insisting on "'freedom provisions'" be given to indentured servants at the end of their indenture, which "generally included at least clothing, tools of some sort, and perhaps such livestock as would enable a servant to start farming on his own account" (Dulles and Dubofsky 10–11).

Coles and Zandy's discourse changes what was once metaphor into empirical reality in attempting to establish working-class people as somehow enslaved, not in the Marxist sense, but in the real sense, claiming that the selling was for all generations and non-commutable, that any attempt to leave this servitude might be met with death, and that some were "sold" as felons to have sentences commuted or reduced; thus, indenturing children or adults is somehow now relational to being captured and sold as slaves.

To maintain that no indentured servants were treated cruelly and exploited beyond what was humanly correct for the time would be an overgeneralization, but it would also be an overgeneralization to contend, by citing a few examples, that all life was miserable and "resistance" was the only option (2). Also, the Marxist metaphor of slavery for the indentured servant must remain a metaphor since, in a literal Marxian sense, money is the universal equivalent standing in for labor-value. What was exchanged, then, between the indentured servant and the bondman through the payment of passage was labor-value, or the promise of a later exchange of labor-value for the payment of it in advance. Even if the exchange was exploitive, it still cannot be considered slavery, not just because most indentured servants sought the contract through their own free will, but also because no real ownership existed. Indentured servants were never considered chattel.

Finally, to contend that indenturing was slavery insults all African Americans living or dead, both those who suffered and those whose ancestors suffered through slavery. Slavery is not about work — it is about ownership of a human by another human, not metaphorically, but literally, as an object. It is about the subjectivity of a human having been taken away and thus relegated to chattel, as texts produced by authors such as Wheatley, Equiano, Douglass, Jacobs, and others argue, seeking to "erect a coherent and reliable slave-subject" (Corley 142). Thus the inclusion of many African American authors in Coles and Zandy's text becomes problematic, particularly Olaudah Equiano and Phillis Wheatley.

Wheatley was a slave, who was treated very well (compared to other slaves), taught to read and write, and allowed to study; later she was manumitted. Her poem, "To the Right Honourable William, Earl of Dartmouth, His Majesty's Principal Secretary of State for North-America, Etc.," which is included in the book, points to a dilemma in Coles and Zandy's text beyond the single-dimensional blurring of the working class with labor struggle and of workers with slaves. The problem it elucidates is the sometimes confusing and unfocused direction the book takes.

Coles and Zandy give one mention of class in their introduction to the two poems of Wheatley's included in the text. "It was at this pivotal point [marriage to a free black man] that the intertwined constraints of caste and class limited her development as a poet" (23). This is an essentialist position. Her development as a poet was not hindered by class. Her difficulty in publishing her works after her marriage had to do with her gender and her race. By marrying a free black man, she found herself outside white society, married to a man with little influence because of his race. Thus her marriage contributed to her marginalization as a poet. Her class is not a cause of her difficulties, but a symptom of the difficulties of race in America.

Coles and Zandy state of Wheatley's poem "To the Right Honourable William, Earl of Dartmouth, His Majesty's Principal Secretary of State for

North-America, Etc." that "she insightfully links the 'iron chains[s]' restraining America's freedom to her own kidnapping and enslavement, persuasively arguing the legitimacy of her own subjectivity as having experienced 'wanton Tyranny'" (23). Nowhere in this poem does Wheatley associate race with class, but, rather, she ironically connects America's "enslavement" to England to her enslavement. The poem, then, is not of class but of race. "Wheatley made the most comprehensive antislavery statements possible for a writer whom society had pre-condemned on three counts: she was a woman, she was an African, and she was a slave" (O'Neale 501). In doing so she subtly questions the legitimacy of slavery in a country that believes in freedom for all.

Equiano becomes even more problematic for the sustaining of Cole and Zandy's implied argument. As Wheatley does, he deconstructs the argument that life was "horrible" for all slaves and servants alike, although for anyone to claim Equiano was treated fairly even by his second owner would be ludicrous. "Fair" would have been to free him immediately, make restitution, and return him home. He was allowed, though, to act on his own behalf, to make his own business deals, to have his own money, to educate himself and finally to buy his own freedom.

Equiano's text questions the argument for the victimization of indentured servants, but not in the way Coles and Zandy believe. If a slave might be allowed education, to earn his own money and to buy his own freedom, though uncommon, how common might the scenario or other fair arrangements have been for indentured servants? By only showing one facet of life in colonial times, authors and editors construct a biased argument for exploitation and victimization, and, as Madden contends of the literature of the 1930s, "we must avoid the preconception that it was primarily an era of radical action, thinking, and literature" (Madden xv). Any construction of a history posited through a single-faceted grouping of literature will be biased.

Unlike their feeble attempt to connect Wheatley's text to class, Coles and Zandy make no attempt to link Equiano's text to class. Ironically, as they and other editors and authors of texts on supposed working-class literature throughout history, or the literary representation of the working class throughout history, are wont to do, they ignore the historicism of the text. Throughout the years Equiano's texts have elicited a broad range of critiques from "questions of authorial intentions" to assertions of "surplus meaning" (Corley 139, 141). The slave narrative was not only a political text written to elicit support for an abolitionist cause, but it was also frequently written in a standard genre form, suggesting standard plotting and themes. The savageness of the white race, shown in the excerpt of Equiano's text used in the anthology, is a common trope in slave narratives. Whether accurate or inaccurate, these tropes were political in purpose, written to disseminate a certain ideology. Robin Sabino and Jennifer Hall state:

> Discomfort regarding the authenticity of Equiano's self-portrayal, apparently initially stimulated by anti-abolitionist interests, seems largely predicated on the elitist assumption an Igbo could not acquire sufficient competency in English language and culture to author such an acceptably English text [5–6].

Very few critics, though, have felt this text was not a product of the slave narrative and thus a negotiation of and between the prominent ideologies of the time concerned with slavery — abolition and proslavery.

Much of the debate about Equiano's books stems from the involvement in picking and purchasing slaves for a plantation on the Mosquito Coast. This anecdote has led to the accusation of Equiano having submitted completely "to Western values" (Sabino and Hall 8). If, as Corley feels, Equiano's text disrupts the genre of the slave narrative through "strategies of subversion," it finally is written as a polemic against slavery in a proslavery world (140). It must put into question the slave narrative as an empirical historical document without the consideration of the constraints on the author. Equiano's story also questions the slave narrative itself as a historical artifact and suggests "slave narratives are 'transcultural' or 'hybrid' productions, written against the terms of the dominant culture" (Murphy 553).

Equiano's and Wheatley's texts included in *American Working-Class Literature: An Anthology*, not only question the authors' construction of indentured servants as "white slaves," but also illuminate the lack of rigor, endemic to the study, continued in the second section of Coles and Zandy's text. This section includes "Sorrow Songs and Spirituals," a title borrowed from W. E. B. DuBois' "The Sorrow Songs," as well as brief excerpts from Frederick Douglass' memoirs of working in the shipyards of Baltimore, Maryland, then a slave-holding state. Notably, these excerpts included are the same section of memoir published in its two versions, the first from *The Narrative of Frederick Douglass, an American Slave, Written by Himself* (1845) and the second from *My Bondage and My Freedom* (1855). The assertion that people of the working class are "white slaves" does not appear in the first version. The second excerpt gives Coles and Zandy justification for their conflation of the working class with slavery.

Again, to maintain the discourse of the working class as slaves, the historicism and political purpose of Douglass' memoirs are ignored. Douglass faced negotiating a place in the abolitionist movement from a distinctly subordinate position, a role he was forced to maintain until his separation from the Garrisonians after having been freed by friends buying him from his former owner. "Even those sympathetic to the abolitionist cause use[d] reductive tropes" toward Douglass (Dorsey 443). Dorsey quotes McFreely, who states that "the antislavery credentials of the Irish publisher Richard D. Webb and his circle did not prevent them from calling Douglass 'a child,' 'a savage,' and 'a wild animal'" (443). Since "Equiano's *Narrative* initiates the tradition of the African American slave narrative and serves as a palimpsest for Frederick Douglass' well-known biography," the slave narrative, also includes Douglass within its sociopolitical boundaries (Murphy 553). As Dorsey states, Douglass' book relies on

> the American success story and an abolitionist rhetoric informed by the discourse of sentimentality and white evangelical Christianity [...] the slave narrative had evolved into a recognized tradition influenced by captivity narratives, criminal confessions, and spiritual autobiographies [438].

Notably, in the *Narrative of the Life of Frederick Douglass, an American Slave, Written by Himself,* no polemic of "white slavery" appears. Only after Douglass split with the Garrisonians, in his rewritten autobiography *My Bondage and My Freedom,* did he minimize the autobiographical account of his life and circumstances in "The Shipyards" and foreground the political rhetoric of similar conditions for white workingmen and slaves. Lisa Yun Lee states, "Not only is Douglass' writing eloquent and moving, it is also carefully planned and sophisticated" (51). She believes Douglass' *Narrative*, and thus *Bondage*, is a "complex rhetorical piece" (51). Dorsey asks, "What caused Douglass to abandon the *Narrative*'s binary religious logic [...] for the more morally ambiguous and richly figurative style more characteristic of canonical writers of the American Renaissance?" (443). His answer is the racism Douglass found in the North (443). This foregrounding of the familiarity between white workingmen and slaves attempts to accomplish an equal-but-opposite placing of "the white workingman, on an equality with Negroes" (Douglass 68). Douglass may have had sympathy for these workers, but this sympathy should not be confused with his political purposes. He blames their racism on their mistaken belief that it is the "slaves as men" competing against them and not enslaved men forced to compete against them (68).

Although Douglass calls the workers "white slaves," he uses the term metaphorically, which is the direct opposite of Coles and Zandy's term. Douglass states, "The white man is robbed by the slave system [...] because he is flung into competition with a class of laborers who work without wages" (68). The "system," as Coles and Zandy call it, slips from the slave system to the capitalistic system in their text. Douglass is speaking of the slave system creating white slaves by pitting unpaid labor against paid labor. Coles and Zandy twist his words to mean that capitalism causes white slavery. Douglass is not attempting to end capitalism but rather slavery, contending that if the slaves were free, they would have to compete fairly in the marketplace.

Coles and Zandy move on to a short section concerned with "factory girls" and their "hard usage." Concerning the conditions of the factory girls, Dulles and Dubofsky, in *Labor in America: A History*, point to Charles Dickens' visit to Lowell, Massachusetts, before the mass immigration of the Irish.[2] Rather than finding the squalor of the English industrial system, Dickens found that "the young women and girls who made up most of the workforce appeared to him paragons of virtue — happy, contented, and exemplary in their conduct" (70).

Although Coles and Zandy contest Dickens' point of view, they provide only weak evidence for their assertion, such as Josephine L. Baker's, "A Second Peep at Factory Life." Josephine states, "Well, you ask, if there are so many things objectionable, why we work in the mill?" (50). She lists the many things that are wrong, but says "every situation in life has its trials" (50). Most significantly for a woman living in a repressive society, she states, "The time we *do* have is our own. The money we earn comes promptly [...] when finished we feel perfectly free" (51). Whether the "usage" was hard, the women gained a freedom and self-reliance not available outside the factory system at that time. Coles and Zandy's point of view here depends on interpreting events of the past through a selective history of the present. Although people working in factories, whether women or men, were not treated as well as society deems today, the working hours and conditions were not so far out of line for their time considering the working day on a farm, although a continual movement to reduce working hours has existed since the inception of the Industrial Revolution until the 20th century, at which point, ironically, working hours became stuck at the forty-hour workweek.

After the short section of writing by factory girls, Coles and Zandy present several canonical writers of the antebellum period: Herman Melville, Whittier, Fern, and Whitman. They include only an excerpt of Melville's "The Paradise of Bachelors" and "The Tartarus of Maids," standard for almost every study on the working class in literature. Coles and Zandy claim these stories are a "mirror of two systems, independent but unequal [...] capital and labor" (32). This, however, is not only a simplistic reading of Melville's diptych, but their hypothesis must also make assumptions based on Marxist tenets with no textual evidence, and must presume that the narrator is Melville himself, thinly disguised, reporting on events he witnessed. This position must assume Melville felt more obligation to report the reality of a condition of both bachelors and maids than to illuminate deeper ills of society. For this to be true, a reader must completely ignore the sleigh-ride section of the "The Tartarus of Maids," or worse, relegate it to simply pornographic writing.

Coles and Zandy's assumption is that, since "The Tartarus of Maids" is about factory girls, "The Paradise of Bachelors" must be about capitalist men. Again, this assumption only works within a Marxist prototype. The theory that

> "The Tartarus of Maids" is actually about factory girls has been disputed. Those who have missed it [the gestation symbolism] can be helped. The problem is with those who understand well enough and continue to think that the tale is essentially a Melvillean denunciation of the industrial revolution. [...] Such critics respond to a story Melville did not write [Young 213].

Melville had deeper depths to plumb than the sterility of factories. Although multiple readings of any work might have legitimacy, assuming that the British lawyers are capitalists is just assuming. The text contains no evidence to back the assertion, and although we do have representations of factory girls, the overt sexual symbolism brings into question the idea that Melville's stories "mirror two systems, interdependent but unequal: lawyers in their 'Temple' and girls in a paper mill, capital and labor" (Coles and Zandy 32). Like many of their assertions, it depends on unstated and faulty assumptions based not on real evidence from the text, but on external assumptions dependent on a Marxist prototype. Much richer and more rewarding readings might be produced of these stories for "English majors" other than one of capitalism versus the working class (Coles and Zandy xv).

However, a "class" reading might be legitimate using textual evidence presented within the story if a Veblenian theory of class is used, negating any comparison of worker to capitalist through his theories of the leisure classes, or violent classes and subordinate classes. This configuration then agrees with Nietzsche's postulations of moralities, noble and slave, although ironically so. If, as Mark Migotti proposes, "in two salient respects Nietzsche's primitive masters resemble to the point of indiscernibility Veblen's leisured classes [...] in their orientation toward intrinsic value, with disdain for goods of mere survival and comfort, and their predilection for boisterous mayhem," then a Veblen reading of "class" might be crafted, although the bachelors have lost their propensity for "boisterous mayhem" (749). Finally, though, the stories separate power along lines of sex. Melville is not concerned with capital dominance and worker subordination, but with male dominance and female subordination. Rather than working-class texts, they are feminist texts.

Again, if both texts are to be read as "mirrors" of each other, then the seedman (the narrator of both stories) and the old bachelor in "The Tartarus of Maids" make any strict reading of class problematic. The old bachelor certainly cannot be considered either a capitalist or a member of the leisure class. The story contains no information to determine the marital status of the narrator. The assumption that he is married because Melville is married is unwarranted.

The bachelors are of a "noble morality," but no longer the "primitive masters" that the original Templars were. Yet, like the monk knights of old, the bachelors, being from the noble (or leisure) class, experience each element in their "'value equation' as part of an indivisible, tangible whole; 'being and doing as we are to do'" (Migotti 750). Unlike the knights of old and the seedman, these bachelors are fruitless, contributing nothing to society, while the maids, who might contribute, are sequestered within a factory producing and reproducing only foolscap, poor representations of themselves.

Another problem with any class reading of these two texts is the idea that, although Melville did experience a dinner with leisure-class bachelors and visited a factory of his day, he felt obligated to report both conditions in any realistic manner. Rather than the depictions of the "working girls" being based on reality, almost all the imagery, at least in "The Tartarus of Maids," is consciously constructed symbolism or metaphor, an "excellent example of Melville's method of artistic concealment [...] expressing controversial, at times scandalous, and usually unpopular views symbolically" (Fisher, "Melville's 'Tartarus'" 80). Fisher states that Melville embedded "his symbols so deeply in situation, description or oblique allusion that few of his contemporaries could fully grasp the multi-leveled meaning" ("Melville's 'Tartarus'" 80). To appropriate a metaphor from *Moby Dick*, the surface of Melville's writing is chiefly the mask and the thing lying behind it is what must be gotten at. These stories are his "response to certain repressive and perhaps destructive forces in life, and the sexuality [...] links what Melville finds most intimately human" ("Melville's 'Tartarus'" 86).

The nine bachelors are not only a counterpoint to the maids, but are also set in juxtaposition to the original nine Templars. The original Templars, according to Melville, were "monk knights; the monk-giver of gratuitous ghostly council; the defender of the sarcophagus; the vowed opener and clearer of every highway leading to the Holy Sepulchre; the knight-combatant of the Saracen, breasting spear points at Acre" (262–63). Now "insulated by layers of tradition, [the] modern Templars protect no Holy Sepulchre" (Fisher, "Melville's 'Tartarus'" 84). The Templars of old, this violent class, these nobles, have passed on because

> the moral blight tainted at last this sacred Brotherhood. [...] The worm of luxury crawled beneath their guard, gnawing the core of knightly troth, nibbling the monastic vow, till at last the monk's austerity relaxed to wassailing, and the sworn knight-bachelors grew to become hypocrites and rakes [Melville, "Paradise" 262].

Melville's modern Templars are not capable of even this infamy. So decorous are the bachelors, an elderly, invalid bachelor sleeping in an adjacent room "sle[eps] undisturbed" (269). The Temple was a "protective cocoon, an envelope of tradition and gentility" (Fisher, "Melville's 'Tartarus'" 82). Melville's modern Templars have lost connection with anything greater than themselves — specifically, for Melville, the spiritual union between man and woman.

The Templars' "holy calling" is not to gain citizens equality under the law but "to check, to clog, to hinder, and embarrass all the courts and avenues of the Law" (Melville, "Paradise" 263). The bachelors control a world that through legal and religious law and societal insistence on decorum, has become sterile and impotent. They have split the world into separate spheres — one of men and one of women — the separation seen in the locations of the stories, England and New England, representing two philosophies, one totally constrained by the other. Melville "seemed to suggest that mid-19 century America had faced a crisis and fallen victim to its moral faults" (Fisher, "Melville's 'Bell-Tower'" 200).

If Melville's description in "The Tartarus of Maids" of the narrator's trip to the factory might be considered more than thinly veiled pornographic writing, one of its purposes is to place the factory inside the woman. The imagery of the landscape is described in terms of a woman's reproductive organs.[3] The Mad Maids Bellows-pipe is described as "bleak hills [that] gradually close in on a dusky pass, which, from the violent Gulf Stream of air unceasingly driving between its cloven walls of haggard rock [...] is called The Mad Maid's Bellows-pipe" (Melville, "Tartarus" 271). The narrator follows the road to its highest point between "the Black Notch" (271). "The ravine now expandingly descends into a great purple hopper-shaped hollow [...] called the Devil's Dungeon" (271). The waters are a "brick-colored stream [...] this strange colored torrent Blood River" (272).

The trip through the countryside is described in terms of copulation. The narrator is a seedman whose seeds have been distributed through all the "Eastern and Northern States and even fell into the far soil of Missouri and the Carolinas," an allusion to biblical "onanism" (Melville, "Tartarus" 272).[4] This onanism might refer to the bachelors and their fruitlessness. Another reading of this passage might assume that this seedman, although his marital status is unstated, attempts what the bachelors do not — to bring fecundity to society. "The forest here and there skirting the route, feeling the same all-stiffening influence, their inmost fibres penetrated with the cold, strangely groaned — not in the swaying branches merely, but likewise in the vertical trunk. As the fitful gusts remorselessly swept through them" (Melville, "Tartarus" 273). "Black [the horse] has been perceived as phallic" (Young 213). The horse was flaked all over with frozen sweat, white as a milky ram, his nostrils at each breath sending forth two horned shaped shoots of heated respiration. Gaining the Bellows-pipe, the violent blast dead from behind, all but shoved my high-backed pung up-hill. The gust shrieked through the shivered pass. [...] Black, my horse [...] slung out with his strong hind legs, tore the light pung straight up-hill, and sweeping grazingly through the narrow notch, sped downward madly past the ruined saw-mill. Into the Devil's Dungeon horse and cataract rushed together [Melville, "Tartarus" 273–74].

As the driver and horse pass into the Devil's Dungeon, "sounds of torrents fall on all sides upon the ear. These rapid waters unite in one turbid brick-colored stream, boiling through a fume among enormous boulders" (Melville, "Tartarus" 271–73).

Melville unites nature and the life force represented by the water with the life force within women by virtue of their monthly cycle. If nature represents female and the horse, pung, and driver represent male, and if the allusion here is of copulation and the wind "shrieked through a shivered pass" and horse and driver are carried away in a sort of animal madness, then this copulation ends in mutual orgasms, the antithetical action of the separation of bachelors and maids.

The factory lies within the hopper, the shape of a uterus. It is "the very counterpart of the Paradise of Bachelors, but snowed upon, and frost-painted to a sepulchre" (275). It is, then, the sepulcher the bachelors no longer protect, the sepulcher where the maids are kept whose "pale virginity" elicits an "involuntary bow" of "pained homage" (286). Thus, within the body of the woman, in her center, lies "the factory," and within the factory the maids produce blank paper as the paper produces blank maids.

Melville is discussing habitus, the inherited ideology perpetuated by family and society—in this case, both patriarchal. "The girls did not so much seem accessory wheels to the general machinery as mere cogs to the wheels," although it is Blood River that "sets our whole machinery a-going" (278, 279). The seedman is taken to the rag room where the girls "like so many mares [are] haltered to the rack" (279). "Before each, was vertically thrust up a long, glittering scythe [...] turned outwards from the girls" (279–80). They are also charged with keeping these "swords" sharp (280). Melville sees women as integral to society not only in a reproductive and sexual sense, but also as the very persons this society depends upon to function.

The narrator asks Cupid, the young assistant to the old bachelor (the overseer of the factory), if the machine ever gets clogged and Cupid states, "No it must go. The machinery makes it go just so [...] the pulp can't help going," an allusion to the perpetuation of "romantic" love by ideological apparatuses, particularly pulp literature aimed at women of his time (284). Thus the machinery of the society of Melville's time is ultimately run by the sacrifice of women for and through love, who, although "pale with work and blue with cold; an eye supernatural with unrelated misery," tend the phallocentric society, knowing no better, having been born a blank piece of foolscap, given a bit of embossing, to finally produce more blank paper (276).

The symbolism depicting the mutual orgasm must be ignored to construct a reading condemning factory work because it takes women away from their real function of producing babies (proposed by Coles and Zandy) since conception is not dependent on a female orgasm. Melville's location of the factory within the uterus, rather than condemning the placement of the woman in the factory, condemns the placement of the factory within the woman. He is condemning, then, the social marginalization of women as baby factories and marriage as a union only meant for the purpose of procreation.

Regardless of whether lawyers are capitalists in the real world, a reading of "The Paradise of Bachelors" as a condemnation of capitalism relies on a Marxist reading of "The Tartarus of Maids" as a condemnation of the exploitation of the proletariat. If "The Tartarus of Maids" is not a condemnation of exploitation of these factory girls, then, as a part of this diptych, "The Paradise of Bachelors" cannot be concerned with capitalism, but with young men of the leisure class who control the rules of the language of the discourse of society and, in doing so, perpetuate a sterile, patriarchic society.

The next section of Coles and Zandy's text is titled "Beneath the Gilded Surface," an allusion to Twain's *The Gilded Age*. At this point in the text the working class melds into the labor movement and hardly deviates from it until the last section of the book some 556 pages later. Even when it does deviate, the selections still focus on struggle, poverty, exploitation, and victimization. The book ignores most non-industrial working-class literature, other than Garland's "Under the Lion's Paw" and a section on Appalachian literature dealing with, again, struggle, this time centered mostly on mineworkers.

The first selection is from Rebecca Harding Davis' *Life in the Iron Mills*, a "novella [...] written for a middle-class audience" (Coles and Zandy 112). The depiction of Hugh Wolfe stands out against the depiction of the other working-class men, and, contrary to Coles and Zandy's assertion, Davis does not ask us to see "workers who have their own needs for beauty, love, and creative expression," but to view the feminized exception of the masculine worker as proving the rule (112). "It is the laborer's body that captures Davis's artistic imagination, that inspires her to write the story of Hugh Wolfe, that reminds us of the signifying power of bodies" (Miles 90). Miles believes the working class' physical and dangerous masculinity is set against the 19th century middle-class "discourse of white male disembodiment [...] that would guarantee the promotion of white manhood masquerading as a homogeneous white national identity" (91).

Ironically, as Coles and Zandy tell the reader, *Life in the Iron Mills* was championed by Tillie Olsen herself, "whose recovery of the text led to republication in 1972 by the Feminist Press" (113). Olsen, a member of the American Communist Party and champion of not only the proletariat but also the female proletariat, seems to have like others, missed the obvious negative renderings of the working class in *Life in the Iron Mills*. Laura Hapke in *Labor's Text*, the second text reviewed in this chapter, has a much deeper, if not stronger, reading of Davis' text, and later in this chapter a more expanded discussion will be given to the problems with the representation of the working class in Davis' text.

As *American Working-Class Literature: An Anthology* progresses from the 1860s to the present, the writings get more and more leftist, as appropriate for a book about labor struggle and not about the working class. This era truly was a time for the need of militant labor, producing militant leftist literature. Many members of the Communist Party in America were intellectuals, including writers such as Langston Hughes and Richard Wright. The party had several magazines where many left-leaning writers were published, such as the *Liberator*, edited for a time by Claude McKay.

Of the six poems of Langston Hughes' included in the anthology, only two could be said to be proletariat: "Let America be America Again" and "Park Bench." "Office Building: Evening" might only be construed as a comment on oppression through race. Although race is mentioned in "Office Building: Evening" as "When white folks get through," no textual evidence exists suggesting Hughes is concerned with class (Hughes, "Office" 1.1). Since the people who "get through" are white folk" and not "rich folk," Hughes is implying the economic differences between the person cleaning and those finished with work for the day are racial. Finally, the other two poems, "Johannesburg Mines" and "Christ in Alabama," deal specifically with race. Although "Johannesburg Mines" mentions working in the mines, it foregrounds "Native Africans working" (1.3). It asks, "What kind of poem / Would you / Make out of that?" (1.4–6). By foregrounding race, the poem paradoxically questions Coles and Zandy's and others' conflation of race and class through essentialist readings of both race and class, of seeing the struggle of 25,000 Africans as a class struggle when they have been forced into the mines in South Africa and have been denied rights to alternate occupations and education because they are black, not because they are working class. It thus deconstructs Coles and Zandy's position once again.

Claude McKay was very much leftist in his politics, believing "racism was inseparable from capitalism" (Baym 1457). However, James R. Keller believes McKay's subversion of the "aristocratic European literary tradition" by using traditional forms, such as the Elizabethan sonnet, to "contain his volatile subject matter" was meant to "challenge white America's claim to cultural superiority and not capitalism" (448). Keller argues that McKay "gains a voice among those whose project of subjugation has been to efface the native cultural heritage of African Americans and to silence the discourse of dissent" (248). Of the three poems of McKay's reproduced in this anthology, only "If We Must Die" might be considered to be anything but concerned with either African American culture, as in "The Harlem Dancer," or racial hatred, as in "The Lynching."

The background of "If We Must Die" questions it as a working-class poem. Although the writing of the poem was precipitated by the Negro Porters' Union strike, the racially motivated murders of the strikers moved McKay to pen the poem. Ironically, as the poem has been subverted to represent the working class, it has also been "appropriated and contained in ways the poet could not have anticipated [...] the public reading of his poem [...] by Winston Churchill" (Keller 450). The "we" in the poem was reconfigured by Churchill to mean British subjects since McKay was a British subject, which renders the poem neither racial nor concerned with class, but rather concerned with nationality. For Coles and Zandy the subject of the poem has been construed to mean working class and, although it is capable of meaning both African American and working class, this is not exactly what Coles and Zandy contend. They argue that African American and working class mean much the same thing — again, essentialist and reductive.

Coles and Zandy include two selections from Studs Terkel's book *Working: People Talk About What They Do All Day and How They Feel About What They Do*: "Dolores Dante," a waitress, and "Mike LeFevre," steelworker. Actually, Terkel's book in its entirety deconstructs the "us and them" argument they have been making for the last 585 pages — that the working class is marked by struggle, exploitation, and victimization and other classes are not. Significantly, both of the texts chosen by Coles and Zandy from *Working* are negative depictions of life as a worker. Many more positive depictions in Terkel's book exist, as well as some negative depictions of life as a CEO, other managerial/professional positions, and many professions not usually discussed within a class dynamic, such as actor or tailor.

Coles and Zandy's text is constrained and constructed by a Marxist argument of labor versus capital. They claim that the people of the working class are and have always been wage slaves. This argument has a certain audacity, seeking to turn metaphor into fact. It diminishes the actual "lived history" of working-class persons and African American slaves. Once they have established this single-dimensional argument, they create a romanticized history through the literature, denying the real humanity of these persons by leaving out aspects of their history outside poverty, or labor struggle, ignoring multitudes of working-class people such as successful small farmers, skilled tradespersons and others whose lives and histories contradict their argument. *American Working-Class Anthology*, then, is not just a poor example of the working class, but it also does real harm to the concept of the working class, especially for students who must then think of their lives within a narrative of antagonistic struggle. If antagonism alone is the basis for the ideology and identity of working-class students (since this is a text for students), this text may work, but if it is a conception of the working class as multifaceted, complex, and with depth, then this is not the text for them to read.

Labor Texts: The Worker in American Fiction

If any text about people of low or medium income might be included in a corpus of working-class literature, whether struggle or exploitation is involved or not, the list of working-class texts becomes extremely large. For Hapke and others, a Marxist point of view provides a mechanism, albeit single-faceted, to categorize and discuss texts, and to create a discourse. This Marxist discourse, however, allows a very narrow perception of the working class. Thompson contends that "at times, too, Hapke's attachment to unreconstructed discourses of labor results in a methodological simplicity" (330).

Laura Hapke constructs her argument throughout her text by first explaining that she is couching her argument within a Marxist ideology. She then contends if the old proletariat fiction is not out of place, then the characters of those fictions no longer represent the laborer (xi). She goes on to postulate that all who work make up the working class since "there is no longer an expectation of bourgeois security" for any worker (xii). Yet the point of view she takes while gathering the texts she refers to within her argument is decidedly proletarian. Hapke continues this discursive shell game through her introduction and much of the rest of her text. She states that at the time of the writing of her book, "one-eighth of the civilian workforce—earn full-time wages below the poverty line" (xii). Eighty-eight percent, then, earn wages above the poverty line. Of those earning wages below the poverty line, she makes the unstated assumption that they are victimized, relying on the stereotype of the exploited worker. Again, it is a sacred-cow argument based on an overgeneralization, questioned by Terkel's book and its later incarnation, *Gig*.

Her simplistic dichotomy covers up a much more complex problem, or problems, at the level of ideology. She quotes Paul Solman, stating "95 percent of those interviewed [...] including those whose income qualified them for the subproletarian one-fifth, called themselves middle class" (xii). She argues against the accuracy of these numbers. If her disputation has substance, then it also brings to light the contradictory frameworks of working-class studies. Hapke understates the problem when she writes, "It does not take a sociologist to notice the tremendous confusion in America about class terms, although it does take one to sort it out" (xii).

Hapke's construction of the working class is an essentialist, theoretical, and political manifestation of the proletariat. "At the core of my inquiry will be the attempt to recover these worker representations" (4). Although she states that "it is important at this point to distinguish between working class and (implicitly pro-) labor fiction," her text, as argument, is pro-labor (as compared to pro–working class) due to her insistence on developing her readings of the works represented in her book through a decidedly antagonistic dichotomy of "them" (the capitalists) and "us" (the workers) (5). Quoting Zandy, Hapke writes, "Zandy observes that 'working-class text centers the lived, material experiences of working-class people.' Attentive to the physicality of suffering, such texts challenge dominant cultural assumptions" (5). She maintains that the "stereotypes" she and others confront are those such as "working-class masculinity," the "burly" or "beefy" male (5). By being "attentive to the physicality of suffering," she also stereotypes the working class as victim. Finally, she believes she has not "confined this study to working-class fiction" (6). She then contends the fiction she is exploring includes working-class fiction (fiction of and about the working class), work fiction (fiction of and about the work of the working class), and proletariat fiction. By not bothering to distinguish one from the other, and giving a Marxist literary overview to all the fiction within her text, she swings the argument of the representation of the working class back to the victim/struggle stereotype of the "heroic worker."

She attempts to "understand what the worker has meant to American fiction, [a] source of information for readers whose knowledge of strikes and sweatshops, child labor and sitdowns, was not firsthand" (6). Hapke has purposely conflated labor fiction with working-class fiction, arguing that class is inexorably "linked with organized labor" (7). She finally slides from her position of "elucidating labor texts" to a position of commenting on working-class texts. By doing so she argues for a stereotypical representation of the working class, the same argument she denies in both her preface and introduction.

Quoting Lise Vogel, believing that at "no time were [workers] a monolithic mass sharing a single consciousness," Hapke does not present her text as such (9). She has allowed her definition of labor texts to include the representation of the working class, and although she emphasizes in her preface that her text should do no such thing, she does not stress, either in her introduction or in her text proper, that her text is a single-faceted representation of the working class constructed through a Marxist lens. She falls into the same essentialist trap as do Coles and Zandy and many others attempting to see the whole of the working class through a Marxist lens.

Although one might say all texts are purposeful — in that an underlying reason exists for their creation — certain texts, especially those of the social realism bent (the slum novel, the proletariat novel, the muckraking texts, and so forth), are created with an overtly political or ideological purpose. Although many of the texts mentioned in Hapke's book are not overtly didactic, the majority of the book's thrust is to illuminate social ills, with many characters being "types" or caricatures, and it cannot be considered a true representation of working-class persons or even of laborers. Thus, as can be seen in *Maggie: A Girl of the Streets*, in the representation of the "Bowery B'hoy," these representations are not necessarily those of the working class and are certainly not representative of the majority of the working class, contradicting a position most of these texts take either explicitly or implicitly (Hapke 10).

As her representation of labor continues, from the beginning of America to the pre–Civil War years, the relationship between the worker and the poor gets stronger. She postulates that the skilled trades people and the artisans were slowly vanishing. This may have been true for some skilled trades in certain places, but the demise of Marx's petite bourgeois has still not been realized. Other than in the very large cities, many of these anachronistic trades existed into the 20 century and still exist in the guise of the independent auto mechanic, the small-appliance repairman, the saw and knife sharpener, the shoe repairman, and the radio and TV repairman, to name just a few that have survived and replaced the wheelwright, the cobbler, and the cooper.

Hapke's readings are well written, but often light on proof and narrow in scope even for Marxist readings. Unlike Coles and Zandy, Hapke seems to feel most of Melville's texts show the working-class person in a negative light. She expresses disapproval of Melville's character Bartleby because he is not stereotypical enough, comparing him to Dickinson's caricatured portraits. "While a veteran of deadening office jobs, [Bartleby] is well spoken and has an aura of gentility" (34). This comparison suggests that Hapke refuses to allow individualistic characterizations of working-class characters. She insists on the romanticized version of the proletariat folk hero as one of the few correct representations of the working class. Thus Hapke endorses the stereotyping of the working class in literature, such as the need for some lack of education in working-class representation, whether it be literacy or in manners.

She again takes Melville to task, stating, "*Redburn* is Melville's most complete repudiation of lumpen proletarians [...] representing the coarseness of the class and their improvidence, ignorance and sexual depravity" (35). Hapke constructs a narrow path for an author to negotiate to correctly represent the working class. According to Marx, the lumpen proletariat was "the 'dangerous class,' the social scum, the passively rotting mass thrown off by the lowest layers of the old society" (Marx and Engels, "Manifesto" 18). Marx had little use for the lumpen proletariat, and according to him, they should be repudiated. However, Hapke probably does not actually mean lumpen proletariat. What she is upset at is Melville's uncovering of what many working-class academics hope to hide — an honest representation of humanity, an unromanticized characterization of the working class. Hapke finally admits "Melville shows a grudging verisimilitude in his accounts of the wretched lot of the common sailor. [...] And he makes gestures toward undercutting the language of class superiority in which *Redburn* and the narrative are steeped" (34).

Her most serious faux pas, for someone writing in literature studies, is her mistaken belief that "*Redburn* is an allegory of his [Melville's] own situation as an underrated, underread, antebellum artist. (*Moby Dick* did not sell well)" (35). Hapke not only makes a judgment while not understanding the text, but she also comes to conclusions lacking a history of the author. *Redburn* (1849) was published after *Typee* (1846) and *Omoo* (1847), both financial successes. *Mardi* (1849) was not, thus spurring on the two sea adventures *Redburn* and *White-Jacket* (1850), both published before *Moby Dick* (1851). At the time of the writing of *Redburn*, Melville was a successful author of popular travel narratives and had yet to find his calling as one of the great American Romantics. *Moby Dick* is his greatest effort and, as Hapke correctly states, sold poorly, but after *Redburn* had sold well.

Hapke finds little useful material for the representation of the working class in *Redburn*, *White-Jacket*, and even *Moby Dick*, since Melville does not seem to represent the proletariat as heroic and does not vilify the pseudo-capitalists, whom Hapke apparently sees in his work as the officers onboard the ships. Although this reading might be easily applied to *Billy Budd*, a text she misses, it is a stretch in other works. Hapke says little of *Moby Dick*, other than to foreground Melville's depiction of Daggoo and Tashteego's "preindustrial nobility" as "greatly at odds with the negative personae of his other black workers: the murderous slave mutineer Babo; the schizoid Pip; the compliant Fleece, 'Baltimore,' and Mongo" (36).

Hapke must inevitably misread Melville. These misreadings, first, stem from an attempt to match characters and plot with real life. They also stem from the attempt to interpret Romantic literature through a socialist-realist lens constructed through attributes of present-day ideology. For Melville the realistic representation of real-life humans or circumstances in his texts was probably not a high priority. He was more interested in exploring the metaphysical or making comments on morality using the plots and characters as metaphors, symbols, or metonymies to explore metaphysical universal questions.

In her statements concerning Melville's story "Benito Cereno," Hapke not only conflates race with class, but she also misunderstands the use of the character Babo. Hapke believes Babo is a "murderous mutineer," a "negative personae of the black worker," rather than a heroic leader of a slave rebellion (36). As in his other stories, Melville presents metaphoric dualities in "Benito Cereno." Similar to *Billy Budd*, in "Benito Cereno" the ships are opposites, the *San Dominick* and the *Bachelor's Delight*. Melville's concept of bachelors was not, as might be depicted today in the mass media, young unmarried yuppies seeming to have a plan and a goal. He saw them as naïve and somewhat sheltered, as can be seen in "The Paradise of Bachelors." Thus the *Bachelor's Delight* has its similarities to the Temple Bar as a vessel housing these naïve men. The *San Dominick*, though, is a very old ship, rotting out from under the owner and captain, both representative of old-world aristocracy. Though Benito Cereno survives all the physical threats to his life, the realization that these Africans are in actuality his equal in all things destroys him. When Delano asks, "What has cast such a shadow upon you?" Cereno replies, "The Negro" (Melville, "Benito Cereno" 257).

Melville also sets Benito Cereno opposite Amasa Delano of Duxbury, Massachusetts, with both of them set against Babo and Atufal, who also are set against each other. Babo is small and appears harmless. He has been a slave all his life, even before being sold to Alexandro Aranda. Babo, then, has been shown nothing but cruelty and returns it with cruelty. He is not Uncle Tom of *Uncle Tom's Cabin*, nor the "happy slave" of plantation fiction. He is intelligent and capable of planning and executing a slave rebellion. He is capable of loving and hating. Melville was critiquing the naïveté of the New England liberals' soft racism so prevalent in works such as *Uncle Tom's Cabin*. For the point of this book's argument, Melville is indirectly critiquing anyone attempting to reduce any person or group to essentialist simplicity.

Most importantly, Melville was a Romantic. His characters or plots were not designed to represent people or real life, but rather to be symbols — representations of higher realities — or to critique what he saw wrong in society, such as transcendentalism in "Bartleby the Scrivener," or the naïve racism of the New England abolitionists in "Benito Cereno," society as a whole in *White-Jacket*, and humanity and its place in the universe in *Moby Dick*.

Hapke also seems to misread "The Paradise of Bachelors" and "The Tartarus of Maids." Although more thorough than Coles and Zandy's interpretation, if a bit radical, it is still a cursory reading of the story. In order to come to her reading, she must also marginalize the other story of Melville's diptych, "The Paradise of Bachelors," and, as others do, ignore the overt attempts of Melville to secure the reader's attention to the fact that the two stories are somehow connected. He mentions twice in "The Tartarus of Maids" that the scene reminds him of "The Paradise of Bachelors."

Hapke erroneously claims "The Paradise of Bachelors" and "The Tartarus of Maids" are Melville's rebuttal to Lowell's "factory-lady iconography" (73). The "mill is a twinned nightmare of industrial over-efficiency and working class exploitation" (73). Hapke focuses on the description of the factory virgins, yet, while elucidating the sexual symbolism of the large scythes within the factory itself, she ignores how this scene must tie in to the other sexualized descriptions outside the factory.

As Hapke's text makes its way chronologically through literature, it finds more solid ground, as does Coles and Zandy's book, in the middle and waning years of the 19 century. Hapke finds the same faults in her critique of the depiction of the working class in Rebecca Harding Davis' *Life in the Iron Mills* as she did in Melville's work. Here, though, Hapke is on firmer ground because the novel was written to bring to light the conditions of the workers in the iron mills of West Virginia while still maintaining the superiority of the middle-class ideology. Hapke states that Davis "is caught between her sympathy for worker sufferings, particularly those of women, and her own classed convictions about lower-class behavior" (78).

Hapke's reading of *Life in the Iron Mills* is feminist, concentrating more on the circumstances of the character Deb than Hugh Wolfe. She states, "These stories were [...] largely the province of women authors and feminine subjects" (26). Regarding Wolfe, she believes he "fashions from its refuse [korl] statues of elemental working-class women [...] responding unconsciously to women's work-sufferings. [...] Wolfe sculpts a 'Korl woman'" (77). Hapke believes this korl woman is "his cousin Deborah transformed" (77). Although

Hapke's reading is interesting and does have legitimacy, the strength of her evidence for the reading must be questioned. Davis does describe the inner Deb as having a "smothered pain and hunger" (Davis 21). The korl woman is described similarly; when Wolfe is questioned as to the meaning of the statue, he replies, "She be hungry" (33). It also has "the power of a desperate need" (65). Yet it is "muscular, grown coarse with labor, the powerful limbs instinct with some one poignant longing" (32).

The relationship between Deb and the korl woman connects through representations of metaphors of the lower classes, but Deb's hunger and pain have nothing to do with class or oppression. Instead, they are from "trying to please the one human being whom she loved" (210). Hapke argues that the lack of an extended description of Deb's job in the textile factory is because "she perceives her work [...] less as a means of self-support than as a contribution to the family economy" (Hapke 78). If Deb and others of the Wolfe clan are forced to crowd a basement, then this stereotypical trope of women's work, applying mostly to the middle class and coming from middle-class thinking, cannot apply to Deb's or any of the Wolfes' circumstances, including Old Wolfe and Hugh. None of their means were self-supporting. In actuality Deb's job is not given extended description because, as only a supporting character, her work is minimal to Davis. As a metaphor of the working class, though, she is as important as Wolfe to the themes of Davis' story.

Again Hapke reads into the text evidence not present. She contends that Deb is "physically powerful" like the korl woman (Hapke 77). Yet Davis describes her as having physical attributes akin to the patriarch of the family. "He was a pale, meek little man, with a white face and red rabbit eyes. The woman Deborah was like him" (16). Davis also states of Deb, "Miserable enough she looked, lying there on the ashes like a limp, dirty rag" (21). Deb is hardly a powerful woman.

Although Hapke positions the korl woman as the product of unconscious manifestations of Deb by Wolfe and thus aligns its symbolism with Deb, most readings align the korl woman and its symbolism with Wolfe himself. The korl woman is described as having "the wild, eager face, like that of a starving wolf's" (Davis 32). Wolfe is also described as feminine, "one of the girl-men 'Molly Wolfe' was his *sobriquet*" (24). This characterization is Davis' attempt to deconstruct the threatening stereotyped characterization of the masculine and dangerous working-class male in society of the time. Thus the korl woman represents both Wolfe and Deb, almost pure metaphor, the artistic rendition of Davis' contention that many of the lower classes hunger for redemption.

Davis' major struggle in writing *Life in the Iron Mills* was reconciling her own and other middle-class people's classism with her and their own moral self-identification. She is repulsed by a class of people she is mandated by her ideological and religious position to feel sympathy toward. Her reconciliation develops in a dialectic between these two opposing paradigms. She is more sympathetic toward the middle class's ambiguity regarding the lower classes than toward the conditions of the working class. She produces an argument reminiscent of Abraham's argument to God for the sparing of Sodom and Gomorrah.

Davis does not attempt to establish a language of equality, but rather reestablishes the lower class as an inferior class of humans and the middle class as the moral and intellectual superiors. She positions her narrator as solidly middle class and establishes the middle class's superiority by locating the narrator on the third floor of the "old house," overlooking the sordid life outside her window (13). In the basement of the home, three floors below, the pack of Wolfes once lived, establishing not only their class inferiority but also their evolutionary inferiority. The narrator readily admits her repulsion for the lower class. "The air is thick and clammy with the breath of crowded human beings. It stifles me" (11). They are "masses of men, with dull, besotted faces bent to the ground, sharpened here and there by pain or cunning" (13). For Davis, many, if not most, of the lower classes were unredeemable. She describes the other workers as "drunken Irishmen [...] puffing Lynchburg tobacco" (11). The Welch immigrants, the "Cornish miners [...] are a trifle more filthy; their muscles are not so brawny; they stoop more. When they are drunk they [...] sulk along like beaten hounds" (15). In describing what Wolfe is not, Davis describes what the typical lower-class worker was for her. "He was never seen in the cockpit, did not own a terrier, drank but seldom; when he did, desperately. He fought sometimes, but was always thrashed, pommelled [sic] to a jelly. [...] He had the taint of school-learning on him,— not to a dangerous extent [...] but enough to ruin him as a good hand in a fight" (24). Finally, using the trope of woman's intuition, Davis asserts through the observations of Deb, "She felt by instinct, although she could not comprehend it, the finer nature of the man, which made him among his fellow workmen something unique, set apart" (22). Wolfe, then, is the exception to the rule of what a working-class person is for Davis.

Davis attempts to create a set of characters redeemable to her and other middle-class people. Although Wolfe, at one level, is used to undercut the dangerous masculinity of the lower classes as a "desperate set" who "bid fair to try the reality of Dante's vision, someday," and to claim that redeemable persons exist in this class, "infant geniuses [...] stray gleams of mind and soul among these wretches," and to reconcile certain opposing impulses in Davis' dialectic, Wolfe's most important metaphoric representation is of the awakened and tragically lost soul, not of Christ, but of the martyr dying while in search of redemption (27, 24).

Hugh Wolfe is not just unlike other lower-class persons in the story; he is also endowed with all that is good and important in the middle class. "It was his nature to be kind, even to the very rats that swarmed in the cellar" (22). He is endowed with a natural sense of the aesthetic, the moral separator of the working class from the middle class. This sense of aesthetic reaches beyond art to the beauty beyond the physical world, and like Davis' middle class, Wolfe has a natural revulsion toward what is not beautiful. Deb "knew, in spite of all his kindness, that there was that in her face and form which made him loathe the sight of her" (Davis 22). Davis does not attempt to reconcile this seemingly unheroic tendency in her hero because she did not see it as unheroic. At the time of the writing of this novel, woman had become fetishized as representative of truth, morality, and beauty. "The late 19 century morality of character was sexist" and deformity of any kind, especially in a woman, was akin to immorality (Gandal 762).

Wolfe, in carving the korl woman, is searching to quell the hunger of his soul. He is searching for enlightenment, to understand God and his place in the universe. He is searching for conversion, to have his soul redeemed. He is the repentant, imbued with romantic irony, becoming the tragic hero for Davis' middle-class audience, awakening while at the same time realizing that he will never know enlightenment. As Wolfe observes Mitchell, he looks "back to himself, seeing as in a mirror, his filthy body, his more stained soul. Never [...] he knew now [...] there was a great gulf never to be passed" (Davis 30). Wolfe's epiphany is not the realization that he will never attain a middle-class lifestyle, but rather, for Davis, that he shall never attain the moral righteousness of the middle class. Something is lacking in his soul.

At no time does Davis reposition the middle class as equal to the lower class, but instead maintains its superiority. "The thirty-year-old author [narrator] is separated by the span of her life and a story or two from the situation of her protagonists" (Hesford 73). Along with the rhetorical spatial position of being above the lower classes, she both positions the middle class higher on the scale of the chain of being and insinuates that they are, in some way, created of better material. Where most statues are made of marble, this "working-class" statue is made of the waste product of steel, the backbone of society.

To reconcile the untenable position of her argument, Davis endows in the character Deb the representation of the lower classes. The lower classes, through Deb, move metaphorically from proto-humans or semi-beasts at the beginning of the story to humans having, as would be said in this epoch, challenges or disabilities. Davis, then, sees the lower classes as redeemable, but never equal, reminiscent of Stowe's positioning of the African American slave in *Uncle Tom's Cabin*. Importantly, the redemption comes not so much through a religious awakening, as suggested by Wolfe, but through submission to a religious philosophy of "Christ-love needed to make healthy this impure body and soul" (Davis 63).

Deb, standing in for the lower classes, possesses no "artist's eye," and although she is a twisted and monstrous thing, "a thwarted woman's form," one should take pity upon her because "was there nothing worth reading [...] nor story of a soul filled with groping, passionate love, heroic unselfishness, fierce jealousy?" (19, 21). Wolfe, except for his stained soul, might have become middle class. However, Deb, and thus most of the lower class, can never hope to do so and within their psyche they are supposedly aware of this fact. Although Deb is endowed with the ability to love deeply and to be devoted to another person, even if love is not returned, Davis seems to argue that love, for the working class, is a miserable thing. Davis asks, "You laugh at it [the idea that a lower-class woman could feel deeply]? Are pain and jealousy less savage realities down here?" (23).

Deb, then, carries the symbolic weight in her physical description of the ugliness of the fallen soul of the working class. All the good in the 19 century middle-class world, of beauty and innocence, is seen in the character of Janey. Janey, like little Eva in *Uncle Tom's Cabin*, is a stock character in sentimental literature, the prepubescent female child. Deb "knew, that, down under all the vileness and coarseness of his [Wolfe's] life, there was a groping passion for whatever was beautiful and pure,— that his soul sickened with disgust for her deformity" (Davis 23). Deb recalls, with "pain and jealousy," how Wolfe looked at the "little Irish girl," Janey, described as having a "vivid glow of beauty and of grace" (23).

Davis' argument can finally only be reconciled through the continued subordination of the lower classes while contending that those exceptional working-class men such as Wolfe exist, equal to the middle-class person, but denied the chance to prove it within the existing circumstances of the working class. In this way she reaffirms the middle class as morally and intellectually superior. She sees the way to redemption for most of the working class as submission to God's will. Finally, by trying to illuminate the conditions of the lower class and alleviate these conditions, Davis creates new stereotypes no less damaging than the old ones.

Another canonical text giving Hapke a bit of trouble is Dreiser's *Sister Carrie*, mainly due to her assumption that Carrie is working class. For Hapke, Carrie is "money hungry" and allows herself to be used by "capitalist men"

(99, 157). However, Dreiser does nothing to place Carrie in either the working class or middle class. Certainly, her sister, Minnie, is working class if one bases a wife's status on her husband's status; however, this assumption is problematic because so little information is provided. Minnie and Carrie's father was a miller, but the text does not mention whether he worked for a large grain company or was a petite bourgeois, who owned his own mill. He might have even been a capitalist.

Hapke calls Carrie a "shoe-factory worker" (56), but this is hardly the case. Carrie works in the factory for just a few weeks. She is appalled by her treatment while employed, more so than the other female workers, who seem to expect the treatment. Whether Dreiser meant to show her naïveté in being from a small town or from a sheltered middle class, he did not place her on a par with the representations of the working women characters in his story.

Carrie does not work at working-class jobs for very long. Dreiser's opening description shows her not to be a worker at all. "She was eighteen years of age, bright, timid and full of the illusions of ignorance and youth" (1). Considering that, in Dreiser's time, a "working girl" would have gone to work long before she reached the age of eighteen, Carrie's lack of work experience and ignorance of her abilities cast doubt on the idea that she is of the working class.

Hapke's reading depends on Carrie having "sexual vulnerability and suggestibility" (156). This is somewhat true because Carrie, at the beginning of the novel, is a bit naïve and shallow. Carrie is more concerned with appearances than with character. Although many critics see Drouet and then Hurstwood as seducing Carrie, she never sees her life in those terms and is never wracked with guilt for her actions.[5] As long as she looks the part of a lady, she is a lady. Whether on stage or off, she is an actress. Hapke contends that Dreiser's point is "even the most refined of workingwomen can ascend only as the mistress of an affluent, capitalist man," but in fact the situation for Carrie is quite the opposite (157). Carrie descends with Hurstwood into poverty only to ascend as a well-known New York actress by her own efforts, leaving him behind to his own feeble devices and finally suicide.

In the final section of her book, Hapke gets to her main point. She blames unions for the condition of the worker in contemporary times, saying, "They discard the language of class for that of (elusive) self-fulfillment" (317). Hapke titles her conclusion "Everything Old is New Again: Working Through Class in the Literary 1990s." Sardonically, she states, "Union leaders over the past twenty-five years have engaged in their own unfair labor practices" (317). Again, this assumption is much too simplistic. She, along with others, ignores the complex interrelations between capital, government, consumers, and technology. If manufacturing and capital have changed in the last one hundred years, the unions should have also changed, and thus the worker, or the theoretical construct of the worker, must also change. Demanding better representation for unskilled workers in a world where nonskilled workers are in overabundance is a study in frustration, not because it is not a noble endeavor, but because the workers themselves cannot and will not band together. To think otherwise is not visionary, but misinformed and utopian.

The chief fault of Hapke, Coles and Zandy, and the many other editors and authors studying and writing about the working class in literature is their refusal to give those they place in the working class a true sense of agency. By promoting such texts as *Life in the Iron Mills* and producing readings of texts like "The Paradise of Bachelors" and "The Tartarus of Maids" that foreground exploitation, victimization, and struggle, they stereotype the working-class person through a simplistic and essentialist paradigm.

Labor Text: The Worker in American Fiction, like *American Working-Class Literature: An Anthology* and many of the other texts constructing the argument for working-class literature through a Marxist lens, whether consciously or unconsciously, whether as anthologies or as scholarly attempts, start with a simplistic theory of the working class and (for Hapke) labor in America. Their lenses come into focus only in the eighty-odd years between the Civil War and the ending of World War II. They are focused on the decades of the Depression when "there was a body of proletarian publishing [...] stereotypical, tendentious, and romantic" (Tyler 324). The lens is very myopic, unable to clearly see, first, all those working-class people, such as Berger's autoworkers and many of Terkel's workers, who have positive attitudes toward their lives, positions, and work. Second, the working class does exist beyond and outside the sphere of work. For many, their "lived experiences" do not include pain and suffering as a daily diet. Third, class is not the driving force in many individuals' struggles. Rather, for many, as in "The Paradise of Bachelors" and "The Tartarus of Maids," it is gender. For others, like Phillis Wheatley, Olaudah Equiano, and the immigrant workers of Hapke's text, it is race or ethnicity.

Labor Texts proclaims itself to be Marxist, and thus it should also claim it does not represent the working class beyond one facet of the working class' history — labor. Although Hapke says just this at the beginning of the book, she makes little attempt to stop her position from finally enveloping all conceptions of the working class, and her implicit argument, if not her explicit argument, is that the concept of working class must be grounded in victimization.

The Stamp of Class, by Gary Lenhart

Gary Lenhart's book is significant in the discussion of working-class literature because it questions how the parameters of the study and the literature should be defined, along with questioning how the working class is configured in literature. However, like others, he sometimes conflates the working class with the poor. He does not believe, though, that the working class is anti-intellectual or anti-education, although he does feel "most working-class Americans have a highly refined and discriminating sense of class" (4). Evidence does not back up this assumption. As Veblen asserts, and the authors in *Cultural Studies and the Working Class* state, many people emulate the middle classes. Many people believe they are middle class, which in many instances is a determining factor in being middle class. Lenhart's mother's belief in education and intellectualism had a direct influence on him becoming a poet. Yet other people from the working class, he implicitly contends, questioned why "a twenty-four-year-old man was still in school," or asked why he hadn't gotten a job (xii).[6] These two opposing impulses complicate any easy delineation of a sense of class.

Lenhart asks, "Why would we, well past the millennium, call attention to class at all, particularly as it manifests in an activity such as poetry, that is by many considered marginal itself?" (4). The first part of his question, "why a concern with class at this time," might be answered in many ways. But the answer this book gives is that we are concerned with class due to the struggle to construct narratives to replace the lost metanarratives. If the question concerns academics, the best answer might be "We're not," if by "we" Lenhart means the population in general, at least not in the way academics are concerned with class. The way class is constructed in the real world is generally much different than the way academics construct it. This answer casts light on the second part of the question concerned with class in poetry. The answers have been supplied by Lyotard and Metzgar in chapter 2, and will be expanded upon in the rest of the book — that there is a need for performativity to ensuring a place within the discourse, thus ensure a place within academia.

Lenhart discusses just this conundrum when he narrates an incident that occurred while he manned a panel at the St. Mary's Poetry Project. The people in attendance "generally responded in two ways. Many took the occasion to stand up and declare themselves more working class than thou" (5). The second response was to disparage "working-class credentials" of poets "not in attendance" (5). The conference, then, seems to have been, among other things, a chance for those in attendance to seek a power network by closing off the avenues to this network for others by controlling the social space within the discourse of working-class poetry. Social space for Pierre Bourdieu is "a structure of objective relations which determines the possible form of interactions and of the representations the interactors can have in them." They "are also strategic emplacements, fortresses to be defended and captured in a field of struggles" (*Distinctions* 244). Thus the discourse of the panel was a way to defend this social field, to limit its members, and to orient the attendees within that field toward a position of power by limiting the number of poets within the field.

Lenhart interviews Ron Padgett, who contends, coming from the working class, that he was influenced in different ways than poets from the middle class, especially in the way he approaches and writes poetry. However, because he does not write in Lauter's style of protest poetry and because he is more concerned with aesthetics than victimization, even writing about non-working-class subjects, he feels he has been ejected "from our class" (qtd. in Lenhart 6).

After the introduction, Lenhart produces a short history of poets he considers to be working class. He moves from poets writing in a working-class vernacular, by which he means writing with "nonstandard forms of speech," such as Stephen Duck and Ann Yearsley, to the poets writing about the working class, such as Whitman and William Carlos Williams (xii). Williams was certainly not working class, but "poetic invention cannot be dismantled from the circumstances of its generation" (35). After World War I and during the Great Depression, Williams, like many other artists concerned with what they were seeing and the experiences of others less fortunate than they, began leaning toward the left, the growing American Communist Party and their ideals, as did McKay and Hughes. Williams contributed poems, stories, and articles first to *The Masses* and then to the *New Masses*. According to Lenhart, as the magazines became more militant, more didactic and more socialistic in the thrust of their submissions, they and Williams parted ways. The question still remains, though, whether Williams' contributions to these magazines might be considered working-class writing, or proletariat writing. Because of theorizing at a surface level, where tenets of vulgar Marxism go unquestioned (although Lenhart does question these assumptions), a paradox exists, suggesting, but never satisfactorily answering, the question of what constitutes working-class writing and working-class authors.

Most academics studying working-class literature position themselves as Lauter does, arguing that working-class literature can be written only by authors from the working class, about conditions of the working class, or protesting, in some way, the working-class conditions. Again, this is a much too simplistic construction and leaves the question open of how much is from and of the working class. If the poet's parents are of the working class, does this mean the poet, by default, is of the working class, or does the poet have to be employed in a working-class occupation? The second part of the paradox of constituting a working-class canon asks this question: what criteria are needed or acceptable to constitute working-class writing? If, as Lauter believes, working-class writing must be socialistic (protest literature), then what is the reason for the narrow scope? This narrowness is often like the other criteria created and contested within the social field, a way to exclude or include authors and academics in the discourse as a bid for a power position. Thus the answer to the question of narrowness of scope is that the criteria are used as a set of rules in the language game to open or close the discourse to certain authors and academics.

Thus the unanswerable question now posed within the field is this: is a working-class writer who writes non-working-class literature still a working-class writer? The bookend question is, of course, whether a writer such as William Carlos Williams is a working-class writer when he writes of the working class and whether his writing can be considered working class. That is to say, can someone like William Carlos Williams write about the working class at all? These questions do not need answering if tenets of vulgar Marxism are not used. No heroic working class writer need exist. This is an artificial construct of proletariat literature, as is "working-class" writing.

Lenhart moves on to a discussion of David Schubert and Marcia Nardi. "Both were damaged humans who harbored special talents" (47). This damage extends from the circumstances of poverty and a discussion of their mental and emotional troubles should not be associated with class. Working class can contain within it people living well above the poverty line. This "line" is a theoretical "line" drawn by the government to distinguish poor from others, including working class. It is also a line sometimes invoked by concerned people to indicate those living within a breath of not surviving — that is, below the survival line. The poor can be only those living below the survival line and, as discussed in the last chapter, are not a class, but people in a set of circumstances. This argument, of course, is not connected to the argument of the haves and have-nots, an argument of the distribution of wealth, and has its own line drawn by those evoking the paradigm.

However, if both Nardi and Schubert's problems were thwarted by their inability to negotiate the various legitimizing power spheres of poetic production, they might be considered working class. They both felt "discomfort when they made rare ventures among 'literary people'" (47). This too is a sign of class shifting, of working-class people moving into other classes, yet being unable to play the game, not knowing the new rules. Schubert ends up institutionalized for the last "years of his life," while Nardi alienates herself from many people, believing her loneliness from lack of "intellectual literary friends [...] explained by her background, not personality" caused the alienation (47). Shubert ends up as "a paranoid schizophrenic" (53). Becoming a schizophrenic from lack of publications seems rather an extreme result. Instead, he may have had these problems all his life and, as many are wont to do, used poetry to express what he was feeling.

Nardi's case is well documented in Williams' writings, especially *Patterson*. She had a history of being poor, unable or unwilling to hold a job, a wanderer in the literary world of the Northeast, and, for Williams, a person constantly approaching him for money, advice (editing) and his profession connections. Like Padgett, Nardi wrote in "nonstandard ways." Yet, unlike Padgett, she could not acquire a reputation in the literary world, as can be seen through Williams' comments on her poetry. She wrote in a time more conservative as concerns poetic production. Nardi was who she was, a complex relationship between experience and ideology — habitus.

At this point of his writing, Lenhart's stamp of class is still undefined, with no solid definition of what or who a working-class writer might be when Duck, Yearsley, Padgett, Schubert, Williams, and Nardi are considered, although he does start to deconstruct the positions of Daniels, Lauter, and Zandy despite claiming that she is a "pioneer," meaning a pioneer in the study of working-class writing (xiii). Lenhart further complicates this position when he brings the poet Melvin Tolson into the discussion, bringing up once again the complexity of class and race — an unanswerable question when looking at both through a Marxist lens. When does a poet's ideology reflect the ideology of class or race, and can it reflect class when the mitigating circumstance of a person's existence is race, as in racial prejudice? This confusion is created with the conflation of class, race, and poverty. Because none of these designations are inclusive of any other, poverty cannot justify putting a poet, writing of poverty because of racism, into a catch-all category of class, as the authors of previously discussed books attempt. The point cannot be overstressed: poverty has nothing to do with class. A person is in poverty owing to their situation, whether they are working class, middle class, or even elite class, male or female, black, hispanic, white, or any other race or ethnicity. Although this statement seems contradictory, Lenhart's well-constructed argument and the above statement bring to light the problems with the constructions of class in academia. As Dickens and Austen have recounted, people from differing classes, when a turn of events casts them into poverty, still retain their class ideologies and do not suddenly switch to a working-class ideology.

Lenhart finally defines his stamp of class when he writes of Walt Whitman and the inheritors of his legacy, the New American Poets. According to Lenhart, despite Emerson calling Whitman a "journeyman printer," Whitman came from the middle class, although "in the poem [*Leaves of Grass*] Whitman chose to represent himself as a rough from the working class" (21). The moniker gave Emerson "a way to approve of a book with 'buffalo strength' but lacking the literary taste that would make it acceptable to his [Emerson's] peers" (21, 22). Echoing the positions of Bridges and Shefter, Lenhart believes the republicanism of America influenced Whitman's writing and way of life, giving him an "advantage over his European contemporary [Marx] of immersion in the flexible class structure of antebellum boomtown New York" (22). Although Lenhart attributes the influence on Whitman to the uniqueness of the American way of life, he, unlike Bridges and Shefter, does not investigate these influences of an underlying and alternative American metanarrative embraced by Whitman and many others, antithetical to the metanarratives proposed (most times implicitly, if not unconsciously) by those positioning their arguments within a Marxist/Weberian/Protestant-ethic/spirit-of-capitalism metanarrative.

"Whitman appreciated money, but never cared to earn much of it, was careless and irresponsible, walked away from good money [...] to devote most of two years to writing the first edition of his little book" (Lenhart 22). This rejection of the Marxist/Weberian/Protestant-ethic/spirit-of-capitalism metanarrative is not unique in American literature. *Walden* is the fruition of an impulse, a metanarrative more native to America than the metanarrative spurring on Benjamin Franklin. "Rip Van Winkle" is a comical rendition of this same narrative. More serious renditions can be found in Abraham "Brom Bones" Van Brunt of *The Legend of Sleepy Hollow*, and Natty Bumppo (Hawkeye) of Cooper's *Leatherstocking Tales*.

Lenhart, avoiding the didactic assertions of those claiming working-class poetry must be "about something" or must be protest socialist literature, finally defines his stamp of class through the language of the poetry, ideals, ideas, and ideologies, and sees Whitman as the purveyor of this poetry with the New American Poets as the inheritors of Whitman. The stamp of class, then, is the breaking away from, and refusal of, the European formalist approaches and poetic language overrunning the American form of poetry during the late 19th and 20th centuries with the advent of high modernism. This new poetry reverts to a looser and more flowing form and common everyday language. Lenhart sees the return to the language and style of Whitman as a return to the language of the people.

Within the New American Poets, Lenhart sees a select group "without the heavy existential angst that affected so many of the New American Poets. Instead they were fresh totally irrelevant smart-asses grabbing words that sailed so near in the air that it was almost impossible to make them stay on the page" (102). To Lenhart the new poets are not the elitists so prevalent in the poetry world, but of "no special privilege" (102). This might be enough to settle the argument of who might be a working-class poet; however, they could have also become the classless poets, who, like Whitman, reject class, but in truth class is foisted upon them by those controlling the legitimatization of cultural production.

Of those he finally cites as models of his working-class poets, he feels a need to explain their working-class background and assert that they actually wrote poems of class protest. This protest, though, is not configured in a Marxist vein, but in a Veblen/Weberian construction. The protest is of "alienation," or, more precisely, exclusion from power networks, configured as moral centers of class because, as Berrigan states, these poets don't "'know' the 'language' and 'the rules'" of class (qtd. in Lenhart 110). This explanation is closer to the realities of class exclusion and separation at the real individual level. The poems Lenhart selects echo class more perfectly in their language than in their subject, although this also echoes the ideologies of class, the confusion, the searching, the embarrassment and even the anger, not of lack of money, but of knowledge of the rules in all their intricacy, of not understanding how or why they have been singled out, what is so different about them.

To sum up Lenhart's assertions, although he wanders into the same traps as others (such as equating class with the lack or possession of money), he does make two very important points. The first assertion is that class is contested in social fields using discourse, language, fashion, and other social and symbolic capital. The rules of these games are many, varied, forever changing, complex, and, for those with a working-class ideology, convoluted and secret. The second assertion (and for discussions of literature, the most important), is that working-class poets, or those with working-class ideologies, have the ability to produce poetry able to survive the scrutiny of aesthetic critiques. Thus geniuses do exist within the working class. A final assertion might be put forth, one discussed further in the next chapter, believing that, because "taste" can be used (and often is) as a device for separation and to gain and control power positions, many times "taste" is nothing more than an exclusionary practice. This position does not negate the idea of quality, but contends that the language used by working-class poets, wielding their "language" as adroitly as other poets wield other "languages," is not a matter for aesthetic judgment. Rather, judgment must be held to the ability to use language well or poorly.

Working: People Talk About What They Do All Day and How They Feel About What They Do, by Studs Terkel

The third text to be explicated for this chapter is Studs Terkel's book *Working*. "Studs Louis Terkel elevates the craft of interviewing and intertwining lives of his interviewees into insightful nonfiction" (Harper 80). Although the book is somewhere between creative nonfiction and ethnographic study, and obviously about work, it is also completely different in range and scope from the other texts explicated in this chapter so far. Published in the 1970s, it is a collection of interviews with diverse working people. In this way it is a collection of short biographical vignettes. "Among those whom [Terkel] counts as 'worker' are a hooker, domestic, piano tuner, news boy, copy boy, stockbroker, TV executive, hockey player, housewife, community organizer, gravedigger, stone mason, mother on relief and retiree" (Tyler 324). Although the interviews are autobiographical, a text such as this is produced by the crafting of the editor no less than an anthology such as Coles and Zandy's. Terkel, placing the reader as the authority of the text, "allows wide latitude to his subjects. [...] They become people first and 'workers' second. Through their eyes — not Terkel's — the reader is allowed to peek at worlds he has never seen or been aware of" (Tyler 324).

As a text concerned with people, *Working* becomes metatextual, commenting on the narrowness of scope of other texts authoritatively proclaiming to represent the working class, questioning their validity of representation. By recording the thoughts of people from a continuum of class positions, Terkel's book grounds itself in the empirical in the same way, if not as scientifically, as Berger's study of the suburban working class in *Working-Class Suburb: A Study of Auto Workers in Suburbia*.[7] Although Richard Ohmann's article "Politics and Genre in Nonfiction Prose" degenerates into an overgeneralized Marxist reading on this type of recorded oral history, he sees Terkel's style as unobtrusive, "simply introduc[ing] edited speech and retreat[ing] into the background [...] supply[ing] a vicarious intimacy" (238). Terkel's scope, also being nonintrusive, does not claim to have exclusive authority over knowledge. *Working* questions, then, the academic authority to determine the concept of work, worker, power, and exploitation.

Edmund J. Farrell, in "The Language Game: Oral Histories as Living Literature," believes "oral histories [such as *Working*] share with autobiographies the verisimilitude that derives from the expressed experiences of real persons, from lives lived" (89). *Working*, then, refutes the argument for the narrow definition of work and working class made by such texts as Kenneth Patchen's "The Orange Bears," promoted by Lauter as working-class literature, and works that Daniels cites as work poetry or working-class poetry. Terkel's text assumes a much more expansive conception of the working class.

In many of the texts and articles concerned with the working class or working-class literature, such as Lauter's article and Coles and Zandy's anthology, the first several lines of the introduction to Terkel's text are quoted, too many times taking this quotation out of context. "This book, being about work, is, by its very nature, about violence — to the spirit as well as to the body. It is about ulcers as well as accidents, about shouting matches as well as fistfights, about nervous breakdowns as well as kicking the dog around" (xi). Purposefully ignoring of the point of Terkel's book, which is elucidated four paragraphs after this passage, seems typical of authors or editors proposing a stance of victimization and exploitation of the working class. "For the many, there is hardly concealed discontent. The blue-collar blues is no more bitterly sung than the white-collar moan" (xi). Also, "the drones [are] in the office as well as the warehouse; at the manager's desk as well as the assembly line; at some estranged companies computer as well as some estranged woman's kitchen floor" (xiii-xiv).

Terkel, stating "the camera, the tape recorder ... misused, well-used," questions, if not the expertise of those who assert their authority to define the working class, then their ability to do so (xix). Texts such as Coles and Zandy's metaphorically announce themselves as cameras. Texts such as Hapke's might be seen as cameras once removed. Cameras not only record what their wielders wish them to record, but they also record the mindset of the photographer. In the case of the many textual cameras trained on the working class, the photographers search for the sensational, whether this stems from blind ideological ignorance, unable to conceive of this class outside the romanticizing of the folk hero, or purposeful skewing of perspective in the effort of performativity.

Terkel questions the premises of much of working-class studies, asserting that most of what is "known" about the working class is a romanticized myth and "the myth dies hard" (xxiii). He believes that when journalists interview those "eminently quotable" worker-philosophers, such as the cab-driver, barber, bartender, and so forth (who are also very "tippable"), the results reflect more on the "slothfulness of the journalists" and the "phenomenon of tipping," than on the nature of the interviewees' work (Terkel xxiii). The proliferation of texts such as those cited by Daniels and Lauter might be, then, a reflection on the slothfulness of publishers by being unwilling or uncaring enough to consider various views and lenses. This slothfulness results in the working class being "romanticized" as it "is caricatured" (Terkel xxii).

Studs Terkel's book is about humans at work. "One must work" (xii). Although his text is not a study in the scientific sense (its methodology is just to interview various people), the shaping and editing of any text suggests a slant and purpose. Terkel states, "I was on the prowl for a cross-section of urban thought, using no one method or technique" (xix). "At one extreme [the author] may simply introduce the edited speech and retreat into the background; close to this extreme [is] Studs Terkel's *Working*" (Ohmann 238).

This text studies people and their relationship to work at the individual level, from CEOs to newspaper boys. In this continuum of work (Terkel does not divide them by economics), a continuum of happiness exists based on a continuum of fulfillment, from the unfulfilled (such as LeFevre, whose story is reproduced in the Coles and Zandy text) to those feeling very fulfilled (such as Carl Murray Bates, the stone mason; Pierce Walker, farmer; Eric Hoellen, janitor; and Vincent Maher, policeman, among others ignored by Coles and Zandy).

Many of the interviews cast doubt on the notion of exploitation of the working class in two senses. The first is that only the working class are exploited. Many interviews exist of people holding occupations considered middle class and upper class where the interviewee, in some way, feels exploited. Thus, in the Marxist meaning of exploitation, many times the exploiter can also be the exploited. Power is relative, viewed from the position in the social field of the viewer. Larry Ross, when interviewed, was a retired president, chief executive officer, and former part-owner of a large corporation bought out by another company, leaving him fairly well off. His memories should be good ones. Yet he says, "Fear is always prevalent in the corporate structure [...] by the slight flick of a finger, your boss can fire you" (Terkel 406). Ross admits he "wasn't in control" (405). He also states, "You get into the corporate structure, you find they all button their pants the same way as everybody else does. They all got the same fears" (405).

Peter Keeley, also a former executive, was not as fortunate as Ross. "I was dropped. It was company policy: no man older than forty-five. [...] I didn't bounce" (401). Keeley was sixty-four and let go along with others. "Just like that, they dropped me. They handed me a couple of checks" (403). He had to start over in the business. At the time of this interview, he was an inventory/purchasing agent for another company and ran a small business of his own that made "about three hundred dollars a month" (402). He was "drawing $128 a week" from his other job (402). Although in 1970s money his earnings were fairly adequate, they were much less than he was earning as an executive.

Exploitation, then, seems universal in a capitalistic system across classes, questioning, among other postulations of Marxist theorists, why the working class is given the majority of attention and is placed in the position of the "innocent." In the assertions of theorists such as Aronowitz and Zweig, at least top management, if not all management, then is included in the capitalist class and thus given little sympathy. Keeley fits into Aronowitz's and Zweig's capitalist class. Unlike the thirty years and out of the working class, of retirement with a pension, the thirty and out for the professional/managerial class speaks of early obsolescence, a time when a person can ill afford to be starting over at the bottom.

The implicit refutation to this argument in *Working*, of universally caring about universal exploitation, is ultimately the position of the exploited to poverty and thus the dangers of succumbing to starvation or exposure. The people of the working class have fewer resources in which to amass capital of any kind to create a protective cushion between them and the elements. This reasoning demands, then, if a person or family whose income puts them squarely in the upper-middle class — for example, Walter Benn Michaels — were to lose the ability to earn a living and had not amassed a cushion of capital to protect them from the elements, others should not care. As Keeley explains, suddenly "people don't know you" (401–2). Once fired, Keeley found a loss of social capital and economic capital with a devaluation of symbolic capital, making it much more difficult to find a job than if he had attempted it while still in a position of power (403).

Thus it is not exploitation of the proletariat Marxists are theorizing about, but the return for the exploitation. The upper-middle class — Keeley, for example — have been exploited, but paid well for it. A better way to understand exploitation is to ask what a person might receive in return and whether that makes him or her happy. Once happiness (subjective well-being) is added to economics and working conditions, the idea of exploitation becomes complex and must be studied at the individual level — whether a person's overall circumstances allow for a feeling of fulfillment. This fulfillment might come from the job (not necessarily from the paycheck) or from the opportunity the occupation gives for other avenues of fulfillment, such as travel, time off, volunteering or pursuing hobbies such as camping or fishing.

Working shows that the argument of exploitation in many working-class texts hinges on the romanticized stereotype of an exploited worker and the narrowing of exploitation to economics based on a framework of inequality — a dichotomy of rich/poor. Michaels and others simplify their dichotomy, speculating "everybody wants to be rich" because "nobody wants to be poor."

As agents inside social fields, people decide, within their options, based on their ideology/habitus and position in a social field, the "cost" of affluence.

Much of Terkel's book bears this out. Pierce Walker, a farmer owning two hundred acres and share-cropping three hundred more, admits, "The return on your investment is so small now that it isn't really worthwhile" (3). Although most of this interview is concerned with the "gambles" in farming, the weather and cost of chemicals and equipment, he states, "When you get a good crop, that's more or less your reward. If you weren't proud of your work, you wouldn't have no place on the farm" (6). Walker believes his son, who graduated from Purdue the previous spring, would have made a good farmer. Of his son, he comments, "I hope he isn't putting money ahead of what he really wants to do" (6).

If fulfillment is the explicit argument of *Working*, "a meaning to their work well over and beyond the reward of the paycheck," then the cost of happiness to happiness's value is the implicit argument (Terkel xi). Happiness in psychology and sociology is understood as "well-being" (King and Pennebaker 53). This state of well-being entails the condition of a person's satisfaction with his or her position in life, love life, family, occupation, and how life seems to him or her in general.

John Stuart Mill's syllogism contends that it is better to be intelligent and unhappy rather than ignorant and happy. This either/or fallacy is questioned by Diener, Sapyta, and Suh as they reconceptualize the syllogism. They state, "Most of us would prefer to be a happy sow rather than an unhappy one, and a happy Socrates rather than a depressed one" (35). Several of the interviewees in *Working* were unhappy in their jobs, such as LeFevre and Steve Dubi, both steelworkers. LeFevre states, "My attitude is that I don't get excited about my job. [...] It's [...] degrading to say *just* a laborer" (xxxii). Diener, Sapyta, and Suh suggest, "Although subjective well-being may not be everyone's highest value, it is likely to be a value that virtually all people hold dear" (35). LeFevre counteracts his frustration with his job of "being a mule" by "blowing up" — going to bars to drink and getting into fistfights (xxxvi). Dubi contends, "You're not regarded. You're just a number out there. Just like a prisoner" (554). He adds, "I told you I am nothing" (557).

Conversely, many interviewees are satisfied, if not happy or fulfilled, such as Bob Sanders, strip miner. "I don't think anybody's gonna say their work's satisfyin', gratifyin' [...] But I make a good livin' at it" (22). Others seem happy and fulfilled, as are Carl Murray Bates, the stone mason, and Roy Schmidt, garbage man, who states "I've been outside for seven years and I feel more free. When I worked in the office [...] it was starting to play on my nerves" (104).

Eric Hoellen had been a janitor for twenty-two years at the time of the interview. His father "did the same kind of work" (120). Even with the slights by the tenants, such as no Christmas tip, he still thinks "there's nothing wrong with a janitor. [...] I come and go as I please'" (119). Hoellen does have complaints. However, he has stuck with this job, not because the material conditions of his life have demanded it, but because he has weighed various "values, goals and life circumstances" contributing to his subjective well-being against the importance (weight) of his subjective well-being (Diener, Sapyta, and Suh 35). Thus, unlike LeFevre and Dubi, who hate their jobs, Schmidt and Hoellen have weighed the importance of being happy against the importance of money, while LeFevre and Dubi have weighed having money against the happiness of doing something they enjoy. They suffer through most of their lives doing a job they hate because they value money more than subjective well-being. Thus, when work is studied at the micro level, as Terkel does, Marxist economics seems less of a factor than Marxism contends. Walker, the farmer, says of the one summer he worked in a factory, "The money part of it is good, but the atmosphere, confined" (6). Walker speaks of the hard work and hard times as a farmer, but he prefers farming over any other occupation.

Terkel's text brings to light another fallacy of many arguments along a Marxist line, and contests many assumptions made by academics writing of class. Their assumption argues that all people weigh public self-esteem (status through conspicuous consumption) or economic security much heavier than other criteria, such as independence, ease of mind, or mental health. This paradigm leaves little choice for a person but to want the responsibility of a white-collar job because of the higher salary potential. It marginalizes the importance of happiness produced by the occupation itself and the weight given to diverse goals and values at the individual level of subjectivity. It does, though, foreground a distinction between the working class and the middle class through the difference in the weighted importance of status or the concept of status itself.

In truth, many people weigh happiness within their job as very important. Philip Da Vinci, a lawyer, found defending an insurance company from "people who had been hit by cars" unrewarding (357). He had the possibility of retiring with a minimum of "$350,000, in profit sharing" (for that time, very lucrative) or he could "jump sides in the game, become a PI — personal injury lawyer for the plaintiffs" (537). He quit this lucrative occupation to drive a cab because he felt unfulfilled. He then learned about a legal aid organization called Uptown. "I finally got into something where I actually felt useful" (537). Romanticizing Da Vinci as a folk hero of sorts, dedicating his life to defending the downtrodden, undercuts the reality of his prioritizing feeling useful to or for society over the importance of material gains. As King and Pennebaker contend, for some people "a sense of purpose is a vital part of feeling happy" (54).

Terkel's interviews question equating happiness with economic equality as a universal constant. Subjective well-being is finally just that, subjective, and any attempt to create a unifying theory of characteristics of good or bad (evil?) is doomed to failure, or worse, doomed to stereotype people. "After all even a science such as physics [...] does not have a fully unified theory" (Diener, Sapyta, and Suh 35). Thus attempting to construct one (through vulgar Marxism) will have disastrous results.

Working shows that, if anything, what constitutes happiness is an ideological construct. In a consumer society driven by the logic of late capitalism, happiness would appear to stem from conspicuous consumption transferring into status and status groups in a straight hierarchy, from which we might deduce that the higher status position a person holds, the happier he or she will be. Happiness is not a constant, nor can it be quantified (or qualified, for that matter) in a straight hierarchy, but even the working-class person has agency in his or her own happiness. *Working* also shows that Marxist theories of exploitation are much too simple. Either exploitation cannot be confined to any one class, or exploitation must be considered alongside ideology at the micro level of individuality to determine whether, or in which instance, it might exist, and where job satisfaction, negating the idea of exploitation, attributes to what Diener, Sapyta, and Suh call "positive self-regard" (35).

Gig: Americans Talk About Their Jobs, by John Bowe, Marisa Bowe, and Sabin Streeter

Gig, like Terkel's *Working*, consists of diverse interviews with people speaking about how they earn a living. Like *Working*, each interview is focused on nothing more than the person's feelings toward his or her occupation and any meaning deeper than their feelings must be drawn from these interviews. Marisa Bowe believes "work defines, to a large degree, your external identity as part of the social matrix. But it also looms very large in your inner sense of how you're traveling through life" (xiii). However, the interviews in the book do not bear out this statement, but instead prove the opposite. How a person narrates him- or herself in the world will define the work he or she picks. This narration depends on diverse criteria, as seen in Evans and Mill's

"Identifying Class Structure: A Latent Class Analysis of the Criterion-Related and Construct Validity of Goldthorpe Class Schema" (mentioned in chapter 2), and on a person's relationship to subjective well-being, as Diener, Sapyta and Suh have explained.

The book *Gig* coalesced from a "webzine *Word*, as a weekly column called 'Work'" (M. Bowe xii). The purpose was to "present the [...] unscripted voice of the individual. Unmediated by TV or magazine editing. [...] It's [the voice] almost always distilled and distorted by high-level media pundits whose last experience of ordinary American life was 10,000 expense account cocktails ago" (M. Bowe xii-xiii). While Terkel's interviews seemed to be directed toward some broad area of inquiry, Bowe, Bowe, and Streeter's are not, having apparently avoided just that scenario by grouping the interviews so as to avoid any implied political thrust. The professions of *Gig*'s interviewees' go far beyond what might be thought of as legitimate professions, although all professions must, in some way, be legitimate if work is involved; however, palm reader might seem to be at the moral edge of work, while drug dealer can hardly be considered legitimate or sympathetic. Yet all the professions, including porn star, escort, and transvestite prostitute, produce a livelihood and for one reason or another were chosen as a profession by those doing them. These reasons, however, are diverse and complicated. The most apparent conclusions garnered from the list of interviewees are, first, that occupation is a poor way to define class, and second, speaking of class within economics is no better since a transvestite prostitute might earn a fairly good wage, but would never be considered middle class by those considering themselves middle class, and the concept "prostitute" evokes a seediness (whether this is actually so or not) many times relegated to the working class, namely, working "girl."

Chris Real is a "forty-year-old temp," an occupation generally evoking victimized and exploited workers, those with little power and few material benefits. However, Chris sees the temp job as an advantage. He does admit the work is "drudgery [...] work people can't keep filled and it's work that will make other people go crazy" (58). However, "it suits me fine" (58). The job allows him to do what he wants when he wants. He decided he wanted to take an extended bike vacation and quit the job he had. As a temporary employee he was not held down to a job. If he doesn't like the employer or boss he is working for, he quits and gets another job in a few days. He doesn't understand why "people take this shit year after year. [...] When you answer the phone for twenty years what have you done?" (62). Chris has evaluated his subjective well-being against ownership of material objects and what most people take for security — a steady job and paycheck — and found he is much happier having fewer material objects and more autonomy in his life.

If, as Weber believes, capitalism needed Protestantism to flourish, then no reason exists to think this ideological point of view might not be rejected wholesale. Once the Protestant moralistic aspect of work is removed, need is satisfied, self-esteem is unhooked from material objects — cultural and social capital — and one realizes that the odds of getting rich are long indeed, the narrative remaining is the older American Dream, one with a core metanarrative of security for self and family and a better life for the next generation. Chris has weighed all his options for subjective well-being and found he enjoys temping and the lifestyle it offers him. Da Vinci, the insurance company lawyer who quit and started driving a cab only to later work in a legal aid organization, is Real's complement in the middle class.

William Rosario is a UPS driver. He seems to have ambiguous feelings toward his job. He likes to drive, but he doesn't like the work. He dislikes the supervisors because they are "company people," but he likes being in the Teamsters' Union and being very well protected (8). "Basically [he has] a problem with authority figures" (8). "I hate wearing a uniform and dealing with people who are real assholes" (8). He goes on to speak about the advantages he sees in the job. One important aspect of the job for him is being away from direct supervision, which gives him opportunities to read porn magazines, drink coffee (and sometimes harder stuff), and to engage in sex on the job. Rosario, although he complains about his job, sees it as an opportunity to live a certain, albeit questionable, lifestyle. Both he and Real have chosen occupations fitting their ideological outlook.

Mike Jackson works at Ford. After starting college and not doing well and having little money, Jackson spoke to his family members who worked for the Ford Auto Company about going to work. After three years, though, he is "getting the hell out" (45). He feels "it's like a prison sentence" and "really hard on your body" (46). Jackson's attitude toward assembly-line work would seem to fit the exploited and victimized worker. His counterparts in *Working*, Phil Stallings and Jim Grayson, have similar attitudes toward working on the line. Stallings finds the work meaningless and mind-numbing, and is thinking about going to college to become a social worker. Jim Grayson is an African American with a college education working on the line because, at that time (mid-1970s), the jobs he was qualified for were not open to African Americans. He believes, "If I had been white, I wouldn't be doing this job" (Terkel 164). However, Hobart Foote, working with both Stallings and Grayson, has a different attitude toward working for Ford. Of Stallings he says, "He's grown to hate the company. Not me. The company puts bread and butter on the table" (170). Jackson's family members and friends do not agree with him. His "buddy Kevin [...] all he ever plans on doing is working here" (47). Of his family, Jackson comments, "You know it's a good life for them — and it's a good life" (47). For a while he had wanted something more than a factory job. In high school he had dreams of being an oceanographer but was talked out of it by his mother (47).

Both Rosario and Real have found jobs fitting their ideology, their belief system, allowing (within their ideology) for subjective well-being. The people of Jackson's family have satisfied their concept of subjective well-being within the narration of their reality; however, Mike Jackson has not. He is the outsider in his family whose dreams (ideology) did not develop in the same way. His mother discourages him from attending college because she adheres to a metanarrative asserting that college is not for working-class people, although within the working-class ideology the narrative exists believing college is the "way out." Importantly, the ideology picks the occupation. The narratives inherited through habitus will construct an ideology and will allow or limit dreams and aspirations both internally and externally.

Also, as proved in *Working*, certain assumptions (such as the one stating that the class people's occupations occupy defines their identity through, or because of, the work they do, so that they see themselves as working class or middle class) must be contested. No substantial evidence exists proving any of these assumptions, although sometimes, through the interview, one or another person does seem defined by the work they do, as with Sandy Wilkens, the slaughterhouse human resource director. Yet her occupation title does not truly fit the work she does. Her job is to hire workers for the slaughterhouse in addition to other administrative duties, a full-time job. She works an average of sixty hours a week trying to keep enough employees working at the company. Sandy states, "Even though we pay a decent wage, the working conditions are terrible" (49). Sandy must work sixty hours a week because people won't and don't put up with the conditions. "Some people will quit fifteen minutes after they get on the floor because it's so ugly to them" (50). Sandy's situation, in a way, is the result of an ideological condition of the workers she hires, of balancing their need for employment with their subjective well-being.

She goes far beyond the definition of her job in trying to keep the workers. "A lot of what I end up doing is kind of like social work. I've gone and gotten dentists for the workers [...] when their babies are sick, I've found pediatricians" (53). Sandy is defined by her occupation because of the overwhelming time and effort she puts into it. However, what truly defines her is not her official occupation, but rather her unofficial one — the occupation of social worker. In truth, her caring personality (identity) defines her job. If she had taken the job to be just a human resource manager, she would have moved on to another company. However, she finds a purpose at this company more fulfilling to her than simply doing a standard human resource manager's job. It is, then, Sandy Wilkins' belief system that keeps her at her job.

Interestingly, the interviewees in *Gig* and in *Working*, have a major difference in the point of view toward their occupations. Some of this is owing to the underlying focus of each collection. However, the interviews in each book create strikingly different cumulative themes when compared. In *Working* more soul-searching seems to be going on, a contemplation of the path each interviewee has chosen in life. Many workers, like Phil Stallings, see themselves as little more than machines. In *Gig*, although some people have questions about their chosen occupation, sometimes believing the job is too demanding or else worrying about what the future holds, only a few, like Mike Jackson and several others forced into demeaning jobs, are dissatisfied. But several people in *Working* seem truly dissatisfied with their occupation from CEOs to line workers. Others, though, seem more than happy. LeFevre and Steve Dubi, both steelworkers, hated their jobs. The tenor of their interviews is negative. Denise Barber in *Gig*, another steelworker, seems satisfied with her job even in a time when steel mills are becoming extinct. She gives partial credit to a strong union, but says, "Even the foremen, they're mostly fine" (42). Her interview is positive even when she warns of other workers who, in these times, believe they have a "right to this good job," by which she means they have no birthright or guarantee to a good job without standing up for themselves and adequately performing (42). Very few interviewees in *Gig* are dissatisfied with their job in the way those *Working* are dissatisfied. The UPS delivery driver, William Rosario, is dissatisfied, but extenuating circumstances for his dissatisfaction seem to exist. Javier Lopez, the undocumented worker, employed illegally in a chicken-processing factory, is also unhappy. Because of his circumstances, he and other undocumented workers are taken advantage of and exist as pseudo "slaves" (228). This slavery, however, cannot be seen as an automatic condition of the working class, as Coles and Zandy contend, because the circumstances of undocumented workers are not the same as those of most working-class people, who have laws protecting them from just such conditions.

Even with all the changes having taken place in the forty-odd years separating the books, only a difference in the ideological makeup of the two groups of people can finally account for this noticeable difference in attitudes, whether this shift might be discussed as a positive or negative attribute. At the time Terkel wrote his book, the nation had yet to experience the devastating crises of the oil embargo, double-digit inflation, two major recessions (not counting this last "recession" of 2009), 9/11 and other terrorist acts, downsizing, the rollback of laws protecting workers and consumers alike, and other varied attacks on the complacencies of 1970s America. If *Gig*'s interviewees might be said to have been taken in by the elitist ideological hegemony, the interviewees in *Working* might be said to have been taken in by the labor hegemony.

A pragmatic attitude seems prevalent in *Gig*, not just because many of the interviewees seem happy to have a good steady job, but also because a belief exists among many that this is the best they can expect unless they are willing to put forth effort to change their own lives. In the 1970s an expectation of success existed. The narratives of expected or promised success and the rights to the American Dream, a career, and a good job have been replaced with mini-narratives of differing ideological aspects.

As examples of real-life feelings of the working class, *Working* and *Gig* claim the academics now producing texts of the working class are attempting to control the discourse of the study through the voice of academic power. While trying to close off this discourse to a discussion of aesthetics, they also create antithetical poles of discourse unable to come to terms with their contradictory construction of the field of study and its many paradoxes and exceptions. This does not, however, allow academics to create, as Pizer argues,

> forced, ingenious, and essentially worthless interpretations [...] which have little support in the work but do confirm his [sic] preconceived notion of the cultural design expressed by the work, [where a resulting] turgid, mind-numbing, tortured prose style can mask the underlying weakness of logic, probability, and common sense which results from the effort to force unrelated parts into a single design ["Bad Critical Writing" 70].

In *Labor's Text* Hapke attempts to control this discourse of study. Although she says the text represents only the "worker," she excludes any non-proletariat representation of the worker that does not show struggle, and does not depict work in a negative light. She then suggests this representation of the proletariat is the correct representation of the working class. Coles and Zandy attempt to establish the discourse for working-class literature studies by boldly proclaiming their anthology contains "working-class" literature. Through this literature they contain the discourse of study within a Marxist paradigm and attempt to bring into this discourse the conflation of race with class.

Both Hapke's text and Coles and Zandy's text are forced to construct direct representations of the working class in American literature to buttress their narrow Marxist paradigm that equates all the working class with the proletariat and class struggle. Their paradigm insists on the existence of a literature deemed working class, capable of being collected into a canon of works. At the same time that it denies its own implicit argument, what it actually studies is proletariat literature, a rather distinct genre involving a Marxist view of exploitation and victimization that dates from a short epoch of the late 19th and early 20th century, and a sub-genre of realism and social realism. These theorists, then, are, encumbered by the paradox of refuting this same paradigm by insisting working-class literature, in the way they conceive it, has existed, and still exists, from the first colonization of America until the present. This leaves them with little choice but to give cursory readings of some texts based on little or no evidence. In doing so, their readings become shallow or off the mark and have to ignore or marginalize contradictory evidence existing in the text, or else make assumptions outside the texts altogether.

Working and *Gig* finally contest the pillars of the study of this working-class-literature theory in the way the theory is implicitly constructed within working-class literature studies at this moment. Lenhart's *The Stamp of Class* questions the necessity of closing the discourse of working-class literature to discussions of aesthetics. At the same time, it questions the standard formulation of what or who might be a working-class author and what might comprise working-class literature. These texts, and many others not reviewed here, cast doubt on an all-encompassing theory of class based on vulgar Marxism. Yet, as is postulated implicitly — negatively in such texts as Coles and Zandy's, Hapke's and others of the same ilk, and positively in texts such as *Working* and *Gig*— class exists, if only ideologically, but it is complicated and resists a simplistic Marxist or other explanation.

Chapter 4

Postmarxist Theories of Class

Within working-class studies and studies of working-class literature Marxism has become hegemonic. As seen in chapter 1, other theorists of class, such as Veblen, Weber, and Durkheim, present alternative and viable theories of class more closely aligned with the social world. Both Weber's and Durkheim's theories were the result of studies concerned with the individual arguing that, rather than economics being the all-pervasive maker of class, status groups create both economic classes and status classes by allowing access to life chances that determine class and economics. As Bourdieu contends, Marxist concepts of class have become an

> intellectualist illusion [...] which leads one to reduce the social field [...] to the economic field alone [...] which leads one to overlook the symbolic struggles that take place in different fields, and where what is at stake is the very representation of the social world [*Language and Symbolic Power* 229].

Cultural Studies and the Working Class: Subject to Change, reviewed in chapter 2, although retaining vestiges of Marxism, actually sits within a postmarxist frame, thus questioning, explicitly and implicitly, many tenets of vulgar Marxism by suggesting class exists within a social field created at the micro level, influenced by individual narratives and ideologies within a social field. Like *Cultural Studies and the Working Class*, the text *Culture Matters: How Values Shape Human Progress* looks at the problems of poverty and inequality as a cultural phenomenon rather than an economic one, or, as Marxists do, as a macro-political one. Both texts' use of the word "culture," though, is problematic.

Again, the term "culture" needs to be defined because the cultural turn of the study of class sometimes suffers from not having the same rigor that other approaches utilize. Usually the term culture is used in three ways, all overlapping, which adds to the confusion within the study of what this term means. The first use is directed toward aesthetics, and is the most common use, concerned with the products of the "best and brightest" through the understanding of aesthetics or a judgment of taste. This use of the term culture might be thought of as qualitative. The first problem with this definition is in defining "brightest." Simply, brightest would seem to mean the most intelligent. However, defining intelligence in a straight-line hierarchy and the measuring of intelligence have come under scrutiny.

Howard Gardner, in 1983, initiated a debate concerning the existence of multiple intelligences. "Gardner's central claim is that what we normally think of as intelligence is merely a single aspect, or two aspects, of a much wider range of aptitudes; he has counted eight so far" (Traub 20). Many psychometricians disagree with Gardner, believing these intelligences to be only aptitudes of a single intelligence. "While psychometricians disagree about the extent to which intelligence is an inherited trait [...] there is broad consensus around the idea that intelligence is a single entity that can be measured with fairly great accuracy" (Traub 20). Scores on IQ tests (the test psychometricians developed, use, and stand behind) by minorities have risen dramatically in the last twenty years, suggesting that whatever IQ tests measure, it is not the brain's inherited ability to learn. If psychometricians' claim is that intelligence may be developed through environment, then what they are measuring is, again, life chances and not inherited intelligence. Since the IQ test is basically understood as a test determining intelligence, it should test only the capacity to learn, not what a person has learned, although what they have learned is exactly what is tested. Thus to state that it measures just intelligence is incorrect. It actually measures the effectiveness of school systems and life chances. "If we limit studies by relying on a single standard for the acceptable measurement of intelligence, our understanding of this most central capacity of human beings will be significantly restrained" (Chen 19).

The theory of multiple intelligences claims different types of intelligences exist. Gardner believes eight exist: "linguistic, logical-mathematical [the IQ ones], musical, spatial, bodily-kinesthetic, naturalistic, interpersonal, intrapersonal, and existential" (Moran, Kornhaber, and Gardner 25). Importantly, "because MI theory is based on the conception of human cognitive functioning in diverse real-life situations, its scientific establishment is grounded in empirical data that describe the functioning of multiple abilities in diverse situations" (Chen 18).

The second problem with the first definition of "culture" lies, obviously, in defining the first term of "the best and the brightest"—"best." According to multiple-intelligence theory, the best and the brightest of an intelligence should excel in the type of artistic endeavor in which their intelligence is most suited. Even if this were so, the question remains as to whether those excelling in an artistic field define art in that field, or whether people lacking artistic ability, but who excel at the ability to manipulate power systems and control the discourse, actually control the artistic output within the field. The decision makers in a field may not be the best and the brightest, nor might they always select the products of the best and the brightest of the field. "All social practice (including art) exists by and in ideology" (Hutcheon 179). This hypothesis can be extended to all fields and all social endeavors.

Bourdieu evokes Weber's position on religion as existing as an autonomous field, arguing that "the 'rationalization' of religion owes its own 'auto-normativity'—relative independence of economic factors—to the fact that it rests on the development of a priestly corps with its own interests" (*Field of Cultural Production* 113). Bourdieu believes the field of artistic production operates in much the same way. He calls this field the "field of restricted production [...] objectively destined for a public of producers of cultural goods" (Bourdieu, *Field of Cultural Production* 115). As Lyotard contends, the field is closed to outsiders or to people or groups challenging this hegemony, and open to those choosing to support the ideology of the field through performativity. Bourdieu states, "The autonomy of a field of restricted production can be measured by its power to define its own criteria" (*Field of Cultural Production* 115). Between artists and critics, those intellectuals, through symbolic capital or knowledge of the field and not necessarily through artistic intelligence, having secured themselves a place of power within the field, create "tiny 'mutual admiration societies'" because "few people depend as much as artists and intellectuals do for their self-image upon the image of others" (Bourdieu, *Field of Cultural Production* 116). However, a struggle always exists for the ownership and control of the discourse defining the legitimate knowledge of a field by insiders and outsiders. As Bourdieu contends, this "field of restricted production can never be dominated by one orthodoxy without continuously being dominated by the general question of orthodoxy itself, that is, by the question of the criteria defining the legitimate exercise of a certain type of cultural practice" (*Field of Cultural Production* 117). The field itself questions the legitimacy of the field, those in a power position within it, and its orthodox discourses. This does not suggest that art has no merit or that criteria within the artistic field are always arbitrary, but within the field a struggle for power exists not only among those who "do" but also among those who "do not" seeking a power position as critics, calling into question any criteria, the products of the field, and especially those controlling the field by controlling the discourse, as well as the discourse of the field itself.

The second use of "culture" entails artifacts (including art and architecture, clothing, and food), rituals (such as mating and religious activities), and pastimes (such as sports, games, dance, and music) defining a separate and unique group. This use of culture might be seen as quantitative. Whereas qualitative demands some criteria to define good and bad, this use only demands adding up or collecting unique "things" of a certain group.

The third use of the term culture is the one used in this text — the manifestation of ideology — encompassing the first two, but not in a simplistic way of adding up artifacts indigenous to a group or adding up the results of a complex process, thus deciding at a certain loci in history what constitutes the products of the best and brightest. M. J. Collier states, "Culture is defined as a historically based, interpretive, constitutive set of practices and interpretive frames demonstrating affiliation with a group" (qtd. in Moss and Faux 22). Culture used as the manifestation of ideologies becomes, rather than the impetus of an action or thought, the result. It becomes the signs of an ideology. Yet too often culture is spoken of as the thing manifesting culture — that is to say, culture manifesting itself—when it is actually the result of the work of ideology.

As with other terms, "ideology," within the study of class, is interpreted in several ways. "Ideology is not only one of the most elusive and colorful concepts in social sciences, it is also among the most loaded and contested. The debate transcends a number of disciplines — philosophy, political science, sociology, and others — and ontological and epistemological positions" (Meyer et al. 1). It can mean a certain political bent, such as conservative or liberal; it can be a pejorative modifier, as in being radical or extremist. However, ideology, as it is used in this text, encompasses all beliefs, from the belief in what might be the correct doneness of toast to how the universe was made, from correct manners to a certain belief in a supreme being or beings. It, like Bourdieu's habitus, exists within a feedback loop. It is created by the narratives and metanarratives generating the schemas and prototypes used to narrate the world and create, mediate, and mitigate those same narratives. It is passed down through families, and modified by state ideological apparatus and various organizations, such as religious groups. Ideology is what is behind culture and Bourdieu's habitus. Ideology is mutable, capable of being modified or altered by outside forces and agency.

Postmarxist theories of class suggest this idea, although many do not foreground ideology within their theories. Gramsci suggests that more is going on in workers' heads than false consciousness when he contends workers are culpable for their own enslavement. Althusser takes up this line of inquiry when he proposes that a person is a subject interpellated, or "hailed," by society as a subject and thus is given a subject position within society, suggesting that some internal mechanism allowing for this subjugation exists. He names it "ideology" and suggests it is all persuasive. Althusser moves the idea of ideology into the realm of Freudian/Lacanian psychoanalysis to recover much of Marxism and although most theorists have moved away from Althusserian Marxism, his construction of ideology, Freud and Lacan aside, allows for the understanding of the mechanisms of separation.[1] Marxism also does not really allow for theories of the individual, while postmarxist theories allow for the consideration of individual agency. Althusserian postmarxism, taking as its departure point Lacanian psychoanalysis, suggests, but does not foreground, individual agency. It also contends that classes still might be conceived as homogeneous. Postmarxism suggests agency is moderated by the dominant ideology. In Althusser's case, through, it is the law-of-the-father.

Pierre Bourdieu and Michel Foucault (two theorists taken up in this chapter) adopt this line of investigation, creating their overarching metaphors of field and discourse. Field and discourse involve the workings of society at the individual/small-group level, although they stop short of considering ideology directly. Importantly, all postmarxist theorists moved away from Marxism. Although Bourdieu and Foucault keep vestiges of vulgar Marxism (causing contradictions and paradoxes in their work), they have broken with several of the major tenets of Marxism — that class is decided through the relationship to the means of production, that economics decides status (class in the social world), and, most importantly, that there exist three antagonistic classes, of which capital (a ubiquitous villain) is somehow consciously engaged in the enslavement of the world. This is not to say persons involved with capitalism (almost everyone in a capitalistic country) may not be unconsciously engaged in the enslavement of the world through the tenets of capitalism.

Chantal Mouffe states, "Within every society, each social agent is inscribed in a multiplicity of social relations. [...] All these social positions determine positionalities or subject positions and every social agent is therefore the locus of many subject positions" (90). Mouffe argues society is "a complex ensemble of heterogeneous social relations possessing their own dynamism" (90). As Katznelson contends and Bridges and Shefter allude to in *Working-Class Formation: Nineteenth-Century Patterns in Western Europe and the United States* (reviewed in chapter 2), rather than collective consciousness acting on a mass of non-individualistic persons, persons with individual interests acting through and with agency, banded together, as Weber contends, out of status groups (at certain times and for personal reasons) to act collectively.

Many postmarxist approaches to the study of class at the micro level exist, most based on Veblen, Weber, or Durkheim. A few are based on Nietzsche's writings, which are, if not explicitly anti–working class, then implicitly anti–working class. However, even these Nietzschian approaches allow for insight into class ideologies at a micro level. Marxist theories do not. Whether Veblen, Weber, Durkheim, or Nietzsche might be considered postmarxist can be debated since the category "postmarxist" does not appear until the mid–20th century. Postmarxist theories move from a Marxist position to a position concerned with culture, identity, ideology, power, and subjectivity. They have come from a direct encounter with Marxism. Although Veblen, Weber, Durkheim, and Nietzsche were contemporaries of Marx, or else wrote shortly after his time, they are not directly influenced by the theories.

Postmarxism mutates to become poststructuralism and postmodernism. Two major theorists evoked in this chapter, Pierre Bourdieu and Michel Foucault, are certainly poststructuralists, at least in their later writings, and have set terms for postmodernism (discussed in chapter 5), but are here because of their relationship to, and final breaking with, Marxism, coming to understand that status groups are the creators of Marx's classes instead of the relationship to the means of production creating classes. That is to say, for the postmarxists, such as Bourdieu and Foucault, the relationship to the means of production is determined by the relationship within a status group determining life chances. These two theorists add complexity to theories elucidating the real working class, such as Veblen's and Weber's theories.

One of the most influential theorists, at least for British cultural studies, is Pierre Bourdieu. He states in the preface of his first major text on the study of class at a micro level, *Distinctions*, that the book is "based on the endeavour to rethink Max Weber's opposition between class and Stande" (xii). At this point Bourdieu is still very much a Marxist materialist, endeavoring to recover Marx's dialectic. This effort produces problems in his early work specifically with his concept of cultural capital. For Kingston, concerned with the application of Bourdieu's theories of cultural capital and the separation of children in school into classes of expectations, the concept of cultural capital "does not substantially account for the relationship between social privilege and academic success" (89). The problem for Kingston rests on how Bourdieu defines cultural capital in his early work, with culture taking on the meaning of those products of the best and brightest. Thus children exposed to museums, classical music, and other products of culture do not seem to have an advantage over those not exposed to this culture. The core of Bourdieu's theories, though, actually lies in what he first calls "distinctions," later to be looked at as "differences"—anything and everything singling out one person from another. For the later Bourdieu, culture takes on the third meaning—the manifestations of ideology.

The first half of *Distinctions* is a study of taste—what it is, how it is acquired, and its manifestations. At this point in his work Bourdieu has already concluded that taste is an exclusionary project related to education, not necessarily formal education. "In matters of taste, more than anywhere else, all determination is negation" (56). Because taste seems linked with types of education, what each class deems important to learn and know, "this predisposes tastes to function as a marker of 'class'" (*Distinctions* 1–2). Importantly, Bourdieu believes "the influence of social origin is the strongest" factor in defining class (*Distinctions* 1). If social origin decides the amount and type of education a person will or might receive, then taste, along with all other characteristics of distinction or difference, originates within social origin, and rather than searching through aspects of education or other criteria of difference, theorists can focus on the origin of difference in social origin: status. This disqualifies occupation or economics as a determinant of class; they are not the origin but the result of social origin, and thus class becomes a synonym of status group, and for the remainder of this text will be evoked in this way.

Bourdieu sees education of the upper classes as teaching the codes needed to decipher art. He believes "popular tastes applies the schemes of the ethos, which pertain in ordinary circumstances of life to legitimate works of art, and so performs a systematic reduction of things of art to things of life" (*Distinctions* 5). John Cook, in "Culture, Class and Taste" (from chapter 2), alludes to just this. Of course, his source is Bourdieu. Other authors have noticed this phenomenon, believing popular taste looks for function over form or meaning over aesthetics. Bourdieu concludes that this function over form comes about because "necessity imposes a taste for necessity" (*Distinctions* 372). However, Bourdieu's definition of popular tastes can be contested. First, it might be contested by arguing that a sign's power comes from its limited access. If popular taste means the majority of tastes, then the separation may not be due to aesthetics alone, but also to power disguised as aesthetics, the need for "artistic tastes" to be held in short supply as a hegemonic power play. If signs of an ideology, or the understanding of the signs themselves, can be limited, the signs, as Bourdieu states, become codes. The secret knowledge of these limited codes allows selective inclusion to a power position within a field and taste becomes inclusionary as well. Certainly artistic merit exists in much art, but merit often is not what is at stake. Rather, it is the control of the signs, what Foucault will come to call the discourse, and what Lyotard, borrowing from Wittgenstein's theories of language, will suggest is control of the rules of the language game.

Bourdieu sees taste as dependent on a person's position to necessity. *Distinctions* was first published in France in 1972 and the assumption of position to necessity can be contested the further away societies move from the devastation of the Great Depression and World War II. Although World War II brought America out of its depression, it was devastating for the French. The class Bourdieu would see as working class sees itself as middle class now, and

Bourdieu's middle class, or petite bourgeois (although this is not strictly a Marxist definition of petite bourgeois), sees itself as bourgeois; as Veblen postulates, each class emulates the one above it.

Some of Bourdieu's propositions are out of date and have been proven wrong — specifically, his assertion that aesthetic competence is tethered to material needs — the further you are from material needs, the more the appreciation of the aesthetic. Instead, this appreciation is an epiphenomenon of material necessity only because material necessity gives less time to learn the rules of the cultural game and likewise places a person within a social group whose ideology or habitus are aimed toward a certain appreciation, or lack thereof, toward art. Most importantly, though, ideology (or habitus), by steering taste toward certain criteria, limits or gives access to codes for entry into power structures within fields. Habitus and ideology, then, are the mediators of cultural competence rather than need, and in so doing, limit or give access to occupations, placing a person in a position to necessity. This phenomenon can be seen in Bourdieu's own example of the *nouveau riche*, who, despite their economic position (position to necessity), do not understand the rules of the game. Because they have not learned to know these rules, their tastes are not in line with their position to necessity. Bourdieu states that "the petit bourgeois or nouveau riche, 'over does it' betraying his [sic] own insecurity" while "bourgeois discretion signals its presence by a show of ostentatious discretion [...] a refusal of everything which is 'showy,' 'flashy,' and 'pretentious'" (*Distinctions* 249). If taste were only mediated by position to necessity, the *nouveau riche*, had they become wealthy gradually rather than suddenly, garnering occupations through education, would have learned the codes and signs necessary to fit in the class their money put them in.

Popular taste might also be described as part of an ideology resisting the ideology of artistic taste proposed by certain hegemonies within certain fields of power. Popular taste, then, becomes a struggle over power or else becomes a resistance to power, a refusal. Without looking at the extremes of any kind of taste, one cannot legitimately say that popular taste is any less valid than any other taste. A judgment of taste, whether popular or elitist, creates within it a legitimacy of an object or process and thus, although each legitimate taste ranges from good to bad, neither has a right to adjudicate the other.

Out of this position Bourdieu develops his four major contributions to the study of class: the habitus, field, types of capital, and practice. Bourdieu's concept of field is analogous to Foucault's concept of discourses, although both contain important differences. "'Field' (*champ*) is a key spatial metaphor in Bourdieu's sociology. Field defines the structure of the social setting in which habitus operates" (Swartz 117). Bourdieu states, "To account for the infinite diversity of practices in a way that is both unitary and specific, one has to break with *linear thinking*. [...] The structural causality of a network of factors is quite irreducible to the cumulated effects of the set of linear relations" (*Distinctions* 107). Fields, then, are theoretical spaces representing social settings in which class is defined at the individual and small-group level. As many social fields exist as areas of human contact. Bourdieu "wants to emphasize the conflictual character of social life. [...] He wants a concept that can cover social worlds where practices are only weakly institutionalized and boundaries are not well established" (Swartz 120). A person takes up a position within a social field depending on how much and what type of economic, cultural, social, or symbolic capital the person has accumulated. This position is in relation to a system or network of power within the field. Not every person is within every field nor is a person's position the same in all fields that he or she may occupy, but within all fields thus occupied a struggle goes on over position for access to power. The largest and all-pervasive field, for Bourdieu, is the field of power. All fields exist within the field of power. For Bourdieu the contest within a field is carried on between those established within the field and newcomers to the field. However, this presupposes several norms. The first is that fields are always established before contestation, and all newcomers align themselves against those established within the field. Bourdieu structures fields as existing stationary within societies when they are constantly coming into existence like new universes, expanding and shrinking, waning and waxing with influence and new power arrangements. Second, as Lyotard has shown, once a hegemonic position is established within a field entrance into the field can often only be accomplished through performativity — that is, through showing an understanding of the system of signs or codes and adherence to those codes as rules. "Individuals do not move about in social space in a random way, partly because they are subject to forces which structure this space [...] partly because they resist [or complement] the forces of the field with their specific inertia" (Bourdieu, *Distinctions* 110). Each person takes up a position within a specific field. For Bourdieu fields may exist separate from each other or alongside, tangent, and inside another. Many fields overlap. The position of a person from field to field is generally congruent, although a position will not necessarily be consistent across these fields. The struggles in one field flow into the struggles in another. What looks like a Marxist version of inequality of economic classes is inequality within separate fields for disparate reason. Through the valuing and devaluing of social, cultural, and symbolic capital, this inequality throughout separate fields relegates a person to a certain economic or social class.

For Michel Foucault discourse is more than language. It is, as Wittgenstein supposes, a set of rules, a language game where the rules go beyond mere grammar and spoken language. Understanding a rule is "not an interpretation, but [...] what we call 'obeying the rule' and 'going against it' in actual cases," which is "a practice" (Wittgenstein 99). We obey rules because "we are trained to do so" (Wittgenstein 99). The rules of the game are made up and enforced by those having been given power to do so by others having relinquished this power voluntarily or by force. To become involved in the discourse demands obeying the rules. "It is part of our language game [...] that a speaker may, without ultimately giving any justification, follow his own confident inclination that this way [...] is the right way to respond rather than another way" (Kripke 87–88).

Discourse "serves as a function of promoting interests in a battle of power and desire" (Alison Brown 31). Its "rules, system, and procedures comprise a discrete realm of discursive practices, 'order of the discourse,' a conceptual terrain in which knowledge is formed and produced" (Hook 101). The rules of discourses, for Foucault, are concerned as much with what cannot be said or done as what may. A discourse, through different language games, disallows certain subjects, approaches, definitions, concepts, philosophies, actions, and points of view by constraining what may be spoken of, thought, and acted out, as well as how it will be spoken of, thought or acted out, and, most importantly, what will be considered knowledge or truth within the field. Discourses are also inclusionary as well as exclusionary. Discourse might be thought of as the mechanism operating below the surface within Bourdieu's social fields.

Foucault by no means argues that truth does not exist, but "truths" are many times historically contingent and certain "truths" may be foregrounded in certain discourses. Foucault sees "a displacement of the will-to-truth by the will-to-power," taking the idea from Nietzsche (what Lyotard calls performativity), and contending that there is a seeking out of power in discursive statements (Hook 105). Within a field certain people hold legitimate rights to certain knowledge; through holding this right, they gain power, and thus through will-to-power attempt to control the discourse giving this knowledge its legitimacy.

Discourses — legitimizing truths — are more than just ways of separating people within fields or distributing power unevenly; they create and maintain fields. The hegemony in power must maintain a position of power in the field by attacking or refuting the challenging discourse, relinquish its position when its discourse is devalued, or modify the discourse, usually by borrowing parts or the whole of another discourse to maintain the position of power in the field.

For Foucault discourses allow for subjectivity — Althusser's concept of interpellation — thus creating or denying access to power. Foucault sees people positioned throughout discourse, interpellated as subjects. He sees the development of the subject, "subjectification," as a historical process, appearing within a historical period created by the historical period, or, to combine Bourdieu's and Foucault's ideas, the subject is interpellated through discourses of a time, of and within social fields, to take up a position within that social field. The subject, then, is given an identity through hailing by the social structure of the time, the position of his or her parents, gender, race, and class.

For Foucault the historical subject has always been attached to a narrative of origin. Not only Marx but also Veblen, Weber, Nietzsche, and other theorists of the 19 and early 20 centuries were caught up in this "subject" discourse of Enlightenment thought proposing the rational "subject," dependent on discourses of origin. Certain discourses of origin are metadiscourses, or Lyotard's metanarratives, such as religious, philosophical, political, and other ideological discourses. These are for Foucault foundational discourses or primary discourses. The major metanarratives throughout history have been "narratives of origins, which make up much of the core of western thought" (Strozier 21). Derek Hook believes "the 'top heaviness' of primary texts [assure] they will remain permanent" (107). However, the opportunity of gaining a power position in an established discourse, one having a very powerful position within the field of power, makes these discourses attractive discourses to perpetuate for persons seeking power positions. Including persons into the discourse allows those who have taken up positions of power within the discourse to ensure the discourse will continue to be valid through time, even when changing interpretations and rules are added and taken away from the game. Significantly, "there are two meanings to the word 'subject': subject to someone else by control and dependence, and tied to his [or her] own identity by a conscious or self-knowledge," a narration of one's own self (Foucault, *Essential* 130). The latter is somewhat affected by the former and the former usually comes into play as a system of power in a social field.

Within all theories of origins, a "Subject," position, a person, deity, idea, or position exists, presupposing some originating Subject, what Jacques Derrida names the transcendental signifier. The Subject is the originating Subject from which all meaning supposedly derives. For discourses, it is "the Word," for Freud the Father, for religion a god or gods, for philosophy rational thought, and for Lacan the Law-of-the-Father. The Subject position as originator contends that the subject was subjugated, or made a subject, through relation to the Subject. The Subject allows for rational subjects and, most importantly, for the argument being made by this book — that hierarchies of Subject/subject positions depend on a supposed relation to the originating subject. Those in the power position, attained through the ownership of the knowledge of the field through the discourse of the field, stand in for the originating Subject and become the Subject within the field where others are subjugated.

In poststructuralism and postmodernism an attempt has been made to dismantle the Subject. However, "as Deconstruction recognizes, for example, the erasure of the subject means its reappearance in another place" (Strozier 29). The trace of its absence can also be reconstituted within discourse to redefine the subject position within the discourse or field, as has been done in feminist studies, minority studies, and postcolonial studies.

A "shift had taken place from the claim that truth could be grounded in the notion of an autonomous subject (as a given) to the notion that the subject was constituted as discourses and/or practices" (Strozier 54). As with Bourdieu, the question of agency comes up when speaking of discourse. "Foucault has a great deal to say about the subject and about resistance, although the insights are heteromorphous and ultimately not very coherent" (Strozier 56). Because Foucault creates the subject as historical, Strozier believes "Foucault is at great pains to exclude subjects [from his theories] who might be assumed to have a potential for resistance even from the 'bottom' or margins of the social structure" (Strozier 57). For Strozier and others writing on Foucault, the discourse always inscribes in itself those positions of resistance negating any true resistance. However, Foucault does allow for resistance, but this resistance only reconstitutes the subject as a subject to the Subject. Minority inner-city youth attempt to change their position as subject to the Subject within the field or discourse of poor, minority, and disenfranchised by forming alliances — gangs — to alter the Subject/subject position, but are reinscribed as gang members — criminals, a similar negative Subject/subject position. Foucault states, "It is not enough to say that these [act of resistance] are anti-authority struggles; we must try to define more precisely what they have in common" (*Essential* 129). Foucault sees, among other attributes of resistance that, "the targets are power effects. [...] They are anarchistic struggles. [...] They are struggles which question the status of the individual. [...] the 'government of individualization' [...] struggles against the privilege of knowledge" (*Essential* 129–30).

This struggle is echoed by Bourdieu when he argues that all fields must have within them contestations of power. All discourses create within themselves alternate discourses. All uses of power must inscribe, as a reaction to this use, a resistance to the use. Foucault's configuration seems to negate true agency if the discourse inscribes within it its own resistance through its Subject/subject position, the same problem existing in Bourdieu's idea of habitus. However, once agency is considered, resistance outside the discourse is possible. This agency does exist within discourses and fields because resistance is not always inscribed in the discourse. The agent can always find new ways to undermine the discourse or his or her subject position in the field. Resistance, in fact, is the introduction of new rules into the language game of the discourse. If enough organized resistance comes to bear within the field, the discourse is changed. Also, the "subject" exists through the interpellation of a person by him- or herself and the groups involved at the locus of contention, allowing for mutability for subject position. Finally, while some persons contest the Subject/subject position, many do not, and must not for a power position to exist.

Again the term "subject" suffers from a slippage of meaning, especially within the contention that the subject is historical and, being a historical product, might not have always existed. If "subject" means to be subjugated to a discourse, then a time could have existed when the subject might not have existed as we understand it, but if "subject" means knowledge of one's existence, of place, even if that place is a position of lack of power, then "subject" has always existed as long as humans or proto-humans understood their "place." If this is true, subjectness is constantly in flux, a play between discourses and agency, and "subject" can never be negated, only transformed and reformed. Since humans, even before they were human, were communal animals, as sentiency developed it must also have developed within a community. Human self-awareness (identity) must also have developed within a community and a predilection for the need to know where a person was placed within the community (subjectivity) probably developed along with self-awareness. Even Foucault could not negate the existence of the subject. To say the subject is historical, as Foucault does, is to say "a subject" is historical, and throughout history different subjects or subject positions existed, as did metanarratives and discourses.

Many discourses now existing still derive from the idea of the originating Subject, giving rise to representative Subjects and Subject positions to which subject positions are subordinate. These discourses, and the concept of Subject/subject itself, suggest a core metanarrative or metanarratives of Subject/subject from which most discourses still arise, or have at their core a discourse allowing and limiting thinking to dominant and dominated as a natural state of being. These discourses, then, suggest the operation of ideology below discourses of Subject/subjectness.

For Foucault and Bourdieu, the idea of power is crucial to their theories. Bourdieu takes his concept of power from Weber and Durkheim while Foucault takes his from Nietzsche. Thus the metaphors used to describe power take differing paths. For Foucault this Subject/subject position created through discourses allows for power. Bourdieu constructs a field of power, the largest social field. All social fields exist within this field. However, Bourdieu does not elucidate where this field of power originated.

"Bourdieu proposes a sociology of symbolic power that addresses the important topic of relations between culture, social structure, and action," offering "a genetic theory of groups. Such a theory would explain how groups [...] create and maintain unity and thereby perpetuate or improve their position in the social order" (Swartz 6, 7). Bourdieu creates a political economy of culture where objects and actions are invested with value beyond the idea of the commodity or action itself. This investment is not simply commodity fetishism. They become capital through their transformation to signs used to delineate status. The position within a field and thus within the field of power — that is, the power given to a person within a field — is dependent on the cultural, social, and symbolic capital the person has to offer. For Bourdieu, power is "access to sources of income in the labor market depend[ing] upon cultural capital in the form of educational credentials and social capital in the forms of networks" (Swartz 74). Thus power for Bourdieu is solidified within the cultural, social, and symbolic capital just as labor for Marx is solidified within the commodity, although he begins by seeing power as still economic; however, his later works move away from this stance.

Foucault starts with the assumption that "power is neither given nor exchanged, nor recovered, but rather exercised, and it only exists in action" (*Power/Knowledge* 89). He first considers power to be repression, "a war continued by other means," rather than the older concept of the analysis contending power is "given up in the establishment of sovereignty [...] with oppression as its limit" (*Power/Knowledge* 90, 91). The newer schema of "war — repression" does not see repression as a limit, but as "the mere effect and continuation of a relationship of domination" (Foucault, *Power/Knowledge* 92). Foucault later develops the theory of power as the necessity of the production of truth — his discourses. However, his theory does not address concepts of competing discourses or discourses competing with agency.

Power for Foucault is "the way a human being turns him — or herself into a subject" (*Essential* 126). Power is mediated by social structure, what Foucault names the "social body," continuing his metaphor of the body of the monarch as the first focus of power (*Power/Knowledge* 55). Social structures are power structures or systems of power within a social field acting on the subject at the level of the individual, "categoriz[ing] the individual, [...] attach[ing] him to his own identity. [...] It is a form of power that makes individuals subjects" (Foucault, *Essential* 130)

For Foucault power is ubiquitous — it exists and has always existed. His best explanation of power is an exercise of force. However, he does not really explain force, or how it is gained, multiplied, used, contested or where it comes from. Force might be considered a potential energy, as work is; however, this still is not much of an answer for this inquiry. Force, this potential energy, must come from someplace. The only place it can possibly originate is within a person. Force, then, rests within each person and must be created by each person as the potential for action. This potential exists in different forms — educational, social, symbolic, cultural, and physical — for both Foucault and Bourdieu, the underlying energies of fields and discourses. This energy is not capital, as Bourdieu describes it, but is rather the underlying mechanism of capital. It is the ability to use force or power against or for another person or group for the advantage of the person or other persons. Theoretically each person is born with an equal amount of force or power, which is added to, or taken away, through position of family, capital, and his or her position within a social field inscribed by the discourse of that field. A person will have more or less power from field to field depending on the weight given to these features within the field.

Foucault comes to know power as the ability to generate or manufacture truths existing in reciprocity to power. Where truths generate power, power also generates truths. Truths are synonymous with Lyotard's metanarratives, or discourses establishing truths, limiting the language games, the ability to think outside these truths, and the narratives themselves.

> In any society there are manifold relations of power which permeate, characterize, and constitute the social body, and these relations of power cannot themselves be established, consolidated nor implemented without the production, accumulation, circulation, and functioning of a discourse [Foucault, *Power/Knowledge* 93].

Truth resides in the dominant discourse. It is not a truly universal truth or necessarily empirical. The impetus for the creation and dissemination of these truths for Foucault is domination. The question he raises is not "why certain people want to dominate," but "how things work at the level of on-going subjugation" (*Power/Knowledge* 97). However, asking why certain people want, or are predisposed, to dominate is also an important question, and for the study of class it becomes a very relevant question. Are certain ideologies more predisposed to be dominated — to allow for subjugation? Are other ideologies more likely to allow for domination? What mechanisms cause this? Obviously some narratives allowing for domination are derived from metanarratives allowing for domination in one form or another. Did ideologies develop together in opposition, allowing for this subjugation and subjugating? If so, how might these ideologies be modified or changed? Finally, for Foucault power is neither good nor bad. It is a force "which circulates [...] employed and exercised through a net-like organization" (*Power/Knowledge* 98). The individual or subject "is an effect of power" and "at the same time its vehicle" (*Power/Knowledge* 98).

The question then becomes how this force or potential energy is created. This potential energy (force) and thus power is, in actuality, agency. Power in this configuration is synonymous with agency "as a temporally embedded process of social engagement, informed by the past (in its habitual aspects), but also oriented toward the future" (Emirbayer and Mische 963).

Agency is the ability to act to satisfy one's needs, but more than that, agency is also the ability to act freely within a society. If people lived in a solitary state and did not depend on a community or group, then agency could be seen as neutral (the person acts only for his or her needs), but within a society, through types of social structures (Bourdieu's fields) created by, maintained through, and producing discourses, a person gains power (agency) or loses power. Thus agency or power can be looked at as neutral (equal to others), negative (restricted within a social field), or positive (multiplied within a social field). When power or agency is positive, it allows one person to act upon others or the social field in a way that is advantageous for the person. If negative, it allows others in the social field or the social field as a whole to act on the person and becomes domination. For Foucault power starts with the individual (your agency) and is given up or taken, first by small groups, then communities, institutions, and states. Through social contracts power is transferred—sometimes voluntarily, sometimes by a larger and more powerful force insisting upon it—from the individual to the state, communities, and groups. In this way persons become subjects before they are born by parents transferring power for the child to the state through their position in the field of power. Power is also given to the child through the parents' positions within the field of power receiving its power from the state and community, sometimes disseminated through a formal institution or ad hoc group. In this way power is distributed unevenly. Importantly, individual power cannot displace individual power if no legitimacy of it by a larger legitimate power exists.

The use of physical power against another human, most times, is illegal, but persons endowed with power through the state, such as police officers, have been given the right to use physical power. The force of punishment, as Foucault contends (seen only in potentiality within Foucault's ideas of the modern system of punishment, his conception of the panopticon), finally centers on physical violence legitimatized by the state, arguing that the losing party must forfeit some form of capital or risk this violence. However, a very important part of power is its attractiveness to others. Through inclusion both parties gain power through the potential use of each other's power. This power is further multiplied through legitimization of the discourse and the ownership of knowledge. This allows the defining of truths within the field through the discourses, legitimatizing the field and the discourse in which the Subject/subject position is defined.

Foucault's theories of power, subjugation or subjectivity, and discourses bridge Bourdieu's social field theory of "habitus + capital + field = practice" (*Distinctions* 101). Bourdieu argues that these

> different forms of capital, the possession of which defines class membership and the distribution of which determines position in the power relations constituting the field of power and also determines the strategies available for use in these struggles [...] are simultaneously instruments of power and stakes in the struggle for power [Bourdieu, *Distinctions* 315–16].

Although Bourdieu uses the term cultural capital in the first configuration of culture, the product of the best and brightest in *Distinctions*, he moves away from the position in later work.

> It is a reminder that comparison is possible only from *system to system* [...] what is commonly called distinction, that is, a certain quality of bearing and manners most often considered innate [...] is nothing other than *difference*, a gap, a distinctive feature in short, a *relational* property existing only and through its relation with other properties. [...] Social space is constructed in such a way that agents or groups are distributed in it according to their position in statistical distributions based on *the two principles of differentiation* [...] economic capital and social capital [*Practical Reason* 6].

For Bourdieu the struggle over the position to and of power within a field is the struggle over what is and is not legitimate capital for a field, ultimately defining the field and manifesting itself in the struggle over dominant and subordinate positions within this field. Over the years since Bourdieu introduced the idea of capital — specifically, cultural capital — much discussion has taken place. Even Bourdieu eventually moved away from his first narrow concept of cultural capital. Randal Johnson explains Bourdieu's later articulation of cultural capital. "Cultural capital concerns forms of cultural knowledge, competences or dispositions [...] a form of knowledge, an internalized code or a cognitive acquisition with equips the social agent [...] in deciphering social relations and cultural artifacts" (Johnson 7). This definition of cultural has been controversial since its inception. However, this definition of cultural capital, the product of the best and brightest, does not include all possible actions within a field, what Bourdieu later calls "practice" — actions mediated by ideology or habitus used as signs. Bourdieu, in *Practical Reason*, has realized culture must be defined in a much wider and deeper way. Culture is becoming, for him, all the attributes of a group, including dress, speech, deportment, education and educational expectations, habits, and propensities manifested through difference. When he is discussing the acquisition of cultural capital within the educational system, he refers to it as educational capital. Yet he contends that "competence, even in areas like cinema or jazz [referring to them as educational capital], which are neither taught nor directly accessed by the educational system," produce signs of exclusion (*Distinctions* 63). When discussing cultural competence, Bourdieu found that "students of working class and middle class origins who had scores similar to those students of the bourgeois origin on classical culture, fell back as the test moved toward 'extra curricular' culture" (*Distinctions* 65). Bourdieu does not explain why questions of extracurricular culture were on the test, what they were, or importantly, who decided what cultural material was important enough to be on a test.

The assumption that cultural capital creates separation in education has been contested by educational theorists. The "acceptance [of cultural capital] seems to proceed without due attention to the related empirical research" (Kingston 88). Kingston believes good study habits and a focus on school were the major causes for differences in test scores. "No other variable came remotely close in its impact" (95). However, Kingston's definition of culture only includes the first definition of culture—of the best and brightest—and does not consider the wider definition.

When the third definition of culture is taken into account, Bourdieu's theories do fit into educational theories. If, within an ideology or habitus, the importance of placement within a class through achievement or knowledge as a sign (or as capital) is marginalized, the student may study less, parents may not insist on achievement and the importance of school, and certain knowledge may be less important. This in turn places the student in a certain social group in the school system. With other manifestations of ideology this lack of knowledge of the importance of good study skills and good marks places the student into a group with pre-assumed expectations. The fact that students from other classes are less knowledgeable than their elite counterparts concerning knowledge of the arts not presented in school suggests, rather than it being an intellectual disparity or even an economic disparity, it is a disparity in knowing the importance of this knowledge as a sign.[2] Educational knowledge in the arts, as Bourdieu alludes to in the first half of *Distinctions*, is used in social fields as signs (cultural capital).

Bourdieu names other capitals producing advantageous positions in specific fields, but like educational capital within those fields, these capitals become cultural and depend on the construction of a personal ideology compatible with the discourse of that field. Of the other types of capital besides cultural capital, symbolic capital seems of special interest to Bourdieu. "*Symbolic capital* refers to the degree of accumulated prestige, celebrity, consecration or honour [sic] and is founded on a dialiectic of knowledge (*connaissance*) and recognition (*reconnaissance*)" (Johnson 7). Capitals such as Bourdieu's academic capital fit within these criteria and are reflected in Veblen's honorific pursuits.

A group is defined by its culture and what culture it feels is valuable, finally revealing that many classes exist and Bourdieu's idea of subclasses or multi-classes is a poor, if not an unwieldy way to look at it, as is a division of capital into ever smaller and diverse groupings. This multitude of capitals finally shows, first, that almost everything is cultural capital, a sign used for separation and movement within a social field — that is, toward a power system within the field. Second, something drives this need for acquisition of cultural capital in certain people and does not in others, or else moderates this drive. Again, it points to a core or core ideologies.

Bourdieu's multiple capitals might be reduced to the following: cultural capital (all property and actions serving as signs for exclusion/inclusion within a social field); symbolic capital (types of degrees, honors and official positions and other titles of distinction, official and ad hoc); and social capital (signs used for membership or association, officially or unofficially, to social groups allowing networking or access to power systems). What Bourdieu considers educational capital can have several permutations. The degree might be considered symbolic capital in one instance, while it may be considered social capital in another, such as what Michaels contends (reviewed in chapter 2) in arguing that certain schools' diplomas are given more value than other schools' diplomas despite the GPA of the graduates. Knowledge as part of an education, when spoken aloud in a certain venue, might be seen as esoteric knowledge, thus becoming cultural capital.

Since culture is the manifestation of ideologies, cultural capital's value comes from the discourse of the dominant ideology creating or controlling the field, and reflects the morals, mores, and values of that ideology. Signs are used to advertise and recognize those manifesting the dominant ideology of a field. Importantly, cultural capital consists of all the signs manifesting a certain ideology. A class may not have a culture in the second definition of culture — artifacts, rituals, and pastimes such as sports, dance, and song — but the third definition sees culture as a mediator of class separation, and thus culture makes class.

Gramsci noticed that, rather than revolution happening through physical violence, a revolution of position, a contestation within the field of power between competing hegemonies, existed, suggesting a coordinated struggle across diverse fields through the use of a mechanism with the ability to affect wholesale change. For Bourdieu this mechanism includes the workings and influence of habitus. Bourdieu, borrowing the term from Thomas Aquinas, calls habitus

> generative principles of distinct and distinctive practices. [...] But habitus are also classificatory schemes, principles of classification, principles of vision and divisions, different tastes. They make distinctions between what is good and what is bad [...] right and wrong [...] distinguished and what is vulgar [...] but the divisions are not identical. [...] Some behavior or even the same good can appear distinguished to one person and pretentious to someone else, cheap or showy to another [Bourdieu, *Practical Reason* 8].

Propensities, habits, tastes, and dispositions are handed down through the family and other institutions contributing to a habitus of the individual. Bourdieu's "concept has broadened in scope over time to stress the bodily as well as the cognitive base of action and to emphasize inventive as well as habitual forms of action" (Swartz 101). For Bourdieu habitus regulates all action, including taste. It is first inherited from parents as one would inherit a spoon. Through the educational system, what Althusser calls a state ideological apparatus, not only are other propensities added to a habitus, but a selection process also goes on though teacher/school-parent/child interface, relegating the child to a certain status group with certain expectations according to habitus and status position of parent/child, or the signs a habitus manifests. Through group and authoritarian expectations, the child learns what is expected of him or her and how to behave properly for his or her status. This, of course, is a greatly simplified explanation. Many other factors come into play, such as resistance.

The idea of habitus has always demanded the concept of cultural capital be expanded beyond products of the best and brightest. Since habitus contains all the actions and propensities of a person (practice) and since all these actions and propensities are used in Bourdieu's exclusionary process within the social field (culture), the signs of what Bourdieu calls habitus, through practice, take on all facets of a person and thus all characteristics become cultural within a certain field. Culture, then, is the manifestation through practice of ideology.

> The essential point is that, when perceived through these social categories of perception, these principles of vision and division, the differences and practices, in the goods possessed, or in the options expressed become symbolic differences and constitute a veritable *language*. Differences associate with

> different positions, that is, goods, practices and especially *manners*, function [...] in the same way as differences which constitute symbolic systems [...] that is as *distinctive signs* [*Practical Reason* 8–9].

For many theorists Bourdieu's concept of habitus negates agency, particularly in *Distinctions*. "Bourdieu's theory lacks an adequate conception of the nature and location of agency, and an adequate conception of the nature of human powers and capacities" (Farnell 403). Although the theory of habitus does not negate the idea of agency, it does seem to assume that people's actions are not completely free and rational.

For Bourdieu habitus is the amalgamation of narratives of correct actions and discourses for and from a position within a social field, specifically, for Bourdieu, for the grouping assigned to a person through the educational systems. This separation is not as simple as many theorists contend. Many believe, that through educational systems, children are separated by the manifestations of signs, arguing this separation is an operation of the school system through middle-class teachers valuing middle-class ideology and devaluing working-class ideology, thus relegating children into groups of expectations. This explanation is too simplistic. A "whole set of factors that enhance academic success, including economic resources, parenting style, encouragement of academic engagement, and assistance with school assignments" exist (Kingston 93).

Kingston implies that working-class parents are seemingly less invested in their children's education. However, this is not usually true. As seen in several articles reviewed in previous chapters, working-class parents see education as a way out of the working class for their children, a manifestation of the old American Dream of the sacrifice of one generation to create a better life for the next. They do have, however, less skill, time, and knowledge, and, importantly, they also lack habitus (or ideology) to know what is required to prepare their children for higher education. The knee-jerk reaction is to see working-class parents as somehow less moral than middle-class parents because of this lack of skill.

Working-class parents may very well think they are investing as much effort as other parents. But besides knowing the importance of good study skills and time management, middle-class parents, as will be discussed in chapter 5, have learned the importance of making their presence known, of networking within the school and with other influential parents, and they have no qualms about using this influence to procure an advantageous position for their children. Because of the lack of ability to negotiate their presence, having never learned the skill of negotiating a power position within a field, or else, because of an ideological position, being loathe to use power — all of which is learned from family — working-class parents, besides passing this lack of ability to their children, sometimes have an aversion to networking, considering it distasteful and dishonest, or learn to distrust authority. Many other factors also exist, making any discussion of class in education complex.

As stated, Foucault's theories of power might be seen to originate with Nietzsche. "Nietzsche is probably the most significant influence on Foucault. [...] Nietzsche is the philosopher who, for Foucault, first begins an analysis of power with clearly productive capabilities" (Alison Brown 15). Catherine Mills states, "In formulating a conception of power that did not presuppose a relation of sovereignty in the form of a centralized origin of power or systematic and interminable domination of one group by another—Foucault drew heavily on Nietzsche's conception of dynamism of force relations" (254). However, unlike Nietzsche, Foucault avoids being trapped by Enlightenment ideals while attempting to negate these same ideals. Like Nietzsche, Foucault sees domination as a natural phenomenon. But while Nietzsche sees it as a positive trait, Foucault sees it as neither positive nor negative. Ideology questions the perception of domination as a natural tendency and suggests it is a socialized tendency; thus the basic assumptions of many arguments based on aggression as normal become suspect and these arguments lose their core ideals.

Nietzsche is often credited for the movement away from Enlightenment thought because he was anti-liberal, anti–Christian, and antidemocratic. However, the assumption that Nietzsche wrote against 19th century Enlightenment thought is erroneous. The Enlightenment thinkers, "whether they were Marxist, liberals or conservatives [...] believed in the ability of Europeans to improve their lives," and thus Nietzsche might be included in this category (Fritzsche 3). Though Nietzsche's ideas of "becoming" or breaking with the established rules of society, setting up one's own moral codes and myths so as to exist in a perpetual transitional state, seem revolutionary, they are not outside Enlightenment ideals. Fritzsche maintains that Nietzsche "removed himself completely from these debates, which he took as systems of increasingly standardized thinking that took as its object the well-being of society instead of the potential of the individual" (3). Yet, for all the radical thinking, Nietzsche did not remove himself far enough from the established discourses of his time and was as much prisoner of the same discourses as the others.

Two major cornerstones of his thinking—evolution based on early Darwinism and the death of God—include positions based on Enlightenment thought. Nietzsche contends, because of Christianity and Enlightenment thinking—specifically, democracy—that the natural evolution of humanity had been stopped; beyond the mere human was the Übermensch. Stern argues that while Nietzsche mocked the "Victorian hope" of a "new morality which has freed itself from a transcendental Christian sanction," seeing it as turning "out to be very much the same," Nietzsche "does not stop to consider the necessary limits of any conceivable moral reform, and thus the inevitable overlap between old and new"; thus Nietzsche's "idea of authenticity lives on the Jewish and Christian moral capital he disowns" (78). Nietzsche's concept of becoming was not, as many authors like to state, for the betterment of the living person, but a means to make way for his superman. For Nietzsche, the reason for humankind's existence was to prepare for this superman, a new species of human.

Nietzsche assumes evolution is teleological and, ironically, because of this stance, Nietzsche's arguments become teleological arguments. Even though he believed history has no other function than to set the stage for the generation of greatness, his argument for the superman is at its core based on some order in the universe, some meaning to man's existence, if only as a rung on a ladder to a higher being, which must itself have a reason to exist since, for Nietzsche, it should exist (Stern 60). A god or some other power needs to exist to direct this evolution, and to give a reason why a superman should exist, especially for Nietzsche's thinking — some moral reason, some right to exist. Of course, these postulations are incorrect. Evolution works on selection for the most fit for the environment of the time. Although scholars of Nietzsche argue that he is proposing exactly this theory, his most fit has these underlying assertions: first, that "fit" implies aggression, and second, man has always been a singular entity and not communal.

"Most fit" does not point to aggression any more than it points to docility, to larger humans or smaller humans or any other trait of humanity. Fit is an adaptation to the environment of the time spurred on by natural and sexual selection. Thus, for this time, most fit would seem to be the "nerd" or "geek," the less aggressive and more cerebral person. The second assumption, that humans have ever been solitary or humanity has been working toward the solitary superman, is by far the most erroneous. "A sick man, he [Nietzsche] imagined superman; a solitary man, he welcomed new creatures 'good Europeans' blond beasts, and, above all, the newborn; a brooding man, he embraced cheerfulness and 'the great Yes to life'" (Fritzsche 3).

History has shown that, if anything, humanity has been moving toward a more communal type of human, one retaining individuality but still more and more aimed at positive action within the group. Thus, where Nietzsche believed society, in searching for its origins (and thus its meaning), had a monkey standing in its way, Nietzsche has a community of apes standing in his way. Nietzsche uses the great men of history as evidence of the truth of what he is postulating. Leaving aside the idea that these "great men" are great because they were the "winners" and controlled the discourses of history, thus writing themselves and others of their ilk as "great," men in history, whether these great men advanced human society more than, say, less great men did, or might have if this violent class had not enslaved or killed them, is debatable. Recently history has shown that Nietzsche's great men have moved and still move the world toward, not the destruction Nietzsche felt important for human evolution, but annihilation, where, afterward, if any humans are left, the best adaptation might be to devolve into some lesser ape. Created without true morality, Christian or otherwise, "the pathos of personal authenticity — was the chief tenet of fascism and national socialism. No man came closer to the full realization of self-created 'values' than A. Hitler" (Stern 79).

Finally, the importance of evolving into a superman must be questioned. History has shown evolution of society has always been through cooperation, albeit often a forced cooperation, as Nietzsche notes. This enslavement for Nietzsche is necessary and in fact morally correct (within his ideas of noble morality). For the development of the superman, "everything is a means and everything must be sacrificed" (Stern 61).

Nietzsche's most famous doctrine is "will-to-power." "The cardinal concept of [his] only systematic venture. [...] The will to power is the agency where by man [...] becomes master of the earth" (Stern 80). As Daigle states,

> Nietzsche is clear: "What is happiness?— The feeling that power *increases*— that a resistance is overcome." Happiness comes upon the exercise of will to power, when one's own self is the expression of this will to power. [Yet] this assertion of power is in no way the same as the contemplative life advocated by Aristotle [3].

Again, for Nietzsche's apologists, will-to-power is a positive attribute. If all humans do not possess it, all should. "The will to power has no teleological purpose; it strives toward no other goal than the eternal iteration of its own functional imperative" (P. Douglas 140).

It is constant overcoming, constant being; the state of a person must always remain in flux. It is a will-to-improvement. However, to see it as only a will-to-improvement or a will-to-freedom, or any such positive attribute, is to leave out much of Nietzsche's philosophy of the will-to-power. In *Beyond Good and Evil*, Nietzsche considers good manners to be the mutual "refraining from injury, violence, and exploitation [...] if the appropriate conditions are present (namely if these men are actually similar in strength and value standards and belong together in *one* body)" (*Basic Writings* 393). If the other person is not of the same strength, value standard or basically one of "us," the use of injury, violence, and exploitation is morally correct. In fact, Nietzsche cautions those with the ability to exercise power over others to guard against becoming weak-willed and extending their "good manners" to everyone, because once "this principle is extended [...] as the fundamental principle of society it immediately proves to be what it really is [...] a principle of disintegration and decay" (*Basic Writings* 393). Thus violence, injury, and exploitation are called for in many situations.

Power is neither good nor bad (evil), as Foucault contends. However, the use of it can be both. Power can be positive, but the potential for harm always exists. Nietzsche's theories on the use of power benefiting the individual and not society have more potential to do harm for society, and since all humans depend on society, they harm the individual as well. Those academics writing about Nietzsche's ideals of becoming frequently neglect to take up Nietzsche's conclusions of his philosophies. He contends that all assumptions, including morals, are just assumptions of a society and might be changed — that is, no reasons exist to care about the weak or to seek justice for anyone but oneself. One of his central ideas is will-to-power, considering any search for knowledge to be a search for power.

> What unifies Nietzsche's seemingly disparate critical remarks — about altruism, happiness, pity, equality, Kantian respect for persons, utilitarianism and so on — is that he thinks a culture in which such norms prevail as morality will be a culture which eliminates the conditions for the realization for human excellence [Leiter 268].

His usage of the term "morality" is also biased. Although several authors separate Nietzsche's theories of morality from the thrust of his moral theory, his beliefs of ideology extend to a worldview. "Although Nietzsche did not use the term 'ideology' [...] he did write of the way culture is made up of ideals, idols, illusions and falsehoods" (Warren 543). Peter Douglas describes Nietzsche's idea of truth (knowledge) similarly to how Somers describes narrativity.

> Knowledge is a network of meanings introduced as truths within a frame of reference. [...] Knowledge must also be, as Nietzsche says, "conditioned." He argues, therefore, that claims to "unconditioned" knowledge are nonsensical, in that coming to know is always "placing oneself in a conditional relation to something" [P. Douglas 136].

Nietzsche's idea of morality, then, extends to ideological constructions of the self. Brobjer contends, "The fundamental aspect of Nietzsche's moral judgment and thinking is his concern and emphasis of personality and character. *Not principles, but personality and character are the determining criteria of value* according to this morality" (66). Nietzsche has little good to say about morality based on principles steering action.

Nietzsche believes two distinct moralities exist in the world. He names them "noble," or master, and "slave." Of course, his discourse is constructed to support and reinforce his position of elitism. As Bourdieu contends, "Nietzsche's 'enlightened elitism' comes close to the scientific truth of the mechanisms of the production in the belief in the value of culture," and thus the name "slave" instead of "nurturer" or "communal" (*Distinctions* 252). Nietzsche believes marked types of people exist in the world — those of distinction and those of the masses — thus resulting in the derogatory moniker for the morality he saw as herd morality, or to say a morality postulating that everyone is equal. Nietzsche saw the predisposition of this morality to care about and for those sick and weak as a weakness in itself. Ironically, Nietzsche spent considerable time in a mental hospital being one of the sick and weak, dependent on someone more powerful caring enough not to euthanize him. The question might also be asked of how noble a person might be who preys on the sick and weak.

What might be taken from Nietzsche, though, is his observation of the differences in the way people constructed their world. He called this morality, but it is ideology. Ideology is the unifying concept of Nietzsche's, Foucault's, and Bourdieu's theories, as well as those of almost all postmarxists, poststructuralists, and postmodernists. It is also the common mechanism of identity making — creating and being created by discourses, thus creating subjects, as Althusser contends, and the mechanism of habitus and, as Nietzsche saw, allowing or disallowing types of agencies.

What Nietzsche actually proposed, once his rantings are separated from his philosophy, is that among many ideologies, two core ideologies exist. The first, his noble or master ideology, contends that virtue is held within the person and not within the person's actions. The other insists virtue is within actions — the altruistic, unprivileged or equalitarian ideology. In a postmodern construction or deconstruction of Nietzsche's concepts of two core ideologies, the difference of worldviews stems from the placement of the originating Subject. or as Derrida names it, a transcendental signifier. Foucault and Derrida contest the existence of a Subject or transcendental signifier, and rightfully so. Although a transcendental signifier may not exist, this "truth" has little effect on ideologies that believe it exists. This signifier is thought to exist either within the self or outside the self, depending upon the core ideology existing within the person. If it exists within the person, then the person, and not the person's actions, define whether the person is good or bad. This allows for unequal positions in a society as moral (a separation by race, class, ethnic group, and gender) and permits the person with an advantageous position to argue that he or she is morally correct in maintaining this position and using this position to gain advantages. When the signifier exists outside the self it demands equal treatment for all; any advantageous position must be earned through moral action, and no position allows for any immoral action or to take advantage of a position.

The theory of core ideologies allows for a more fecund approach to the study of class than other theories based on economics or occupation. That this concept of ideology and many other postmarxist theorists are not being studied to any extent in class studies is not due to Marxism being a better set of theories, since contradictions abound, but to the fact that Marxism is hegemonic within academia, so much so that it is not questioned. Since the mid–20th century, a movement away from Marxism (except in working-class studies) has taken place along with a shift within the paradigm of the concept of history; this major change occurred after World War II, and is seen as a condemnation of, or reaction to the ideological discourses behind, controlling, and driving two major lines of thought of the Enlightenment or modernity: philosophical and scientific thought. Throughout history these lines have had an antagonistic relationship. Philosophy took up the banner of a displaced religion, becoming religion's apologist for the primacy of humans over all other species, against scientific thought's displacing of humanity as the center of the universe. Philosophy sought to recoup what it could through rhetorical methods of the old logocentric man/God-centered universe, of the world existing before scientific thought.

Two-hundred-fifty-plus years have passed and humanity still struggles along these lines, due mostly to the two autonomous groups, religious and philosophical, still holding power positions in society. Because they exist as power positions, the "tooth for tooth" philosophy is dominant and the "brotherly love" philosophy (a major tenet within their discourses), whose narratives insist on altruism, is subordinate to all their actions except the production of rhetoric.

The two lines of thought, scientific and philosophical/religious, combined in the 20 century to create devastation on a scale never known in history. The result of this devastation precipitated a paradigm shift by the common people in disrupting long-held beliefs in the major metanarratives of society. This epoch we are now in has been labeled postmodernity. Postmodernity has been, and still is, argued about — what is it, what does it entail, is it at its beginning, its zenith, or its end?

Postmarxism, as is poststructuralism, is a first impulse of postmodernism — a searching for answers in the inconsistencies of the major metanarratives, including Marxism. Theorists, having lost faith in the old Marxist metanarratives of society, turned to other theorists of society — Veblen, Weber, Durkheim, and Nietzsche, to name a few of the more important ones.

Pierre Bourdieu and Michel Foucault are two of the more influential postmarxist/poststructuralist theorists of class, both moving away from vulgar Marxism early in their careers. Both challenged the economic paradigm of class structure. Bourdieu postulates that class is formed at the individual level through distinctions, or difference. He theorizes a sphere of struggle at this level, calling these spheres social fields. People vie for advantageous positions through the use of various types of capital. The accumulation of capital depends on position, determined by capital itself, practice, and habitus — his configuration of ideology. Foucault postulates that discourse creates subjectivity by determining truths — knowledge of reality. The position of a person to these truths, his or her placement in the discourse, determines his or her subjectivity. Both Foucault's theories and Bourdieu's theories are compatible once discourse is thought of as the apparatus working within the social field. They see the relationship to power as the most important result of these struggles. However, neither explains what power might be. Power is ultimately agency, a potential to act. In theory, everyone is born with the same agency. In truth, agency is regulated by social structure, state, community, and group, by denying it or giving it to certain persons.

Nietzsche's philosophy of power (which Foucault reconstitutes), with his elitist philosophy of noble/master and slave morality, was a contributor to the crisis that spurred on the paradigm shift of postmodernity. His philosophy allowed for both world wars and the Holocaust. His moral and slave morality, although conceptually incorrect, points to two differing core ideologies; however, the world would seem to be a better place if, rather than privileged ideology being centered (as Nietzsche believes), the unprivileged, equalitarian ideology is placed above its privileged counterpart. Maybe not as many "good" great men would come to the forefront of civilization, but then not as many "evil" great men would either. A few evil great men can undo all that many good great men have accomplished.

The shift in paradigm called postmodernity allowed two things to happen. The first was the questioning of both modern and ancient metanarratives. The second was the freeing of marginalized voices. Both allow for the questioning of Marx's theories of class and movement toward other theorists. This spurs on new ways to consider class and the working class, leading to the understanding that class is contested at the micro level, showing the macro level to be a reflection of this phenomenon.

So far these alternate theories of class, having existed for more than half a century, have had limited success in making inroads into academia as far as studies of the working class are concerned, due to their complexity, the effort to use them, and the performativity of Marxism within academia. However, because the underlying mechanism of the diverse theories seems to be ideology, the complexity of the theories might be centralized into a theory of differing ideologies, the manifestations through culture and the interplay of these ideologies. In the next chapter a theory of ideology as it concerns two core ideologies will be developed, first considering how ideology works, and finally how it creates and informs identity.

Chapter 5

Postmodern/Poststructuralist Theories of Class and a Theory of the Working Class

Poststructuralist and postmarxist theories have foregrounded questions of discourses, social fields, habitus, and ideology. Postmodernism takes up these questions as concerns identity, identity making, and the negotiating of identity in a postmodern society. The importance of postmodernity for identity making lies in its displacement of the hegemonic metanarratives, its reconfiguration of class, and its consideration of how ideology and identity are negotiated within society. Postmodern theories investigate these questions, contending a person will have multiple identities, these identities becoming salient at the locus of interpellation, and that identity is never simplistic but complex, constructed through ideology, which is itself constructed through narratives, prototypes, and schemas.

Linda Hutcheon states, contesting the negative positions of many theorists on postmodernity and the postmodern, that "of all the terms bandied about in both current theory and contemporary writing on the arts, postmodernism must be the most over-theorized and under-defined" (3). Although a few theorists contest postmodernity, such as Jürgen Habermas (who sees it as a "conservative ideology attempting to devalue emancipatory modern theories of value"), most see a rupture within the fabric of modernity extending to philosophy, science, ways of viewing art, and ways of living (Best and Kellner 3). Much has been written about the postmodern turn in philosophy, science, and the arts, but much less has been written on the shift in paradigms among those living postmodernity.

Postmodernism and modernism are a set of theories and acts attempting to define and redefine the epochs they purport to represent, comment on, critique, and study. To understand the theories of postmodernism, both modernity and postmodernity need to be defined—not a small task, as Hutcheon has implied. Theorists have been attempting to define both for a very long time. Best and Kellner state:

> We might distinguish between "modernity" conceptualized as the modern age and "postmodernity" as an epochal term for describing the period which allegedly follows modernity. There are many discourses of modernity, as there later would be postmodernity, and the term refers to a variety of economic, political, social, and cultural transformations [2].

These diverse discourses cannot even agree on when both epochs began and what their length might be. For some modernity began after feudalism in Europe through the spread of knowledge, writing, and art, what is commonly called the Renaissance. For others it started at the beginning of the Enlightenment period, punctuated by Newton's discovery of the natural laws of the universe and the postulation of natural laws of man.

When it actually began is not important for this argument of how the cultural turn of postmodernity has allowed for a movement away from metanarratives of modernity such as Marxism. Two of modernity's founding principles are important, though: the belief that man could know the universe through scientific thought and the equality of humans — that is, that humankind could understand its place in the universe and all humans held the same place. As equalitarian as most humanistic thinking proposed itself to be, including philosophy (often bordering on theology), the ideologies of the times, still dependent upon a meaning and a purpose of and for man in a God-driven universe, paradoxically allowed for inequality, and produced discourses reaffirming the natural state of inequality through the closing of the discourses to alternate voices, positioning the elite class as not only proper creators of discourses, but also proper creators of other classes', ethnic groups', and genders' discourses, creating and perpetuating domination as a natural state of being or portraying such a condition as a natural state itself.

When modernity ended has some bearing on the argument for this text. The usual date for the start of postmodernity is the 1960s. However, manifestations of the postmodern exist as early as the 1900s. The counterculture of the 1960s, usually touted as the manifestation of the postmodern period, is only an open manifestation. Countercultures have been recorded well back before World War I, manifesting in alternate ideologies such as the loss of confidence in the states to solve the growing problems in society, actual movements away from Enlightenment thought of equality and democracy. The American counterculture manifested itself in the expatriate writers near the beginning of the last century, in the hipsters of the 1930s and 1940s, metamorphosing into the beatniks of post–World War II, thus leading to the hippies of the 1960s.

The hippies were a manifestation of a counteraction brewing within

America against the repressive discourses of the depression, war, and especially the post-war era, what is now called the McCarthy years. The McCarthy years are much more than HUAC. "Never before had a war found the American people so united behind a government" (Dulles and Dubofsky 321). The war allowed those in power to solidify their power through sociopolitical means, thus marginalizing all other discourses and creating almost two decades of repressive culture in America, closing off other discourses as to what might be acceptable actions for a "good" American, being race, class, and gender specific.

Labor was able to gain power after World War I. During the Great Depression, although many people were out of work, the threat of the American Communist Party gaining real ground in the political arena allowed labor to obtain influence beyond what it had before the Civil War through the enactment of many pro-labor laws. "Many observers thought that labor had become a new power in the land" (Dulles and Dubofsky 341). Not since the beginning of the Industrial Revolution had labor been in this position. However, "a major reason for the CIO's more radical position on many issues was that many of the organization's secondary leaders and cadres came out of the Socialist and Communist parties" (Dulles and Dubofsky 289). During the McCarthy years, unionism, being associated with socialism and communism, if only in its ideology of collective bargaining, turned conservative public opinion against them. The large labor unions' repudiation of communism and backing of the conservative right-wing or "hawk" politics ("both the AFL and CIO supported the foreign policies of President Truman and Eisenhower") turned the liberal and leftist opinion against them (Dulles and Dubofsky 354). This left labor in an untenable position. Coincidently, the high point of labor corresponds with the rupture of the modern, but, unlike most of society, labor could not distance itself from the old narratives. Their failure to change with the times, falling into the trap of their own rhetoric, and being unable and unwilling to change as manufacturing and the world changed, has been their undoing.

One of the first public signs of a countermovement becoming strong enough to contest the hegemony, creating a revolution of position, was the election of John Kennedy at a time when conservative politics seemed to have a chokehold on the nation. Other public manifestations include the civil rights movement and antiwar movement. After Kennedy's death, this counterculture, feeling itself ignored and closed off by an ongoing conservative propagandist backlash, found other ways to revolt, such as dropping out altogether, attempting to create an alternate society based on pacifism and love. This culminated in Woodstock, a celebration of strength and solidarity of, if nothing else, thought, but also of a lack of focus, organization, and commitment (if not a lack of real courage) to harvest what they had sown — the incredulity toward metanarratives. The movement also created its binary opposite the — formation of radical groups, some militant.

A sea change has taken place in America, a postmodernist cultural (ideological) turn. What this change has been, what has changed, and what it portends has been a subject of discussion, sometimes heated, for the last fifty years. "This break is most often related to notions of the waning or extinction of the hundred-year-old modern movement" (Jameson 1). Although Jameson argues that this epoch is nothing more than a stage of late capitalism, a "*purer* stage of capitalism," and comes closer than many theorists to viewing the workings of postmodern society, he frequently misses the point by adhering to a strict Marxist paradigm, anchoring class within the position to the means of production and value. However, he understands postmodernism is not a "style but a cultural [ideological] dominant: a conception which allows for the presence and coexistence of a range of very different yet subordinate features" (4). Whether this rupture has affected art and architecture (one of the thrusts of Jameson's text) is beyond the focus of this book. What is within the scope of this book, though, is understanding how this rupture has affected society and the discourses concerned with both defining society and studying society.

The major prevailing attitude of postmodernity is, as Lyotard contends, "incredulity toward metanarratives," including, sadly, those of the counter-culture of the 1960s (xxiv). This does not so much suggest a type of nihilism, but a turning from metanarratives to mini-narratives, constructing individual ideologies fitting the everyday use of everyday people. This turning away from the meta for the mini may suggest this mini, which theorists such as Jameson decry as somehow connected with "a new wave of American military and economic domination throughout the world: in this sense as throughout class history, the underside of culture is blood, torture, death and terror," has always existed and been marginalized by the metanarratives. Jameson's postulation also suggests a disconnect exists between these historical mininarratives and the official or dominant metanarratives (5). This likewise suggests adherence to mininarratives is, in fact, a more natural state. If macro discourses are considered the realm of the elite (those with power), constructed for the elite (to construct a basis of power) and not the rank and file, the idea that mininarratives have always existed becomes plausible, suggesting they have always been marginalized within the meta discourses. This disconnect suggests Jameson's theories may have substance if the American people, now more attuned to mininarratives, have allowed those in power to run amok with their elitist metanarratives of power. Ironically, these alternate voices of sex, gender, ethnicity, and class have been marginalized by both those denying they have been marginalized and those insisting they have.

Although a multi-voiced world has always existed, with different interpretations of the world and history (an ironic position for those contesting postmodernity's opposition to totalizing theories), certain assumptions of modernity and postmodernity might be agreed upon. Although some theorists, such as Habermas, argue against the demise of modernity, two major paradigm shifts existing in Western society in the last two hundred and fifty years are not usually contested, as Jameson claims. "What I want to call postmodernism is fundamentally contradictory, resolutely historical, and inescapably political. Its contradictions may well be those of late capitalist society, but whatever the cause these contradictions are certainly manifest in the important postmodern concept of 'the presence of the past'" (Hutcheon 4). Yet the presence of the past is a historical, a past reconceived as a myth in reaction to the loss of faith in the historic metanarratives of the past, the unanchoring of identity from history, and the attempt to regain a historical perspective through nostalgic myth.

Two tenets of postmodernism are important for the discussion of class. The first is the making visible of the discourses behind institutions such as philosophy, the sciences, art, literature, and everyday practices. The second is the repudiation of totalizing theories. By contesting any totalizing theory, postmodern theories apparently become totalizing theories themselves. However, the source of the paradox is in the approach to postmodernism theories, in the use of an ideological approach that is modernist in its concept. Postmodernism, at its core, is a set of theories not attempting to make some universal claim, but only to fit a certain situation. Postmodernism asks us to consider how our ideologies inform our approach to knowledge, truth, and reality.

Postmodernity exists as a set of actions or reactions, making visible the metanarratives through the failure of the metanarratives to continue to retain truths. This causes loss of belief in these metanarratives. The reaction to this loss of belief is, again, the making visible of these metanarratives — that is, the unanchoring of identity to history — as well as attempting to recover these identities through recovery of the metanarratives. Most postmodern theorists agree a loss of historicity has taken place, but they are divided as to whether it is unfortunate or fortuitous. A notable argument, Jameson's pastiche and Hutcheon's parody, seems at first to be irreconcilable, and may be until the whole of the population is considered. For Jameson, "pastiche is, like parody, the imitation of a peculiar or unique, idiosyncratic style, the wearing of a linguistic mask, speech in a dead language [...] without any of parody's ulterior motives" (Jameson 17). However, Hutcheon contends that parody points out the desire (nostalgia) for the stability of the old metanarratives by exposing these narratives as narratives and nothing more. "It is precisely this that is contested in postmodern parody where it is often ironic discontinuity that is revealed at the heart of continuity [...] it paradoxically both incorporates and challenges that which it parodies" (Hutcheon 11).

Neither explanation is incorrect. As Foucault contends, all discourses create alternate discourses and a postmodern world contains both of these discourses, and a lack of faith in both discourses disallows either becoming hegemonic. The two impulses are first, as Hutcheon explains, a questioning of the validity of metanarratives of history, and second, as Jameson sees them, a nostalgia attempting to reconstitute the old metanarratives in an almost mythological way.

The name "postmodern" only argues for an ending, and for many theorists contending a type of entropy, but as realized through chaos theory, disorder is only an interlude to new order. Postmodernity might be, and most likely is, pre-something, but what pre-something is almost impossible to know. Most of the more radical speculations of theorists such as Deleuze, Guattiari, Baudrillard, and others have yet to come true. If anything might be learned through the speculations of both modernity and postmodernity, it is that both utopian and distopian speculations are inaccurate.

The most liberating aspect of postmodernity, and, conversely, for those basing their identity on metanarratives of power — white, male, educated, middle/upper class — the most frightening aspect, is its liberating of marginalized voices that illuminate (although the term is passé) the pluralism of society and the world. However, because of the freeing of marginalized voices, the elitist, fascist, and right-wing radicals, normally marginalized for their absurd positions in reacting against a polyphonic society, have also gained a voice within the discourse. Their racism, sexism, and classism are said to be a reaction against dilution, what Robert J. Antonio calls new tribalism. "New tribalism bears the imprint of and helps drive postmodernization, especially its centrifugal forms of cultural fragmentation, antiuniversalism, and identity politics" (55). This phenomenon is actually a reaction against postmodernity, yet within postmodernity, a reaction against the loss of hegemonic power in social and political fields, as are all politics of ultraconservative or neoconservative or neoliberal (as in libertarianism) groups advocating, in any way, purity of races/culture or any non-equalitarian discourses, including rights of private property. It is a type of fascism playing on the confusion of people resulting from this unanchoring of identity, assuring them of a position of power no less than Hitler did in post–World War I/depression Germany, an assurance that culminated in the Holocaust. "Radical conservatives decried liberal-left efforts to impose formal and substantive equality, holding that allegedly suppressed natural inequalities ought to be cultivated and employed within the ranks of the domestic sociopolitical order. Overall they envisioned an 'organic' hierarchy of corporate groups and loyal subjects, regimented in a pseudo-communal way under natural leaderships" (Antonio 58). Thus inequalities of birth — class, race, sex, gender (what they actually mean) — created by categorization, and thus position to power networks, should not be rectified, giving the privileged an advantageous position to power. If intelligence is evenly distributed among humans without regard to sex, gender, class, or race (and all real studies show this to be true), then the idea of corporate groups — groups of privileged people — and loyal subjects — subjugated people — does not speak of any natural selection, but of privileged selection by those in power. Those groups promoting this political logic ignore the other side of the equation, as Nietzsche did and as other elitists of power also do. According to these thinkers, those out of power have the right to seize power in any way available, and thus those out of power, being the mass of human beings, can and should overrun those in power, taking their power and most likely their lives. The argument immediately becomes absurd. Thus, as those enlightened Enlightenment thinkers came to understand, the masses will not go away or, to corrupt Dylan Thomas' poem, "will not go gentle into that good night"; for any civilization to remain in existence, equality of all people must be established. Postmodernity brings to the forefront the existences of these diverse people and their needs.

Through making the scholars of diverse disciplines such as philosophy, anthropology, social anthropology, sociology, psychology, and other sciences aware of their role and the role of their own ideology within their observations and conclusions, postmodernity has allowed a multitude of voices to be heard, especially those within minority or disenfranchised groups — religious, ethnic, racial, and gendered groups. It has, however, also allowed for identity politics because the approaches to studying the voices were based on modernist methods of developing totalizing theories of identity when identity is complex, and a certain identity, such as one based on gender, ethnicity, and class, becomes salient only at the locus of interpellation in a complex relationship to other identity factors. For class, it questions any theoretical approach that designates three classes to actually be twelve, or any number at all. Postmodernity and this book questions the theories of class and how they do not reflect the way class is conceived in the real world. Finally, postmodernity puts into question the old theories of identity itself.

Thus, to assume that postmodernism, "an emerging intellectual and cultural orientation," is only an abstract theory, as Aronowitz claims, is to think of postmodernism as detached from what it might theorize — postmodernity, "a set of historical conditions" (Aronowitz 159; Pescosolido and Rubin 57). Aronowitz is not discussing a cultural orientation, although his complaint is that the theory "deprives groups of levers of power" and "postmodernist [...] thought deconstructs the goal of 'emancipation' by showing that those who adhere to this goal are infected with the virus of essentialism" (159). Aronowitz is mistaken in his assertion. Postmodernism does, however, question the essentialism of totalizing theories of society.

Pescosolido and Rubin, in "The Web of Group Affiliations Revisited: Social Life, Postmodernism and Sociology," contend that "in the pre-modern network [feudalistic] the local polity circumscribed the world" (55). They do not describe the mechanisms creating and maintaining these networks other than to hint at the advantages and disadvantages for individuality within each network, thus suggesting the existence of metanarratives — overarching discourses limiting the allowable choices of identities within each social network.

An individual in the pre-modern world existed within a hierarchy of group membership, creating a very stable network yet having little freedom, but "with modernity comes a greater element of choice [and] the uncertainty that comes with new freedoms" (Pescosolido and Rubin 56, 57). Pescosolido and Rubin argue, "The price individuals pay for modernism is a weaker personal and local safety net in which multiple groups pull the individual in different directions" (57). This pull is accomplished through metanarratives, or discourses. "Metanarratives have been the epic dramas of our time[s]," or at least the understanding of the themes of these dramas (Somers, "Narrative" 619). Within these narratives is the closure of discourse to other ideas of conceptualizing the world. "Perhaps the most paradoxical aspect of metanarratives is the quality of denarratization. [...] built on concepts and explanatory schemes" (Somers, "Narrative" 619). Thus class consciousness can arise in the Marxist sense only when the language game limits the possible allowable identities of the working class to the proletariat, but, as Pescosolido and Rubin state, "The world is socially constructed and [...] our old constructions are inadequate for understanding new realities" (61). Margaret Somers states that Marxist theories of class "presume what has not been empirically demonstrated — namely that identities are foundationally constituted by their categorization in the division of labor" ("Narrative" 624). Somers concludes, "Identity formation takes shape within this relational setting [narratives and practices] of contested but patterned relations among people and institutions" ("Narrativity" 609).

Finally, if both modernity and postmodernity are shifts in paradigms, with modernity disallowing plurality of being and postmodernity giving a voice to the voiceless, then multiple voices and identities must have always existed in one form or another. People did not fall neatly into assigned groups for a certain society, but because of limited agency, they had little recourse other than to act within the narratives they were given or react against what society allowed with a limited repertoire of discourses/narratives.

Postmodernism does not contest that humans live in a world of material reality, but rather that this world might be viewed in exactly the same way by all. "There is no question that contemporary research reveals and analyzes various crises of confidence" in the old approach to identity study (Howard 387). Howard argues, "Most human actors experience simultaneously a multiplicity of relationships and identities" (387). Postmodernism also allows for the concept of individual agency rather than both collective class interest and passive acceptance of dominant ideologies through metanarratives. The study of agency—its mechanisms, and the way individuals construct identities within social fields—allows for the study of how individuals narrate their selves into existence. The concept of narration of identity allows for multiple diverse identities to be conceptualized within the study of class. These multiple identities suggest that different ideologies exist, manifesting themselves through signs designated through difference. Class, then, must be studied not as a group of individuals with similar interests, but as attributes, judged by others as either in-group or out-group attributes, along with the reasons for these judgments.

Class attributes and reactions to class attributes might be studied within literature as a way to study the negotiating of class in society. Here again, the danger is to speak of the manifestations of attributes as attributes in and of themselves, as many studies speak of the manifestations of culture as culture. What might appear to be an attribute, such as Nietzsche's concepts of resentment by those having (what he titles) a slave morality, is actually a manifestation of the attribute of an ideology basing good and bad on a person's actions—the belief that you gain respect through certain honest action. Thus certain proclivities of the noble morality—such as insisting on privilege— create a sense of injustice and resentment in those with an identity based on moral actions, a moral action in itself.

What might be considered signs of class, such as fashion, or, as Aronowitz suggests, the "little blending of people," are actually manifestations of ideologies. What Aronowitz and others mistake as economic signs, as Bourdieu suggests, actually stem from the different levels of importance, within a certain ideology, of cultural and social capital, tied to the ability or importance of negotiating power networks. Although identity exists within a continuum and is fluid, these manifestations of ideologies seem to suggest, as Nietzsche glimpsed, two core ideologies or metanarratives existing at a very deep level of the subconscious. If "core" ideologies do exist, signs, although changing over time, will be reproduced by these core ideological positions consistently enough to allow for a consistent designation of in-groups/out-groups. Many of these attributes should reflect a core ideology capable of being studied as a "working-class" core ideology.[1] Where "Weberian-inspired scholars [...] treat culture as an independent causal force that both reflects and shapes material relations [there] are analyses by postmodernist scholars, who describe values, identities, and ideologies as primary generative forces in modern stratification systems" (Charles 42–43).

What postmodernist theories contend is this: identity is fluid based on individual ideology. This ideology is constructed through habitus influenced by ideological apparatus, such as educational and religious institutions, and mass media, allowing for different identities to become salient at certain times. These identities are both limited, and, more importantly, negotiated within the locus of subjectivity through power dynamics. Thus the individual is not passive in this construction of identity, nor does the individual have unlimited resources. Agency and its limits must be considered when studying class.

"Many theorists have failed to distinguish agency as an analytical category in its own right — with distinctive theoretical dimensions and temporally variable social manifestations" (Emirbayer and Mische 962–63). This may be caused by the reciprocal nature of the agency/ideology relationship. This interaction between agency/ideology and social structure — fields and discourses — causes a continued self-reassessment of individual identities, both personal and social; thus no intra-class uniformity exists, and proposing a prototype of a universal "actor" in literature with universal interests automatically stereotypes the working class by marginalizing their individual voices. However, "our personal narratives are not entirely confabulated. They are constrained by the world around us and from corrections by others. [...] Ourselves are a fiction in the sense of always being constructed, subject to constant revision" (Hardcastle 117).

Identities are fluid, salient, and dependent upon the occasion, but identities available to one person are limited in range and number. The possible number and range of identities are influenced by habitus, ideology, narratives, and social structure. "We select from all the stimuli falling on our senses only those which interest us and our interests are governed by a pattern-making tendency" (M. Douglas 156). These stimuli become "cues" for the "building up" of our personal identity or characteristics for categorization in in-group/out-group social identity (M. Douglas 156). "The human cognitive capacities are limited; that therefore, we process information as cognitive misers streamlining information to manage the demands of everyday interaction" (Howard 368).

Because "all our impressions are schematically determined from the start," an ideological apparatus, such as the myth of America, helps to standardize a prototype suggesting America is a classless society where, paradoxically, everyone might someday be allowed into the upper class (M. Douglas 156). A schema, for Mary Douglas, is "a pattern-making tendency" using available narratives to develop prototypes and stereotypes. The "discordant ones [schemas] tend to be rejected" (M. Douglas 156). Many times, "uncomfortable facts, which refuse to be fitted in [to the prototype,] we find ourselves ignoring or distorting so that they do not disturb the established assumptions" (M. Douglas 156). Yet because "it is through narrativity that we come to know, understand, and make sense of the social world, and [...] constitute our social identities," the breakdown of older metanarratives of class allows for different voices to be heard and different rules to be added to the language game (Somers, "Narrative" 606). This is prototype theory.

Prototype theory asserts that humans categorize stimuli into discrete groupings. Humans hail (categorize) others and are hailed by society through prototyping whose categories come from and are influenced by habitus (the ideologies of parents, family, and community), the ideological state apparatus (specifically, the educational system), and mass media. Humans are also hailed by groups through professional, social, and ad hoc organizations. Human response to interpellation (hailing), mediated through habitus, limits the types and numbers of identities becoming salient in a given situation. The concrete subject is interpellated within the categories of common and accepted prototypes, making salient certain identities in certain situations. Prototypes, according to Mary Douglas, change not just from one group to another, but also through time as they are acted upon by outside stimuli, especially (in our time) mass media (156).

Mary Douglas, using Durkheimian analysis, argues that stimuli are categorized as sacred, profane, or indeterminate (157). Categorizing stimuli in this way affects prototype construction by changing or creating new categories of prototypes at the individual or small-social-group level. Cues ingested by individuals become prototypes and are used by people to define themselves and others. These cues are gathered, for the most part, from mass media, controlling and disseminating the stimuli with which individuals define themselves and others.

Aspects of ideology are handed down through family and other institutions contributing to the habitus of the individual. Status groups, then, are not homogeneous groups acting as a one, but a conglomeration of actors with agency acting individually at the site of subjectification — the social field. These actors construct their identity at the site by interpellating each other and many times "othering" those manifesting signs not of their group. This interpellation "may be categorized along cognitive, attitudinal, and behavioral lines. Social stereotyping is primary among the cognitive outcomes" (Stets and Burke 226).

These cognitive, attitudinal, and behavioral prototypes used to construct one's identity and to hail or "other" another now come primarily through mass media, with the portrayal of stereotypical characters and narratives, and through corporate advertising. Corporations create authority by generating what Nick Couldry calls "'meta-capital' [...] power over other forms of power [affecting] social space through the general circulations of media representations" (667–68). He believes this "symbolic power" operates in two ways: first, "by influencing what counts as capital in each field; and second, through the media's legitimation of influential representations of, and categories for understanding, the social world that, *because of their generality*, are available to be taken up in the specific conflicts in *any* particular field" (668). They define the social space and the discourse of that space, thus defining the limits of the imaginary and, as a result, the limits of identities in which a person might be hailed. The tension in this process is derived from the need for a person to constitute his or her subjectivity. Through the meta-capital of mass media, manufacturing constantly shifting types of capital and signifiers, class is contested on an individual level or local-group level.

Prototypes are the primary building blocks of identity. They produce the schemas, signs, and narratives (ideology) out of which people build or narrate their identities. Again, the term identity is in need of defining.

> The language of identity is ubiquitous in contemporary social science, cutting across psychoanalysis, psychology, political science, sociology, and history. The common usage of the term *identity*, however, belies the considerable variability in both its conceptional meanings and its theoretical role [Stryker and Burke 284].

The usage of the word "identity" is as varied as "culture." It

> includes a number of distinct connotations. It refers first to the structures of things that remain the same, to that which is seen to constitute their "essence" across all transformations. But it also refers to the relation of the singular human being to him- or herself, to their actions, experience, wishes, dreams memories, and thus to the various instances of the "self." [...] And the term always contains a reference to time [Friese 1].

Signs produced by prototypes are used for exclusion and inclusion into a small group or status group. Thus the working class can only exist in comparison between status groups. A small group (as opposed to a theoretical "class") ingests practices, philosophies, and points of view that separate the group from other groups. They then maintain and pass down this separation to their children by what Mouffe calls "antagonisms" to and by the other groups, confirming identities (91).

The proposition that people are agents in the construction of their own identity does not negate the idea of ideology mitigating the formation of identity, but questions the correctness of assuming identity to be a collective or social category or common culture without agency. Identity theorists propose that, rather than society being divided into graduated classes of wealth and power, "society [should be] seen as a mosaic of relatively durable patterned interactions and relationships, differentiated yet organized" (Stryker and Burke 285).

Identity theorists propose that multiple identities exist within a single person. These identities become salient at different times and in different circumstances. However, a person is always a member of multiple groups, sometimes seeing him- or herself as a member of the working class in one situation and of the middle class in another. Stryker and Burke assert that "two important processes in social identity formation, namely self-categorization and social comparison" exist (225). Operario and Fiske believe

> (1) People are motivated to maintain a positive self concept; (2) the self-concept derives largely from group identification (in addition to personal identification, as stressed by American social psychologists); and thus (3) people establish positive social identities by comparing the ingroups favorably against outgroups [42].

This "leads the in-group to be judged positively and the out-group to be judged negatively" (Stets and Burke 225). The criteria used to judge in-group/out-group lead to one manifestation of stereotyping. Since groups vary through time and space, social identity is positional, becoming salient at different times and in different locations. A person may find some of his/her values reflecting middle-class values at one time within one group and at another time reflecting working-class values with a different group — thus different identities will be salient at different times. This scenario may well be reversed. Importantly, though, through different social signs noted and judged by others, a person without a salient identity — not adhering to in-group categorization is designated a member of an out-group.

For identity theory, "categorization depends upon a named and classified world. Among the class terms learned within a culture [society] are symbols used to designate positions," such as "working class" or "middle class" (Stets and Burke 225). Importantly,

> social categorization produced distinct and polarized ingroup — and outgroup — defining prototypes that assimilate relevant group members [...] when applied to self (i.e., self-categorization), transforms one's self-representation, perceptions, cognitions, feelings, and behavior so that they are governed by the ingroup prototype [Hogg and Abrams 10].

A person attempts to name him- or herself, and others, trying to construct salient identities within a distinct circumstance. Thus there is a high probability that people could be, and are, hailed as a middle-class subject in one instance and a working-class subject in another.

Although "two theories currently prevail in the [sociological] literature on the fundamental interplay between the individual and social world, identity theory [...] and social identity theory," a third — personal identity theory — is "posit[ed] but rarely address[ed]" (Hitlin 118). Hitlin states, quoting Hewitt, "Personal identity thus emphasizes a sense of individual autonomy rather than communal involvement" (118). Kristen Monroe, in discussing how identity constrains moral choice, using narratives and interviews of rescuers and rescued from the terror of the Third Reich, suggests, "It was the integration of values into identity that imposed constraints on their actions" (417). Personal identity, then, stems from the integration of "values" in the widest sense. Hitlin also proposes that personal identity is constructed from socially structured values (119). However, he believes "a simple causal relationship between a person's values and his or her behavior" does not exist (120).

If a person has a salient "working-class" identity, it is evoked in two ways: voluntarily and involuntarily. The first is when the person's signs are designated as "working class" and he or she becomes a member of a working-class in-group, always situational, perpetuating those practices and philosophies designated "working class" (a positive instance). When a person's signs are designated "working-class" and do not fit within those practices and philosophies of a group, that person is othered, or rejected, from the in-group and thus the working-class identity is evoked, this time negatively. However, if the person is able to produce signs consistent with what, for the group, are middle-class signs, that person will take on the identity of a middle-class person, whether positive (the group is middle class) or negative (the group is working class).

Identities, like values, are ordered by relative importance.[2] Hitlin states, "I place personal identity at the core of the self, experienced as unique but subject to social patterning through the concept of values" (121). Each person assembles values from others, including mass media. If habitus reflects signs of certain prototypes used for in-group and out-group interpellation of small groups at the site of interpellation, and even if almost no one can be contained solidly within a working-class prototype, the idea of a social grouping called the working class might still be conceptualized through status. A class theory might be developed based on prototypes of status where certain people's situational salient identity does not match the prototype of what might be considered middle class.

Identities are many and varied, and, most importantly, negotiated within ideologies. Identity politics has opened up the discourse to marginalized voices, but "identity politics, by portraying identity group members as ideologically monolithic, distorts public forum debate [...] by converting a diverse array of individual viewpoints into a few identity group meta-ideologies" (Knouse 763). Rather than an identity existing within a single category of experience, Somers proposes that "through narrativity that we come to know, understand, and make sense of the social world, and it is through narratives and narrativity that we constitute our social identities"—that is, the self is narrated through complex narratives ("Narrativity" 606).

Within these narratives lies not only the meaning-making process but also the "self"-making processes. These processes are mediated by metanarratives—controlling, through dominant ideologies, the discourses of possible "selves," or at least possible socially acceptable "selves," by controlling and managing the language games of such discourses. This limits the available prototypes. By limiting the available prototypes, metanarratives affect how an individual conceives him- or herself and the surrounding world. Ratner argues, "Social institutions structure behavior [...] by imposing rules of behavior, benefits, and punishments" (418). Meaning-making must reflect the available discourses of the place and time, allowing and disallowing certain utterances of meaning.

"Our current stream of consciousness selectively uses the past to create an on-going and continuously changing sense of self" (Hardcastle 49). Humans take from the past to both understand the present and project the future. Through the construction of prototypes created in the past (memory), actors make decisions about the present.

> Memory is understood as a process of re-presenting and re-membering by bringing past experiences [narratives] into the present. [...] Hence, re-presentations refers to the self-organized dynamics by virtue of which a previous construction [prototypes and schemas] is re-constructed (re-presented) from memory, given that there is some sensory interaction (perturbation) with the environment [Arnellos, Spyrou, and Darzentas 302].

The present is understood through the past by means of each person's constructed narrative of the past — their interpretations of the past filtered through prototypes and schemas making up a habitus or ideology. Within a society mediated by grand narratives, "all social groups possess repertoires of stories that serve as temporal framing resources and that help to define membership in a community" (Emirbayer and Mische 989).

Importantly, these plots are complex stories locating actors within a social field where their identities are negotiated at the locus of interpellation. Thus, within in-group/out-group dynamics, an actor's agency, mediated by his or her narrative conception of the situation, the narrative conception of others, and the social structure, will be decided and will also determine how that actor will be recognized and what identity might become salient.

> The shape of our narratives is shaped by our cultural milieu. Though our affective reactions are all our own and emerge from horrifyingly complex interplay between cortical and sub-cortical brain circuits, the environment, our genes, and our unique cognitive histories, our stories about them are sieved through and by the norms of our individual communities. These guiding — more accurately coercing — norms are so powerful that we revise, edit, and alter our personal reactions and concomitant stories to force them to meet social expectations [Hardcastle 91–92].

Narratives are the way we think ourselves into existence, or at least explain our existence to ourselves. "Ontological narratives, for instance, process events into episodes. People act, or do not act, in part according to how they understand their place in any number of given narratives — however fragmented, contradictory" (Somers, "Narrativity" 603). However, social actors are not free to fabricate narratives at will. Their agency is limited. They must choose from a set of limited discourses, often disseminated through mass media, constructed within, for, and from multiple power struggles in multiple fields. Thus agency also depends on the allowable narratives available in a social field or structure.

Sheelagh Drudy's article, titled "The Classification of Social Class in Sociological Research," is concerned with "the existence of varying theoretical approaches to class structure [that] leaves a problem of classification for the empirical researcher," and is a comparison of different classification schemes, such as the three-tiered system of Marx or the seven-tiered system of Goldthorpe (21–22). This article also points to different ideological habitus of expectations. It is also a good example of how ideology, passed down through individuals, can affect and limit possible narratives for a person's identity.

Drudy puts the cart before the horse (something many sociologists seem prone to do) by assuming the father's occupation directly correlates with the child's occupational expectations (32). It is related, but only indirectly, through the ideology of the parents being passed to the child through habitus. The occupational position of the father (or mother, for that matter) does not drive the ideology as much as their ideology, driving their choices, spurs on the occupational choices of the child — that is, the child's ideology. Drudy, like others, surmises that the belief systems of children whose fathers occupy different occupations have different occupational expectations. The uncomplicated assumption would be to believe that the occupation of the parents directly affects the parents' ideology, so that they then pass the ideology on to their children. This automatically assumes that the ideology of the parents' parents had no effect on them as children. It is a sociological chicken-and-egg question.

The conclusion is less uncomplicated than those hoping to elicit strong results from empirical studies would like. Although finding a correlative between occupations and occupational expectations of children is not difficult, finding the underlying connection is more difficult. This underlying determining factor must be ideology, since it must always precede the choice of occupation as far back as the conundrum might go. This problem is also evident in Evans and Mills' assumption that one can "construct social classes out of combinations of occupational unit groups and employment statuses," and this correlation might be useful in the study of class (90). As Drudy has indirectly shown, occupations should be considered epiphenomena of ideology because, within life chances, ideology is the strong influence on choice. A person's agency, and the possible narratives available to the person, is greatly influenced by the ideologies of people around him or her.

A person is always negotiating these positions in a complex relationship to his or her world. Class is not a designation of a homogeneous group of people, but a function of conglomerations of signs designated as class signs, or, as Bourdieu understands, the construction of designations called "classes" in a social field can only come from "*difference*, that is, they occupy *relative positions* in a space of relations [...] and the real principle of the behavior of individuals and groups" (*Practical Reason* 31). Difference can only exist through a manifestation of differing signs. These signs are used to name persons as belonging to one class or another at the locus of interpellation (in-group/out-group). These signs are varying and intricate, changing almost daily, but these signs, most of the time, are manifestations of attributes of ideology. Cultural manifestations might finally point to ideology.

In academia a tendency exists to assign attributes to the working class through a middle-class lens even if the academic claims that he or she is from the working class, having ingested middle-class narratives while negotiating higher education and academic departments, thus acquiring a penchant to attribute all class designations through a Marxist discourse. This creates a propensity to ascribe attributes of the working class at a shallower level of theorizing than meaning-making and narrativity, which marginalizes agency.

Multiple voices and locations of identity exist within the self and society. The individual is not passive within the interpellation of self, but must first narrate his or her self (agency) within the confines of a social field (social structure), space and time specific. Like the concepts of culture and ideology, "agency" may connote several levels of abstraction; at its most basic level, agency is the ability to make meaning, without which action, be it physical or mental, is not possible.[3]

The concept of agency in the guise of free will and determinism (power) has been one of the grounds for debates concerning not only society, but specifically the working class and the poor, suggesting, as Michaels does, calling the effects of free will and determinism "egalitarianism — or anti-elitism, [that] we pretend everybody had an equal chance" (104). Much of his book, *The Trouble with Diversity: How We Learned to Love Identity and Ignore Inequality*, contests the libertarian ideal of everyone being positioned equally within social fields as concerns access to power and thus life chances. He believes the equality deck is so stacked against the working class and poor that they have little or no agency, but his is a slightly different meaning of agency.[4]

"People play an active role in making and remaking culture. [...] Agency is the intentional causal intervention in the world, subject to the possibility of a reflexive monitoring of that intervention" (Ratner 413). Agency, though, is not a simplistic set of actions. "Any action the individual agency initiates including action to transform society always takes place from a social basis" (Ratner 421).

During September 2006 in Jena, Louisiana, several incidents involving black and white students ended with a civil rights march of some twenty-thousand African Americans and others through the streets of the small town after one of the black students was jailed for an act of reprisal. The white students' part in the incidents was considered a student prank, but not so for the black students. While some people point toward racism as the reason for the unequal interpretation of the incidents, others do not. Obviously the unequal interpretation was racism. This racism, however, was of a subtler form than the social discrimination starting the chain of events leading to the march — the separation of white students from black students and the effort by one student to change this situation. The racism was perpetuated by what must be called "white privilege." O'Connor quotes Ferguson, who found that,

> black boys more often find themselves in trouble because of how their performances are interpreted, rather than how they actually perform. [...] When white boys transgress, school officials presume that boys will be boys, attribut[ing] "innocence to their wrong doing," and believe that "they must be socialized to fully understand the meaning of their acts." [...] black boys [...] are "adultified" [...] "stripped of any element of childish naiveté" [162].

The narratives (discourses) school officials and others in power use for meaning-making allow for different levels of agency depending on race. These narratives, as O'Connor suggests, function together as a social structure, distributing power and privilege unevenly throughout the social field — in this case, a public school system and judicial system (162).

Ideology, acting through meaning-making, is reflected through agency and structure. Agency as power can be seen as the performance of personal identity. Structure equals how those in a power position react to this performance. These performances of agency and structure are very complex, as well as reciprocal. In the case of the "Jena Six," privilege was defined in terms of race and (somewhat) of gender. In other loci of interpellation, privilege might be defined through class. Although race and gender are based on the "normalcy" of white and male, class divisions are much subtler.

O'Connor first makes the mistake of incorrectly believing wealth creates privilege and power (160). Wealth as a distinction, although used much in theory, is not and cannot be very well defined when speaking of class. Since the author also includes middle-class families (a very large and ill-defined economic group), wealth must be discounted as a marker. Power, the use of the power by institutions, and social and cultural capital gain privilege, creating advantageous positions without wealth. Institutions of power might be some organization given legitimate power by the state, such as schools, or some institution given power by society at large, or often by ad hoc groups of people in the majority in a certain locus of performance. O'Connor undoes the assumption that wealth creates power later in her article (or contradicts her own argument) by postulating that privilege is based not on wealth, but singularly on power, such as men over women, white over black, and middle class over working class. She also constructs classism in a non-economic way (160). What she does assume is that somehow a "middle class" has more power than a "working class" within a social field, classifying people into middle class and working class. This power is not always directed from a middle-class person toward a working-class person, but a middle-class person knows how to acquire power, if only through the manipulation of institutions and the use of social and cultural capital, and also knows how to use this power for his or her benefit. Since a middle-class person is the beneficiary of this power arrangement, working-class people are the recipients of the negative results such as being marginalized regarding life chances. In a study of ideology and how it works for middle-class mothers as concerns their children's advantageous positioning in education, Brantlinger, Majd-Jabbari, and Guskin note that the middle class's "advantaged position depends on the poor's [and working class's] inferior status" (574).

Although ideologies, narratives, schemas, and prototypes are many and varied, especially in a time when metanarratives have less power to create, control, and negate individual narratives, two core metanarratives seem to still hold sway, providing primary lenses through which to view the world. These core narratives might be seen as the basic plot schemes in which attributes might arise used as signs for separation (classes). This core narrative or plot structure seems to revolve around the relationship to "privilege." Thus, wealth or power are not privilege in and of themselves, but can allow privilege. Privilege may still exist without real wealth or power.

Privilege is an ideology allowing (morally) for the positioning of oneself in a hierarchy of power, sometimes gained by positioning oneself with someone or some group having access to power in a distinct social field. Part of privilege involves having the skill to position oneself within the power arrangements in such a way as to take advantage of the arrangement, as well as, importantly, believing one has not only the right to do so but also the birthright. This allows for a power position without real wealth while still allowing for privilege, although some sort of "wealth" usually follows.

Notably, this concept of power is different from the concept of power Aronowitz or Zweig put forth (autonomy in the workplace), but it is the power spoken of by Bourdieu and Foucault. Michaels comes close to this concept of power when he contends that a form of power resides in the unequal distribution of school taxes within a community or state when money is doled out through a system designed to disperse money based on the property taxes collected within the school district through property value, a result of power influencing legislation at the state level through political networks. Michaels believes, "If we are committed to equality of opportunity, we should be funding all school districts equally and abolishing private schools" (135–36). However, just putting more money into schools or bringing better schools to disenfranchised neighborhoods would not solve the problems of those children living in the disadvantaged neighborhoods or effect a large change because, although poorly funded schools are part of the problem, they are a result of a larger ideological problem of disenfranchisement. Michaels' assumption also cannot explain the varying outcomes of success for students within the same school. If identity is conceived as a function of agency and narrativity mediated through ideology, produced by positions in a social field or structure, and inherited through habitus, then the unequal outcomes of students within the same school can be explained through conceiving inequality, not as wealth, but as a function of power through discourses within social fields — ideology.

"Class identity and unity are ideologically constructed through exclusions and the creation of borders. [...] Hence outsiders [...] reciprocally affect power holders" (Brantlinger, Majd-Jabbari, and Guskin 574). Power is reciprocal. On the one hand, power arrangements demand in-group/out-group designations. On the other hand, by virtue of having power, one gains more power through others attempting to associate themselves with this power arrangement through inclusion and performativity. For the working class, not only are they denied entrance into certain networks, but they also are either not taught the nature of power networks, and thus are inept at negotiating these power webs, or, whether adept or not, they find negotiating within power networks contradictory to their moral beliefs, constructed through ideology. As Trotsky states, "Morality is a product of social development; there is nothing immutable about it; it serves social interests; these interests are contradictory; morality more than any other form of ideology has a class character" (qtd. in Cloud 531).

Those manifesting middle-class signs have the advantage of gaining power through social and cultural capital because both reflect the ideologies, if only in emulation, of those already with power, allowing the system to perpetuate itself. "Social structures produce orientations toward action, which in turn reconstitute knowledge," or, in Lyotard's configuration, performativity (Brantlinger, Majd-Jabbari, and Guskin 575). These social structures evolve into physical institutions, such as the PTA, or institutions of thought "that resist change and generate ideologies that naturalize their existence" (Brantlinger, Majd-Jabbari, and Guskin 575). These social institutions exclude those manifesting signs that are unaligned with the ideologies of its members. Concerning systems of power within a social field, those excluded are usually showing what can be labeled "working-class" signs — signs different from those of the middle class. People manifesting working-class signs do not produce the signs that legitimatize and reflect the ideology of the systems of power or the totality of signs for in-group participation.

Life chances come from acquiring, wanting to acquire, and, most importantly, knowing how to acquire social and cultural capital, and also by understanding power dynamics and how these dynamics can be manipulated by social and cultural capital, along with believing in the right to do so. It is a "privileged" ideology. Ideology allows or disallows this understanding of power dynamics and not intelligence, or lack thereof. Thus another aspect of the differences in the core narratives of the working class and middle class is the way their narratives allow or preclude a relationship to power.

This relationship might be suggested by splitting ideology, at a primary level, into the two divisions glimpsed in Nietzsche's theories of noble and slave morality. For Nietzsche, a noble person understands instinctively who he or she is by his or her place in a social field, often placed in the field through birth and maintained through power networks inherited from parents. It is elitist and sometimes narcissistic. A slave is a person who constructs a morality through actions or places himself, or herself, and others within a social field through good or evil deeds. It is, as Michaels suggests, equalitarian and sometimes altruistic. Importantly, the idea of privilege stems from these two interpretations of the world. Those believing in privilege, Nietzsche's nobles, do not judge acts as right or wrong, but "worthy or unworthy" (Brobjer 72). Virtue for those of privilege comes from the inside, from character, which is inherited and thus needs no proof, and can be used to rationalize an unfair or unearned advantageous position as deserved through character. For an equalitarian ideology virtue can only exist through good or evil action and needs proof. Owen terms the difference in virtue as "self-respect" (114). The concept of self-respect, though, depends on an ideological concept of good and bad.

The concept of "privilege" as inherited character comes down through history, as Nietzsche suggests, from those believing they were of the elite, bolstered by the major disseminator of the major metanarratives — the church through the "great chain of being," which posits, similar to Greek and Roman myth, that differing levels of humans exist, some more divine than others. This concept was taken up again in a new guise as the "elect" by Calvinistic Protestants, and is reflected in the concept of the "saved" or "born again" in many fundamentalist churches. Habitus passes these prototypical ideologies to the children. For the middle-class child, having been taught to emulate the mores and values of the upper class, these prototypes are then used to complement his or her understanding of power and the importance of social and cultural capital. Working-class prototypes produce signs of the working class because they differ from middle-class signs produced by middle-class prototypes — Bourdieu's difference. Also for the working class, as a way to legitimize the identities of self and a particular in-group, habitus can also pass on the resistance to capitulating to a different ideology by rejecting the signs of upper-class ideology, contending that the actions producing the signs are immoral. Habitus will pass on the signs of the working class: a lack of knowledge of the importance of power systems, in addition to the manipulation of this power (privilege), and the lack of the knowledge of the importance of social and cultural capital. Middle class might be conceived as a group existing in the tension between both core metanarratives, creating a group of people who, at one time, base their self-esteem on moral actions, and, at another time, emulate the upper classes, disregarding, or rationalizing, actions they might have regarded as immoral (or at least unfair) at another time.[5]

Since the locus of interpellation is the site of identity making, it is also the site of identity contestation and the struggle over narratives. "Struggles over narrations are thus struggles over identity" (Somers, "Narrative," 631). Struggles over the signs of ideologies are also struggles over identity. Obviously, as many working-class academics demonstrate, not all people hailing from working-class parents remain within the working class by displaying signs of a working-class ideology. With the breakdown of the metanarratives of class, the signs once reserved for the middle class are now readily available to the working class, one of the main thrusts of this book. A continuum is now evident, rather than segregated groups, although this continuum probably has always existed in some form, from a person displaying working-class signs all the time to persons showing no working-class attributes. Marianne Conroy, in her study of the significance of factory outlet malls, argues that these malls

> highlight the fracturing of middle-class identity. [...] The vast range of merchandise offered at a discount underscores the emergence of new discriminations in the status signification of commodities for which the traditional Marxist language of class seems inadequate. [This suggests] the sheer volatility of class categories in the United States [...] insofar as outlet malls [among many other institutions] encourage a mode of consumption grounded in a performative attitude toward middle-class identity [...] enabl[ing] consumers to impersonate class positions [64].

Through Veblen's emulation, then, a blending of classes takes place and thus to speak of classes in a Marxist sense is to misconstrue the actuality of real-world class separation. By themselves, "working-class" signs are quite meaningless in the definition of class, but when compared to "middle-class" signs, they are used as separators in in-group/out-group designations. Since people are separated into classes through in-group/out-group separation, and, as Conroy contends, through signs such as fashion, which also confuse class boundaries, alternative signs manifesting themselves, for better or for worse, exist as attributes of working-class identities — manifestations of an ideology's core attributes, displayed and used for class separation. These signs may change in their manifestations over time, but attributes exist of a primary ideology driving a worldview. This primary "equalitarian" ideology might be discovered through difference and applied to literature as an alternate way to study the working class. Some differences between working-class attributes and other class attributes — the difference between privileged and unprivileged — are the ideological position toward power caused by the in-group/out-group separation of the working class from power networks as a way for other classes to narrate themselves, the ineptness of working-class persons regarding the skills of negotiating positions in power networks, the refusal to negotiate within power arrangements in a moral connotation, and the resistance to negotiate positions in power networks as an exercise of agency in an attempt to construct and maintain a viable identity.

An amazing text, not for its self-conscious thrust of attempting to define the working class, but for its incidental elucidating of working-class attributes, is *Writing Work: Writers on Working-Class Writing*, edited by David Shevin, Larry Smith, and Janet Zandy, a coauthor of *American Working-Class Literature: An Anthology* (reviewed in chapter 3). "By challenging stereotypical views of working-class culture and art with the authentic accounts of those who live and work there," these editors give the authors free reign to "relate their own experience" (5). However, the editors of this text seem to conceive "culture and art" at the second level of theorizing, seeing "culture" as artifacts of a people, and thus miss the ideological aspect of this culture.

Joe Mackall's essay, "The Stories of Working-Class Lights," in the text elucidates the awareness of another ideology, that of privilege, though he does not articulate it as such. His ideology is grounded in the narration of family and, for him, a solid working-class ethos of hard work. Although Mackall grew up in a time when heavy industry was booming in the northeast, and thus should have had a feeling of security, he had an ever-present, distressing "feeling [of] the sense of something lost [...] I would be on the silent side of the secret people like me would never know" (15). Although unable to articulate his observation of others not sharing his ideological worldview of hard work equaling success, he observed, somehow, that others were not only successful but seemed to know a secret that made them successful without hard work or struggle. The secret, of course, was perceiving and understanding power systems, social and cultural capital, and language games — the rules of the discourses of the social fields. He has glimpses of another core ideology not based on deeds, but on the position one's family and oneself hold in power networks within specific social fields.

One reason working-class individuals do not pursue social networks with the same enthusiasm as do other classes is because the pursuit of positions in power networks is much more difficult for those persons showing working-class signs. This is reflected in Mackall's insecurity. In order for the "middle class" to be the "middle class," and to benefit from being the middle class, when so much confusion is presented by class mimicry (as Conroy suggests), and since class can only exist through difference, the working class (as

Brantlinger, Majd-Jabbari, and Guskin contend) must be the significant "Other." The working class becomes the "Other" designating the standard, which, through power networks and mass media, is the middle class. By showing signs of being working class, a person finds him- or herself denied access to these power networks, or at least the pursuit of power networks is more difficult for those showing signs of the working class because the middle class "dominates by controlling cultural capital that generates distinctions and by putting forth their knowledge as *the* legitimate knowledge" (Brantlinger, Majd-Jabbari, and Guskin 574).

Brantlinger, Majd-Jabbari, and Guskin, in a study of the use and manipulation of power networks within school systems found that middle-class mothers separated people into, not the haves and have-nots, but "normal" and "not normal." They were able to legitimize their knowledge of working-class children (and thus middle class as the standard) as coming from "multiproblem families" even though they had no factual evidence for their claim, othering working-class children and families and justifying their privileged position (Brantlinger, Majd-Jabbari, and Guskin 579).

How do middle-class persons distinguish not only working-class persons but also signs of the working class if the signs of the middle class are now so easily acquired by people designated as working class or out-group? Whether because of this ostracism, or because many working-class people come from the poor peasantry of Europe (as did Mackall's family), and thus have no pedigree to speak of, working-class ideology is a "deed" or action-based ideology where self-esteem is based on good or bad actions. Thus the concept of "equalitarianism," which might also be seen as unprivileged. Who you are does not matter, but what you do and how you act does matter, and people with working-class or action ideologies are loath to use influence to deal with situations.

Persons holding a working-class ideology will approach situations differently from those with a middle-class or privileged ideology. Horvat, Weininger, and Lareau, studying class differences in relations between parents and schools, notice that even when working-class parents knew of "an undesirable teacher [...] they simply 'hoped' that their children would avoid him or her. [...] Many working-class and poor parents assumed they had neither the capacity nor right to intervene in such matters" (338). These individuals do not see themselves as somehow better than others or above the rules. Horvat, Weininger, and Lareau also state, "When working-class parents are confronted with a problem in school they handle these [...] incidents in a more individual fashion" (333). An equalitarian ideology insists on noninterference of power systems for unfair advantage.

The difference between equalitarian and privileged ideologies creates a difference in the concepts of organization, institution, and networking. A privileged ideology conceives any grouping of people, official or ad hoc, as a power system with influence in a certain field. This power can and will be used by people to position themselves and others in an advantageous position. Since they perceive this manipulation of power as one of the primary rules of the game, people with privileged ideologies see themselves as entitled to use the power for their advantage.

An equalitarian ideology conceives organizations, institutions, and networks as existing to exercise power to enforce the rules, assuming that, whether these rules are just or unjust, they will be enforced equally for all. For a person whose ideology is equalitarian the conception of the game is different from that of one who adheres to a privileged ideology. The person with the equalitarian ideology believes power is always present outside him- of herself, conceiving the transcendental signifier as existing externally to the self, while privileged ideology conceives it as internal to the self. This ideology of equalitarianism demands people face problems head on and solve these problems themselves rather than calling on other people (social networks) to intercede. An equalitarian ideology also contends that use of influence is dishonest. By adhering to the principles of this ideology, an ineptness is present in negotiating power networks and in understanding the concept of social and cultural capital. This lack of skill limits access to the use of a power base by becoming a sign itself.

When middle-class parents have a problem in school, they are likely to use the power networks consisting of other middle-class parents. This not only solves the problem, usually in favor of the parent, but also reestablishes both their rank within the network and the network's power base within the school system. Horvat, Weininger, and Lareau refer to an incident concerning a teacher pushing a student during an argument. The boy's mother did not learn of the incident from her son, but from a slew of phone messages from other parents waiting for her when she arrived home. "By then the members of the school board were getting calls" (332). The result of this incident was that "the teacher was suspended for a week" (333).

Another attribute of the working class designated as out-group within social networks is their disinclination or refusal to "network." Because their ideological makeup insists that self-esteem is predicated on correct action, people with a working-class ideology deemphasize certain signs of a character-based ideology, such as the importance of the ever-changing signs of class. These ever-changing signs of class include the correct hairstyle, correct clothes, correct books to read, correct music to listen to or movies to see, correct places to go, and, importantly, not only the correct subjects for conversation but also the correct lexicon and viewpoint in which to speak about them. Michaels gives a good example of just this problem while reviewing two books, Wolfe's *I Am Charlotte Simmons* and Sittenfield's *Prep*. Although Michaels has bigger fish to fry than worrying about the crisis of the inability for a character in a novel to reproduce correct signs of class, his refusal to confront inequality within the same school avoids the question of class separation not directly based on economic life chances. This allows for a deconstruction of his argument that only the rich and the poor now exist in America. The main characters in both stories are concerned (Michaels thinks maybe overly concerned) with showing and producing the correct signs of class — an attribute of the middle class or middle-class wannabes, as these two girls are (91–95).

When attempting to reproduce signs of the middle class, persons with working-class ideologies do so through their understanding of the middle-class through actions — the wearing of certain clothes, the doing of certain deeds (such as going to the correct restaurant or movie), reading the correct books, and even knowing the correct people. But because they interpret these signs of cultural capital as actions, they miss the subtlety, or sometimes intricacy, inherent in the makeup and display of the signs, or the complexity of the rules to the game, and at certain times and places they will reveal themselves as one of the out-group and thus initiate an opportunity for people entrenched in power groups to "other" them, narrating their own identity as middle class, an incident the characters of Wolfe's *I Am Charlotte Simmons* and Sittenfield's *Prep* feared. Much of the knowledge games of fashion, art, music, and even knowledge of "celebrities" depends on the middle class' need to construct ever-changing signs in an ongoing war for power, allowing for "othering" or, through recognizing of those not of their class, gaining power through the closure of systems, thus concentrating societal power into a smaller group.

Action-driven ideology has a plethora of signs of its own. Joe Mackall argues that families, like nations, are narrated into existence as a myth (12). Through these narrations — stories — they narrated their identity. "All my cousins — particularly male cousins — measured themselves, as I did, against the story of my grandfather leaving kith and kin and sailing from Italy to the United States as a twelve-year-old" (11). Mackall and his male cousins defined themselves through their grandfather's deed of sailing off into the unknown, a deed of bravery and self-sacrifice, and through his actions in the New World, as in the story of his grandfather's humanity while working as a milkman, giving his products away free of charge when people had no money (11). However, Mackall's uncles also judged his grandfather through other deeds, for being "a man who pushed his sons ruthlessly and showed them his love not at all" (11). The actions of Mackall's grandfather were viewed by the uncles not as laudable but as contemptible. Because the grandfather's lineage did not enter into the arguments of whether he was good or bad, the story of the grandfather was narrated through his actions from several points of view. If their ideology had been privileged, the narrations might have been less diverse so as to reinforce a character-driven, privileged ideology. The core of this ideology is action-based rather than character-based, contesting the belief that the working-class is "solidaristic," as Metzgar and others contend, but rather arguing that their ideology is individualistic and altruistic more than it is an ideology that seeks out power groups (207).

Because this ideology is individualistic, it demands at least the appearance of agency, and, though mediated by structure, working-class agency frequently resists a passive acceptance of allowable identities within the social structure, although even certain negative identities might be said to be allowable, and even resistance is in its own way a passive acceptance of the structure, as Foucault suggests. Paul Christensen alludes to the idea of resistance when he says, "I was unwilling to play the games that led to success. Teachers favored those who made their jobs easier, and rewarded them for their willingness to behave, to do the work" (52).

If one's identity is based on an ideology of action, resistance becomes an action pitting a "moral" person against an "immoral" system or people, based on the concept of moral and immoral actions. Thus, if standing on one's own is moral, then using the system is immoral, and kowtowing to power brokers can only result in a negative view of one's own identity, perpetuating a feeling of powerlessness, as seen in Terkel's text and *Gig* (see chapter 3). Rather than aligning themselves with power, Berger's workers in *Working-Class Suburb: A Study of Auto Workers in Suburbia* (reviewed in chapter 2) try to avoid power networks altogether and seek freedom from them, often in "'a little business of my own'" (Berger 96).

Within an ideology of action, the concept of justice and injustice must be based on action. To Mark Migotti

> the nobles described in GM I [volume I of *On the Genealogy of Morals*] form a leisure class in Thorstein Veblen's sense of that term; they belong to those classes that are "by custom exempt or excluded from industrial [work] occupations and are reserved for certain employments to which a degree of honor attaches" [749].

An ideology based on hard work and good deeds would see the actions of this class as an example of laziness and the fact that these people succeed as an example of injustice. However, an ideology based on privilege would see these people as unmitigated successes and through emulation would attempt to attain the same status. Bourdieu, like Veblen, sees the working-class ideology as stemming from necessity, from the need of thrift and the nearness to necessity, and although this nearness to necessity may no longer exist for the working class, some remnants of the ideology remain. This leads to several manifestations of this action ideology. The first is the idea of real work, or hard work being real, meaning that the production of a tangible object constitutes real work. Conversely, easy work and non-tangible work became a sign of laziness, indicating that men are less than men when afraid to get their hands dirty or to work up a sweat.

Another aspect of working-class ideology is an underlying fear of injustice, passed down through habitus from parents experiencing "othering." This fear marks the children as "others" within a small social group, perpetuating the ideologies. As Heidi Shayla states, her father "always told me to prepare for the worst. [...] Optimism, in his mind, was shortsighted" (19). Whether grounded in reality or not, Paul Christensen felt that because he failed to play the "games" leading to success, he "failed at everything" (52). Christensen's essay is focused on the fear of failure, not just the fear of poverty or starvation. Since a working-class person's identity is based on actions, failure, rather than being a turn of events, is a direct reflection on a person, so much so that many times this fear of failure, combined with an unnerving suspicion that others are some how privy to secrets, borders on a superstition and may be one of the reasons Thaddeus Coreno sees a connection between class and Protestant fundamentalism.

> Those who occupy the lower tiers of class fractions have limited access to the power, wealth and respect enjoyed by those in more privileged locations. [...] Those who lose prestige and/or gain only limited material rewards from these institutional arrangements and value commitments are more likely to find traditionalist critiques of society appealing [345–46].

These critiques range from the immorality of the rich to the inscrutability of fate.[6] "Failure was a return to the wilderness, and to a dependency on forces that were outside the human brain [...] an overpowering force of ancient gods" (Christensen 53). The "gods," in fact, are those controlling power networks in social fields, expecting, often unconsciously, reciprocation through performativity. Thus another attribute of the working class is a belief in fate, however it might be expressed. Fate, or what might be a belief in direct divine intervention of God or the fates, or an "overpowering force," also manifests itself in success.

However, success — the accumulation of property and goods for a working-class person — is not, as it is for a middle-class person, a manifestation of cultural capital through conspicuous consumption, but a sign of the success of actions and the reaching of a goal, as seen through Berger's workers. Material goods for those possessing an equalitarian ideology are not used as capital, but as manifestations of success and of goodness — a sign that they have lived a good and decent life, worked hard, obeyed the rules, and so forth. In "More Is Better: Consumption, Gender, and Class Identity in Postwar America," Shelley Nickles writes of working-class women's attitude toward kitchen appliances.

> These machines were primary tools for work, and this concern primarily shaped women's purchasing decisions.[...] Working-class women's preference for up-to-date, substantial, shiny appliances was an expression of their distinctive domestic lifestyle. [They] saw their primary role as houseworkers, whereas middle-class women defined themselves more as wives [Nickles 595, 600].

Women with working-class ideologies saw improvements in appliances as a function of the appliances' practical working capability, and as symbols of "respectability which gave them a 'sense of security'" (Nickles 601). Nickles concludes that, rather than relating to their appliances as symbols of their worth, "middle-class women named possessions that appealed to 'aesthetic sensitivities,' [social and cultural capital] such as living-room furnishings" (602).

Though the women studied did much the same tasks and their positions were much the same within the household, their narration of their selves was informed by different ideologies, as reflected in their primary role as "houseworker" or wife. This narration was manifested in the type and style of the appliances they chose, allowing for comparison and in-group/out-group designations. A cursory look, though, of these manifestations of class through a Marxist prototype would see little difference in the choices made in this acquisition or consumption, other than the price as a sign of class.

Finally, in what must be one of the great paradoxes of society, this working-class equalitarian ideology is actually perpetuated by elitist, privileged ideology (the dominant ideology) that believes little of it, or at least does not adhere to its tenets. A comparison can be made between mass media's dissemination of an equalitarian metanarrative and the actions and rationalizations of those involved in its dissemination. The examples of this double standard are too numerous and obvious to require citation. The middle class, through emulation, also promotes this paradox.

Postmodernity has given voice to once-marginalized ideologies and identities, and has not only questioned all totalizing theories but in doing so has also provided a space in which to question what is known about identity making itself. This has allowed for identity politics to study these marginalized voices, while also threatening to conceive identity in essentialist paradigms when identity is always a complex negotiation of class, age, gender, sexual orientation, and race/ethnicity mediated between agency and social structure.

Thus to speak of class as a group of homogeneous people is to be essentialist, and to speak of class in its relation to other identity signifiers, such as race or sex, is still essentialism. If class is to be spoken of and for in academia and is to be useful — without the problems of inconsistencies and contradictions now plaguing the study — a different way to speak of class needs to be created. Rather than speak of class as a group of people, class needs to be spoken of as attributes and propensities of a core metanarrative showing itself within changing signs — manifestations of an ideology through the negotiating of identity in a complex relationship to society.

These signs might only exist through difference and can only be designated as working class by a system that holds the power to do so. Thus "working-class" attributes only exist opposite to and outside of middle-class attributes. To study the working class in literature, then, is to discover the core ideology producing the attributes and signs. In Nietzsche's noble and slave morality can be found the clues to these separate ideologies, the idea of privilege — ideology based on character — and equalitarian — ideology based on moral action. By studying the signs of these core ideologies (and this chapter can only be the beginning), a better understanding of persons manifesting working-class attributes might be developed.

As with Marxist theories, any theory or class is in danger of becoming rigid and thus totalizing, especially if the major metaphor constructs a "place" or category for class designations rather than holding a temporary position within a matrix. A working-class, equalitarian identity or ideology should be thought of as a pole at one end of a continuum of an ideological schema, with elitist or privileged identity or ideology as the opposite pole. A character's identity might exist as anything from a completely working-class ideology to a completely elitist or privileged ideology. Since a character will be located within at least one social field, placed in position to other characters and the social structure of the field(s), different ideologies will be manifested, making up different identities.

A Working-Class Theory of Literature

Class in the Western world, excluding those arguments purposely exposing a Marxist point of view, is spoken of within the terms of Weber's status groups. Class is contested within social fields through the use and control of discourses at the small-group or individual level by means of in-group/out-group interpellation through difference. Discourses are established and implemented that legitimize knowledge as truths (self-constituting), thus establishing a power position, which, through performativity, (inclusion/exclusion), further legitimizes the discourses and the power position. This legitimizing of knowledge, which creates a locus of power, allows for subjectification of a person as a "subject" by those legitimized as the "Subject" by the discourses. This subject position, through inclusion/exclusion, is determined through the manifestations of ideologies through signs — culture.

A person has many complex identities, both personal and social, derived from both self-categorization and social categorization — in-group/out-group interpellation in a complex play of signifiers including, sometimes, forms of resistance. These signs are garnered through narratives passed down through habitus existing throughout social fields suggesting schemas and prototypes of objects, ideas, and beliefs. Through schemas, prototypes, and narratives a person constructs a reality, and thus an identity is given agency and constrained by social structure within the field.

Although the postmodern era has allowed for a reassessment of many metanarratives, two core metanarratives, as Nietzsche understood them, still seem to hold sway: equalitarian and privileged. These core metanarratives produce other narratives and are reproduced by even more narratives. Since a position of power cannot exist without exclusion and inclusion, the privileged ideology (the dominant ideology at this time), besides reproducing itself, adds to the production and maintenance of the equalitarian ideology in what might be termed "lip service." It legitimizes and at the same time denies an equalitarian ideology. Part of its narrative is to propound tenets of equalitarianism while repudiating it in practice through exclusion.

This act of inclusion/exclusion, now that almost everyone can attain signs of the many and varied classes, takes on a subtle understanding of the importance of signs themselves. To wear a certain piece of clothing or own a certain commodity within a certain social field is not enough. A person must have an understanding of the importance of this clothing or commodity as a sign and thus the importance of the correct type, or the correct time — in the case of clothing, this means the correct shade, style, fit, and so forth. This need for the understanding of signs goes beyond commodities to actions, such as gait, stance, and speech — which means not only knowing the correct vocabulary for the field, but also the correct usage of the terms for the field and what to speak of, or not to speak of, and how to speak of it (that is, the correct opinions).

Privileged ideologies, using inclusion/exclusion within social fields, construct hegemonies controlling the discourse and create the rules to the language games that influence and decide what might count as social and cultural capital. A privileged ideology, through habitus (ideology plus practice), perpetuates the importance of signs as capital in gaining a power positions within the social fields. This power position within a field makes of itself a social situation and, through discourses distributes power, allowing or disallowing agency. Agency allows a person or persons to act on their own behalf or others to gain access to life chances.

Equalitarian ideology is the binary opposite of privileged ideology. Equalitarian ideology demands fairness and thus the dismantling of a power position within a social field. It is based on the metanarrative of all humans being equal, of fair play on a truly even playing field. A truly equalitarian ideology must open space within the field for minority and gendered players. Equalitarian ideology denies capital in all its forms except for actions and performance (not to be confused with performativity), which is an underlying reason why professional athletes are so revered by working-class people, yet considered selfish when they demand exorbitant salaries. A "good name" for a person of an equalitarian ideology does not come from lineage, but from correct, honest, and sometimes heroic actions. This "good name" becomes more important than power.

For persons or characters situated somewhere on the continuum between equalitarian and privileged (meaning in the majority of people and characters in literature other than those created to espouse some socialistic theory), a tension develops between adhering to and perpetuating, or denying, the language games of a social field. For those nearer to the equalitarian pole this tension results in a negative attitude toward playing the game, passing down this attitude through habitus. Because these individuals do not instruct the next generation on the importance of the use of signs, the next generation becomes inept at "playing the game." Resistance to playing the game is also passed down. These propensities allow those leaning more toward a privileged ideology to separate themselves from those of equalitarian ideologies.

This text has been working toward an understanding of these differing ideologies. It questions any category placing an author or book into a canon titled "working-class literature," but contends that, rather than attempting to shoehorn authors or books into ill-fitting, ill-conceived categories, all books might be subjected to a class reading, as all books can be subjected to feminist, African American, Native American, and LBGT and alternative theoretical readings. As with any theory, a book may not be germane to the theoretical position. For class this would mean little or no separation of people into groups. A book that contains depictions of class (meaning almost all literature) may be subjected to a class reading. This reading can produce insight into the workings of class — in the case of the working class, how class is played out external to a stereotypical socialist paradigm or labor versus capital. A piece of literature may also represent the working class in a negative or stereotypical way, creating caricatures rather than rounded characters whose attributes reflect real-life people.

Stereotyping, while seemingly obvious, is usually the most difficult aspect to discover because of Marxism's hegemony within class studies. Marxism has created criteria demanding that working-class characters be stereotyped. As seen in Melville's "Tartarus of Maids," the female characters worked in a factory, but beyond this setting, no other criteria is presented to judge them as representations of working-class people. Other works have been written purposely to espouse a Marxist view and take as a starting point the assumed stereotyped characters as the correct interpretations of the working class. As seen in the analyses of the characters presented in *Life in the Iron Mills*, the supposedly positive viewpoint is actually a negative one. This new theory of class in literature allows for the consideration of texts by exposing narratives of class that perpetuate hegemonic discourses or alternate discourses; a working-class or class reading can expose the real workings of class and how class, through power, can give or deny access to life chances.

A text under consideration might be approached in several ways, such as internally (the fictive world as a representation of the real world) or externally (the text as an ideological product produced to disseminate class ideology or some sociopolitical point of view). This point of view is usually not consciously illustrated in the text, but is still very much present. However, a text written to espouse a point of view concerning class is probably already at fault in certain ways and would garner a negative class reading. Instead, the job is to discover the underlying ideological influence on the text.

To really study class within the fictive world of the text, or to subject a story to a class reading, is to discover the social fields within the text where class is contested and to ask the following questions:

What might be the major and controlling discourses and language games played out in the text?

How do they legitimize truths, and what are these truths?

How do they establish a power position configuring the criteria for inclusion/exclusion and further legitimize the discourses and power position?

What social, cultural, and symbolic capital are presented within the constructed social fields of the text?

How is power manifested within the social fields through discourses?

How do the discourses distribute power throughout the fields? Who wields it and whom is it wielded against?

How does power influence the characters?

How does it place characters as Subject/subject?

How do characters play out their roles through performativity, agency, and resistance to the power of the field?

A major concern is uncovering the ideologies of the characters of the text and placing them within the continuum between the two metanarratives where each character's ideology and identity is shown through their actions, reactions, and dialogue within a social field. This might be shown through their performativity toward the legitimate discourses of the field. The manifestations of signs showing privilege or equalitarian ideologies will need to be discovered, including the following:

The use or denial of social capital;

A character's attempt to position him- of herself within a power network to gain agency, whether successfully or unsuccessfully;

The use of power or a power position to produce an advantageous position, a power network denying agency to a character or the resistance to a power network within a field in an attempt to gain agency.

External to the Text

A text can also be looked at as a product of a discourse within a social field. A text might elucidate the discourses, social field, and the powers and ideologies within that field. In an approach closer to New Historicism than Marxism, the text might be questioned as to its representation of differing classes as a way to reinforce certain ideologies. This becomes a more complex and complicated reading. In *Life in the Iron Mills*, Davis seems to explore the victimization of the working class in the West Virginia iron works, when she is, in actuality, attempting to shore up discourses of the "moral" middle class and the contradictions within them — that is, to explain an ideology that allows for a moral position while exploiting or allowing the working class to be exploited. By positioning the people of the working class as children or somehow slightly lower on the evolutionary scale, yet still human, she reclaims the moral high ground of the middle class, reconstituting the truths of the middle-class discourses by separating the classes intellectually, and thus she reclaims the middle-class discourses from their contradictions and repositions the middle class within the sphere of power in the large social field.

A reading of this type might first consider:

The social viewpoint the text is attempting to present. What seems to be the overall thrust of the text?

How the text develops or shows the characters and the classes, and how those characters interact.

A reading might also question the narrator's position to the classes of the book. If the narrator is first person, how does the author depict him or her? If the narrator is third person how does this narrator react to the characters, the situation, and the actions of the characters?

A reading might investigate the relationship of the author's social field to the field of the narrator, and the connection of both to the field of the characters to see how they play off one another or give clues to the discourses of the social fields affecting the author's writing. As an example, an author may be writing against the dominant discourses of a social field, yet be caught up within a discourse of another social field, such as an author writing against the discourses of capitalism only to be caught up within a socialist or Marxist metanarrative that disallows the true development of a character, instead stereotyping both character and situation.

A reading should notice any underlying narratives permeating the text with ideological viewpoints, sometime contradictory to the supposed thrust of the text itself. It should likewise question any type of capital seemingly important to the author, and reconsider whether the text truly does show working-class people in a fair light as individuals as different from each other as they are from people of other classes.

Chapter 6

A Working-Class Reading of *Maggie: A Girl of the Streets* and *The Great Gatsby*

A major argument of this text that has not yet been fully addressed is whether literature can or should actually represent "real" people. Many scholars will argue against literature having to represent reality in any form; however, this statement is not really accurate. At some level literature has to make sense to the reader, even if a tree might speak or a horse might have interiority. People commonly personify inanimate objects in real life and anthropomorphization is a common occurrence in literature, especially children's literature (although it is not uncommon in adult literature). What this suggests is that at some level, humans need to recognize and associate themselves and their lives with the characters of a work. Although the "reality" of the story may be set in some fantastic world of dragons, demons, and fairies, or in a future world, the actions, thoughts, and reactions must reflect a certain concept of verisimilitude of the readers based on prototypes the reader has constructed through the intersecting of ideology and schema used to narrate his or her self and world. As the previous chapters have argued, for academics studying working-class literature, this literature "represents the lived experiences" of the working class. Too many times, though, representations of the working class have been stereotypical. Rather than attempting to create actual representations of working-class people, the authors have attempted to create banners for a cause whether they are knowledgeable of a situation or misinformed. Authors have also written to a "genre"—a literary or editorial expectation of what a piece of working-class literature should read like with expected plots, characters, situations, and meanings all coming out of an entrenched Marxist paradigm. Using literature to represent people as a stultified class has no real legitimacy in literature studies, but at a certain level characters in literature must represent realistic human attributes, which casts doubt on the idea that literature need not represent real people. Real people find narratives of identity within literature through, first, the ideological aspect of literature, and second, the narrative aspect of identity. If what Margaret Somers proposes is true, humans narrate their identity into existence through available choices within a social structure, meaning that literature of all kinds supplies raw material for the stories used to "tell" "selves" into existence.

The stories people tell themselves to construct complex and multiple identities can be influenced by literature when literature contributes to the language game through adding new rules — new ways of creating plots, characters (identities), and themes in life. "Narrative can order our thoughts and real-world experiences by offering a mimetic parallel to our own lives" (Oatley 60). Oatley correctly states, "Literature exists on 'a spectrum.' At one end is transportation: fiction can be an escape, the pleasurable occupation of time. At the other end is transformation: fiction can change the self" (42). Literature affects people because it provides alternate narratives in a world of limited narratives while reinforcing existing narratives. Whether or not literature represents reality faithfully, it does add rules to the language game of self-narration and social structure. Literature may also illuminate the inconsistencies or paradoxes inherent in social structures of a given time or place. Literature, when it is not deliberate propaganda of a sociopolitical theory attempting to establish the authority of a discourse, elucidates the complexity of class and identity in the real world.

Classes, as Bourdieu contends, are separated by difference. Thus a way to recognize classes in literature without reverting to the constraints of a Marxist prototype is to consider how characters react within social fields set up within the text. Using the existence of social fields as a starting point (configuring class as a play of difference), many texts, even those seemingly not directly concerned with class issues, have clues of class difference throughout in the actions and reactions of one class to another, between characters in the plot, or in the way the author constructs both. A text such as *Sister Carrie*, when unpacked using this working-class theory, shows concern with the dissemination and appropriation of the signs of class. Although Dreiser does not directly allude to Carrie being concerned with appearance as cultural capital, Carrie is constantly concerned with the appropriation of signs of class. Dreiser states of Carrie after she has left her sister and moved into an apartment supplied by Drouet, not a bit worried about the social stigma of being a kept woman, "Carrie's state was remarkable in that she saw the possibilities in it. [...] Carrie was an apt student of fortune's ways — of fortune's superficialities. Seeing a thing, she would immediately set to inquiring how she would look, properly related to it" (74, 99).

Rebecca Harding Davis' *Life in the Iron Mills* is not just about the working class, but is also unconsciously concerned with the paradoxes in "upper-class" ideology. As a member of the upright and moral middle class, Davis, like her narrator, is morally bound to help those persons whom she feels are below her and believes are, in certain ways, immoral. She is not so much attempting to change the working conditions, as Upton Sinclair was in *The Jungle*, as attempting to save souls. The factory workers' actions allow Davis to place the workers into a class somehow less human than her own class. She actually categorizes class through the physical levels of living in the boarding house — the Wolfes in the basement, her narrator on the top floor looking down, albeit benevolently. Henry James writes about the paradox inherent in a class positioning itself as morally superior to other classes because of birth. Winterbourne's judgments of the title character in *Daisy Miller* create a paradox in which he, a person of upstanding moral virtue, judges her as somehow from a lower class than himself, making the love he feels for her impossible to bring to fruition. The paradox for Winterbourne is that, by assuming his superiority, he shows his inferiority.

Maggie: A Girl of the Streets a Study in Class Theory

Steven Crane's *Maggie: A Girl of the Streets*, whether considered canonical literature, as are his other works, such as *The Red Badge of Courage* and "The Open Boat," has been touted as a representation of the working class in the Bowery of New York City and other cities in America mainly because *Maggie: A Girl of the Streets* lends itself well to Marxist readings. For Marx, in a capitalistic system, because of the trend toward accumulation through competition, and labor being a cost of competition, the expenditure of capital on labor should only be enough to maintain the labor force. "Capital cares nothing for the length of the life of labor power [laborer]. All that concerns it is simply and solely the maximum of labor power that can be rendered fluent in a work day" (Marx and Engels, *Basic Writings* 148). This is the Marxist background of *Maggie: A Girl of the Streets*.

For Marxists the Bowery is a place where little capital is spent maintaining the labor force, and violence and struggle are the norms. In a Marxist reading of *Maggie: A Girl of the Streets*, the reader is presented with the working class as a proto-class only just beginning to become aware of things. This proto-proletariat is a section of humanity produced by capitalism, maintained at the level of existence, and sedated by false thought material, thus producing a false ideology.[1] Thus their "consciousness is [...] a social product" and their "life is not determined by consciousness, but consciousness by life" (Marx and Engels, *German* 57). The proletariat, Marx's working class, consisted of people employed in manufacturing for wages, "a class of laborers, who live only so long as they can find work, and who find work only so long as their labor increases capital" (Marx and Engels, "Manifesto," 14). These workers, by attaining class consciousness, would enter into political struggles with the bourgeoisie, ultimately creating the revolution many Marxists believed was on the historical agenda.

In the opening paragraphs a young Jimmy is standing on a rubble pile, defending it for the honor of Rum Alley. Marx believes that "the proletariat goes through various stages of development. [...] The organization [...] into a class [...] is continually being upset [...] by the competition between the workers themselves" (Marx and Engels, "Manifesto," 15). Marx also believed the lack of power in the working class was due to the lack of a class consciousness. Once the proletariat class united and the power of the capitalists was waning due to competition and attrition, the proletariat would rise up and create a new world order. The people of the Bowery in Crane's fictive world have yet to attain a class consciousness. They are an incoherent mass "struggling against each, other as of yet not a class" (Marx and Engels, "Manifesto," 15).

According to Marx, the violence perpetrated on the proletariat by the bourgeoisie manifests itself through one worker to another. Life for workers at the bottom is violent and they react to it with violence, but they have no focus for this violence. This, to Maggie, is life. She has no other example with which to compare her existence. "All family ties among the proletarians are torn asunder" (Marx and Engels, "Manifesto," 25).

This violence is mediated by the false thought material perpetuated within the Bowery. Engels states,

> Ideology is a process accomplished by the so-called thinker consciously, it is true but with a false consciousness. The real motive forces compelling him remain unknown to him. [...] Hence he imagines false or seeming motive forces. [...] He works with mere thought material which he accepts without examination as the product of thought ["To Franz Mehring" 408].

Pete takes Maggie to a burlesque show where a ventriloquist "held two fantastic dolls on his knees. He made them sing mournful ditties and say funny things about geography and Ireland" (Crane 23). According to Marx, this is the bourgeoisie's attempt to disseminate false thought material. The bourgeoisie are not only pulling the strings of the lower classes but also providing their voice. Although Jimmy, at moments, has a sense of community (a collective consciousness, according to Marx), competition in the marketplace undercuts this sense. Maggie becomes the commodity being bargained and fought over.

The obvious problem with this reading, and indigenous to many Marxist readings, is the complete ignoring of agency by authors of the close reading, or the argument that somehow ignorance is equal to innocence. Once ignorance is separated from innocence and agency is given to the characters, a Marxist reading loses its heroic construct. Jimmy and Pete become nothing but small-time criminals and brutal toughs, Maggie a whore, and Jimmy and Maggie's parents something vile and less than human. However, if the text is considered a product of a set of competing discourses within mulitple social fields promoting and working within different sets of metanarratives, thus producing different ideological perspectives on competing hegemonies vying for a power position within several social fields, many completely different readings might exist that would allow for complexity of character and identity not dependent on a dichotomy of innocence/corrupt or a reading outside the text considering the impetus of the writing and publication of the text.

As stated in chapter 5, several close readings of a text might exist interior to the text, helping to unpack the text as a representation of real life. A reading can also be done exterior to the text, exploring the text as a product of discourses within social fields. Two readings will be done for *Maggie: A Girl of the Streets*. The first reading will be interior, considering how Maggie, Jimmy, and Pete negotiate their identities within the social fields, and with and against the discourses and narratives presented to them. The second, an exterior reading, will explore the origins of the text as a cultural artifact.

When considering a work of a different epoch, consideration must be given to the prevailing metanarratives of the time and alternative metanarratives, and how these construct differing ideologies. Thus a working-class or middle-class ideology of the last century will differ from the ideologies manifested within these classes today. However, aspects of the ideologies will be similar, especially in the knowledge and use of social, cultural, and symbolic capital, and also in the skill, or lack thereof, in negotiating power networks within the existing social fields. Since the discourses will be different, the social fields will also be different from those existing today.

The major social field existing in the text seems a brutal one. This brutality is perpetuated not by one social field, or one discourse, but by overlaying fields and competing and irreconcilable metanarratives. Within a page of her introduction in the novel, Maggie is being beaten by her brother and is cursing him back. Her mother beats her brother when he gets home, soon followed by an all-out battle with her husband as Jimmy and Maggie quickly hunt for places to hide. After Pete "ruins" Jimmy's sister, Jimmy and a friend hunt down Pete and brawl in the bar where Pete is employed, almost destroying it.

A clash, a misalignment of narratives and reality, exists. This clash is created through habitus and the popular entertainment of the day, which contend that the correct way to live is with honor, demanding justice. Because of this misalignment, people of the Bowery like Jimmy and Pete have difficulty reconciling their beliefs with the reality demanding survival at the cost of honor. Several times Jimmy questions the inconsistencies within these narratives. When Jimmy's father steals the pail of beer Jimmy returned with for a neighbor woman, Jimmy says, "Ah come off! I got dis can for dat ol' woman an' it 'ud be dirt teh swipe it" (Crane 11). Although unable to develop his thoughts into a coherent philosophy, Jimmy understands that what has been done is somehow morally wrong, but his father, needing alcohol and not having the money to acquire it, automatically takes it from his son. Later in the story Jimmy again questions the disparity between the discourses and reality when he thinks maybe "it wasn't common courtesy for a friend to come to one's home and ruin one's sister. But he was not sure how much Pete knew about the rules of politeness. [...] It occurred to him to vaguely wonder, for an instant, if some of the women of his acquaintance had brothers" (31–32). This conundrum is not unknown today for those males who find womanizing an easy way to bolster their self-esteem — a type of honorific pursuit, albeit dishonorable.

The social fields of the Bowery have been created by opposing discourses, paradoxically created within the discourses of privileged metanarratives. The first discourse demands honorific pursuits, a public display of prowess, whether in combat or love. This display becomes even more important since little ability exists to garner and display other types of capital. However, this middle-class ideology, when mixed with a working-class ideology demanding honesty, or that actions be honorable (not honorific), creates a type of schizophrenia in characters such as Pete, Jimmy, Maggie, and their parents. For women the middle-class discourse of the time leaves little agency, with honor being contained in the female body itself, while the female body is a commodity that might have exchange value. The working-class ideology, though, seems more practical.

"Jimmy publicly damned his sister that he might appear on a higher social plane. But arguing with himself, stumbling about in ways that he knew not, he, once, almost came to a conclusion that his sister would have been more firmly good had she better known why" (42). Maggie misunderstood the narratives, the rules of the game and her place as a pretty, but poor, girl in the social field. In the world of this text, the metanarratives disseminated throughout the Bowery are of romance and sentimentality. Within the plays and dancehall music, Crane demonstrates the tenets of these metanarratives. Of the shallow melodramatic plays Crane writes, "To Maggie and the rest of the audience this was transcendental realism. Joy always within, and they, like the actor, inevitably without" (27).

These metanarratives enable these people, with little positive in their lives, to construct an identity enabling them to confront the reality of their subject/Subject position through not confronting it, and instead of using these narratives to construct a romantic identity. Pizer, speaking of Crane's "intense verbal irony," proposes "Crane suggests that the idea of honor is inappropriate to reality [in the Bowery], that it serves to disguise from the participants in the fight [...] that they are engaged in a vicious and petty scuffle" (Pizer, "Stephen," 187–88). They are not dishonorable. They conduct themselves as honorably as possible, but "since there are no meaningful alternatives to a life of violence, conventional notions of morality are without application" (Fitelson 110). Their morality (ideology) must be adapted to the reality of their lives, mediated by their narratives.

The impasse precipitating Maggie's "fall" is shaped by an ideology created from two contradictory and irreconcilable metanarratives existing in the Bowery. The discourse of the ideology contends that one should act honorably even though opportunities to do so are few. This romantic metanarrative is counterproductive to negotiating an existence in the reified reality of the Bowery. Thus Pizer's Bowery knights fight many battles to secure the romantic illusion, the largest battle being resistance to their subject position by the dominant ideology, one they do not understand. Pizer believes that "Crane's irony emerges out of a difference between a value which one imposes on experience and the nature of experience itself" (Pizer, "Stephen," 187). He argues that the values the Johnsons apply to their situation come from middle-class discourses hiding the "truth" of their situation from them. These values are disseminated by ideological apparatus such as the reformists' tracts, the melodramatic plays, and sentimental songs.

To Jimmy and especially to Pete, one's public identity becomes very important, particularly within a subject/Subject paradigm. Consumed with being the chivalrous knight, Pete does not start out by subjugating Maggie and treats her very well, partially because she reaffirms his beliefs about himself. By treating her well he likewise reaffirms his position as the chivalrous knight within the local social field, placing him closer to the power structures. Maggie invests Pete with the symbolic value of a knight, also elevating his subject position. She thought "his mannerisms stamped him as a man who had a correct sense of his own superiority" (17). He also reasserts her romantic beliefs by posing as the knight. He takes Maggie to places to be seen by people and leaves her once Nell discounts his subject position when discounting Maggie's subject position, contending that Maggie is only a little maiden hardly worth fighting for.

When Pete rejects Maggie for the second time, Maggie finally sees the reality beyond the imaginary and not, as Gandal suggests, the reality of her condition, just before she kills herself (768). "Astonishment swept over the girl's features. [...] 'But where kin I go?' [...] She wandered aimlessly for several blocks. She stopped once and asked aloud a question to herself: 'Who?'" (Crane 50). Notably, she does not ask Pete who might take her in. Nor does she ask of herself where she might go. She can only be asking herself who she might become. The romantic narrative given to her through the dominant middle-class metanarrative has been found to be false. The real world is laid out before her and she becomes aware of her devalued position within the social fields. This is her epiphany.

The last words of Chapter XVII, the last the reader sees of Maggie, state that "the various sounds of life, made joyous by distance and seemingly unapproachableness, came faintly and died away in silence" (53). This is not Maggie's epiphany, but the author's and, hopefully, the reader's, having the romantic illusion stripped away to see the reality of Maggie's existence.

Maggie has now renarrated her self through different narratives, what Bourdieu calls "the choice of the necessary" (*Distinctions* 372). Before late modernity and postmodernity this narrative seems to have been a part of a working-class metanarrative. Yet, as Carrie does in *Sister Carrie*, Maggie develops attitudes of conspicuous consumption, part of a middle-class ideology. She has, then, moved along the continuum of class, not toward a more working-class ideology, but, by being devalued through the narrative of what constitutes female honor, she seeks to narrate herself through the discourses valuing symbolic and cultural capital, moving more toward an elitist/middle-class ideology. She does not see herself through what she does or has done, but through who she is, mediated by outward appearances.

Reconsidering Maggie's position within the social fields of the Bowery and New York City as a poverty-stricken, young and pretty girl at a time when most discourses disallowed agency to almost all women, and considering how opposing ideologies supplied inconsistent metanarratives in which to narrate a self and reality, as well as the brutality of the Bowery, the reading of Maggie's "downfall" as a prostitute and her suicide might be questioned. In a later edition of the book, Jimmy states to Maggie in a matter-of-fact way while she is still quite a young girl, "Mag, I'll tell yeh dis. See? Yeh've edder got to go to hell or go to work" (Crane 16). According to the *Norton Critical Edition of Maggie: A Girl of the Streets*, edited by Thomas A. Gullason, in the 1896 edition (an earlier edition), Jimmy says, "Go on d' toif," meaning to walk the streets. Jimmy is informing Maggie of the choices for a young woman of the Bowery. Marriage does not seem an option Jimmy has considered for his sister, maybe because his parents' marriage was akin to war and he sees it as less viable, if not less safe, than his sister becoming a prostitute. The passage questions whether Maggie's prostitution is ultimately a downfall or a choice of occupation. Though Jimmy does publicly condemn her, the condemnation is more show than fact.

The choice of prostitution might also constitute a form of resistance to the discourses of the time. Maggie's subject position as a poverty-stricken woman in the mid–19th century allows her few options: remain chaste and, for her, poor and exploited by factory owners; marry, more than likely remaining poor and exploited and abused by a husband; or become a prostitute and be publicly condemned, although, like Nell, not privately. Pragmatically choosing the third option allows her freedom from the major discourses of the major social field and gives her power in another social field. Although Maggie is exploited in the shirt-collar factory, whether she is, in a concrete sense, exploited in any worse way on the street may be debated.

Prostitution would seem to be exploitation. If, as Gandal believes, "the slum is [...] a separate moral universe" (760), then one cannot judge the morals of those in the Bowery by metanarratives developed outside the Bowery, and a woman such as Nell (and later Maggie) might be considered less a fallen woman than petite bourgeoisie. As is seen in Berger's study of working-class factory workers, and also in *Gig* and Terkel's text, "a small business of their own" was an attempt by the working class to sidestep and resist the power networks and the discourses of certain social fields. Prostitution gave Nell independence and thus must have given Maggie the same independence.

Ethics of character, of honor, seem to have been handed down, but not recognized, by those narrating their identity through a middle-class moral metanarrative. As brawling and womanizing may seem dishonorable to the middle class, prostitution may also seem dishonorable, but to others, such as Maggie and Nell, it brought a freedom allowing for a positive narration of self. Although considering a prostitute petite bourgeoisie seems a slightly outrageous assertion, to suggest prostitution in late 19th century slums was looked at in the same way it is now, with middle-class sensibilities, is also an assumption.

Gandal sees the rise in power of an alternate discourse, a movement away from the Enlightenment idea of equality toward one of privilege and aristocracy. He states, "Crane perceives an alternative morality" (759). Though the people of the Bowery lack skill in understanding and using conspicuous action and consumption as cultural capital, they do understand both as leading to self-esteem within the possibilities allowed by lack of agency. Without a hint of irony, Crane describes Nell as "a woman of brilliance and audacity" (43). Not quite the standard adjectives for a mere prostitute. At the end of the story Maggie seems to be, if not capable of reaching the "brilliance" of Nell, then at least a reasonable facsimile of her, and the only true difference between the two, as characters, is the middle-class symbolism of purity and innocence invested in Maggie by readers.

Jimmy's suggestion to Maggie to become either a factory girl or a prostitute undercuts the idea of the suicide in the East River. The reader gets little reflection of what Maggie is feeling before her end and must infer these thoughts from her last moments. Because a tradition existed in 19 century sentimental literature of a fallen woman contemplating suicide — a strict tenet of the genre — this ending is usually foregrounded. Jimmy's suggestion lends credence to her death being homicide by questioning her supposed, and conjectured, shame through lending credence to the notion that prostitution was a legitimate alternative to working in a factory.

David Fitelson sees *Maggie: A Girl of the Streets* as Darwinistic in that only the fittest survive, using Jimmy and Pete as examples of adaptation and Maggie as "merely an instance of self-destruction and failure" (110). This interpretation assumes that Maggie kills herself because she sees her life as a failure of character, but if, as Gandal perceives, an alternate morality (ideology) exists and Maggie no longer perceives her reality within a middle-class moralistic paradigm, but narrates her self through a discourse of privilege, of character, based on social, cultural, and symbolic capital, then suicide seems less logical as an ending. If her death is homicide, the suggestion of Maggie as failure is put in doubt. Certainly she was not a financial failure. She is described as "bending forward in her handsome cloak, daintily lifting her skirts and picking for her well-shod feet the dryer spots upon the pavements" (52).

The penultimate chapter, which includes Maggie's death and "the fat man," was left out of several editions. Joseph Katz believes the reason for the omission of this chapter and several sentences from the preceding chapter is that they "make the fact of her prostitution inescapable" — too inescapable for the editors and readers (195). Parker and Higgins contend that Appleton, the editor of the 1896 edition, "ultimately removes the focus from her degradation so that she hardly seems more than incidental to Crane's depiction of the evils of the Bowery" (239). The removal of the penultimate chapter, then, was intended to bring the book more into line with the slum genre of the time.

"The varied sounds of life, made joyous by distance and seeming unapproachableness, came faintly and died away to a silence" (Crane 53). This is the last sentence written of Maggie's life. This passage is meant to point to Maggie's disillusionment, but it hardly seems strong enough to indicate that Maggie was distraught enough to kill herself. She had much more reason to kill herself when Pete left her or when she was sent away from her mother's home. The death of Maggie at the hands of the fat man seems as plausible as suicide and also better fits a story whose underlying premise is the incompatibility of ideologies, their effect on identity, and the manifestation of power by a corrupt society. "When almost to the river, the girl saw a great figure. On going forward she perceived it to be a huge fat man in torn and greasy garments. [...] Chuckling and sneering he followed the girl of the crimson legions" (53). If the fat man has any non-symbolic purpose in the story, this purpose must be to kill Maggie.

Crane's descriptions of the fat man and the factory owner are similar. The fat man wore "torn and greasy garments. His gray hair straggled down over his forehead. His small, bleared eyes, sparkling from amidst great rolls of red fat [...] his brown, disordered teeth gleaming under a gray, grizzled moustache" (Crane 53). The proprietor of the factory "was a detestable creature" (25). Maggie "felt she would love to see somebody entangle their fingers in the oily beard of the fat foreigner who owned the establishment" (25). Both the fat man and the factory owner are manifestations of power and power networks. Configuring the factory owner as a representation of capitalism stretches the evidence in the text beyond the point of believability. He is, by a Marxist account, not truly a capitalist — that is, the reader does not have enough evidence to assume he is a capitalist — although he can be seen as a representation of the capitalistic system. He could very well be a petite bourgeoisie. Maggie hates him because of the power he wields over her and her lack of power in this social field. The fat man might be seen as a representation of society — a fat, bloated, truly ugly, man lusting after what is beautiful and innocent (in a way Maggie is still innocent of the knowledge of society at the time of her death), not to possess it, but to exercise complete power over it — to destroy.

The second reading of *Maggie: A Girl of the Streets* is external of the text. As Lukács contends, literature is a product of an ideology. It is produced by the discourses within multiple social fields to disseminate certain metanarratives supporting specific ideological positions within fields, often in competition with other ideologies, to gain and control power within multiple social fields. Literature, then, is created through discourses within a dominant ideology, or within another subordinate ideology contesting or supporting the hegemony of the field. "Possibly the most arresting critical problem posed by Stephen Crane's first novel is that of the disposition of mind that lies behind and shapes it — ideology, so to speak, that it communicates" (Fitelson 108).

From a working-class theoretical perspective two external readings of *Maggie* are possible. One reading questions the text as a product of a hegemonic discourse disseminating certain narrative truths and promoting a certain ideological position, such as those in the mid–19 century attempting to gain authority in the American literary world by challenging the hegemony of the parameters of what might be called "literary" in American literature through the promotion of realism, and later naturalism. The other reading positions *Maggie* as an ideological product seeking to disseminate discourses from within the text that address the ills of late 19 century society while maintaining the dominance of middle-class morality.

Crane is sometimes extolled as the first American naturalist, if not one of the first realists. However, the style of *Maggie* is not realism or naturalism, and it is probably not a hybrid form, but a very dark slum novel written before Crane was famous and republished later in his career; it was received not so much for its literary genius, which is still doubted, but because it fit into three social-political discourses of the time. The first discourse concerns the hegemonic struggle of a group of literati — Howells, Garland, and others — trying to gain and control power in and over the production of American literature. "The freedom promised to him by Alden [*Harpers*] [...] presented just the opportunity that Howells could use at that time to develop and broadcast his growing interest in realism" (Lutwack 195).

The second discourse is a set of narratives seen in the popular sentimental novel's functional bent of the reformist movement. Although *Maggie* was deemed vulgar at the time, it found champions among the reformists. Finally, *Maggie* was written and published during a crisis in the middle class's moral ideology and thus is concerned with the reconstruction of the truths of the discourses of the moral middle class. "The cornerstone of [middle-class morality] was the supremacy of the moral sense over all other aspects of the mind" (Gandal 761).

Frow explains, "The process of literary evolution occurs in two contradictory ways: discontinuously, through the production of deviant forms of textuality, and continuous, through the reproduction of the literary norm" (105). At the time of *Maggie*'s publication, Romanticism, in its sentimental form of romance found in women's popular literature, stood against the idealistic realism of Howells, James, Twain, and others establishing a foothold in literary culture. *Maggie: A Girl of the Streets* is purposefully praised by Howells, who proposes that the story is not sentimental literature, but realism. He states, "[Crane] never shows his characters or his situations in any sort of sentimental glamour" (155). Donald Pizer believes that Howells finds similarity between his critical realism and Crane's naturalism in "a belief in the social function of the novel in delineating the evils of social life" (Pizer, "Stephen," 193).

Maggie: A Girl of the Streets was first published at the expense of the author, sold little and had very mixed reviews; many reviews, such as Hamlin Garland's, were negative. Only after Howells championed the novel did it find a publisher and notice. *Maggie*'s canonical status, then, has more to do with Howells' political leanings than *Maggie*'s literariness. "Between the years 1889 and 1894 [...] the major novels of William Dean Howells were markedly economic and even socialistic in their criticism of American life" (Arms 260). George Arms suggests Lawrence Gronlund, "a leading member of the Socialist Labor Party," was a major influence on Howells. "Yet the significance of Gronlund on Howells is that he influenced Howells' philosophy and not his literary form" (261, 263). Daniel Aaron believes Howells "balked at the prospect of filling in the sordid backgrounds" of the type of realism he championed in writers such as Garland, Norris, and Crane (89). "As editor and assistant editor [of *Harpers*] Howells both decided on the publication of such articles [socialist] and must have been stimulated by them" (Arms 265).

Crane's novel may have had much of its success not because it is an exemplary example of naturalism or critical realism, but because it appeared in its tenement literature form at a very opportune time for such work, a time when several different hegemonies in literature were contesting the position of the dominant narratives. Crane, by the time of *Maggie*'s second publishing, had garnered notice as the author of *The Red Badge of Courage* and Howells was a powerful editor with an ideological ax to grind.

Howells' agenda was the writing and promotion of realism. As Frow states, "Textual events are not arbitrary in relation to the system which structures their occurrence" (1). Although Crane may have originally written *Maggie* as an impulse to elucidate a condition within America he felt needed to be brought to light, "environment is a tremendous thing," and its canonical standing, its subsequent second publication, depended more on how it fit into the discourse of Howells' realism than its literary merit (Crane 132). *Maggie* thus became an ideological apparatus for those promoting realism.

Howells asserted that *Maggie*, rather than being a clichéd product of slum literature, was a work of high art. Howells says of *Maggie*, "Another effect [of Crane's] is that of an ideal of an artistic beauty which is as present in the working out of this poor girl's squalid romance as in any classic fable. This will be foolishness, I know, to the foolish people who cannot discriminate between the material and the treatment of art" (154).

Yet Keith Gandal believes *Maggie* is "a story about temptation, fall and remorse," several tropes indigenous to slum literature (760). Frank Norris writes:

> Good though the story is and told in Mr. Crane's catching style, the impression left with the reader is one of hurry, the downfall of Maggie, the motif of

the tale, strikes one as handled in a manner almost too flippant for the seriousness of the subject. [...] The reader is apt to feel the author is writing, as it were, from the outside [151].

If the idea that *Maggie* is realism might be contested, *Maggie* as sentimental literature might also be contested. Solomon believes, "*Maggie* involves a complete reversal of the sentimental themes of the 19 century best sellers that dealt with the life of a young girl" (117). Yet Cunliffe contends, "Crane's sources might lie [...] in the mass of literature produced by Americans on the evils of slum life: ill-health, intemperance, immorality, and the like" (94). The textual evidence seems to suggest Crane's short novel is sentimental or slum/tenement literature.

As discourses are concerned with the production of ideology, ideology is concerned with "the production and the conditions of production of categories and entities within the field of discourse" (Frow 61). Certain discourses will exist in certain ideologies, and vice versa. Sentimental literature is a very visible example of just this condition in American literature. Because of the "cult of economic masculinity"—masculinity judged by wealth and influence perpetrated by men working outside the home, brought on by the rise of industrialism in the 19th century—the nonworking wives and daughters of an affluent male became a symbol of his masculinity. Although most families did not achieve this affluent status, with many women doing "putting-out" work, this status ideal became part of the ideology of the time, as did conspicuous consumption and the importance of social, cultural, and symbolic capital. Women came to be looked upon as frivolous, lazy, and irresponsible—essentially large children. Women lost any power and agency they once had. In the 19th century women were not only restrained from writing certain types of literature but also from reading literature that men thought did not fit their nature. The sentimental novel was among the allowable literature.[2]

Although Joanne Dobson takes a rather high road in defining sentimental literature, forgetting or ignoring how it is tied intimately to regenerating narrow middle-class morality (including the repression, if not the oppression, of women), she does make some claims that ring true.[3] Sentimental literature of the 19th century has, for the most part, not been considered literary until recently. "Long castigated as inferior aesthetically and intellectually to other literary movements such as romanticism and realism, sentimentalism is now recognized on its own terms and for its enormous cultural and literary influence" (Harris 606). Dobson believes that "sentimental writing can be seen in a significant number of instances to process a conventional sentimental aesthetics," depending on "an idiom whose tropes are designed to elicit feelings of empathy and concern, and whose language, like the language of realism, is intended to communicate meaning with minimal impediment" (265, 268). However, "it is a mistake to ignore the origin of the sentimental novel, especially its ideological foundation which must be seen alongside its literary nature" (Hansen 41). Dobson does not argue that all texts falling under the designation of sentimental literature are of literary quality, stating that they may run the spectrum of quality from stereotypical and formulaic to using the genre to elucidate the human condition in insightful ways (Dobson 268). These sentimental tropes "often serve as vehicles for depictions of all too-common social tragedies and political outrages stemming from the failure of society to care for the disconnected" (Dobson 272).[4] This impetus, however, is tied directly to the discourse of the moral middle class in maintaining "a middle-class culture and ideology" and its effort to retain a power position within a social field (Hansen 41).

After the Second Great Awakening (1800–1830s), revivalism became rampant in America, calling for active participation in society through "good works." The reformist movement came out of the ideology of this time as much as it did out of need. It was the physical manifestation of the belief of the middle class that they held the moral high ground in America. Since most workers in these movements were women, reformist writings were developed within the women's genre — sentimental literature — thus the existence of the slum or tenement novel as a sub-genre of sentimental literature.

In the slum story of the late 19 century, the young woman "undergoes an internal transformation as she succumbs to her passions or transcends them with her will" (Gandal 760). In the average slum novel the innocent girl is seduced, usually by a middle-class male, and left to deal with the consequences. "Sullivan's *Tenement Tales of New York* includes two stories about slum women. [...] In both stories the women contemplate suicide," with one having her seducer propose marriage, while the other goes through with the act (Gandal 763). Sullivan states of the suicide in his novel, "She had chosen between death and degradation. So I rejoiced with her and her choice" (qtd. in Gandal 763).

Understanding the ideology and historical background surrounding *Maggie* becomes important in deciphering any meaning of the text. Attempting to explain away the vagueness of character development in the story, Robert Stallman claims, "*Maggie* is a tone painting rather than a realistic photograph of slum life, but it opened the door to the Norris-Dreiser-Farrell school of sociological realism" (xix). Yet Cunliffe states, "It could be said that this [suicide] is a naturalist convention. Possibly, but is it not, even more, a moralist convention" (100). Edward Bright, in condemning *Maggie* as an "immature effort," states that the slum in sentimental slum literature is "either

[...] a locale replete with the raw material of sentiment, or it is a battleground of unspeakable sordidness, a loathsome pit infested by monsters in human form" (152).

Importantly, "value systems have the function of realizing relations of power" (Frow 60). Crane's *Maggie* reconstitutes the ideological moral imperative of the middle class in a world where contradictions in the truths of the discourses of the middle class help create a crisis within the ideological makeup of this class. Charles Loring Brace, in "The Dangerous Classes of New York and Twenty Years' Work Among Them" (1872), commenting on the vagrants of the slums, contends that "there is no reality in the sentimental assertion that the sexual sins of a lad are as degrading as those of a girl. The instinct of the female is more toward the preservation of purity" (66). This is obviously a sexist comment, but one elucidating the feelings and narratives of the period. Because the female "child" was symbolically invested with all that was pure, only through death or marriage (a sort of death) could she be redeemed.

As a "grown child," a woman was invested with the "heart," and thus became the keeper of Christian morality and all that was good and missing in post–Industrial Revolution America. Reform, then, took on the imperative of reconstituting a middle-class ideology, and other than being left to the religious reformists, this reconstitution became the profession of sociologists such as Jacob Riis, stating, "If it shall appear that the suffering and the sins of the 'other half,' and the evil they breed, are but as a just punishment upon the community that gave it no other choice, it will be because that is the truth" (Riss 76). Yet the "spectacle" of this debauchery and the final punishment for the loss of innocence, in such stories as *Maggie*, "served to define middle-class authority" (Schocket 111). The slum novel not only illuminates the problems in the ideological makeup of the middle class but texts such as *Maggie* also reinforced this ideology with the promise of fit and just punishment. *Maggie*, then, fit into a preconceived genre while also evolving enough to be of use by those (Howells and others) promoting realism, yet not enough to undercut the purposes of slum literature — to pressure reform while maintaining a middle-class ideological moral authority.

A Class Reading of *The Great Gatsby*

The Great Gatsby is considered one of the finest examples of contemporary American literature. It is also Fitzgerald's condemnation of modern American society, or, more specifically the American class system and the discourses perpetuating it, especially metanarratives promoting the belief of a classless society located in the discourses perpetuating the myth of the American Dream. *The Great Gatsby* contends that the discourses arguing for a classless society are more damaging to the American people than those discourses admitting that class exists in America. The characters in *The Great Gatsby* move through social fields, attempting to negotiate locations within the fields to align themselves with positions of power. The great irony of the story is that Nick never realizes he, almost as much as Tom and Daisy, is culpable for Gatsby's death through his perpetuation of the discourses of class.

Unlike *Maggie: A Girl of the Streets*, written within the genre of slum literature, toward a sociopolitical point of view, thus creating caricatures rather than realistic characters, *The Great Gatsby* attempts to capture the essence of people of a certain place, more social than geographical, between World War I and before the Great Depression. Within this social milieu Fitzgerald proposes that many classes exist within a matrix of class positions rather than in a straight Marxist hierarchy.

The Great Gatsby is a novel concerned with class, but a strictly Marxist reading leaves out the nuances of class Fitzgerald hoped to capture, as well as how America defines class and how class functions in America. Fitzgerald shows class in America to be decidedly Weberian. The relationship to the means of production is not a factor; rather, class is defined through difference in social fields through language games—discourses and metanarratives in relation to power networks.

The story is told in the first person by a narrator recounting the events of a year gone by to better understand them, his part in these events, and, most importantly, his crisis of identity caused by the breakdown of the metanarratives he has used to narrate it. Through his ideology, Nick, by the way he has lived (sheltered from the harsh reality of life by his privileged position within the social fields of his social network), perpetuates the narratives of the American Dream as much as any other character in the story. While commenting on the elusiveness of the American Dream, contending that this dream may now be too idealistic, he reconstitutes the narrative perpetuating the dream. As Nick states in the last page of his book, "Gatsby believed in the green light, the orgastic future that years by years recedes before us. It eluded us then—tomorrow we will run faster, stretch out our arms further ... and one fine morning—So we beat on boats against the current bourne back ceaselessly into the past" (Fitzgerald 189).

Almost no one, when asked to define the American Dream, would say it is the ability (agency) to move from one class position to another—that is, to move from one set of social fields to another and, importantly, to be accepted within a position aligned with a power network within the field.

They would probably say it is the dream of success (which is now apparently equated with money). However, this is not exactly true. The discourses of the American Dream have never claimed that a Marxist three-tiered class system existed, or, paradoxically, that no class system exists at all (as many theorists argue), but still proclaim that many rungs on the ladder to success exist (classes), and these can only be reached through hard work and diligence. The idea of success, then, the American Dream, is more than wealth. It is acceptance into a higher class, as Veblen notes. *The Great Gatsby* challenges the discourse of the American Dream by asserting that certain social arenas (fields) are closed off to certain people whether or not they achieve wealth and success.

The social fields in *The Great Gatsby* are many, intricate, and blur into one another. Nick associates with Tom and Daisy within their field through performativity and emulation spurred only by his ideology of privilege, and because of this he is accepted as a subordinate, as is Jordan. Because of their birth, lineage, and the reproduction of the correct signs (the correct social and cultural capital such as owning polo ponies, being a member of an older and more established society in the Midwest, and graduating from the right university), Tom and Daisy are entrenched in a social field positioned closer to power, East Egg, effectively closing off the field to those of the out-group — West Egg.

Separate positions (classes) exist within the middle class also, of which Nick is a member, separated by the same discourses as those separating East and West Egg. George Wilson's wife, Myrtle, after meeting Tom on the train, has pretensions of moving into a higher class than her husband might provide by acquiring from Tom the economic ability to assume the signs of higher classes. Myrtle's acquaintances at the apartment Tom has rented for their liaisons are mostly of the middle class, yet of a different middle class than Nick. The group, including Myrtle, is oblivious of the fact that money — economic capital — will not gain them access to Nick's middle class. Nick would seem economically positioned within this class, yet, as Callahan points out, his "middle-class background [comes from] the role of his ancestors in American history, and his application of those values to the experience under scrutiny" (31). Nick, in the first few pages of the text, seems almost obsessed with establishing his identity to his reader through lineage. "My family have been prominent, well-to-do people in this middle-western city for three generations. [...] We have a tradition that we're descended from the Dukes of Buccleuch, but the actual founder of my line was my grandfather's brother who came here in fifty-one, sent a substitute to the Civil War" (7). The characters in Tom and Myrtle's apartment speak of what they do, rather than who they are, taking photographs and such, overly concerned with the proper actions of someone in the middle class. They are upstarts, as is Myrtle, and, as Bourdieu argues, misinterpret not only the signs of class but also the correct way of producing the signs of class, a sign in itself. They do not understand the rules of this social field as Nick understands them, who, being of an older middle class with connections to Tom and Daisy's elite class, has the power to establish the discourses legitimizing truths.

By employing a metanarrative of character, a "privileged" ideology, Nick assumes his education, upbringing and family allow him a class position above many of the characters in the story and some of the *nouveau riche* attending Gatsby's parties, including Gatsby himself, who "represented everything for which I have unaffected scorn" (Fitzgerald 6). Gary J. Scrimgeour hints at the class paradox when he suggests Jordan's accusation about Nick's carelessness echoes his "same attack on the Buchanans and the rest of the world" (75). Nick, then, like Winterbourne in *Daisy Miller*, is a hypocrite. Like Tom, Daisy, and Jordan, he places himself in a superior position to others for no other reason than having been born into a situation providing better life chances. One of the more condemnatory statements of Nick's classism is in his recounting of Gatsby and Daisy's first affair. He writes, "Eventually he took Daisy one still October night, took her because he had no real right to touch her hand" (156). Through his Midwestern, middle-class lineage, Nick retains vestiges of the 19 century moral middle class. Intertextually he is connected to Davis' unnamed narrator in *Life in the Iron Mills*. He narrates his identity and his class position from the assumption that his moral upbringing and magnanimous relationship with people of classes lower than himself make him better than many people he meets. "As my father snobbishly suggested and I snobbishly repeat, a sense of the fundamental decencies is parceled out unequally at birth" (Fitzgerald 6).

Nick's opinion of the people he meets in the city apartment Tom has rented for his and Myrtle's liaisons reflects those of Tom, Daisy, and other persons of established birth who consider themselves, through their birth, as somehow better than others—Nietzsche's noble morality (privileged ideology). Nick alludes to the West Eggers as being of a lower class than the East Eggers, although possibly having as much money. Nick "rented a house in one of the strangest communities in North America. [...] I lived in West Egg, the—well, less fashionable of the two, though this is a most superficial tag to express the bizarre and not a little sinister contrast between them" (9).

The difference has become an obsession of Tom's. He sees the old metanarrative of class breaking down and fears, not for the dilution of his race, but for the loss of a power position if too many people gain the symbolic, cultural, and social capital of his class, as Gatsby and others from West Egg have done. Tom devalues symbolic capital for ever more minute distinctions in social and cultural capital. Tom discerns, through Gatsby's incorrect presentation of the signs of the elite class, that Gatsby is not who he makes himself out to be. Although Gatsby may be as wealthy as Tom, Tom's discourses of class, involving more than money as a signifier, allow him to "other" Gatsby as "Mr. Nobody from Nowhere" (137). "One's house, one's clothes: they do express one's self and no one more than Gatsby. It is in a good part because of the clothes he wears that Tom Buchanan is able to undermine him as competitor for Daisy" (Donaldson 188).

Nick, Tom, Daisy, and Jordan are members of a group under siege. Their power is in jeopardy due to the assault on their position within the field of power by the *nouveau riche*. By constructing narratives of birth and inherited social position, they have maintained a power position, but it is slowly withering as the rules to the game, or the language games within the discourses, are being changed by the devaluing of the discourses of class constructed through 19 century metanarratives. For Nick, Tom, Daisy, and Jordan, this new permeability of class has precipitated a crisis in identity. They are "concerned with the real or imaginary fluidity of class positions — the apparent increase in the permeability of the upper social strata" (Seguin 922). The permeability of the upper social strata has caused Tom to turn to radical ideas of class and race. "Something was making him nibble at the edge of stale ideas as if his sturdy physical egotism no longer nourished his peremptory heart" (Fitzgerald 25). Tom is losing his identity as class becomes more fluid in America, with Gatsby and other *nouveau riche* blurring the lines of social class. As Will points out, "This is a problem for [...] Nick and the Buchanans, whose own sense of location [...] is very much dependent upon a clear distinction between truth and lies, insiders and outsiders, natives and aliens" (Will 128). Nick, Tom, Daisy, and Jordan depend very much on a standardization of the prototype of class disseminated throughout society, disguising the paradox inherent in the reality of this configuration. For characters such as Myrtle, Gatsby, and many others, the breakdown of the old established metanarratives of class allows them to appropriate new class roles and to modify the signs of those roles. Gatsby and others have constructed prototypes of class, devaluing the power networks and the subtle signs that signify membership in the networks so important to the upper classes by appropriating the signs of these same upper classes, rendering them meaningless for class separation. As the signs are appropriated, they are changed through the misinterpretation of their meaning.

Thus *The Great Gatsby* is also a story of the breakdown of the old metanarratives of class and the adding of new rules and truths to the discourses of class. Class, at least in the East, is no longer constructed from the old hierarchical prototype Nick, Tom, Daisy, and Jordan have used to create their identity, but rather in a complex matrix. Through Nick's judgments of people he meets, Fitzgerald divides the classes into the two major groups, the old and the new — equalitarian (who believe all should have access to advantageous positions so they might move up in class, the new American Dream) and privileged (who believe class is restricted to those chosen by others and thus the elite class is truly elitist). Fitzgerald brings to light the existence of the two major core ideologies while still maintaining a class matrix structure. Nick is positioned with Tom, Daisy, Jordan, and the other East Eggers as privileged. Gatsby and the West Eggers are positioned with Myrtle and George Wilson, many of the partygoers, and Myrtle's friends at the apartment, who believe in equalitarianism.

Several critics have attempted to racialize the classes portrayed within the novel, discovering, but mis-recognizing, that Fitzgerald presents, among the multitude of class positions, two different groups — these groups are not based on race, but rather on ideological positions. However, the critics see the two divisions in *The Great Gatsby* as "white" and "nonwhite." Jeffrey Louis Decker believes that, in *Gatsby*, there exist "racialized forms of nativism [that] create the conditions under which Fitzgerald's narrator imagines Gatsby" (56). Meredith Goldsmith believes, "If the scandal of Gatsby's success lies in his ambiguously ethnic, white, working-class origins, the success of his scandalous behavior resides in his imitation of African American and ethnic modes of self-definition" (443). Decker and Goldsmith have noticed ideological differences between the groups. Goldsmith makes the assumption that only African Americans or other ethnic groups must perform their identity. Gender and class are always performances. Both Decker and Goldsmith assume, judging by several of Tom's remarks that he sees the lower classes as nonwhite. Goldsmith contends, "Gatsby's wooing of Daisy is tantamount to 'intermarriage between black and white'" (443). The section she quotes, though, does not contend Tom thinks Gatsby is not white.

> I suppose the latest thing is to sit back and let Mr. Nobody from Nowhere make love to our wife. Well, if that's the idea you can count me out. [...] Nowadays people begin by sneering at family life and family institutions and next they'll throw everything overboard and have intermarriage between black and white [137].

The statement suggests that whatever Tom fears (intermarriage) has yet to happen. Tom does not see Gatsby as nonwhite, but as a lower class, and believes that if his class allows their women from his class to make love to men of lower classes, next they will be marrying men from other races. Tom fears his privileged class is under attack from lower classes who no longer respect the old metanarratives of class. He worries that if class separation is no longer respected, then someday race separation will not be respected. He does not separate the inferiority of race from the inferiority of class. They are both inferior to him.

Gatsby, like others of his class, does not perceive the nuances of the signs of this elite class. Tom lives in East Egg to separate himself, and, as others of his ilk do, use space as a sign of class, as shown in Gatsby's parties. "Instead of rambling this party had preserved a dignified homogeneity. [...] East Egg condescending to West Egg, and carefully on guard against its spectroscopic gaiety" (Fitzgerald 49). Gatsby (James Gatz), though he has realized the importance of having the correct name — one less ethnic and more "American" — Fitzgerald, through Gatsby's ignorance, points out that names, like clothing, cars, houses and places of residence and education, have certain value and become signs of difference in which to divide the people into classes. Fitzgerald points out the importance of producing the correct signs of class through the names of the partygoers. Significant differences exist in the names.

> [From East Egg:]Chester Beckers and the Leeches and a man named Bunsen whom I knew at Yale and Doctor Webster Civet [...] and the Hornbeams and the Willie Voltaires [...] Blackbuck [...] Ismays [...] Christies [...] Aurbach [...] and Beaver. [...] From West Egg came the Poles and the Mulreadys [...] Cecil Roebuck and Cecil Schoen and Gulick [...] Orchid [...] Cohen [...] Schwartze [...] McCarty [...] Catlips and Bembergs [...] Muldoon [...] Da Fantano [...] Legos and James B. ("Rot gut") Ferret [...] de Jongs. [65–66].

Only if race is conceived in very broad terms can the names of the West Eggers be considered racial. The names fit better into a class paradigm where the names designate new immigrants, indicating the "once poor" and now *nouveau riche*. Tom is bothered by these inferior classes making their way into his world, appropriating the signs used to determine class positions, changing both them and their importance.

The crux of the conflict in *The Great Gatsby* is of the two separate metanarratives constructing two core ideologies, resulting in two ideas of America and of the American Dream. This quest for the American Dream is not only Gatsby's quest but also that of Wilson, Myrtle, all those orbiting around Tom and Myrtle's apartment, those from West Egg, and even Nick, who travels to the East to sell bonds and hopes to make his fortune allowing access to the same positions within the same social field as Tom and Daisy. It is a romantic quest perpetuated by those of Tom and Daisy's class to gain power and at the same time separate themselves from others to maintain this same power through exclusion/inclusion to the power networks demonstrated through specific signs.

Holquist may be the most accurate when he calls *The Great Gatsby* a "quest romance" (468). Similarly, D. G. Kehl and Allene Cooper see it as no less than the "grail quest" (203–17). To assume, however, that the quest is only Gatsby's is to miss much of the significance of the story. Because late modernity, or the beginning of postmodernity, is facilitating a breakdown in the metanarratives constructing the prototypes of class, the fictional narration of this story by Nick Carraway is a quest to construct a viable ideology in which to understand the world, now that his romantic quest of moving East to make his fortune has ended so disastrously. The story of Gatsby, then, is the story of Nick's attempt to re-narrate himself within a paradigm that does not contain an obvious paradox based on the belief that the more well off you are, the more honest and virtuous you are. He states, "Conduct may be founded on the hard rock or the wet marshes but [...] when I came back from the East last autumn I felt that I wanted the world to be in uniform and at a sort of moral attention forever" (Fitzgerald 6).

Nick narrates the story of the summer he went East so he might re-narrate his world and himself. He has had a crisis of identity perpetuated by a crisis in the American identity of class, "a generalized recognized unsettling of the sense of American cultural identity," where the breakdown of the metanarratives constructing the myth of America has caused a dilemma for those whose class position is dependent on the signs of status perpetuated by these metanarratives (Stavola 11). In the East, the old designations of class seem to no longer apply. The crisis, for Nick, is caused by the paradox of the two opposing ideologies: in Gatsby there is an ideology of actions, equalitarian (or, for the purpose of this argument, a working-class ideology), and in Tom there is an ideology of character (or privileged ideology). Nick's personal crisis is the bankruptcy of the discourses of the upper classes, which he had learned to emulate through habitus inherited from family and community. Nick is left with the problem of re-narrating himself in a manner that will allow him to retain certain aspects of his personality he feels are honorable and virtuous. He must narrate Gatsby in this manner since the events of that summer make narrating Tom and Daisy in a positive way impossible.

At first Nick seems enthralled with Daisy, almost as much as Gatsby himself. She is, in fact, for him, as for Tom and Gatsby, a symbol of the ephemeral and elusive dream so indigenous to Americans. She is "the golden girl" whose "voice is full of money" (Fitzgerald 127). She is also the symbol of America as the virgin land both pure and fecund, a symbol Nick alludes to in the final pages of the story as he "became aware of the old island here that flowered once for the Dutch sailors' eyes — a fresh, green breast of the new world" (189). Daisy alludes to the purity and virginity of her "white girlhood" (24). Lockridge believes that "Daisy Fay became Gatsby's version of the Virgin Mary, both mother and bride that Gatsby founded his church upon"— that is, his belief system, his ideology (14). When Nick firsts meets his cousin and Miss Baker in East Egg, the scene seems reminiscent of an ethereal experience of a first meeting with two virgin goddesses. He states:

> The breeze blew through the room, blew the curtains [...] twisting them up toward the frosted wedding cake of the ceiling. [...] Two women were buoyed upon [the couch] as though upon an anchored balloon. They were both in white and their dresses were rippling and fluttering as if they had just been blown back in after a short flight around the house. [...] The two young women ballooned slowly toward the floor [Fitzgerald 12].

The two women are described later, while lying on another enormous couch, as "silver idols weighing down their own white dresses against the singing breeze of the fans" (Fitzgerald 122). Daisy is described by Nick in several instances as aloof, where she speaks "with a bantering inconsequence that was never quite chatter, that was as cool as their white dresses and their impersonal eyes in the absence of all desire" (16–17). She must always remain "the 'nice girl' and 'spotless,'" the symbol of the dream (Ornstein 58).

Glenn Settle is among the large contingent of critics who see Daisy as culpable for her enchantment of Gatsby and for directly causing his death. "Fitzgerald's artful handling of the quality of her voice allows a reading of Daisy as classical Siren" (Settle 116). For critics such as Leland S. Person, Jr., this condemnation of Daisy and expiation of Gatsby seems unfair and unwarranted. He suggests that Daisy is no less a romantic than Gatsby. "Daisy becomes his [Gatsby's] female double" (251). She becomes this personification of the American Dream because she, a woman in the 1920s, is a member of another subordinate class (female), and is given only so many options by the metanarratives of the time in which to narrate her identity. She has romantically constructed herself, and has been constructed by others, as the universal American object of desire. Tom, whose class insists on this romantic version of woman, has failed to allow her agency to maintain the romantic illusion of herself. "Daisy, in fact, is more victim than victimizer: she is victim first of Tom Buchanan's 'cruel' power, but then of Gatsby's increasingly depersonalized vision of her" (Person 250). To acquire Daisy is to successfully attain the American Dream, to finally achieve the goal Gatsby set for himself many years ago when devising a list of self-improvements written on the back of a comic book.

By the time Daisy's daughter is born and Tom has had several affairs,

Daisy is conscious of the illusion and hollowness of herself as this symbol. She says to the nurse, "I'm glad it's a girl. And I hope she'll be a fool — that's the best thing a girl can be in this world, a beautiful little fool" (21). Gatsby, though, allows Daisy to recover her illusions. Yet it finally leads to her corruption in the same way Gatsby's quest for her leads to his. "If she is corrupt by the end of the novel [...] that corruption is not so much inherent in her character as it is the progressive result of her treatment by the other characters" (Person 251). Like Gatsby, then, what is inherent in her character is a romantic narration of reality, allowing the "foul dust [that] floated in the wake of" her dreams to prey on her (Fitzgerald 6).

The motif of the American Dream, or the discourse constituting the narrative of the American Dream, is prominent in much of the work written on *The Great Gatsby*. When Margaret Lukens studies "the marine motifs," she still sees "another variation on the failure of the American Dream — the one that got away" (44). Lionel Trilling believes Gatsby "comes inevitably to stand for America itself" (qtd. in Watkins 249). Bewley proposes that the theme of *The Great Gatsby* "is the withering of this American Dream" (37). Decker believes readings such as those created by Bewley and others are a misreading through late 20th century eyes, and that "the 'American Dream' is not a trans-historical concept, but [...] a term invented after the Twenties in an effort to address the crisis of the Great Depression" (56). Roger L. Pearson states in contrast:

> The American dream, or myth, is an ever recurring theme in American literature, dating back to some of the earliest colonial writings. Briefly defined, it is the belief that every man, whatever his origins, may pursue and attain his chosen goals, be they political, monetary, or social. It is the literary expression of the concept of America: the land of opportunity [638].

The American Dream that Marius Bewley and others speak of is an older concept than Decker's, tied more to the idea of independence and freedom, living a life without the constraints of an entrenched class system, more attuned to an equalitarian ideology. It is constructed from an older myth of America contending that America is a classless society and, with hard work one might prosper; while one will not necessarily become rich, one will still become an American — a member of a classless society.

> Of course what is problematic about Gatsby's dream is that it not only has roots in the past, but that it is intended to remake the past. In short, it is temporally disoriented, for the dreams of Columbus and the others, including the Dutch sailors, are keyed to the possibilities of the future [Monteiro 165].

Bewley contends, "The American dream is anti–Calvinistic, and believes in the goodness and nature of man. It is accordingly a product of the frontier and the West rather than of the Puritan Tradition" (37).

Tom and Daisy's class, and, through emulation, Jordan and Nick's class, constructs the metaphor of America and the American Dream in a different way. Tom and Daisy's privileged ideology contains vestiges of the Puritan tradition of the elect.

> The Puritans were Calvinists [...] but the sovereignty of God was so total that the inequality of men had to be in God's plan. Once they arrived here they enjoyed a special sense of their historic virtuousness. [...] Partisan theology played a decisive role in creating, within the Puritans feelings that the elect must come from among them [Kazin 344].

John A. Pidgeon explains the origins of the paradox within this American Dream metanarrative. He suggests that the only way to tell an elect from a person who was not elect was by signs from God — in this case, the reward of wealth and health. "Wealth came to be a sign of goodness" (178). The other factor is "founded upon the philosophical fundamentals on which our nation was built [...] that all men were created equal" (Pidgeon 178–79). Thus, "out of the combination of Puritanism, democracy and transcendentalism has emerged the term 'rugged individualism' [...] an inner-directed, individualistic approach to the acquisition of material wealth" (179). And so "out of this comes the idea [narrative] of the American dream" (179). Bewley suggests, "The simultaneous operation of two such attitudes in American life created a tension out of which much of our greatest art has sprung" (37). In *The Great Gatsby*, this tension creates a separation of people and causes for Nick, Tom, Daisy and Jordan a crisis in their identities.

For Tom, Daisy, Jordan, and Nick to narrate their identity, they must have separation from others by creating a multitude of classes based on minutia. To do so, they must constantly redefine and refine the prototypes of class through constantly changing what counts as social and cultural capital. Because people of other classes are also constantly attempting to appropriate these signs of social and cultural capital — that is, attempting to infiltrate the upper classes — a real threat exists for these elitist classes. This infiltration by others into the elite class would deny some of the easy access to life chances, repositioning Tom, Daisy, Jordan, and Nick in the social field and thus the field of power, diluting the power networks they have inherited through privilege. It would also change the rules to the game, which would, again, put them in a less advantaged position.

Power networks — the alliances of family, educational, and fraternal networks — are important for in-group/out-group designation. For a person with an equalitarian ideology these power networks seem to allow for immoral and unjust actions, such as access to better education and better jobs, and thus better life chances, without earning them. Wolfshiem and Gatsby, players in a different but related social field, hint at the appropriation and perversion of just these power networks by those seeing the signs of class through actions. Gatsby perceives little difference between his actions and those of Tom and his class. When Tom accuses him of being a bootlegger, he retorts, "What about it? I guess your friend Walter Chase wasn't too proud to come in on it" (141). Wolfshiem, Gatsby, and others seek to be "American" within the narratives they've constructed of what it is to be an American perpetuated through the ideology of Tom and Daisy's class.

Callahan sees "archetypically American are the materials of his [Gatsby's] self-creation" (54). These materials are of the self-made man, of Franklin and Lincoln, perpetuated by the state ideological apparatus through educational systems and mass media. This creation myth, though, is perverted through the medium used to disseminate it. "Yet annihilating it all to the sixteen-year-old's imagination is the paper it is written on. No tabula rasa this Hopalong Cassidy comic book [which] utters the fantasy far more graphically and kinetically" (Callahan 55). Callahan sees Gatsby as starting his journey to corruption before he attempts self-improvement, furthered along by Cody. Ornstein believes Jay Gatsby's "career begins when he met Dan Cody [...] an education in ruthlessness" (58). Yet he contends that Gatsby is "not really Cody's protégé. [...] Jimmy Gatz inherited an attenuated version of the American Dream of success, a more moral and genteel dream" (58). The assumption that Gatsby was a criminal in mind, if not action, by the time he first meets Daisy must overlook Gatsby's attending Oxford. Certainly, for someone already corrupted, this is taking the long way around to power and wealth. Gatsby left Oxford only when he received the letter of Daisy's marriage. This precipitates a change in him that Fitzgerald never really explains, other than implying it was to regain Daisy.

If Gatsby's ideology is based on equalitarianism, and his appropriation of the signs of class seems to allude to this, and if a person having this ideology believes he or she is judged on what they do, then someone with this ideology could not construct themselves as "good" if they believed their actions to be immoral, whereas a person with a privileged ideology could view their actions as bad, but their own character as good, as Tom must to allow himself to take mistresses and yet condemn Gatsby while not condemning Daisy. For Fitzgerald's character to ring true, and Gatsby does, readers must accept that some rationalization has allowed Gatsby to reconstruct his narratives of good and evil, something not stated within the text, but which readers have little trouble assuming as true and logical for a man in Gatsby's position. As mentioned before, other than this rationalization, his actions are no different from those of the upper classes.

The change in Gatsby from the man attending Oxford to the man associating with criminals may point to a crisis in his identity. Like Maggie, Gatsby moves along the continuum of identity, moving toward an identity of character; like Carrie, he believes the signs of class constitute class itself, precipitating Gatsby's misunderstanding of the rules of the new game he is now about to play. First he does not understand why Daisy would choose money over love, but believes she must have done so, leading to his inability to believe Daisy ever loved Tom. Having been indoctrinated into the American Dream of the lone male and self-made man through popular fiction, and unable to separate the real Daisy from the personification of his dream, Gatsby must search for seemingly logical reasons this dream has been denied him, why fate has dealt him this hand. Good and evil, right and wrong, he might have felt his actions thus far had been incorrect — there were secrets he did not know. Once in New York, Gatsby's self-improvement regimen changes to accumulating money and the signs of the elite class as he interprets them. Gatsby's self-esteem, being based on good or bad actions, demands of him that he conceive what he was doing as good, though it was illegal. His love for Daisy, having been merged with the narration of his self as good or bad in the pursuit of his goal of attaining the American Dream, justifies his actions to many readers. It did for him, and, finally, for Nick.

Not satisfied with living the life of his parents, Gatz sets out to make the myth tangible. His action-based ideology drives him, believing within himself that it will help him achieve the goal of upward mobility, but "Gatsby is defeated externally in his identity [...] by evil, incarnated in the organized forces of Tom and Daisy Buchanan and the other seductive traps of American society" (Stavola 132). Significantly, for Gatsby and others upward mobility not only means having financial security but also being accepted into the society of the upper class.

They see class as Marx did, only a separation of people by their position to the means of production — that is, their wealth. *The Great Gatsby* argues this to be a misunderstanding of class in American. Class involves much more than wealth. This is why Gatsby and many others move to West Egg, hoping that, by living in what they think is the right neighborhood (although it is not), they will be privy to, as Mackall calls them, "the secret[s]" of this class (15). Nick says of meeting his cousin for the first time in East Egg, "She looked at me with an absolute smirk on her lovely face as if she had asserted her membership in a rather distinguished secret society to which she and Tom belonged" (Fitzgerald 22). Nick later discovers the secret society, this ingroup, is made up of "careless people" who "smashed up things and creatures and then retreated back into their money or their vast carelessness or whatever it was that kept them together, and let other people clean up the mess they had made" (187–88).

Although Gatsby is certainly naïve, not understanding the complexity of class in America — not understanding the rules governing those people with character-driven ideologies and how this concerns the designations of signs of class, and not realizing Daisy would reject him once she found out about his association with Meyer Wolfshiem — is a much too simplistic assumption. When Tom confronts Gatsby in the hotel room, Gatsby does not deny the accusation. Instead, he attempts to rationalize his actions by indicting one of Tom's class, Walter Chase (141). Nick says of Gatsby after Gatsby's exposure, "He looked [...] as if he had killed a man" (142). Gatsby "began to talk excitedly to Daisy, denying everything, defending his name against accusations that had not been made" (142). Gatsby's association with Meyer Wolfshiem suggests another possible reading for Gatsby's actions. He not only might not have understood the consequences of his actions, but might also have felt he had been left with little choice in this matter if he were to see justice done.

A possible explanation for Gatsby's actions might be seen in the actions of Wilson in the mistaken killing of Gatsby. Wilson's dream seems to have been much smaller than Gatsby's, Nick's, Jordan's, Daisy's, Tom's, or even Myrtle's. His goal, like that of Berger's workers, seems to focus on independence.[5] As a person showing significant working-class attributes, Wilson's subjective well-being would seem to come from the freedom from power arrangements that must be negotiated when working for someone else. Obviously Wilson was inept at understanding power arrangements, or he would have realized Tom was never going to sell him his coupe and Tom was playing him for a fool.

Wilson's core ideology, being equalitarian, centers on a sense of justice — good actions should be rewarded and evil ones punished. While he had believed he had been good to Myrtle, she had not been honest with him. He feels justified in locking her up as punishment. He drags Myrtle to a window and forces her to look outside at the eyeless spectacles of Doctor T. J. Eckleburg. He says to her, "God knows what you've been doing, everything you've been doing. You may fool me but you can't fool God!" (167). As John W. Bicknell believes, these spectacles "reappearing throughout the story eventually become a symbol of what God has become in the modern world, an all-seeing deity — indifferent, faceless, blank" (568). Wilson's belief in just actions being rewarded and unjust actions punished is shaken after he realizes his wife has been unfaithful, and also after her death. His belief system, through which he narrates the world into existence, comes apart after the killing of his wife by the man he thinks is her uncaring lover. Wilson comes to believe justice will only be served by his hand.

Nietzsche had a name for this type of action and philosophy — resentment. "It is a state of 'repressed vengefulness'" (Reginster 286). Yet "the validity of any judgment, including presumably any value judgment, is relative to the perspective formed by the 'affects,' 'needs,' 'desires,' and 'interests' of the agent who endorses it" (Reginster 284). Again, Nietzsche's bias was obviously turned toward the noble or privileged ideology, and thus he misreads the ideology of the group he called slaves, the unprivileged or those seeing privilege as immoral because their morality is based, not on resentment, but on moral action. Staring out at the sign Wilson says, "God sees everything. [...] He stood there a long time, his face close to the window pane, nodding into the twilight" (167).

Gatsby comes from the same stock as Wilson. He once believed he could make it on his own through hard work and diligence. After receiving the letter of Daisy's marriage, Gatsby quits Oxford and returns to Louisville. When he locates Tom and Daisy in East Egg, Gatsby travels to New York City. When he arrives in New York, though, he does not contact Daisy right away, and when he finally does contact her, it is not directly, but rather through Jordan, then Nick. Gatsby has been obsessed with the idea of regaining Daisy. Two possibilities for his actions might exist if Gatsby manifests this working-class ideology, an ideology of just actions. Like Wilson, Gatsby seeks justice for the injustice of privilege, of Tom using his money to take Daisy away from him. Gatsby has little chance of combating this injustice in his original state. This cosmic injustice necessitates an acknowledgment by Gatsby of a change in the rules of the game and a shift in the narration of his world and ideology, so that he sees his actions as a bootlegger as now moral. Existing in a universe with an uncaring God, he must seek justice himself. If he is rich, Daisy will have reason to leave Tom and come back to him. However, Gatsby misinterprets the rules, not understanding the importance to Daisy of the social and cultural capital Tom provides.

Gatsby's actions might also be seen as a form of resistance — of evoking agency to narrate his identity. Gatsby has invested in Daisy, as the personification of his version of the American Dream, his belief system, and through her he constructs the narration of his self and his reality. Tom, by taking Daisy away, has forcefully re-narrated Gatsby's self, denying Gatsby the right to narrate his existence (as Tom also does to Daisy). Tom has altered the discourses within the social field through his position to power, effectively re-narrating Gatsby's identity. This ability to narrate one's own identity, agency, is a fundamental aspect of the American Dream. By acting, Gatsby and Wilson recoup a narration of their selves and the world that not only makes sense to them but also allows them to reclaim their identities. "Gatsby creates his own identity, his own God, is own private morality" (Lockridge 16).

After Gatsby's death Nick can no longer believe the upper classes are, in some way, more moral than the lower classes. To narrate his identity Nick must find something good in the American identity. Nick is caught between narrating himself using an ideology bankrupted by its own paradoxes and amorality, and using one that has lost its morality in the pursuit of the American Dream. Where Tom's ideology must exist within the paradox of claiming America to be classless while also claiming moral superiority, Gatsby's ideology allows for his use and corruption in pursuit of the American Dream and justice.

Nick may have finally chosen to view Gatsby as "all right in the end" for several reasons, but the main reason seems to be his need to reconstruct a discourse allowing him to see himself as honest and virtuous, and only Gatsby showed any signs of either of these tendencies (6). Nick has lost all belief in the metanarratives of Tom and Daisy's class. He can no longer ignore Jordan's faults, or his own. He says to Jordan before they part for the last time, "I'm five years too old to lie to myself and call it honor" (186). He comes to this decision after he has had three affairs in one year, including the one with Jordan, the one precipitating his move to the East, and the third affair "with the girl in the bond office" (Callahan 36). He has chosen Gatsby because he can align Gatsby's hopes, dreams, and struggles with the old myth of America. To do so Nick must erase all of Gatsby's faults and failures, as he must also erase the obscene word on Gatsby's steps. "As critics have often noted, the text stakes its ending on the inevitability of our forgetting everything about Gatsby that has proved troublesome about his character" (Will 126). Nick must ultimately see Gatsby as a symbol of "the sustaining belief in the value of striving for a 'wondrous' object, not its inevitable disappearance and meaninglessness" (Will 126). Nick needs to believe in the goodness of life. He relates a memory of Christmas, a time when all of life seemed to stretch out before him in a long straight line like the track taking him home from Chicago for the holidays, when Nick, like the others, was "unutterably aware of our identity with this country for one strange hour before we melted indistinguishably into it again" (Fitzgerald 184). Nick must somehow narrate Gatsby as good. He must ignore Gatsby's corruption or see it as unimportant, as he did Jordan's dishonesty when he first met her.

Nick must do this to narrate himself as good, to reconceive the American past through the discourses of Emerson and Whitman and, notably, to reconstruct a myth of America starting with the Dutch sailors — an America fresh and new and full of hope, unsullied by the touch of civilization, symbolized by the snow-covered landscape he remembers viewing from the window of the train as it rushed him home for Christmas in a simpler and more innocent time when the metanarratives he used to construct his identity had not been tested and found wanting. He must reconstruct an ideology through narratives foregrounding hope in the American Dream because, for Nick, in order to be an American, to be who he is, he must have "an extraordinary gift for hope" (6).

The Great Gatsby rings true for readers because it touches on the unnamed narratives of class and the myth of America, if not the American Dream — the former being unconsciously constructed out of our daily experiences and habitus, and the latter from mass media and ideological state apparatus. *The Great Gatsby* not only transports us to another place and time, a bit more romantic than real life, where fateful, coincidental encounters play out, but it also transforms the reader by allowing him or her to test narratives of class against those of the story, whether they be true or false. In this a reciprocal testing of text against discourses comes about. This testing of *The Great Gatsby* against the readers' discourses of class shows by its continued popularity not only that Fitzgerald understood how class was constructed by American readers but also how American readers understand how class is conceived in America. Class for Fitzgerald and the reader is constructed through difference at the locus of interpellation, through in-group/out-group signs of class based on discourses of class.

Conclusion

Many academics who study and write about the working class in literature maintain that working-class literature encompasses a broad and diverse field of inquiry as it now exists in academia; however, the opposite is true. Through the basing of their assertions about class on a Marxist prototype, these academics narrow and close the discourse of class in literature, especially concerning the class they call the working class. They construct a corpus of working-class literature and authors using, at its core, a narrow range of literature — proletariat and labor literature — and then attempt to shoehorn literature from other periods into this narrow prototype. Although a text might have many diverse readings, often the result is a cursory or shallow reading, or else a purposeful misinterpretation.

In defense of the way the study is now constructed, several academics writing on working-class literature have set up a very exclusive and closed discourse, arguing that, because working-class literature "does something," it cannot be studied through a theory expressed in "inaccessible jargon" — that is, mainstream literary theory (Christopher and Whitson 73). Christopher and Whitson see texts that "do something" as exempt from the scrutiny of literary analysis, whether a critique of the author's abilities or alternate readings of a text through the lenses of other theories, though they do not prevent a "working-class" critic from critiquing any text through his or her working-class lens.

Christopher and Whitson, in fact, contend that working-class literature must be written by authors from the working class. Other academics insist that any text speaking of the working class at all (or work, for that matter) is working-class literature and the author a working-class writer. This allows the corpus to be so open that it becomes unusable for any study of the working class. Lauter subscribes to the position that the author is not as important as the configuration of the text. It must be literature about the violence of work of the working class — a form of protest/proletariat literature. As defined by academics, foregrounding victimization, exploitation, and "industrial violence with its disorder injury and death," working-class literature must be made up of mostly socialist realism, realism, and labor protest literature (Lauter 67). Much of this literature is, as Waldo Frank states, "dull novels about stereotyped workers" (qtd. in Madden xviii).

If this literature is to be viewed as a serious attempt at literariness, especially by those academics who make their living in literature departments, this literature must stand up to the test of writing aesthetics. These configurations of working-class authors and works, while attempting to control and close the discourse to other rules, stereotype the working-class person and author, relegating him or her to folk-hero status. This is why many authors who have been designated as working class, or whose work has been categorized as about the working class, reject these labels — they find the title too constricting.

The work to be done in literary studies is to metamorphose the study, freeing it from the chains of a totalizing Marxist prototype of class that insists the working class be conceptualized through a three-tiered system based on simplified prototypes of victimization, exploitation, some vague idea of "manual" work based on a root prototype garnered from social realism, and labor protest literature. As the study exists now, it creates a corpus of work that needs to be defended against not only essentialism (the study of white males) but also aesthetic criticism.

In academia, at least concerning new working-class studies, an attempt to create or maintain a hegemonic metanarrative of class as a reaction to the crisis of postmodernity exists, the very same postmodernity allowing for discordant voices to be heard; importantly for this book, these include the voices of those individuals titled "of the working class." The impulse to control the study of the working class derives from the breakdown of the old metanarratives once used to construct identity. Thus the study, in one sense, is used to reconstruct identity. A second reason, ironically, lies in the middle-class impulse to construct, or become attached to, power systems. Through positioning themselves as authorities and maintaining authority through performativity and controlling the rules of the language game in which the working class might be discussed, certain academics legitimize themselves as authorities and thus create and have access to valuable cultural capital.

Although the academics who study the working class or working-class literature do not always evoke Marx or his theoretical positions, their work is often decidedly Marxist in philosophy, which is frequently caused by theorists, rather than looking to real life and the sciences to establish a theory, finding one that fits a prototype taken from the study of socialist realism, labor protest literature, and proletariat literatures, along with fitting the sociopolitical thrust of the literature and the sociopolitical bent of the academics. Thus Marxism has become hegemonic in the study of working-class literature by providing an easy way to view class and a very simplified discourse in which to speak of class, as long as many of the paradoxes and contradictions are ignored — such as the contradictory belief in individual upward mobility, individual identity, agency (all ideals contingent to the "American Dream"), and subjective well-being — while still endorsing theories of exploitation and victimization that argue for an absence of agency. Sadly, no room is left in this Marxist prototype for stories about working-class people who are happy and content with their lives.

Although Marxism claims that it gives voice to the working class in a capitalistic system allowing them no voice, as a totalizing theory it must close the discourse to the voices that contradict its own theories. Postmodernist and poststructuralist theories, having contested Marxism's totalizing positions along with other totalizing theories, suggest that a multitude of individual voices exists. By allowing for discordant voices within society to be heard, postmodernist and poststructuralist theories add new rules to the language game of class. In doing so, postmodernist and poststructuralist theories question the way class is conceived and studied within literature studies, thus questioning the tenets of a study not truly reflecting class negotiation within American society or class perception by Americans.

Postmodernist and poststructuralist theories, while permitting alternative voices to be heard, must guard against essentialism. For the study of class this means conceptualizing class at the point of interpellation as an in-group/out-group designation based on signs of differences. In this way identity can still be studied as a complex construction of race, gender, sex, and class. For literature studies this means understanding what aspect of a character's identity is foregrounded within the text — the overarching mechanism restricting the actions of the protagonist. Conceptualizing class at the individual level allows class to exist in much of literature by determining class through difference as some "standard" and dominant set of attributes foregrounded implicitly or explicitly within the text.

This configuration of class would seem to make speaking of class in literature all but impossible. Yet class does exist in everyone's life in the everyday world. It exists in core ideologies not unlike Nietzsche's concept of noble and slave moralities. Nietzsche, being biased toward the aristocracy and seeing the social contract and altruism as a Christian constraint on his superman, could not or would not conceive of an ideological position asserting that men and women might be judged as equals through their actions against a set of defined moral laws in an equalitarian society — thus the biased names. Rather, these ideologies might be titled equalitarian ideology or privileged ideology. Both these ideologies are passed down by the parents to the children through narratives with which they construct their reality.

The equalitarian ideology conceives systems, whether official, societal, or even ad hoc, as bodies set up to maintain order by establishing and maintaining implicit rules (manners and decorum) or explicit rules (laws and edicts) based on some moral precept. A person with an equalitarian ideology, because his or her ideology is action based, sees the use of influence to circumvent rules as immoral and thus never learns, or refuses to learn, the finer points of negotiating and gathering power, or the gathering and disseminating of social, symbolic, and cultural capital. These actions of the equalitarian person may also be a form of resistance to the encroachment of discordant prototypes into his or her narrations. In this way the equalitarian ideology is perpetuated by the privileged ideology in a Gramscian form of "revolution by position" as a way of reciprocal "othering."

People whose ideologies are privileged construct their identities based on their position in power networks, such as family, society, or class within the community and small groups. They attempt to align themselves with power networks, or to create power networks (which, at times, might oppose other power networks), as a way of negotiating their place in the community. Unlike the equalitarian individual, the privileged person believes rules are a function of power systems. For people with privileged ideologies these rules, then, are not at heart either moral, or immoral, since their concept of morality is internal, based on who they are rather than what they do. Power networks are to be manipulated to create advantageous positions for a person and his or her family.

In order for power networks to exist, exclusion must exist, a valuing of the cultural capital associated with any power network or status group. As a way of creating this value of cultural capital, middle-class persons attempt to control the discourses legitimizing the truths or legitimate knowledge of signs in order to exclude those persons who show signs of the working class. Because middle-class signs are now so easily obtained by others, the signs must constantly change and must, sometimes, be so subtle that only those who believe these minute differences are important will notice the differences. Thus the purchase of an item looking very much like another item, but purchased for its function rather than for its value as a sign (a purchasing of a simulacra of a simulacra), might be a telltale sign of a person who does not know the importance of the difference, even if that difference is only a manufacturer's label. This importance of knowing the signs also leads to a rejection of this same importance in a form of resistance.

The close readings of *Maggie: A Girl of the Streets* and *The Great Gatsby* illuminate an alternate way to conceive class not only in literature but also in the real world. It is a class theory based on the intersecting of ideologies at the micro level, the level of the individual, contesting in-group/out-group selection through the use of signs of difference embedded within discourses. These discourses construct social fields, which, in turn, construct and maintain these discourses. These discourses are used by persons within a social field to separate themselves from others vying for positions of access to power. The readings in this book do not depend on assumptions not found in the text or on intentional or affective fallacies. Both readings are rather straightforward and are only the beginning of the work that might be done in this new field.

This book's overarching argument is a result of observations of the many real-world inconsistencies of Marxism and the way it has been applied to working-class studies and working-class literature studies in America. The theory is a result of a search for other theories that better relate to the way class is performed in the real world, and an attempt to bring rigor into the study.

Unlike Marx, who constructs class through economics and the position to the means of production at the macro level, Thorstein Veblen, Max Weber, and Emile Durkheim contend that class is created within status groups at the micro level allowing or denying access to life chances, and economics is an epiphenomenon of status groups. The mechanism of separation is ideology, which is more complex than Marx's false consciousness. Through the employment of narratives, ideology constructs the self while pretending to be natural, a fable masquerading as a history. A person's ideology, and thus identity, comes from the world around him or her through habitus, social structure, what Althusser termed ideological apparatus, and through mass media. However, ideology, and thus identity, is mutable. Agency, a person's "power," can act upon ideology, and influence, revalue, and reconstruct prototypes and schemas used to narrate the self and world. Identity in most of the social sciences, sociology, anthropology, and psychology is seen as fluid and mutable, becoming salient at the locus of interpellation through an exchange of signs filtered through prototypes and schemas garnered through habitus, systems, and mass media, which provide the major signs for in-group/out-group separation.

Contemporary theorists employing Veblen's, Durkheim's, and especially Weber's theories have developed alternate theories of class focused on identity at the micro level concerned with the locus of identity, social structure (fields), belief systems (metanarratives), and personal beliefs (habitus). Bourdieu develops a theory of social fields—fields of social power—that includes habitus (Veblen's propensities); cultural, symbolic, and social capital; and signs manifested through what he names "practice," all mediated by ideology. These signs become differences for small-group inclusion and exclusion. Foucault conceives the area of contestation as discourses perpetuating "truths." These discourses are analogous to Bourdieu's social fields, although they might be seen as operating within the social fields, creating social fields as the fields create them. They are metanarratives controlling the rules of the language games within the fields, allowing certain narratives while disallowing others, inscribing for each individual within a field a Subject/subject position.

Although Bourdieu and Foucault are concerned with how power is created and dispersed in society, neither explicitly explains the origins of power. For Bourdieu social fields are inscribed within the larger social field of power, and people take up positions in relation to the power in the field. Foucault's ideas of power, however, come from Nietzsche.

This book establishes an alternate way to view class, constructing a new theory of class capable of being used at the micro level without fear of contradictions and inconsistencies, seeing class as determined by access to power and in-group/out-group selection. It brings together tenets to be used in a working-class reading of any text, seeing class as decided through difference and power mediating agency through social structure. The book does not, however, argue that only two poles exist, but rather that ideology, and thus identity, exists on a continuum from privileged to equalitarian, and a character might change throughout a story as a person might change throughout life. This change, often, becomes the crux of the story.

This new field of class theory adds complexity to texts normally thought of as classed texts (but not didactically so), such as Dos Passos' works or Carver's stories. This new theory can also be applied to texts not normally considered classed texts to show how texts incorporate class into their plots unknowingly and unwittingly, and how within these texts class is defined and redefined through power, agency, and signs of capital at the locus of interpellation, questioning the author's position within his or her real-world class system, the ideology producing the text, and the ideology reproduced by the text. Thus it solves the inconsistencies and contradictions inherent in attempting to form a working-class corpus.

Class can be seen in such works as those of Melville, to use Hapke's example of an author who elucidates text poorly, although he actually elucidates class very well, showing its complexity. *Billy Budd* is a very good example of the interplay of positions within a social field, that of the H.M.S. *Bellipotent*. Billy is naïve, a new entrant to this new social field bringing with him his equalitarian ideologies. He does not understand the new rules to the game, but then again, neither does Captain Vere, born of the nobility, who is forced to execute Billy in order to maintain his status and position to power, if only in the eyes of the sailors. Claggart, however, is very aware of how the game is now played, although, because he is so sure of himself and his ability to play the game, he does not foresee Billy's working-class reaction, although one could suggest he foresaw it, but not the results. His adeptness at playing the game within the social sphere of the ship forces both Billy's hand (literally) and Vere's.

"Benito Cereno," although its major thrust is concerned with race and the soft racism of the American middle class, illustrates a play of two classes coming about within the text. Amasa Delano is a new man of the New World, as Melville contends through his initials ("A.D."), just as Benito Cereno is from the Old World ("B.C.") with an entrenched class system. Delano, being of the middle class and of a different social field, is able to adjust his prototype of the African slaves he meets onboard Cereno's ship without destroying his narrations of his world. Cereno cannot. Delano's ideology is more mutable than Cereno's, having internalized narrations of republicanism, whereas Cereno's ideology is dependent on an older set of metanarratives perpetuated by the Catholic Church, those of the great chain of being. Cereno, believing in Nietzsche's noble and slave moralities, cannot see someone such as Babo as being able to outwit him, and capable, mentally and emotionally, of pulling off a mutiny and enslaving him.

In Hawthorne's work, too, class is played out. Much of *The Blithedale Romance* is concerned with sex and gender roles. Yet instances of class exist between the transcendentalists themselves and between them and the local farmers. Struggle for class position and the signs of class are factors in the plots of both *The House of the Seven Gables* and *The Marble Faun*. However, neither of these texts fits well into a Marxist paradigm. In fact, class exists through difference in much of American literature.

Class can be seen in works penned as early as America's own origin in works by John Smith, John Winthrop, Thomas Morton, Sarah Kimble Knight who provides a humorous perspective, William Byrd, and Washington Irving. This play of class can also be discovered in 19th century texts outside the realist literature so touted as working-class literature.

Class is prevalent in Twain's essays and his novel *The Gilded Age*, but it is also prevalent in his two most famous works: *The Adventures of Tom Sawyer* and *The Adventures of Huckleberry Finn*. These books, when compared, bring to light the two differing core ideologies, privileged and equalitarian. Although Tom acts as if he is from Huck's class, he is really a tourist. His actions are tolerated by the adults of his class, who know that he will, at some time, choose to return to his middle-class roots. Tom is allowed to pretend because he has a network that will tolerate his childish foolishness, whereas they will not tolerate the same foolishness from Huck. Tom's games are practice in manipulating signs and people, a skill the middle class sees as important due to its being practice for the negotiation of class in a social world. Pretending to be a pirate and the leader of a robber gang is practice for assuming leadership in other roles later on in life. Tom learns to recognize when opportune times exist to advance the value of his social, cultural, and symbolic capital, as when picking the day of the funeral to arrive back in town and taking the blame for Becky, influencing her and her father. Becky, then, becomes symbolic capital for Tom in negotiating class within the social field of Hannibal, an upper-middle-class girlfriend. Finally, his privileged ideology allows him to believe he has a right to steal Injun Joe's gold for no other reason than class differences. Huck does not understand the importance of signs and thus does not understand the importance of acting and dressing correctly. Huck judges all his actions as right or wrong, and thus judges himself through those actions. His equalitarian ideology is the heart of *The Adventures of Huckleberry Finn*. Being honest, and believing a person is judged by their actions, he must judge Jim by his actions and not the color of his skin, as he must finally confront slavery itself as unjust because it separates people by race and not deeds.

Other local colorists or regionalists, such as Sarah Orne Jewett and Willa Cather, write of class in rural areas. The working out of class likewise takes place in the plays of Eugene O'Neal and Tennessee Williams. In Williams' *The Glass Menagerie*, three classes clash: Amanda's upper-middle-class, privileged ideology, now bankrupt in the Depression years; Tom's lower-middle-class ideology; and the ideologies of the workers at the shoe warehouse where Tom is forced to work. Tom struggles to redefine himself outside Amanda's narratives and the ideologies in the warehouse, and finally, in desperation, leaves his mother and sister, joins the merchant marines, and is caught up in the greater clash of ideologies of World War II (outside the play), returning to the family's apartment years later. He comes to understand that, like the memory of his sister, the narratives of his past will always haunt him. In other narratives of class, the struggle may not be over the position of a person within the networks of power, but rather what constitutes the signs of class within the social field. Wharton's *Age of Innocence* concerns just this struggle, as does Williams' *Cat on a Hot Tin Roof*.

Hopefully, by presenting a discussion of how working-class studies and working-class literature studies are now configured in academia — centered around a totalizing Marxist prototype of class — and providing alternatives for a new theory of class, a new beginning, a new study of the working class, might be instituted in academia that will allow for a wider and less rigid concept of the working class in literature, reflecting the complexity of class in the real world. Rather than attempting to name a corpus of authors and works, a theory of the "working class," or class itself, in literature, based on the interactions of ideology, should be constructed that will permit readings of texts, which will then allow for the understanding of how class is negotiated within these texts and how these texts reflect real-world experiences.

Postmarxism, postmodernism, prototype theories, identity theories, theories of narrative identity, agency, and other theories of identity formation fit better in establishing a study of class in literature that truly reflects the real world. In the future, working-class theory must develop deeper understandings of these alternative viewpoints and begin to explore fecund areas of research, such as tapping research done in areas as diverse as cognitive science and psychology. Much work still needs to be done, and this book is only the beginning of a study that, if it can avoid essentialism or the propensity of theories to establish themselves as hegemonic through the attempt of academics to close the discourse through performativity, can bring to literature a new area of knowledge in which to study texts.

Chapter Notes

Preface

1. Within the discourse of working-class studies as it now stands, the concept of the working class (and thus the term "class") has been "framed," as Russo and Linkon contend. However, this framing actually refers to the closure of the discourse within strict Marxist criteria. Thus the discourse of the working class starts by disregarding alternate conceptions of the working class. This book attempts to open the discourse. The use of the term "working class," then, as a "framed" class, is evoked throughout this text only as a way of discussing the conception of class by others, such as in authors' critiques, and to attempt to come to terms with the discourses through which academics understand literature supposedly of, about, and often by the working class. As will be expanded upon in later chapters, the position of this text is that class is an identity narrated through ideology that does not exist within a solid framework — it is fluid and exists in a continuum constructed through the narration of identity. Thus "working class" ceases to exist except at the locus of interpellation.

Chapter 1

1. These assumptions will be discussed in chapters 2 and 3.
2. This is not the same as payment later.
3. Ideology will be discussed in depth in chapters 4 and 5.
4. This complicates the concept of "value," a word bandied around as much or more than the other terms this text is attempting to define. Value can only be realized at the point of sale and not before, although most economists would dispute this when considering the transformation of raw material into a finished product, an extreme case of the emperor not wearing clothes; however, if that product is damaged to the point of being scrapped, the only value comes from the salvaging of the material. Thus everything before the sale is actually cost. In reality, no value can be added to a commodity until it is sold. Simply, if it is not sold, the owner of the commodity must "eat" the cost, not the value. If the commodity becomes damaged within the manufacturing process, the cost, including labor, must be borne by the capitalist.
5. Subjective well-being is taken up in later chapters.
6. The idea of laborers having agency will be discussed in later chapters.
7. The concept of habitus is taken up in later chapters.
8. See Max Weber, *General Economic History*, chapters 1–4.
9. How ideology works and is developed is taken up in chapter 5.
10. G. Domhoff William, in *Who Rules America: Power, Politics and Social Change* (New York: McGraw Hill, 2006), better explains the real-world mechanisms of how a dominant ideology is disseminated.

Chapter 2

1. "Labor" in this essay, as in much of Zweig's text (and several other texts reviewed), has little to do with work, but is rather used to identify a very limited faction of people in a narrow range of occupations. It should not be confused with all those who work and earn a wage, or a salary.
2. The purposeful conflation of indentured servants with African slaves will be discussed in chapter 3.
3. This conflict of metanarratives is taken up in chapter 4.
4. An explanation of Bourdieu's configuration of class, habitus, and class struggle will be provided in chapter 4.
5. Agency will be taken up in chapter 4. Subjective well-being will be taken up later in this chapter and expanded upon in chapter 3.
6. Contradictory statistics are prevalent in both new working-class studies and working-class literature studies.
7. The exact quote will be cited in chapter 3.
8. Michaels does not use the term "culture" in the ideological sense, but in the same way others use it — as a set of acts and objects that can be used to separate one group from another.
9. This is a much higher percentage than others have stated and higher than that recorded by the U.S. Census.
10. These are taken up as core ideologies in chapter 5

Chapter 3

1. Chapter 2 shows how the complexity of labor — specifically, skilled trades — complicates a simple division of classes by both power and economics.
2. Unlike England, where industrial manufacturing evolved over time, the beginning of America's Industrial Revolution can be pinpointed to Lowell, Massachusetts, where the first textile mill was opened in 1820. Even before this industrialization, labor was scarce, allowing for those in poverty in Europe to sell their labor in advance in America as indentured servants. Although Coles, Zandy, and others choose several of the horror stories, there exist in print many more articles, letters, and tracts of a positive nature about indentured service.
3. For background information on Melville's knowledge, and/or lack of knowledge, of the female reproductive system, see Philip Young, "The Machine in the Tartarus: Melville's Inferno," *American Literature* 63.2 (June 1991): 208–24.
4. See Genesis 38:9–10 for the sin of Onan.
5. Refer to the reading *of Maggie: A Girl of the Streets* in chapter 6 for the standard plot of the "fallen woman" in the fiction of this time.
6. This ideological belief of having to have a job is much more complicated than it first appears and will be elucidated in later chapters
7. Refer to chapter 2.

Chapter 4

1. In chapter 5 ideology will be investigated.
2. This importance of knowledge becoming a sign for exclusion and inclusion will be discussed in chapter 5 within the idea of in-group/out-group separation.

Chapter 5

1. Here working class is used as a way to speak of persons who are defined through signs or attributes (difference) against what, at that time, was posited as the "norm"—the "middle class"—because of its position of power in such power systems as academia. Thus working class is the class, or sometimes any class, seen through the manifestation of signs as "below," "less than," or "different from" the middle class.

2. For an in-depth reading of personal identity theory and how it relates to other theories of self, refer to Steven Hitlin, "Values as the Core of Personal Identity: Drawing Links Between the Two Theories of Self," *Social Psychology Quarterly* 66.2 (2003): 118–37.

3. Emirbayer and Mische's concept of agency is complex and involves several different types of schematizing processes. For a more in-depth study, see Emirbayer and Mische, "What Is Agency?"

4. As has been cited in former chapters, Michaels refuses to envision those who are not rich as being happy and thus must conceive subjective well-being as ideologically constructed, or as a false consciousness perpetrated by the dominant ideologies.

5. Thanks to Dr. Jason Marc Harris for suggesting the idea of tension between metanarratives creating the (sometimes) split personality of the middle class.

6. This inscrutability of fate is usually a misunderstanding or ignorance of the actual situation (the game of power), thus leading to confusion over why opportunities (life chances) seem to always go to other people.

Chapter 6

1. False consciousness differs from the postmarxists' conception of ideology in that it might be defined as a confusion or distraction from reality.

2. As one of the few major outlets left for women to disseminate their beliefs, the sentimental novel in the hands of many women writers was refined well beyond those novels of the bulk press. For further study, see Jane Tompkins, *Sensational Designs: The Cultural Work of American Fiction, 1790–1860* (New York: Oxford University Press, 1985); Susan K. Harris, *Nineteenth-Century American Women Novelists: Interpretive Strategies* (New York: Cambridge University Press, 1990); Suzanne Clark, *Sentimental Modernism: Women Writers and the Revolution of the Word* (Bloomington: Indiana University Press, 1991); Ann Douglas, *The Feminization of American Culture* (New York: Avon, 1978); Fred Kaplan, *Sacred Tears: Sentimentality in Victorian Literature* (Princeton, NJ: Princeton University Press, 1987); Nina Baym, *Woman's Fiction: A Guide to Novels by and about Women in America, 1820–1870* (Ithaca, NY: Cornell University Press, 1978); and others.

3. However, critics such as Joan N. Radner and Susan S. Lanser in "The Feminist Voice: Strategies of Coding in Folklore and Literature," *Journal of American Folklore* 100 (1987): 412–25, speculate that alternate discourses were coded into the text of sentimental literature.

4. The obvious problems with this high-road point of view are too long and complex for this chapter and are not all that germane to this text, but, like much of what is purported to be working-class literature, sentimental literature has been put to blatant ideological use. Several times Dobson cites *Uncle Tom's Cabin*, ignoring the explicit and implicit patriarchal ideological symbols invested in the female characters, including "Little Eva."

5. Refer to chapter 2.

Bibliography

Aaron, Daniel. "Howells' 'Maggie.'" *New England Quarterly* 38.1 (1965): 85–90. Print.
Althusser, Louis. *Lenin and Philosophy, and Other Essays*. Translated by Ben Brewster. New York: New York Monthly Review Press, 1972.
Antonio, Robert J. "After Postmodernism: Reactionary Tribalism." *American Journal of Sociology* 106.2 (2000): 40–87.
Arms, George. "The Literary Background of Howells's Social Criticism." *American Literature* 14.3 (1942): 260–76.
Arnellos, Argyris, Thomas Spyrou, and John Darzentas. "Towards the Naturalization of Agency Based on an Interactivist Account of Autonomy." *New Ideas in Psychology* 28 (2010): 296–311.
Aronowitz, Stanley. *How Class Works: Power and Social Movement*. New Haven, CT: Yale University Press, 2003. Print
Baker, Josephine E. "A Second Peep at Factory Life." In *American Working-Class Literature: An Anthology*, edited by Nicholas Coles and Janet Zandy, 49–52. New York: Oxford University Press, 2007. Print
Baudrillard, Jean. *The Mirror of Production*. Translated by Mark Poster. St. Louis: Telos Press, 1975.
Baym, Nina, ed. *The Norton Anthology of American Literature*, 1456–57. 6th ed. 5 vols. New York: Norton, 2003.
Berger, Bennett M. *Working-Class Suburb: A Study of Auto Workers in Suburbia*. Berkeley: University of California Press, 1960.
Best, Steven, and Douglas Kellner. *Postmodern Theory: Critical Interrogations*. New York: Guilford Press, 1991.
Bewley, Marius. "Scott Fitzgerald's Criticism of America." In *Twentieth Century Interpretations of America*, ed. Ernest Lockridge, 37–53. Englewood Cliffs, NJ: Prentice-Hall, 1968.
Bicknell, John W. "The Wasteland of F. Scott Fitzgerald." *Virginia Quarterly Review* 30 (1954): 556–72.
Bourdieu, Pierre. *Distinctions*. Translated by Richard Nice. Cambridge, MA: Harvard University Press, 1884.
———. *The Field of Cultural Production*. Edited by Randal Johnson. New York: Columbia University Press, 1993.
———. *Language and Symbolic Power*. Translated by Gino Raymond and Matthew Adamson. Edited by John B. Thompson. Cambridge, MA: Harvard University Press, 2001.
———. *The Logic of Practice*. Translated by Richard Nice. Stanford, CA: Stanford University Press, 1990.
———. *Practical Reason*. Translated by Richard Nice. Stanford, CA: Stanford University Press, 1998.
Bowe, John, Marisa Bowe, and Sabin Streeter. *Gig: Americans Talk About Their Jobs*. New York: Three Rivers Press, 2001. Print.

Bowe, Marisa. Introduction. *Gig: Americans Talk About Their Jobs*. Ed. John Bowe, Marisa Bowe, and Sabin Streeter. New York: Three Rivers Press, 2001. xii–xiii. Print.
Brace, Charles Loring. "The Dangerous Class of New York and Twenty Years' Work Among Them." In *Stephen Crane, Maggie: A Girl of the Streets*, edited by Thomas A. Gullason, 65–67. New York: W. W. Norton, 1979.
Brantlinger, Ellen, Massoumeh Majd-Jabbari, and Samuel L. Guskin. "Self-Interest and Liberal Educational Discourse: How Ideology Works for Middle-Class Mothers." *American Educational Research Journal* 33.3 (1996): 571–97.
Bridges, Amy. "Becoming American: The Working Class in the United States Before the Civil War." In *Working-Class Formation: Nineteenth-Century Patterns in Western Europe and the United States*, edited by Ira Katznelson and Aristide R. Zolberg, 157–96. Princeton, NJ: Princeton University Press, 1986.
Bright, Edward. "A Melodrama of the Streets." In *Stephen Crane, Maggie: A Girl of the Streets*, edited by Thomas A. Gullason, 152–53. New York: W. W. Norton, 1979.
Brobjer, Thomas. "Nietzsche's Affirmative Morality: An Ethics of Virtue." *Journal of Nietzsche Studies* 26 (2003): 64–78.
Brown, Alison Leigh. *On Foucault: A Critical Introduction*. Belmont, CA: Wadsworth/Thompson Learning, 2000.
Brown, Andrew. "A Materialist Development of Some Recent Contributions to the Labour Theory of Value." *Cambridge Journal of Economics* 32 (2008): 125–46.
Brown, Kenneth D. *The English Labor Movement 1700–1951*. New York: St. Martin's Press 1982.
Callahan, John F. *The Illusions of a Nation: Myth and History in the Novels of F. Scott Fitzgerald*. Chicago: Illinois University Press, 1972.
Camfield, David. "Review of *What's Class Got to Do with It? American Society in the Twenty-First Century*." *Industrial Relations* 60 (2005): 198–99.
Carlson, Arvid J. "Review of *How Class Works: Power and Social Movement*, by Stanley Aronowitz." *International Social Science Review* 80 (2005): 64.
Carter, Everett. "William Dean Howells' Theory of Critical Realism." *ELH* 16.2 (1949): 151–66.
Charles, Maria. "Culture and Inequality: Identity, Ideology, and Difference in 'Postascriptive Society.'" *Annals of the American Academy of Political and Social Science* 619.1 (2008): 41–60.
Chen, Jie-Qi. "Theory of Multiple Intelligences: Is It a Scientific Theory?" *Teachers College Record* 106.1 (2004): 17–23.
Christensen, Paul. "Failing." In *Writing Work: Writers on Working-Class Writing*, edited by David Shevin, Larry Smith, and Janet Zandy, 47–58. Huron: Bottom Dog Press, 1999.
Christopher, Renny, and Carolyn Whitson. "Toward a Theory of Working Class Literature." *NEA Higher Education Journal* (Spring 1999): 71–81.
Clawson, Dan. "Review of *How Class Works: Power and Social Movement*, by Stanley Aronowitz." *American Journal of Sociology* 110 (2004): 236–37.
Cloud, Dana L. "Beyond Evil: Understanding Power Materially and Rhetorically." *Rhetoric & Public Affairs* 6.3 (2003): 531–38.
Cobble, Dorothy Sue. "When Feminism Had Class." In *What's Class Got to Do with It? American Society in the Twenty-First Century*, edited by Michael Zweig, 23–34. Ithaca, NY: Cornell University Press, 2004.
Coles, Nicholas, and Janet Zandy, eds. *American Working-Class Literature: An Anthology*. New York: Oxford University Press, 2007.
Conley, James R. "'More Theory, Less Fact?' Social Reproduction and Class Conflict in a Sociological Approach to Working-Class History." *Canadian Journal of Sociology* 13.1–2 (1988): 73–102.

Conroy, Marianne. "Discount Dreams: Factory Outlet Malls, Consumption, and the Performance of Middle-Class Identity." *Social Text* 54 (1998): 63–83.
Cook, John. "Culture, Class and Taste." In *Cultural Studies and the Working Class: Subject to Change*, edited by Sally Munt, 97–112. London: Cassell, 2000.
Coreno, Thaddeus. "Fundamentalism as a Class Culture." *Sociology of Religion* 63.3 (2002): 335–60.
Corley, Íde. "The Subject of Abolitionist Rhetoric: Freedom and Trauma in *The Life of Olaudah Equiano*." *Modern Language Studies* 32.2 (2002): 139–56.
Corra, Mamadi. "Separation and Exclusion: Distinctly Modern Conditions of Power?" *Canadian Journal of Sociology* 30.1 (2005): 41–71.
Couldry, Nick. "Media Meta-Capital: Extending the Range of Bourdieu's Field Theory." *Theory and Society* 32.5–6 (2003): 653–77.
Crane, Stephen. *Maggie: A Girl of the Streets*. Edited by Thomas A. Gullason. New York: W. W. Norton, 1979.
Crompton, Rosemary. "Class Theory and Gender." *British Journal of Sociology* 40.4 (1989): 565–87.
Cunliffe, Marcus. "Stephen Crane and the American Background of Maggie." In *Stephen Crane, Maggie: A Girl of the Streets*, edited by Thomas A. Gullason, 94–103. New York: W. W. Norton, 1979.
Daigle, Christine. "Nietzsche: Virtue Ethics ... Virtue Politics." *Journal of Nietzsche Studies* 32 (2006): 1–21.
Daniels, Jim. "Work Poetry and Working-Class Poetry: The Zip Code of the Heart." In *New Working-Class Studies*, edited by John Russo and Sherry Linkon, 113–36. Ithaca, NY: Cornell University Press, 2005.
Dauber, Kenneth. "Realistically Speaking: Authorship in the Late Nineteenth Century and Beyond." *American Literary History* 11.2 (1999): 378–90.
Davis, Rebecca Harding. *Life in the Iron Mills*. Edited by Tillie Olsen. New York: Feminist Press, 1985.
Dawahare, Anthony. "Langston Hughes's Radical Poetry and the 'End of Race.'" *Melus* 23.3 (1998): 21–41.
Decker, Jeffrey Louis. "Gatsby's Pristine Dream: The Diminishment of the Self-Made Man in the Tribal Twenties." *NOVEL: A Forum on Fiction* 28.1 (1994): 52–71.
DeFreitas, Gregory, and Niev Duffy. "Young Workers, Economic Inequality, and Collective Action." In *What's Class Got to Do with It? American Society in the Twenty-First Century*, edited by Michael Zweig, 143–60. Ithaca, NY: Cornell University Press, 2004.
DeGenaro, William. "Review: Work as Text." *College English* 66.6 (2003): 229–37.
Diener, Ed, Jeffery J. Sapyta, and Eunkook Suh. "Subjective Well-Being Is Essential to Well-Being." *Psychological Inquiry* 9.1 (1998): 33–37.
Diggins, John P. "Animism and the Origins of Alienation: The Anthropological Perspective of Thorstein Veblen." *History and Theory* 16.2 (1977): 113–36.
Dobson, Joanne. "Reclaiming Sentimental Literature." *American Literature* 69.2 (1997): 263–88.
Donaldson, Scott. "Possessions in *The Great Gatsby*." *Southern Review* 37.2 (2001): 187–211.
Dorsey, Peter. "Becoming the Other: The Mimesis of Metaphor in Douglass's *My Bondage and My Freedom*." *PMLA* 111.3 (1996): 435–50.
Douglas, Mary. "Symbolic Pollution." *Culture and Society: Contemporary Debates*. Edited by Jeffrey C. Alexander and Steven Seidman, 156–59. Cambridge: Cambridge University Press, 1990.
Douglas, Peter. "Nietzschean Geometry." *25th Anniversary Issue*. Special issue of *SubStance* 25.3 (1996): 132–52.
Douglass, Frederick. "In the Shipyards (1855)." In *American Working-Class Literature: An*

Anthology, edited by Nicholas Coles and Janet Zandy, 67–68. New York: Oxford University Press, 2007.

Dreiser, Theodore. *Sister Carrie*. New York: Signet Classic-Putnam, 2000.

Drudy, Sheelagh. "The Classification of Social Class in Sociological Research." *British Journal of Sociology* 42.1 (1991): 21–41.

Dulles, Rhea, and Melvyn Dubofsky. *Labor in America: A History*. Arlington Heights, VA: Harlan Davidson. 1993.

Durkheim, Emile. *The Division of Labor in Society*. Translated by George Simpson. New York: Free Press, 1993.

———. *Ethics and the Sociology of Morals*. Translated by Robert T. Hall. Buffalo, NY: Prometheus Books, 1993.

Eby, Clare Virginia. "Thorstein Veblen and Rhetoric of Authority." *American Quarterly* 46.2 (1994): 139–73.

Emirbayer, Mustafa, and Ann Mische. "What Is Agency?" *American Journal of Sociology* 103.4 (1998): 962–1023.

Engels, Friedrich. "Preface to the English Edition of 1888 'Manifesto of the Communist Party.'" In *Basic Writings on Politics and Philosophy* (Karl Marx and Friedrich Engels),edited by Lewis S. Feuer, 1–6. New York: Doubleday, 1989.

———. "Engels to Franz Mehring." *Basic Writings on Politics and Philosophy*. Karl Marx and Friedrich Engels. Ed. Lewis S. Feuer. New York: Doubleday, 1989. 407–12. Print.

Evans, Geoffrey, and Colin Mills. "Identifying Class Structure: A Latent Class Analysis of the Criterion-Related and Construct Validity of Goldthorpe Class Schema." *European Sociological Review* 14.1 (1998): 87–106.

Fairbanks, Michael. "Changing the Mind of a Nation: Elements in a Process for Creating Prosperity." In *Culture Matters: How Values Shape Human Progress*, edited by Lawrence E. Harrison and Samuel P. Huntington, 296–308. New York: Basic Books, 2000.

Farnell, Brenda. "Getting Out of the Habitus: An Alternative Model of Dynamically Embodied Social Action." *Journal of the Royal Anthropological Institute* 6.3 (2000): 397–418.

Farrell, Edmund J. "The Language Game: Oral Histories as Living Literature." *English Journal* 71.4 (1982): 87–92.

Faue, Elizabeth. "Gender, Class, and History." In *New Working-Class Studies*, edited by John Russo and Sherry Linkon, 19–31. Ithaca, NY: Cornell University Press, 2005.

Finney, Russ L., Maurice D. Weir, and Frank R. Giordano. *Thomas' Calculus Early Transcendentals*. 10th ed. New York: Addison Wesley Longman, 2001.

Fisher, Marvin. "Melville's 'Bell Tower': A Double Thrust." *Part 1*. Special issue of *American Quarterly* 18.2 (1966): 200–207.

———. "Melville's 'Tartarus': The Deflowering of New England." *American Quarterly* 23.1 (1971): 79–100.

Fitelson, David. "Stephen Crane's *Maggie* and Darwinism." In *Stephen Crane, Maggie: A Girl of the Streets*, edited by Thomas A. Gullason, 108–11. New York: W. W. Norton, 1979.

Fitzgerald, F. Scott. *The Great Gatsby*. Edited by Matthew J. Bruccoli. New York: Macmillan, 1992.

Fletcher, Bill, Jr. "How Race Enters Class in the United States." In *What's Class Got to Do with It? American Society in the Twenty-First Century*, edited by Michael Zweig, 35–44. Ithaca, NY: Cornell University Press, 2004.

Foucault, Michel. *The Essential Foucault*. Edited by Paul Rabinow and Nikolas Rose. New York: New Press, 2003.

———. *Power/Knowledge: Selected Interviews and Other Writings, 1972–1977*. Edited by Colin Gordon. New York: Pantheon Books, 1980.

Friese, Heidrun. "Introduction." *Identities: Time, Difference and Boundaries*. New York: Berghahn Books, 2002.

Fritzsche, Peter. "Introduction: Nietzsche's Life and Works." In *Nietzsche and the Death of God: Selected Writings*, translated by Peter Fritzsche, 1–39. New York: Bedford/St. Martin's, 2007.
Frow, John. *Marxism and Literary History*. New York: Blackwell, 1988.
Gandal, Keith. "*Maggie* and the Modern Soul." *ELH* 60.3 (1993): 758–85.
Goldsmith, Meredith. "White Skin, White Mask: Passing, Posing and Performing in *The Great Gatsby*." *Modern Fiction Studies* 49.3 (2003): 443–68.
Gordon, Colin. "Introduction." In *Power/Knowledge: Selected Interviews and Other Writings, 1972–1977*, edited by Colin Gordon. New York: Pantheon Books, 1980.
Hall, Robert T. "Introduction." In *Ethics and Social Morals*, translated by Robert T. Hall. Buffalo, NY: Prometheus Books, 1993.
Hansen, Klaus P. "The Sentimental Novel and Its Feminist Critique." *Early American Literature* 26.1 (1991): 39–54.
Hapke, Laura. *Labor's Text: The Worker in American Fiction*. New Brunswick, NJ: Rutgers, 2001.
Hardcastle, Valerie Gray. *Constructing the Self*. Philadelphia: John Benjamins North America, 2008.
Harper, Dean. "Recommended: Studs Terkel." *English Journal* 72.7 (1983): 80.
Harris, Sharon M. "'A New Era in Female History': Nineteenth-Century U.S. Women Writers." *American Literature* 74.3 (2002): 603–18.
Hesford, Walter. "Literary Contexts of *Life in the Iron Mills*." *American Literature* 49.1 (1977): 70–85.
Hitchcock, Peter. "They Must Be Represented? Problems in Theories in Working-Class Representation." *PLMA* 115.1 (2000): 20–32.
Hitlin, Steven. "Values as the Core of Personal Identity: Drawing Links between Two Theories of Self." *Social Psychology Quarterly* 66.2 (2003): 118–37.
Hogan, Patrick Colm. *Cognitive Science, Literature, and the Arts: A Guide for Humanists*. London: Routledge, 2003.
Hogg, Michael, and Dominic Abrams. "Social Identity and Social Cognition: Historical Background and Current Trends." In *Social Identity and Social Cognition*, edited by Dominic Abrams and Michael A. Hogg, 1–25. Oxford: Blackwell, 1999.
Hollander, Jocelyn A., and Judith A. Howard. "Social Psychological Theories on Social Inequalities." *Special Millennium Issue on the State of Sociological Social Psychology*. Special issue of *Social Psychology Quarterly* 63.4 (2000): 338–51.
Holquist, Michael. "Stereotyping in Autobiography and Historiography: Colonialism in *The Great Gatsby*." *Poetics Today* 9.2 (1988): 453–72.
Hook, Derek. *Foucault, Psychology and the Analytics of Power*. New York: Palgrave Macmillan, 2007.
Horvat, Erin McNamara, Elliot B. Weininger, and Annette Lareau. "From Social Ties to Social Capital: Class Differences in the Relations between Schools and Parent Networks." *American Educational Research Journal* 40.2 (2003): 319–51.
Howard, Judith A. "Social Psychology of Identities." *Annual Review of Sociology* 26 (2000): 367–93.
Howells, William Dean. "New York Low Life in Fiction." In *Stephen Crane, Maggie: A Girl of the Streets*, edited by Thomas A. Gullason, 154–56. New York: W. W. Norton, 1979.
Hughes, Langston. "Johannesburg Mines." In *American Working-Class Literature: An Anthology*, edited by Nicholas Coles and Janet Zandy, 371. New York: Oxford University Press, 2007.
———. "Office Building Evening." In *American Working-Class Literature: An Anthology*, edited by Nicholas Coles and Janet Zandy, 374. New York: Oxford University Press, 2007.

———. "Park Bench." In *American Working-Class Literature: An Anthology*, edited by Nicholas Coles and Janet Zandy, 371. New York: Oxford University Press, 2007.
Hull, Gloria T. "Notes on a Marxist Interpretation of Black American Literature." *Black American Literature Forum* 12.4 (1978): 148–53.
Huntington, Samuel, P. "Foreword." In *Culture Matters: How Values Shape Human Progress*, edited by Lawrence E. Harrison and Samuel P. Huntington, xiii–xvi. New York: Basic Books, 2000.
Huspek, Michael. "Oppositional Codes and Social Class Relations." *British Journal of Sociology* 45.1 (1995): 79–102.
Hutcheon, Linda. *A Poetics of Postmodernism: History, Theory, Fiction*. New York: Routledge, 1992.
Hyman, Richard. "Marxist Thought and the Analysis of Work." In *Social Theory at Work*, edited by Marek Korczynski, Randy Hodson, and Paul Edwards, 26–55. New York: Oxford University Press, 2006.
Jameson, Fredric. *Postmodernism or, the Cultural Logic of Late Capitalism*. Durham, NC: Duke University Press, 2005.
Jensen, Barbara. "Across the Great Divide: Crossing Classes and Clashing Cultures." *What's Class Got to Do with It? American Society in the Twenty-First Century*. Ithaca, NY: Cornell University Press, 2004. 168–83.
Johnson, Randal. "Introduction." In *The Field of Cultural Production* (Pierre Bourdieu), edited by Randal Johnson, 1–25. New York: Columbia University Press, 1993.
Katz, Joseph. "Art and Compromise: The 1893 and the 1896 *Maggie*." In *Stephen Crane, Maggie: A Girl of the Streets*, edited by Thomas A. Gullason, 194–202. New York: W. W. Norton, 1979.
Katznelson, Ira. "Introduction." In *Working-Class Formation: Nineteenth-Century Patterns in Western Europe and the United States*, edited by Ira Katznelson and Aristide R. Zolberg. Princeton, NJ: Princeton University Press, 1986.
Kazin, Alfred, ed. *F. Scott Fitzgerald: The Man and His Work*. New York: World Publishing, 1951.
Kehl, D. G., and Allene Cooper. "Sangrai in the Sangreal: *The Great Gatsby* as Grail Quest." *Rocky Mountain Review of Language and Literature* 47.4 (1993): 203–17.
Keller, James R. "'A Chafing Savage Down the Decent Street': The Politics of Compromise in Claude McKay's Protest Sonnets." *African-American Review* 28.3 (1994): 447–56.
King, Laura A., and James W. Pennebaker. "What's So Great About Feeling Good." *Psychological Inquiry* 9.1 (1998): 53–56.
Kingston, Paul W. "The Unfulfilled Promise of Cultural Capital Theory." *Sociology of Education* 74 (2001): 88–99.
Knouse, Jessica. "From Identity Politics to Ideology Politics." *Utah Law Review* 3 (2009): 749–814.
Korczynski, Marek, Randy Hodson, and Paul K. Edwards. "Introduction." *Social Theory at Work*. London: Oxford University Press, 2006. 1–25.
Kripke, Saul A. *Wittgenstein on Rules and Private Language: An Elementary Exposition*. Cambridge, MA: Harvard University Press, 1982.
Lacey, Joanne. "Discursive Mothers and Academic Fandom: Class, Generation and the Production of Theory." In *Cultural Studies and the Working Class: Subject to Change*, edited by Sally Munt, 36–50. London: Cassell, 2000.
Lauter, Paul. "Under Construction: Working-Class Writing." In *New Working-Class Studies*, edited by John Russo and Sherry Linkon, 63–77. Ithaca, NY: Cornell University Press, 2005.
Lawler, Steph. " Escape and Escapism: Representing Working-Class Women." In *Cultural Studies and the Working Class: Subject to Change*, edited by Sally Munt, 113–28. London: Cassell, 2000.

Lee, Lisa Yun. "The Politics of Language in Frederick Douglass's *Narrative of the Life of an American Slave*." Before the Centennial. Special issue of *Melus* 17.2 (1992): 51–59.
Leiter, Brian. "Nietzsche and the Morality Critics." *Ethics* 107.2 (1997): 250–85.
Lenhart, Gary. *The Stamp of Class Reflections of Poetry and Social Class*. Ann Arbor: University of Michigan Press, 2006.
Lin, Nan. "Inequality in Social Capital." *Contemporary Sociology* 29.6 (2000): 785–95.
Lockridge, Ernest. "Introduction." In *Twentieth Century Interpretations of* The Great Gatsby, edited by. Ernest Lockridge, 1–18. Englewood Cliffs, NJ: Prentice-Hall, 1968.
Lukens, Margaret. "Gatsby as a Drowned Sailor." *The English Journal* 76.2 (1987):44–46. Print.
Lutwack, Leonard. "William Dean Howells and the 'Editor's Study.'" *American Literature* 24 (1952): 195–207.
Lyotard, Jean-François. *The Postmodern Condition: A Report on Knowledge*. Translated by Geoff Bennington and Brian Massumi. Minneapolis: University of Minnesota Press, 1984.
Machin, Steve. "The Economic Approach to Analysis of the Labor Market." In *Social Theory at Work*, edited by Marek Korczynski, Randy Hodson, and Paul Edwards, 182–207. New York: Oxford University Press, 2006.
Mackall, Joseph. "The Stories of Working-Class Lights." In *Writing Work: Writers on Working-Class Writing*, edited by David Shevin, Larry Smith, and Janet Zandy, 8–16. Huron: Bottom Dog Press, 1999.
MacLaury, Robert E. "Prototypes Revisited." *Annual Review of Anthropology* 20 (1991): 55–74.
Madden, David. "Introduction." *Proletarian Writers of the Thirties*. Carbondale: Southern Illinois University Press, 1968. xv–xlii.
Marx, Karl. *Capital: A Critique of Political Economy*. Translated by Samuel Moore and Edward Aveling. Vol 1. New York: International Publishers, 1967.
Marx, Karl, and Friedrich Engels. *The German Ideology: Part One with Selections from Parts Two and Three and Supplementary Texts*. Edited by C. J. Arthur. London: International Publishers, 1970.
———. "Manifesto of the Communist Party." In *Basic Writings on Politics and Philosophy*, edited by Lewis S. Feuer, 6–41. New York: Doubleday, 1989.
Medhurst, Andy. "If Anywhere: Class Identifications and Cultural Studies Academics." In *Cultural Studies and the Working Class: Subject to Change*, edited by Sally Munt, 19–35. London: Cassell, 2000.
Melville, Herman. "Benito Cereno." In *Herman Melville: Billy Budd and Other Stories*, edited by Frederick Bush, 159–258. New York: Penguin, 1986.
———. "The Paradise of Bachelors and the Tartarus of Maids." In *Herman Melville: Billy Budd and Other Stories*, edited by Frederick Bush, 259–86. New York: Penguin, 1986.
Metzgar, Jack. "Politics and the American Class Vernacular." In *New Working-Class Studies*, edited by John Russo and Sherry Linkon, 189–208. Ithaca, NY: Cornell University Press, 2005.
Meyer, Renate E., Kerstin Sahlin, Marc J. Ventresca, and Peter Walgenbach, eds. *Institutions and Ideology*. Bingley, UK: Emerald Group, 2009.
Michaels, Walter Benn. *The Trouble with Diversity: How We Learned to Love Identity and Ignore Inequality*. New York: Henry Holt, 2006.
Migotti, Mark. "Slave Morality, Socrates, and the Bushmen: A Reading of the First Essay of *On the Genealogy of Morals*." *Philosophy and Phenomenological Research* 58.4 (1998): 745–79.
Miles, Caroline S. "Representing and Self-Mutilating the Laboring Male Body: Re-examining Rebecca Harding Davis's *Life in the Iron Mills*." *ATQ* 18 (2004): 89–104.
Mills, Catherine. "Contesting the Political: Butler and Foucault on Power and Resistance." *Journal of Political Philosophy* 11.3 (2003): 253–72.

Moberg, David. "New Concepts of Class." *The Progressive* 64.9 (2000): 41–43.
Monteiro, George. "Carraway's Complaint." *Journal of Modern Literature* 24.1 (2000): 161–71.
Monroe, Kristen. "How Identity and Perspective Constrain Moral Choice." *International Political Science Review/Revue Internationale de Science Politique*. 24.4 (2003): 405–425. Print.
Moran, Seana, Mindy Kornhaber, and Howard Gardner. "Orchestrating Multiple Intelligences." *Educational Leadership* 64.1 (2006): 22–27.
Moss, Kristin, and William V. Faux II. "The Enactment of Cultural Identity in Student Conversations on Intercultural Topics." *Howard Journal of Communications* 17.1 (2006): 21–37.
Mouffe, Chantal. "Hegemony and New Political Subjects: Toward a New Concept of Democracy." In *Marxism and the Interpretation of Culture*, edited by Cary Nelson and Lawrence Grossberg, 89–104. Urbana: Illinois University Press, 1988.
Munt, Sally. "Introduction." In *Cultural Studies and the Working Class: Subject to Change*, edited by Sally Munt, 1–16. London: Cassell, 2000.
Murphy, Geraldine. "Olaudah Equiano, Accidental Tourist." *African-American Culture in the Eighteenth-Century*. Special issue of *Eighteenth-Century Studies* 27.4 (1994): 551–68.
Nickles, Shelley. "More Is Better: Mass Consumption, Gender, and Class Identity in Postwar America." *American Quarterly* 54.4 (2002): 581–622.
Nietzsche, Friedrich. *Basic Writing of Nietzsche*. Translated by Walter Kaufmann. New York: Modern Library, 1968.
———. *Nietzsche and the Death of God: Selected Writings*. Translated by Peter Fritzsche. New York: Bedford/St. Martin's, 2007.
Norris, Frank. "Stephen Crane's Stories of Life in the Slums: Maggie and George's Mother." In *Maggie: A Girl of the Streets*, edited by Thomas A. Gullason, 151. New York: W. W. Norton. 1979.
Oatley, Keith. "Emotions and the Story Worlds of Fiction." In *Narrative Impact: Social and Cognitive Foundations*, edited by Melanie C. Green, Jeffery S. Strange, and Timothy C. Brock, 39–70. Mahwah, NJ: Lawrence Erlbaum, 2002.
O'Connor, Carla. "Comment: Making Sense of Complexity of Social Identity in Relation to Achievement: A Sociological Challenge in the New Millennium." *Extra Issue: Current of Thought: Sociology of Education at the Dawn of the 21st Century*. Special issue of *Sociology of Education* 74 (2001): 159–68.
Ohmann, Richard. "Politics and Genre in Nonfiction Prose." *New Literary History* 11.2 (1980): 237–44.
O'Neale, Sondra A. "Challenge to Wheatley's Critics: 'There Was No Other Game in Town.'" *Journal of Negro Education* 54.4 (1985): 500–511.
Operario, Don, and Susan T. Fiske. "Integrating Social Identity and Social Cognition: A Framework for Bridging Diverse Perspectives." In *Social Identity and Social Cognition*, edited by Dominic Abrams and Michael A. Hogg, 26–54. Oxford: Blackwell, 1999.
Ornstein, Robert. "Scott Fitzgerald's Fable of East and West." In *Twentieth Century Interpretations of* The Great Gatsby, edited by Ernest Lockridge, 54–60. Englewood Cliffs, NJ: Prentice-Hall, 1968.
Owen, David. "Equality, Democracy, and Self-Respect: Reflections on Nietzsche's Agonal Perfectionism." *Journal of Nietzsche Studies* 24 (2002): 113–31.
Pakulski, Jan, and Malcolm Waters. "The Reshaping and the Dissolution of Social Classes in an Advanced Society." *Theory and Society* 25.5 (1996): 667–91.
Panitch, Leo. "September 11 and Its Aftermath through the Lens of Class." In *What's Class Got to Do with It? American Society in the Twenty-First Century*, edited by Michael Zweig, 77–93. Ithaca, NY: Cornell University Press, 2004.

Parker, Hershel, and Brian Higgins. "Maggie's 'Last Night': Authorial Design and Editorial Patching." In *Stephen Crane, Maggie: A Girl of the Streets*, edited by Thomas A. Gullason, 234–44. New York: W. W. Norton, 1979.

Pearson, Roger L. "Gatsby: False Profit of the American Dream." *English Journal* 59.5 (1970): 638–45.

Person, Leland S., Jr. "'Herstory' and Daisy Buchanan." *American Literature* 50.2 (1978): 250–57.

Pescosolido, Bernice A., and Beth A. Rubin. "The Web of Group Affiliations Revisited: Social Life, Postmodernism and Sociology." *Looking Forward, Looking Back: Continuity and Change at the Turn of the Millennium*. Special issue of *American Sociological Review* 65.1 (2000): 52–76.

Pidgeon, John A. "*The Great Gatsby.*" *Modern Age* 49 (2007): 178–82.

Pinker, Steven. *The Blank Slate*. New York: Viking, 2002.

Piven, Frances Fox. "Neoliberal Social Policy and Labor Market Discipline." *What's Class Got to Do with It? American Society in the Twenty-First Century*. Ed Michael Zweig. Ithaca, NY: Cornell University Press, 2004. 113–24.

Pizer, Donald. "Bad Critical Writing." *Philosophy and Literature* 22.1 (1998): 69–82.

———. "Late Nineteenth-Century American Realism: An Essay in Definition." *Nineteenth-Century Fiction* 16.3 (1961): 263–69.

———. "Stephen Crane's Maggie and American Naturalism." *Stephen Crane, Maggie: A Girl of the Streets*. Ed. Thomas A. Gullason. New York: W. W. Norton, 1979. 186–193. Print.

Quan, Katie. "Global Strategies for Workers: How Class Analysis Clarifies Us and Them and What We Need to Do." In *What's Class Got to Do with It? American Society in the Twenty-First Century*, edited by Michael Zweig, 94–110. Ithaca, NY: Cornell University Press, 2004.

Ratner, Carl. "Agency and Culture." *Journal for the Theory of Social Behaviour* 30.4 (2000): 413–34.

Reginster, Bernard. "Nietzsche on Ressentiment and Valuation." *Philosophy and Phenomenological Research* 57.2 (1997): 281–305.

Riis, Jacob. "From How the Other Half Lives." *Stephen Crane, Maggie: A Girl of the Streets*. Ed. Thomas A. Gullason. New York: W. W. Norton, 1979. 75–84. Print.

Russo, John, and Sherry Linkon, eds. *New Working-Class Studies*. Ithaca, NY: Cornell University Press, 2005.

———. *Steel-Town U.S.A.* Lawrence: University Press of Kansas, 2002.

Sabino, Robin, and Jennifer Hall. "The Path Not Taken: Cultural Identity in the Interesting Life of Olaudah Equiano." *Melus* 24.1 (1999): 5–19.

Schocket, Eric. "Undercover Explorations of the 'Other Half,' or the Writer as Class Transvestite." *Representations* 64 (1998): 103–33.

Scott, Alan. "Capitalism, Weber and Democracy." *Max Weber Studies* 1.1 (1997): 31–53.

Scrimgeour, Gary J. "Against *The Great Gatsby*." In *Twentieth Century Interpretations of The Great Gatsby*, edited by Ernest Lockridge, 70–82. Englewood Cliffs, NJ: Prentice-Hall, 1968.

Seguin, Robert. "Ressentiment and the Social Poetics of *The Great Gatsby*: Fitzgerald Reads Cather." *Modern Fiction Studies* 46.4 (2000): 918–40.

Serravallo, Vincent. "Review of *How Class Works: Power and Social Movement*, by Stanley Aronowitz." *Social Science Review* 78.3 (2004): 514–16.

Settle, Glenn. "Fitzgerald's Daisy: The Siren Voice." *American Literature* 57.1 (1985): 115–24.

Shayla, Heidi. "Working Poor." In *Writing Work: Writers on Working-Class Writing*, edited by David Shevin, Larry Smith, and Janet Zandy, 17–23. Huron: Bottom Dog Press, 1999.

Shefter, Martin. "Trade Unions and Political Machines: The Organization and Disorganization of the American Working Class in the Late Nineteenth Century." In *Working-Class Formation: Nineteenth-Century Patterns in Western Europe and the United States*, edited by Ira Katznelson and Aristide R. Zolberg, 197–276. Princeton, NJ: Princeton University Press, 1986.
Shevin, David, Larry Smith, and Janet Zandy, eds. *Writing Work: Writers on Working-Class Writing*. Huron: Bottom Dog Press, 1999.
Shweder, Richard A. "Moral Maps, 'First World' Conceits, and the New Evangelists." In *Culture Matters: How Values Shape Human Progress*, edited by Lawrence E. Harrison and Samuel P. Huntington, 158–76. New York: Basic Books, 2000.
Skeggs, Beverley. "The Appearance of Class: Challenges in Gay Space." In *Cultural Studies and the Working Class: Subject to Change*, edited by Sally Munt, 129–50. London: Cassell, 2000.
Smith, Larry. "Introduction." In *Writing Work: Writers on Working-Class Writing*, edited by David Shevin, Larry Smith, and Janet Zandy, 5–8. Huron: Bottom Dog Press, 1999.
Solomon, Eric. "Maggie and the Parody of Popular Fiction." *Stephen Crane, Maggie: A Girl of the Streets*. Ed. Thomas A. Gullason. New York: W. W. Norton, 1979. 116–120. Print.
Somers, Margaret R. "The Narrative Construction of Identity: A Relational and Network Approach." *Theory and Society* 23.5 (1994): 605–49.
———. "Narrativity, Narrative Identity, and Social Action: Rethinking English Working-Class Formation." *Social Science History* 16.4 (1992): 591–630.
Sørensen, Aage B. "Toward a Sounder Basis for Class Analysis." *American Journal of Sociology* 105.6 (2000): 1523–58.
Stallman, Robert W. "Introduction to *Stephen Crane: An Omnibus*. New York: Alfred A. Knoph, 1970. Print.
Stavola, Thomas J. *Scott Fitzgerald: Crisis in American Identity*. London: Vision Press, 1979. Print.
Stern, J. P. *Nietzsche*. London: Fontana/Collins, 1981.
Stets, Jan E., and Peter J. Burke. "Identity Theory and Social Identity Theory." *Social Psychology Quarterly* 63.3 (2000): 224–37.
Strozier, Robert M. *Foucault, Subjectivity, and Identity: Historical Constructions of Subject and Self*. Detroit: Wayne State University Press, 2002.
Stryker, Sheldon, and Peter J. Burke. "The Past, Present, and Future of an Identity Theory." *Social Psychology Quarterly* 63.4 (2000): 284–97.
Swarts, Heidi. "Review of *How Class Works: Power and Social Movement*, by Stanley Aronowitz." *Perspectives on Political Science* 33 (2004): 187.
Swartz, David. *Culture and Power: The Sociology of Pierre Bourdieu*. Chicago: University Press of Chicago, 1997.
Swedberg, Robert "Introduction." In *Essays in Economic Sociology*, edited by Richard Swedberg, 3–39. Princeton, NJ: Princeton University Press, 1999.
Terkel, Studs. *Working: People Talk About What They Do All Day and How They Feel About What They Do*. New York: Pantheon Books, 1974.
Tester, Keith. "Between Sociology and Theology: The Spirit of Capitalism Debate." *The Sociological Review*, 48.1 (2000): 43–57.
Thompson, Graham. "Review of *Labor Texts: The Worker in American Fiction*, by Laura Hapke." *Yearbook of English Studies* 34.1 (2004): 329–30.
Tokarczyk, Michelle M. "Promises to Keep: Working Class Students in Higher Education." In *What's Class Got to Do with It? American Society in the Twenty-First Century*, edited by Michael Zweig, 161–68. Ithaca, NY: Cornell University Press, 2004.
Traub, James. "Multiple Intelligence Disorder." *New Republic*, October 26, 1998: 20–23.

Tyler, Gus. "Review of *What's Class Got to Do with It? American Society in the Twenty-First Century*. Ed. Michael Zweig." *New Leader* 83.9 (2003): 27–28.

———. "Review of *Working: People Talk About What They Do All Day and How They Feel About What They Do*." *Industrial and Labor Relations Review* 28.2 (1974): 324–25.

Veblen, Thorstein. "The Instinct of Workmanship and the Irksomeness of Labor." *American Journal of Sociology* 4 (1898): 188–202.

———. *The Theory of the Leisure Class*. New York: Dover, 1994.

Walton, Mary. *The Deming Management Method*. New York: Perigee Books, 1986.

Warren, Mark. "Nietzsche's Concept of Ideology." *Theory and Society* 13.4 (1984): 541–65.

Watkins, Floyd C. "Fitzgerald's Jay Gatz and the Young Ben Franklin." *New England Quarterly* 27.2 (1954): 249–52.

Weber, Max, and Frank H. Knight. *General Economic History*. New York: Collier Books, 1961.

Weber, Max, and Richard Swedberg. "The Area of Economics, Economic Theory and Ideal Types." In *Essays in Economic Sociology*. Princeton, NJ: Princeton University Press, 1999.

———. "The Spirit of Capitalism." In *Essays in Economic Sociology*. Princeton, NJ: Princeton University Press, 1999.

Will, Barbara. "*The Great Gatsby* and the Obscene Word." *College Literature* 32.4 (2005): 126–44.

Williams, Damian T. "Review of *New Working-Class Studies* by John Russo and Sherry Linkon." *Work and Occupations* 34.1 (2007): 102–4.

Wittgenstein, Ludwig. *The Wittgenstein Reader*. Edited by Anthony Kenny. Oxford: Blackwell, 1994.

Wright, Thomas. *Some Habits and Customs of the Working Classes by a Journeyman Engineer*. New York: Augustus M. Kelley, 1967.

Young, Philip. "The Machine in the Tartarus: Melville's Inferno." *American Literature* 63.2 (1991): 208–24.

Zandy, Janet. *Hands, Physical Labor, Class, and Cultural Work*. New Brunswick, NJ: Rutgers University Press, 2004.

Zweig, Michael. "Introduction." *What's Class Got to Do with It? American Society in the Twenty-First Century*. Ithaca, NY: Cornell University Press, 2004. 1–18.

Index

Aaron, Daniel 277, 260
Abrams, Dominic 192, 265
academic capital *see* capital, academic
The Adventures of Huckleberry Finn 254
The Adventures of Tom Sawyer 254
African American 5, 54, 55, 118, 145, 196, 211, 235; culture 118; genre 98, 107; slaves 119, 107, 119, 128
The Age of Innocence 254
agency 1, 7, 8, 21, 32, 48, 67, 70, 92, 130, 143, 153, 154, 161–163, 165, 170, 173, 177, 187, 188, 190, 191, 194–198, 202, 206, 209, 210, 211, 213, 219, 220, 222, 223, 228, 231, 238, 244, 249, 251, 252, 255, 257, 258, 259
Althusser, Louis 6, 42, 43, 94, 153, 154, 169, 175, 251, 260; *Lenin and Philosophy, and Other Essays* 6, 42, 43, 94, 153, 154, 169, 175, 251, 260
altruism 7, 174–176, 200, 206, 249
American Dream 50, 51, 86, 145, 148, 170, 231, 232, 235, 236, 238, 239, 240, 241, 242, 244, 245, 246, 249; hyper 51
American identity of class 237, 245
anti-capitalist economists and philosophers 20
Antonio, Robert J. 184, 185, 260
Arms, George 227, 260
Arnellos, Argyris 193, 260
Aronowitz, Stanley 50, 58, 64–68, 82, 84, 87, 140, 186, 187, 198, 260
Austen, Jane 134
autonomy 4, 45, 53, 73, 87, 144, 152, 192, 198

"Bad Critical Writing" 148, 268
Baker, Josephine E. 111, 260
barbaric stage 36
Barber, Denise 147
"Bartleby, the Scrivener: A Story of Wall-street" 121
Basic Writing of Nietzsche 173, 174
Basic Writings on Politics and Philosophy 218
Bates, Carl Murray 139, 141
Baudrillard, Jean 11, 12, 17, 26, 33, 184, 260; *The Mirror of Production* 11, 12, 17, 26, 33, 184, 260

Baym, Nina 118, 259, 260; *Woman's Fiction: A Guide to Novels By and About Women in America, 1820–1870* 259
Becker, George 97
"Becoming American: The Working Class in the United States Before the Civil War" 78–79, 80
belief systems 92, 146, 147, 195, 238, 243, 244, 251
Berger, Bennett M. 38, 48, 50, 52, 61, 74, 85–87, 130, 137, 206, 223, 260; *Working-Class Suburb: A Study of Auto Workers in Suburbia* 49, 50, 52, 74, 86–87, 137, 206
Berrigan Ted 136
Best, Steven 179, 180, 260
Bewley, Marius 239, 240, 260
Beyond Good and Evil 173
Bicknell, John W. 243, 260
Billy Budd 122, 123, 254
Billy Budd and Other Stories 103, 111–116, 121–124, 130, 212, 252, 253, 258
The Blithedale Romance 253
Bourdieu 6, 7, 66, 94, 153, 161, 162, 163, 164, 166–170, 177, 187, 195, 200, 207, 216, 251, 252, 258, 260; *Distinctions* 132, 154–158, 166, 167, 175, 222; *The Field of Cultural Production* 45, 152, 260; *Language and Symbolic Power* 32, 150, 260; *Practical Reason* 33, 100, 166, 169, 170, 195, 260
bourgeoisie 17, 29, 31, 33, 36, 37, 53, 81, 94, 119, 218, 121, 157, 167, 218; ideology 18; thought 33
Bowe, John 6, 24, 69, 260; *Gig: Americans Talk About Their Job* 24, 143–147, 260
Bowe, Marisa 6, 24, 69, 143, 144, 260, 261
Bowery 217, 218, 220, 221, 222, 223, 224
Bowery B'hoy 121
Brace, Charles Loring 230, 261
Brantlinger, Guskin 198, 199, 203, 261
Brantlinger, Majd-Jabbari 198, 199, 203, 261
Bridges, Amy 49, 76, 77, 81, 105, 154, 261; "Becoming American: The Working Class in the United States Before the Civil War" 78–79, 80
Bright, Edward 229, 261

271

Brobjer, Thomas 174, 200, 261
Brown, Alison Leigh 159, 171, 261
Brown, Andrew 11, 261
Brown, Kenneth D. 15, 29, 261
Burke, Peter J. 190, 191, 192, 269

Callahan, John F 231, 241, 245, 261
Camfield, David 53, 261
capital 28, 33, 47, 57, 76, 80, 100, 105, 111, 112, 129, 130, 136, 140, 153, 157, 158, 163, 164, 165, 166, 167, 168, 177, 190, 208, 211, 212, 214, 216, 217, 218, 220, 232, 252; academic 100, 168; cultural 7, 37, 67, 87, 145, 155, 158, 163, 166–169, 187, 197, 199, 200, 202, 203, 204, 205, 208, 211, 212, 219, 222, 223, 224, 228, 232, 234, 240, 244, 248, 250, 251, 254; educational 1, 167; moral 172; social 7, 37, 100, 140, 145, 158, 163, 166, 168, 187, 197, 199, 200, 202, 208, 211, 212, 213, 219, 224, 228, 232, 234, 240, 244, 250, 251, 254; symbolic 7, 37, 74, 97, 95, 140, 145, 152, 158, 163, 212, 219, 222, 224, 228, 233, 234, 250, 251, 254
Capital: A Critique of Political Economy 10, 11, 12, 13, 15, 25, 27, 28, 29
capitalism 7, 14, 18, 20, 25–31, 33, 37, 39, 42, 52–59, 67, 76–78, 80, 81, 103, 111, 112, 116, 118, 120, 128, 129, 140, 143, 145, 153, 182, 214, 217, 218, 225, 257; domination 53; economy 11, 25; enterprise 81; epoch 42, 56; forces 2; manufacturing 29; narratives 50; philosophy 86; pseudo 122; society 20, 42, 183; system 110, 140, 217, 249
Carlson, Arvid J. 65, 261
Carter, Everett 97, 261
Cary, Alice 102
Cat on a Hot Tin Roof 254
Cather, Willa 101, 254; "Neighbor Rosicky" 101
Charles, Maria 188, 261
Chen, Jie-Qi 151, 261
Christensen, Paul 206, 207, 261
Christopher, Renny 48, 98, 99, 247, 261
civil rights 65, 66, 181, 196
Clark, Suzanne 259; *Sentimental Modernism: Women Writers and the Revolution of the Word* 259
class 31–43; conflict 68; consciousness 77, 86; culture 82; designation 4; divisions 87; dominance 23; economic 30; identity 93; in literature 6; managerial 31; middle 4, 30, 38, 47, 52, 53, 56, 57, 61, 62, 66, 67, 70, 72, 73, 74, 75, 80, 81, 83, 85, 86, 87, 92, 93, 95, 96, 116, 120, 124–129, 131, 132, 134, 135, 139, 140, 142, 144, 145, 146, 156, 157, 167, 191, 192, 193, 197, 199, 200, 201, 202; signs 6; struggle 33, 41, 53, 57, 79, 98, 117, 148, 258; theories 6, 7, 8, 9, 46, 53, 54, 55, 65, 69
classism 84
Clawson, Dan 65, 67, 68, 261

Cloud, Dana L. 199, 261
Cobble, Dorothy Sue 54, 55–56, 57, 261
Coles, Nicholas 6, 56, 98, 99, 102, 103, 104–119, 130, 138, 139, 148, 149, 258, 261
collective consciousness 85, 154, 218
college graduates 168
Collier, M.J. 153
commodity 10–19, 21, 22, 24–28, 30, 31, 37, 39, 88, 163, 210, 218, 220, 257
communal group 31
communal house 22, 24, 39
communism 18, 25, 30, 35, 36, 39, 79, 181; primitive 35
The Communist Party 181, 263; American 98, 117, 1–32, 181
Conley, James R. 70, 261
Conroy, Marianne 201, 262
consciousness, (working) class 34, 50, 71, 77, 86, 121, 186, 217, 218
conspicuous: achievement 74; action 223, 228; consumption 18, 37, 38, 39, 87, 142, 143, 208, 222; waste 18, 37
construction of class 6
Cook, John 94–95, 156, 262; "Culture, Class and Taste" 94–95, 156, 262
Cooper, Allene 237, 265
core metanarrative 64, 95, 145, 162, 198, 201, 209, 210
Coreno, Thaddeus 207, 262
Corley, Íde 107, 108, 109, 262
Couldry, Nick 190, 262
counterculture 47, 180, 181, 182
Crane, Stephen 218, 220, 221, 223, 224, 225, 226, 227, 228, 230, 262; *Maggie: A Girl of the Streets* 217–230
crisis in identity 231, 233, 237, 242
Crompton, Rosemary 73, 262
crossover experience 64
cultural capital *see* capital, cultural
cultural studies 69, 85, 91, 92, 155
Cultural Studies and the Working Class: Subject to Change 92–96, 265
cultural turn 154, 180
culture 32, 48, 49, 50, 60, 63, 67, 69, 70, 72, 73, 74, 78, 82, 83, 84, 88–93, 95, 98, 104, 105, 109, 150–156, 163, 166–169, 174, 175, 178, 182, 184, 186, 187, 188, 190, 191, 196, 202, 210; middle-class 229, 258, 259; repressive 181
Culture and Society: Contemporary Debates 188, 189, 259, 262
"Culture, Class and Taste" 94–95, 156, 262
Cunliffe, Marcus 228, 229, 262

Daigle, Christine 173, 262
Daniels, Jim 69, 72, 96, 99, 101, 134, 138, 262
Dante, Dolores 118
Darwinism 23, 34, 171, 224
Darzentas, John 193, 260
Da Vinci, Philip 142, 145
Davis, Rebecca Harding 2, 116, 117, 125, 126,

213, 217; *Life in the Iron Mills* 117, 124, 125–128, 213, 215, 262
death of god 7, 171
Decker, Jeffrey Louis 235, 239, 262
Deconstruction 1, 56, 161, 175, 205
deed(s) 24, 200, 202, 203, 205, 206, 254
DeFreitas, Gregory 59–62, 63, 64, 262
DeGenaro, William 84, 262
Deleuze and Guattiari 184
Deming 17
Democracy 88, 171, 180, 240
Derrida, Jacques 160, 175
Dickens, Charles 111, 134
Diener, Ed 50, 141, 142, 143, 144, 262
differences 7, 8, 155, 156, 166, 167, 169, 170, 177, 187, 195, 200, 201, 202, 209, 210, 216, 236, 246, 249, 251, 252, 253, 259
Diggins, John P. 18, 262
discourses 1, 7, 47, 62, 65, 66, 82, 85, 93, 99, 136, 154, 156–170, 177, 179, 180, 182, 183, 184, 186, 187, 188, 191, 193, 194, 197, 199, 202, 210–214, 219, 220, 222, 224, 225, 226, 228, 231, 233, 259; meta 182
distinctions 36, 37, 94, 156–158, 166, 169, 175, 177, 203
division of labor 20–23, 30, 35, 41, 98, 186
The Division of Labor in Society 22, 23, 42, 150
Dobson, Joanne 228, 229, 259
domestic workers 4
dominant class 99
Donaldson, Scott 234, 262
Dorsey, Peter 110, 262
Dotson, Floyd 86, 262
Douglas, Ann 259
Douglas, Mary 188, 189, 259, 262
Douglas, Peter 174
Douglass, Frederick 57, 105, 107, 109, 110, 262; *The Narrative of Frederick Douglass, an American Slave, Written by Himself* 109, 110
Dreiser, Theodore 97, 263; *Sister Carrie* 128–129, 216, 222, 242
Drudy, Sheelagh 94, 195, 263
Dubi, Steve 141, 142, 147
Dubofsky, Melvyn 76, 105, 106, 111, 181, 263, 154, 155, 162, 176, 251, 263
Duffy, Niev 59–64, 262
Dulles, Rhea 76, 105, 106, 111, 181, 263, 154, 155, 162, 176, 251, 263; *Labor in America: A History* 76, 105, 106, 111, 181, 154, 155, 263
Durkheim, Émile 2, 3, 6, 20, 22, 23, 24, 35, 41–42; *The Division of Labor in Society* 22, 23, 42, 150

economic capital *see* capital, economic
education systems (school) 38, 42, 63, 151, 167, 169, 170, 197, 203, 204, 241
Edwards, Paul K. 9, 265
elite class 19
Emirbayer, Mustafa 165, 188, 194, 259, 263
Engels, Friedrich 10, 173, 174, 217; *Basic Writings on Politics and Philosophy* 218; *The German Ideology: Part One with Selections from Parts Two and Three and Supplementary Texts* 99, 217; "Manifesto of the Communist Party" 29, 30, 33, 34, 122, 218
"Engels to Franz Mehring," *Basic Writings on Politics and Philosophy* 218, 263
The English Labor Movement 1700–1951 46, 49, 75, 77, 76, 77, 78, 80–81, 135, 154, 260, 265
The Enlightenment 1, 7, 12, 13, 17, 22, 25, 26, 35, 160, 171, 176, 180, 185, 223
equalitarianism 8, 175, 180, 200, 209, 235, 237, 249, 250; ideology 177, 200, 201, 203, 204, 208, 209, 211, 213, 235, 239, 241, 243, 249, 250, 252, 253
erasure 161
Essays in Economic Sociology 21, 26, 270
The Essential Foucault 106, 160, 161, 163
essentialism 91, 100, 105, 107, 117, 118, 120, 121, 124, 139, 186, 209, 249, 255
Evans, Geoffrey 33, 73, 87, 143, 195, 263
evolution 3, 7, 20, 22, 23, 34, 35, 39, 126, 171, 172, 173
exchange-value 14, 15, 18, 20

factory girls 111, 112, 116
factory worker(s) 53, 129, 217, 223
Fairbanks, Michael 88, 263
false consciousness 3, 6, 14, 15, 26, 35, 38, 42, 67, 153, 218, 251, 259
family norms 64
farm workers/farmers 21, 79, 101, 104, 119, 139, 141, 142, 253
Farnell, Brenda 170, 263
Farrell, Edmund J. 137, 263
fascists 185
Faux, William V., II 153, 267
feminist movement 65, 66
feudal lords 37, 39
feudalism 180, 186
field of power 1, 7, 158, 160, 163, 165, 166, 169, 234, 240, 252
Finney, Russ L. 10, 263
Fisher, Marvin: "Melville's 'Bell Tower': A Double Thrust" 114, 263; "Melville's 'Tartarus': The Deflowering of New England" 113, 114, 253
Fiske, Susan T. 191, 267
Fitelson, David 221, 224, 225, 263
Fitzgerald, Scott F. 230, 231, 233–239, 241, 242, 244, 246; *The Great Gatsby* 230–246
Fletcher, Ben 56
Fletcher, Bill, Jr. 55, 56, 57, 263
Foote, Hobart 146
Foucault, Michel 6, 7, 154–161, 162, 163, 164, 166, 171, 174, 175, 177, 184, 198, 251, 252, 263; *The Essential Foucault* 106, 160, 161, 163; *Power/Knowledge: Selected Interviews and Other Writings, 1972–1977* 163, 164, 165
Frank, Waldo 98
Freud, Sigmund 37, 42, 153, 154, 160
Friese, Heidrun 190, 263

Fritzsche, Peter 171, 172, 264
Frow, John 226, 227, 228, 230, 264

Gandal, Keith 127, 222, 223, 224, 226, 227, 229, 264
Gardner, Howard 151, 153, 267
gemeinschaft 40, 79
gender 4, 49, 52, 54, 55, 56, 63, 91, 92, 100, 104, 105, 107, 130, 160, 175, 181, 182, 185, 197, 209, 235, 259, 253; biases 55
General Economic History 20, 21, 23, 27, 39–41, 257
The German Ideology: Part One with Selections from Parts Two and Three and Supplementary Texts 99, 217
gesellschaft 78, 79
Gig: Americans Talk About Their Job 24, 143–147, 260
The Gilded Age 253
Giordano, Frank R. 10, 263
"The Glass Menagerie" 254
Goldsmith, Meredith 235, 264
Gramsci, Antonio 3, 6, 42, 65, 66, 153, 168, 250
Grayson, Jim 145
The Great Gatsby 230–246
Gronlund, Lawrence 227

habitus 7, 8, 34, 35, 66, 115, 134, 141, 146, 153, 157, 162, 166, 167, 169, 170, 175, 177, 179, 188, 189, 190, 192, 194, 195, 199, 200, 207, 210, 211, 219, 237, 246, 251, 257, 258
Hall, Jennifer 109, 268
Hall, Robert T. 35, 264
Hall, Stuart 92
Hands, Physical Labor, Class, and Cultural Work 9, 98
Hansen, Klaus P. 229, 264
Hapke, Laura 6, 99, 101, 102, 103, 117, 119–130, 138, 148, 149, 264; *Labor's Text: The Worker in American Fiction* 6, 99, 101, 102, 103, 117, 119–130, 138, 148, 149, 264
Hardcastle, Valerie Gray 188, 193, 194, 264
Harper, Dean 137, 264
Harris, Sharon M. 229, 264
Harris, Susan K. 259; *Nineteenth-Century American Women Novelists: Interpretive Strategies* 259
Harvard 84
have nots 82, 88, 133, 203
haves 82, 133, 203
Hawthorne, Nathaniel: *The Blithedale Romance* 253; *The House of the Seven Gables* 253; *The Marble Faun* 253
Haymarket hangings 97
hegemony 1, 2, 42, 65, 148, 152, 159, 181, 225, 226; of Marxism 1, 10, 32, 212
Hesford, Walter 127, 264
Hewitt, John P. 192
Higgins, Brian 224, 268
high school graduates 60

Hitchcock, Peter 48, 264
Hitlin, Steven 192, 259, 264
Hodson, Randy 9, 265
Hoellen, Eric 139, 142
Hogg, Michael 192, 265; *Social Identity and Social Cognition* 192, 265, 191, 267
Hollander, Jocelyn A. 45, 87, 264
Holquist, Michael 237, 264
honorific 24, 30, 31, 36, 37, 38, 168, 220
Hook, Derek 159, 160, 264
Horvat, Erin McNamara 203, 204, 264
The House of the Seven Gables 253
How Class Works: Power and Social Movement 64–68
Howard, Judith A. 45, 87, 187, 189, 264
Howells, William Dean 97, 98, 226, 227, 230, 264
HUAC 181
Hughes, Langston 5, 117, 132, 264; "Johannesburg Mines" 117; "Office Building Evening" 117; "Park Bench" 117
Hull, Gloria T. 100, 265
Huntington, Samuel, P. 49, 88, 89, 265
Hutcheon, Linda 7, 152, 179, 183, 184, 265; *A Poetics of Postmodernism: History, Theory, Fiction* 152, 179, 180, 183, 184
Hyman, Richard 9, 29, 265

identity 6, 7, 8, 32, 42, 47, 48, 58, 69, 70, 71, 79, 86, 96, 98, 105, 119, 143, 146, 155, 160, 162, 163, 175, 178, 179, 183–194, 196–199, 201, 202, 205–9, 213, 216, 219, 221, 225, 232, 233, 235, 242, 244, 245, 249, 251, 252, 255, 257, 259; class 60, 199; equalitarian 209; formation 185, 191; making 84, 179; markers 105; narration of 187; personal 188, 192, 197, 259; politics 91, 185, 193, 208; privileged 209; salient 191, 193; study 187; theory 185, 191, 192; working-class 93
ideology 1, 2, 3, 7, 8, 14, 32, 34, 35, 41–43, 47, 49, 63, 66, 73, 78, 82, 86, 92, 93, 99, 120, 134, 141, 143, 152, 153–157, 162, 166, 170, 171, 174, 175, 179–214, 215, 217, 218, 221, 224, 225, 228, 229, 237, 238, 241, 244, 245; altruistic 7; apparatus 38, 42, 43, 68, 115, 153, 169, 188–190, 221, 227, 241, 246, 251; bourgeois 18; concept 3, 12, 17, 200; construct 25, 57, 82, 143, 174; core 8, 25, 188, 202, 209, 243; discourses 160, 176; dominant 21, 23, 42, 154, 168, 208, 221, 225, 257; of emulation 38; equalitarian 175, 177, 201, 203, 204, 208, 209, 210, 211, 239, 240, 241, 249, 250, 254; individual 188; makeup 76; master 175; middle-class 124, 170, 218, 220, 222, 230, 254; of ownership 36; personal 168; point of view 77; position 77, 170, 188, 202, 225, 226, 235, 249; practice 169; privileged 177, 198–202, 203, 204, 206, 209, 210, 211, 233, 237, 240, 241, 244, 249, 250, 254; subordinate 225; upper-class 200, 246, 251, 252, 253, 255, 257, 258, 259;

Index

working-class 50, 134, 136, 146, 170, 201, 203, 204, 207, 209, 220, 222, 237, 244
"If We Must Die" 118
immigrants 76, 79, 105, 126, 237
imperial consciousness 56
imperialism 13
indentured servants 56, 105–9, 258
individuality 2, 76, 143, 172, 186
Industrial Revolution 111, 112, 181, 230, 258
industrial system 111
industrial working class 49, 68, 78, 79, 81, 116
inequality 49, 50, 51, 56, 59, 69, 82, 84, 87, 88, 103, 140, 150, 158, 180, 199, 205, 240
in-group/out-group 8, 41, 66, 94
instinct of workmanship 34
"The Instinct of Workmanship and the Irksomeness of Labor" 19, 270
intelligence 151, 152, 185, 199; tests 151
interpellation 7, 8, 43, 55, 94, 160, 162, 179, 185, 189, 190–197, 201, 210, 246, 249, 251, 252, 257
Invisible hand 16

Jackson, Mike 145, 146, 147
James, Henry 97, 217, 226
Jameson, Fredric 6, 182, 183, 184, 265; *Postmodernism or, the Cultural Logic of Late Capitalism* 182, 183, 184
Jensen, Barbara 63–64, 93, 265
Jewett, Sarah Orne 102, 254
"Johannesburg Mines" 117
Johnson, Randal 166, 168, 265
Jones, Jacqueline 105
joy of workmanship 18
The Jungle 217

Kaplan, Fred 259; *Sacred Tears: Sentimentality in Victorian Literature* 259
Katz, Joseph 224, 265
Katznelson, Ira 46, 49, 75, 77, 154, 265; *Working-Class Formation: Nineteenth-Century Patterns in Western Europe and the United States* 46, 49, 76–81, 154
Kazin, Alfred 240, 265
Keeley, Peter 139, 140
Kehl, D.G. 237, 265
Keller, James R. 118, 265
Kellner, Douglas 179, 180, 260
King, Laura A. 141, 143, 265
Kingston, Paul W. 155, 167, 170, 265
Knouse, Jessica 193, 265
Korczynski, Marek 9, 265
Kornhaber, Mindy 153, 267
Kripke, Saul A. 159, 265; *Wittgenstein on Rules and Private Language: An Elementary Exposition* 159, 265

Labor in America: A History 76, 105, 106, 111, 181, 154, 155, 263
labor-value 13, 15, 18, 21, 24, 28, 30, 31, 37, 107

Labor's Text: The Worker in American Fiction 6, 99, 101, 102, 103, 117, 119–130, 138, 148, 149, 264
Lacey, Joanne 94, 265
language game 2, 9, 10, 11, 45, 47, 61, 62, 75, 85, 92, 93, 96, 100, 101, 133, 156, 159, 162, 164, 186, 189, 193, 202, 211, 212, 216, 231, 234, 248, 249, 252
Lanser, Susan S. 259
Lareau, Annette 203, 204, 264
"Late Nineteenth-Century American Realism: An Essay in Definition" 97, 268
Lauter, Paul 69, 70, 71, 72, 96, 132, 133, 134, 138, 247, 248, 256
law-of-the-father 154, 160
Lawler, Steph 95, 265
Lee, Lisa Yun 110, 266
LeFevre, Mike 118, 139, 141, 142, 147
Leftists 58, 64, 68, 71, 104, 117, 181
leisure class 35–37, 112, 113, 116, 206
Leiter, Brian 174, 266
Lenhart, Gary 6, 100, 102, 131–136, 149, 266; *The Stamp of Class Reflections of Poetry and Social Class* 6, 100, 102, 131–136, 149
Lenin and Philosophy, and Other Essays 6, 42, 43, 94, 153, 154, 169, 175, 251, 260
libertarianism 184
life chances 2, 38, 39, 40, 41, 43, 48, 94, 150, 151, 155, 195, 196, 198, 199, 205, 211, 212, 234, 240, 251, 259
Life in the Iron Mills 117, 124, 125–128, 213, 215, 262
Lin, Nan 56, 266
Linkon, Sherry 8, 48, 51, 68–75, 257, 268
"Lion's Paw" 101, 116
Lockridge, Ernest 238, 244, 266
Lopez, Javier 147
low-income families 60
Lowell, Massachusetts 111, 124, 258
Lukens, Margaret 239, 266
Lutwack, Leonard 226, 266
Lyotard, Jean-François 10, 45, 47, 48, 61, 70, 86, 100, 101, 152, 156, 158, 159, 160, 182, 266; *The Postmodern Condition: A Report on Knowledge* 10, 45, 47, 48, 61, 70, 86, 100, 101, 182

Machin, Steve 16, 17, 266
Mackall, Joseph 202, 203, 205, 206, 242, 266
macro theory 1, 3, 49, 56, 84
Madden, David 98, 101, 103, 108, 266; *Proletarian Writers of the Thirties* 98, 101, 103, 108, 266
Maggie: A Girl of the Streets 217–230
Maher, Vincent 139
"Manifesto of the Communist Party" 29, 30, 33, 34, 122, 218
The Marble Faun 253
Marx, Karl 2, 3, 6, 9, 10–18, 19, 20, 22, 24–30, 33–34, 35, 36, 37, 38, 39, 41, 42, 43, 98, 121, 122, 135, 155, 160, 163, 173, 174,

201, 217, 218, 248, 251; *Basic Writings on Politics and Philosophy* 218; *The German Ideology: Part One with Selections from Parts Two and Three and Supplementary Texts* 99, 217; "Manifesto of the Communist Party" 29, 30, 33, 34, 122, 218
Marxism 1–6, 9, 10–11, 14, 17, 25, 26, 27, 30, 34, 38, 48, 52, 58, 78, 80, 85, 91, 101, 130, 135, 140, 149, 150, 158, 171, 217, 218
"Marxism and the Interpretation of Culture" 154, 191, 267
Masses 132
McCarthy Era 181
McFreely, William S. 110
McKay, Claude 117, 118; "If We Must Die" 118
Medhurst, Andy 92–93, 96, 266
Melville, Herman 103, 104, 111, 116, 121–124, 254, 258, 266; "Bartleby, the Scrivener: A Story of Wall-street" 121; "Benito Cereno" 103, 123; *Billy Budd* 122, 123, 254; *Billy Budd and Other Stories* 103, 111–116, 121–124, 130, 212, 252, 253, 258; "The Paradise of Bachelors" 111–116, 123, 124, 130; "The Paradise of Bachelors and the Tartarus of Maids" 111–116, 212; *Redburn* 103, 121, 122; "The Tartarus of Maids" 212, 111, 114–116, 124, 258
"Melville's 'Bell Tower': A Double Thrust" 114, 263
meta-capital 190
metanarratives 1, 7, 11, 23, 26, 31, 35, 47, 48, 64, 66, 70, 76, 82, 90, 93, 95, 131, 135, 145, 146, 153, 160, 162, 164, 176, 177, 179, 180, 182–184, 186–189, 193, 198, 199, 201, 208–211, 213, 214, 219–223, 225, 230, 231, 233, 234, 236; of class 47
Metzgar, Jack 47, 67, 69, 72–75, 83, 206, 266
Meyer, Renate E. 153, 266
Michaels, Walter Benn 48, 70, 74, 81–84, 85, 140, 168, 196, 198, 200, 205, 258, 259, 266; *The Trouble with Diversity: How We Learned to Love Identity and Ignore Inequality* 48, 70, 81–84, 85
Migotti, Mark 112, 113, 206, 266
Miles, Caroline S. 116, 266
Mill, John Stuart 141
Miller, Daisy 217, 233
Mills, Catherine 171, 266
Mills, Colin 33, 73, 87, 143, 195, 263
minimum wage 16, 58
The Mirror of Production 11, 12, 17, 26, 33, 184, 260
Mische, Ann 165, 188, 194, 259, 263
Moberg, David 53, 267
Moby Dick 122, 123
modernism 135, 179, 187
modernity 176, 179, 180, 193, 184, 186, 187, 222, 237
money equivalent 14
Monroe, Kristen 192, 267

Monteiro, George 239, 267
moral action 176, 187, 201, 209, 244
moralities 7, 95, 112, 174; master/noble 175, 176; slave 175, 249, 253
Moran, Seana 153, 267
Moss, Kristin 153, 267
Mouffe, Chantal 154, 191, 267; "Marxism and the Interpretation of Culture" 154, 191, 267
multiple intelligence 151
Munt, Sally 49, 91, 92, 267; *Cultural Studies and the Working Class: Subject to Change* 92–96, 265
Murphy, Geraldine 109, 110, 267
My Bondage and My Freedom 109, 110

Nardi, Marcia 133, 134
Narrative Impact: Social and Cognitive Foundations 216, 267
The Narrative of Frederick Douglass, an American Slave, Written by Himself 109, 110
narratives 7, 26, 47, 49, 50, 52, 56, 76, 84, 86, 92, 93, 94, 96, 98, 119, 122, 131, 135, 145, 146, 148, 149, 153, 160, 164, 170, 176, 179, 184, 186–190, 193, 194, 195, 197, 189, 200, 201, 210, 212, 214, 216, 219, 220, 221, 222, 225, 226, 227, 230, 231
naturalism 98, 226, 227
Negro Porters' Union Strike 118
"Neighbor Rosicky" 101
neoconservative 185
neoliberal 185
Nesbit, Robert 32
New Masses 132
new working-class studies 1, 51, 68, 73, 75, 77, 248, 258
New Working Class Studies 8, 48, 51, 68–75, 257
Nickles, Shelley 208, 267
Nietzsche, Friedrich 7, 95, 112, 154, 155, 159, 160, 162, 171–178, 185, 187, 188, 209, 210, 233, 244, 249, 253, 267; *Basic Writing of Nietzsche* 173, 174; *Beyond Good and Evil* 173; *Nietzsche and the Death of God: Selected Writings* 171
Nietzsche and the Death of God: Selected Writings 171
Nineteenth-Century American Women Novelists: Interpretive Strategies 259
Norris, Frank. 227, 229, 267; "Lion's Paw" 101, 116
nostalgia 83, 184

Oatley, Keith 216, 267
O'Connor, Carla 196, 197, 267
"Office Building Evening" 117
Ohmann, Richard 137, 139, 267
Olsen, Tillie 104, 117
O'Neal, Eugene 254
O'Neale, Sondra A. 108, 267
Operario, Don 191, 267
Ornstein, Robert 238, 241, 267

Owen, David 200, 267
ownership 18, 19, 24, 30, 34, 37, 38, 39, 107

Padgett, Ron 132, 135, 267
Pakulski, Jan 32, 267
Panitch, Leo 57, 267
"The Paradise of Bachelors" 111–116, 123, 124, 130
"The Paradise of Bachelors and the Tartarus of Maids" 111–116, 212
"Park Bench" 117
Parker, Hershel 224, 268
parody 183, 184
Parrington, Louis 97
pastiche 183
Patterson 134
peaceable savage 18
Pearson, Roger L. 239, 268
Pennebaker, James W. 141, 143, 265
performativity 4, 10, 61, 62, 70, 75, 96, 101, 131, 138, 152, 158, 159, 177, 199, 207, 210, 211, 213, 232, 248, 255
Person, Leland S., Jr. 238, 239, 268
personal identity theory 192, 259
Pescosolido, Bernice A. 186, 268
petite bourgeoisie 33, 53, 81, 121, 129, 157, 223, 225
Pidgeon, John A. 240, 268
Pinker, Steven 34, 268
Piven, Frances Fox 59, 268
Pizer, Donald 97, 148, 221, 226, 268; "Bad Critical Writing" 148, 268; "Late Nineteenth-Century American Realism: An Essay in Definition" 97, 268
pluralism 184
A Poetics of Postmodernism: History, Theory, Fiction 152, 179, 180, 183, 184
political blocs 65
polyphonic 7, 184
Porter, Carolyn 99, 268
post–Althusserian 92
post–Marxism 2, 3, 6, 18, 25, 35, 42, 66, 96, 154, 155, 175, 176, 177, 255, 259; terminology 35; theories 6, 9, 65, 99, 150–178, 179
The Postmodern Condition: A Report on Knowledge 10, 45, 47, 48, 61, 70, 86, 100, 101, 182
postmodernism 7, 25, 47, 66, 155, 161, 175, 176, 178–180, 182, 183–187, 208, 210, 222, 237, 248, 255
Postmodernism or, the Cultural Logic of Late Capitalism 182, 183, 184
poststructuralism 155, 161, 176
poverty 4, 49, 51, 54, 60, 62, 70, 73, 82
Power/Knowledge: Selected Interviews and Other Writings, 1972–1977 163, 164, 165
power network 87, 131, 136, 185, 188, 199, 200, 202, 203, 204, 206, 207, 213, 219, 223, 225, 231, 234, 237, 240, 241, 250
practice 7, 33, 45, 55, 69, 129, 136, 152, 153, 157–159, 161, 166, 169, 170, 177, 183, 186, 191, 192, 210, 211, 251, 253, 254

pre-capitalistic society 21
pre-capitalistic spirit 26
"Preface to the English Edition of 1888 'Manifesto of the Communist Party'" 29, 30, 263
pre-modern network 186
Proletarian Writers of the Thirties 98, 101, 103, 108, 266
proletariat literature 71, 98, 133, 149, 157, 249
propaganda 66, 67, 91, 216
propensities 7, 34, 96, 167, 169, 209, 210, 251
propensity for workmanship 19, 34, 36
Protestant work ethic 21, 26, 39, 135
The Protestant Work Ethic and the Spirit of Capitalism 9
Protestantism 12, 20, 39, 145
prototype 8, 45, 52, 61, 100, 112, 153, 179, 188–94, 198, 200, 210, 215, 234, 235, 237, 240, 247, 248, 249, 250, 251, 253, 254, 255

Quan, Katie 50, 58–59, 64, 65, 268

race 5, 34, 49, 52, 54, 55, 56, 57, 63, 68, 79, 82, 86, 90, 91, 92, 100, 104, 105, 107, 108, 113, 117, 123, 128, 130, 134, 148, 160, 175, 181, 184, 185, 197, 209, 233, 237, 249, 253, 254
Radner, Joan N. 259
Ratner, Carl 193, 196, 268
Ray, Debraj 88
Real, Chris 144, 145, 146
realism 5, 8, 97, 98, 100, 101, 103, 123, 226, 227–230, 253
red scare 69
Redburn 103, 121, 122
Reginster, Bernard 244, 268
resentment 187, 244
resistance 98, 107, 157, 161, 162, 169, 173, 200, 202, 206, 210, 211, 213, 221, 223, 244, 250
revolution 2, 23, 25, 42, 50, 58, 64, 65, 66, 98, 112, 168, 169, 181, 218, 250
revolutionary consciousness 77
Riis, Jacob 230, 268
Rosario, William 145, 146, 147
Ross, Larry 140
Rubin, Beth A. 186, 268
rural workers 80
Russo, John 8, 48, 51, 68–75, 257, 268; *New Working Class Studies* 8, 48, 51, 68–75, 257; *Steel-Town U.S.A* 51, 68, 69, 70, 84, 268

Sabino, Robin 109, 268
sacred cow argument 51, 119
Sacred Tears: Sentimentality in Victorian Literature 259
safety net 186
salaries 29, 142, 211, 258
salient identity 191, 193
Sanders, Bob 142
Sapyta, Jeffery J. 50, 141, 142, 143, 144, 262
Schmidt, Roy 141, 142
Schocket, Eric 230, 268
Schubert, David 133, 134

Scott, Alan 20, 21, 268
Scrimgeour, Gary J. 233, 268
Seguin, Robert 234, 268
Sensational Designs: The Cultural Work of American Fiction, 1790–1860 259
Sentimental Modernism: Women Writers and the Revolution of the Word 259
sentimentality 110, 220, 259
Serravallo, Vincent 65, 268
Settle, Glenn 238, 268
seven-tiered system 194
Shayla, Heidi 207, 268
Shefter, Martin 49, 76, 77, 78, 80–81, 135, 154, 269
Shevin, David 202, 269
Shweder, Richard A. 89, 90, 269
Sinclair, Upton 217; *The Jungle* 217
Sister Carrie 128–129, 216, 222, 242
Skeggs, Beverley 94, 269
skilled labor 12, 15, 16, 21, 28, 30
slave: narrative 108, 109, 110; system 110, 229, 230
slum novel 121, 224–231
slums 223
Smith, Adam 16
Smith, Larry 202, 269
social agent 155, 166
social capital *see* capital, social
social field 7, 8, 13, 38, 41, 49, 94, 132, 133, 136, 139, 141, 150, 158–160, 163–170, 177, 179, 187, 190, 194–202, 207, 209–214, 216, 219–223, 229, 231–233, 236, 240, 241, 244, 251, 252, 253, 254
Social Identity and Social Cognition 192, 265, 191, 267
social identity theory 192
social realism 8, 121, 149, 248
socialism 64, 76, 79, 98, 173, 181
Socialist Labor Party 227
Solman, Paul 120, 269
Solomon, Eric 228, 269
Somers, Margaret R. 174, 216, 269
Sørensen, Aage B. 46, 269
Spenser, Herbert 22
spirit of capitalism 35
"The Spirit of Capitalism." *Essays in Economic Sociology* 21, 26, 270
Spyrou, Thomas 193, 260
Stallings, Phil 145, 147
Stallman, Robert W. 229, 269
The Stamp of Class Reflections of Poetry and Social Class 6, 100, 102, 131–136, 149
stande 40
status consciousness 74, 87
status group 2, 7, 39–41, 44, 78, 94, 143, 150, 154–156, 169, 190, 191, 209, 250, 251
"The Statute of Artificers" (1563) 15
Stavola, Thomas J. 237, 242, 269
Steel-Town U.S.A 51, 68, 69, 70, 84, 268
stereotype 45, 54, 63, 81, 93, 96, 98, 100, 119, 120, 125, 128, 130, 140, 143, 188, 189, 212, 248

Stern, J.P. 171, 173, 269
Stets, Jan E. 190, 191, 192, 269
Stowe, Harriet Beecher 128
stream of consciousness 193
Streeter, Sabin 6, 24, 69, 260
strikes 23, 58, 72, 81, 118, 120, 228
Strozier, Robert M. 160, 161, 269
Stryker, Sheldon 190, 191, 269
subject 6, 7, 43, 56, 108, 153–154, 160–163, 165, 166, 175, 185, 188, 189, 192, 210, 213, 221, 223, 252
subjectification 160, 190, 210
subjective well-being 2, 31, 49, 50, 51, 67, 83, 87, 140–146, 247, 258, 259
subjectivity 4, 8, 66, 94, 107, 108, 142, 155, 160, 162, 166, 177, 188, 190
Suh, Eunkook 50, 141, 142, 143, 144, 262
superman 172, 173, 249
survivor guilt 63, 64
Swarts, Heidi 65, 269
Swartz, David 157, 158, 163, 169, 269
Swedberg, Robert 20, 26, 39, 269
symbolic capital *see* capital, symbolic
system, class 31, 43, 50, 61, 75, 76, 230, 232, 239, 252, 253; of discourse 159; formal 10, 12, 45, 52; of interpretation 11; power 8, 39, 41, 78, 85, 94, 151, 160, 163, 168, 171, 199, 200, 202, 203, 204, 248, 250, 259; punishment 165; reproductive 45; of signs or codes 158; society 12; stratification 188; symbolic 170; university 91; value 95, 230

"The Tartarus of Maids" 212, 111, 114–116, 124, 258
taste 66, 94, 95, 136, 150, 155–157, 169
tenement literature 227–29
Terkel, Studs 6, 24, 38, 50, 69, 71, 102, 118, 120, 130, 137–143, 144, 145, 147, 206, 223, 269; *Working: People Talk About What They Do All Day and How They Feel About What They Do* 6, 24, 71, 102, 118, 137–143
Tester, Keith 17, 269
The Theory of the Leisure Class 17–19, 24, 30–31, 34–38, 83, 270
theory of workmanship 18
Thompson, Graham 103, 119, 269
three-tiered system 52, 73, 82, 194, 232, 248
Tokarczyk, Michelle M. 62–63, 64, 269
Tompkins, Jane 259; *Sensational Designs: The Cultural Work of American Fiction, 1790–1860* 259
trade unions 78, 80, 81, 105
transcendental signifier 40, 160, 175, 204
Traub, James 151, 269
tribalism, new 185
Trilling, Lionel 239, 269
Trotsky, Leon 199
The Trouble with Diversity: How We Learned to Love Identity and Ignore Inequality 48, 70, 81–84, 85
Twain, Mark 97, 116, 226, 253; *The Adven-*

tures of Huckleberry Finn 254; The Adventures of Tom Sawyer 254; The Gilded Age 253
Tyler, Gus: "Review of What's Class Got to Do with It? American Society in the Twenty-First Century" 53

Übermensch 171
Uncle Tom's Cabin 123, 128, 259
unions 50, 54, 55, 57, 58, 59, 60, 61, 65, 78–81, 84, 86, 98, 105, 118, 129, 130, 145, 147, 181
unskilled labor 3, 12, 16, 21, 28, 41, 60, 78, 83, 105
use-value 10–13, 14, 15, 18, 19, 20, 24, 37
utopia 1, 17, 18, 43, 48, 130, 184

value 11–13, 15, 17, 18
Veblen, Thorstein 2, 3, 6, 7, 17–19, 20, 22, 23, 24, 30–31, 34–38, 39, 83, 112, 131, 136, 150, 154, 155, 157, 160, 168, 176, 201, 206, 207, 232, 251, 270; "The Instinct of Workmanship and the Irksomeness of Labor" 19, 270; *The Theory of the Leisure Class* 17–19, 24, 30–31, 34–38, 83, 270
village systems 39
Vogel, Lise 121

wage system 81
wages 4, 15, 16, 17, 26, 28, 29, 31, 43, 48, 59, 60, 69, 78, 80, 110, 119, 218
Walker, Pierce 139, 141, 142
Walton, Mary 17, 270
Warren, Mark 174, 270
Waters, Malcolm 32, 267
Watkins, Floyd C. 239, 270
Weber, Max 2, 3, 6, 12, 13, 14, 17, 20–22, 23, 25, 26, 27, 30, 32, 33, 35, 38–41, 64, 78, 79, 80, 90, 94, 135, 136, 145, 150, 152, 154, 155, 160, 162, 176, 188, 209, 231, 251, 270; *Essays in Economic Sociology* 21, 26, 270; *General Economic History* 20, 21, 23, 27, 39–41, 257; *The Protestant Work Ethic and the Spirit of Capitalism* 9
Weininger, Elliot B. 203, 204, 264
Weir, Maurice D. 10, 263
Wharton, Edith 254; *The Age of Innocence* 254
white slaves 105, 106, 109, 110

Whitejacket 122
Whitson, Carolyn 48, 98, 99, 247, 261
Wilkens, Sandy 146
Will, Barbara 235, 245
Williams, Damian T. 70
Williams, Raymond 104
Williams, Tennessee: "The Glass Menagerie" 254
Williams, William Carlos 5, 132, 133, 134; *Patterson* 134
Wittgenstein, Ludwig 156, 159, 270
Wittgenstein on Rules and Private Language: An Elementary Exposition 159, 265
Woman's Fiction: A Guide to Novels by and about Women in America, 1820–1870 259
work 10–22; as occupation 22–31
worker (laborer) 24–31
Working: People Talk About What They Do All Day and How They Feel About What They Do 6, 24, 71, 102, 118, 137–143
working class: canon(s) 4, 99, 133; culture 202; folk hero 103, 122, 138, 142, 248; literature 1–8, 9, 22, 69, 70–72, 96, 97–49, 150, 202, 211, 215, 247, 248, 251, 253, 254, 258, 259; redefinition 43–44; studies 2, 3, 6, 8, 10, 22, 24, 31, 32, 47, 52, 55, 56, 60, 63, 64, 67, 68, 70, 73, 96, 97, 104, 120, 138, 150, 176, 251, 254, 257; writers 133, 134, 247
Working-Class Formation: Nineteenth-Century Patterns in Western Europe and the United States 46, 49, 76–81, 154
Working-Class Suburb: A Study of Auto Workers in Suburbia 49, 50, 52, 74, 86–87, 137, 206
working girls 113
workmanship 19, 30
Wright, Thomas 26, 270

Young, Philip 112, 114, 258

Zandy, Janet 6, 9, 56, 98, 99, 102, 103, 104–120, 130, 134, 138, 139, 148, 149, 202, 258, 261, 269; *Hands, Physical Labor, Class, and Cultural Work* 9, 98
Zweig, Michael 48, 50, 52–54, 58, 64, 65, 69, 87, 140, 198, 258, 270

www.ingramcontent.com/pod-product-compliance
Lightning Source LLC
Chambersburg PA
CBHW051212300426
44116CB00006B/535